William Bede Dalley
Silver-tongued pride of old Sydney

Also by Robert Lehane and published by Ginninderra Press
Irish Gold
Forever Carnival

Robert Lehane

William Bede Dalley
Silver-tongued pride of old Sydney

Front cover image: Government Printing Office collection,
State Library of New South Wales

William Bede Dalley: Silver-tongued pride of old Sydney
ISBN 978 1 74027 437 1
Copyright © text Robert Lehane 2007

First published 2007
Reprinted 2016

GINNINDERRA PRESS
PO Box 3461 Port Adelaide 5015
www.ginninderrapress.com.au

Contents

Foreword		7
Introduction		9
1	Looking up	13
2	Into the fray	26
3	Assembly and Circuit	40
4	In and out of office	54
5	Twank and Tiptop	68
6	The other side	82
7	Among bushrangers	97
8	The journalist	111
9	Libel and murder	124
10	Parkes and the Irish assassin	138
11	Settling down	151
12	The dolphin and the anchor	165
13	A married man	179
14	Robertson's Attorney-General	194
15	Three more governments	206
16	Political battles and a busy pen	220
17	Dark times	233
18	In praise of troubled genius	245
19	He's back	259
20	The 'Dining-out Administration'	274
21	The land war won	288
22	In charge	302
23	To Sudan	318
24	Back to earth	331
25	The aftermath	346
26	Church and state	360

27 Looking back   374
28 Centenary   387
29 'Tongue of silver, heart of gold'   401
Notes   410
Bibliography   431
Picture credits   436
Index   438

Foreword

I became interested in William Bede Dalley – found him an intriguing, and clearly historically significant, character – when working on my last book, *Forever Carnival: a story of priests, professors and politics in 19th century Sydney*. Like this one, it is set in the 1850s to 1880s, but with a church rather than state focus. Dalley makes frequent appearances.

Others who have encountered Dalley in their research have found surprising, as I did, the lack of an extended account of his life. Judge G.D. Woods, author of a recent history of criminal law in colonial New South Wales, concluded from his reading of court reports and political speeches that at the height of his powers Dalley's 'gift of speech was spellbinding'; he was 'probably the most charming and eloquent of 19th century Sydney barristers and public speakers'. Malcolm Saunders, also much impressed by the man, observed in his centennial account of the Sudan military adventure of 1885 instigated by Dalley that Australian historians had 'virtually passed him by'.

I am particularly grateful to two others who thought a book about Dalley overdue. T.W. Campbell, biographer of Sir George Dibbs, three times Premier of New South Wales, gave me access to a large amount of relevant material he had collected. Also valuable was an index he prepared of references to Dalley in Sydney's *Freeman's Journal*. The late Bede Nairn, author with Martha Rutledge of the fine account of Dalley's life in the *Australian Dictionary of Biography*, offered valuable insights into the man and prominent contemporaries in a discussion in early 2006. I remember warmly his enthusiasm and encouragement. Special thanks also to priest/historian Rev. Brian Maher, who put me in touch with both men, for his interest and help during the writing of this book and the two that preceded it.

Dalley's statue, Hyde Park, Sydney.

Introduction

> And only he the glorious triumph knows
> Of fighting oft, yet never making foes.
> At his command, care flies the human race,
> And laughter beams o'er every happy face...

So wrote a rhymester of 34-year-old William Bede Dalley – barrister, politician, journalist, orator, patron of literature – in *Sydney Punch* in 1865. His popularity remained undimmed up to his death in Sydney in 1888 and, when his statue was unveiled at the northern end of Hyde Park on a sunny April afternoon nine years later, some 10,000 people gathered to pay their respects. But how many of those who wander past this cheerful bronze today know anything of the man, whose fame seems to have been lost in the mists of time?

The statue, by Sydney sculptor James White, shows the short, dapper Dalley in a typical pose – frock coat, flower in the lapel, addressing a meeting. The Governor of NSW, Lord Hampden, performed the unveiling, pulling aside the flag that had draped the figure. The Governor of Victoria, Lord Brassey, was there with him, along with Cardinal Moran, Archbishop of Sydney – Dalley was a Catholic – and a long list of notables, mainly from the law and politics.[1]

The pedestal bears the portentous inscription 'Scholar, Patriot, Statesman', and much of the oratory at the ceremony, focusing on the last two words, was in praise of Dalley's offer, as acting Premier in 1885, of a New South Wales contingent to help Britain in its troubles in Sudan. Dalley combined colonial patriotism with a romantic view of the empire that gave rise to this act of 'chivalry', as he described it at the time. But just as he deplored religious bigotry he rejected the popular notion that British civilisation was inherently superior to others. He was criticised for welcoming, rather than wanting Britain to resist, the growing French and German presence in the Pacific.

The speaker who best captured the real Dalley was Sydney University's classics professor, Thomas Butler, whose task was to speak of him as a scholar. Dalley had read avidly and widely, and his writing displayed the 'same grace and distinction of style, choice diction, sparkling wit, genial humour, keen satire and fertility of illustration' as his oratory. He had been 'in some ways the most brilliant perhaps of a brilliant circle'. Friends included the early patron of colonial literature Nicol Drysdale Stenhouse and the classics scholar Professor Charles Badham. He was also close to the ill-fated 'brilliant Dan' Deniehy and Premier and Chief Justice James Martin. 'Those men were young in stirring times and were quickened by them', Butler said, referring to the movements for self-government and democratic reform in the 1840s and '50s. He hoped 'the great movement towards federation' might produce a crop of comparable talent, but as yet saw no sign of it.

Genial good nature, buoyant spirits, and unfailing courtesy and urbanity were characteristics of Dalley noted by Butler. Another was his 'boundless stock' of anecdotes; 'of courts and lawyers he could tell stories of every kind with exquisite power of imitation'. Some of those stories survive in early accounts of Dalley's life, which are peppered with references to the oratory he employed in defence of men charged with bushranging, murder and other heinous crimes, and the reputation his eloquence won him, not least among criminal defendants.

Major-General John Antill, a visitor to the Dalley home as a youth in the 1880s, wrote of the barrister's ability 'to bring tears even to his own eyes… there have been known occasions when hard-hearted juries have sobbed and rocked with anguish and indignation…'[2] One story tells of an occasion when, during 'a moving and almost tearful passage' in his successful defence in a trial for robbery under arms, Dalley was 'not a little disturbed at seeing a broad grin on the face of the accused'. Outside the court the liberated man went over to his defender to thank him.

> 'What in the devil's name were you grinning at just now?' asked Dalley.
> 'Well Sir, it's this way. Until I heard that speech of yourn, I didn't believe I was innocent.' Having thus delivered himself, happy in heart and satisfied in his conscience, the fellow put out his hand. 'Now that we've both

come through all right, let's shake hands!' 'What, you infernal scoundrel!' Dalley replied, in the tone of mock indignation he knew so well how to assume; 'how dare you? I know I have incurred the vengeance of heaven and imperilled my immortal soul by saving you from the gallows; but I'm not going to load myself with the greater sin of shaking hands with you.'³

Presumably Dalley was the source of another tale, recounted by Antill. He and crown prosecutor William Charles Windeyer were proceeding by Cobb & Co. coach to Forbes for criminal hearings when a gang bailed them up. The bushrangers

> promptly stripped all the passengers of cash, watches and other convertibles. Dalley had something like £200 on him, gold watch and fob. Who's them blokes in the top hats?' asked the head of the gang to the coachdriver. 'The little fellow is the lawyer Dalley, going up to defend your pal. The big bloke's Windeyer, out to hang him!' Thereupon, Dalley's watch and wad were returned to him, with profuse apologies; as for Windeyer, they took him, neck and crop, and heaved him into a waterhole!

Newspaper court reports often used phrases such as 'eloquent and feeling' to describe Dalley's addresses to juries, but he varied his pleading techniques. For instance, a reporter at the Bathurst Circuit Court in April 1865 found his summing up for the defence in an arson trial 'very amusing and ingenious'. Prosecutor Edward Butler had a clever response: 'if fun and amusement were sufficient to secure the freedom of prisoners all that would be required would be for persons charged with offences to secure the assistance of his learned friend, Mr Dalley, and there would be an end to all difficulty.'⁴ In this case, the prisoner was acquitted.

Another story tells of a case where Butler won out. Three men were on trial for cattle stealing.

> Full two hours Dalley held the Court as by a spell, and even the unsentimental Judge seemed to melt as the master of picturesque and pathetic phrases arrayed his arguments and poured out his persuasive pleadings. Had the twelve good men and true gone straight off to their room, acquittal was a certainty. But Edward Butler had to have his say. Rising in his affectedly easy-going manner, Butler quietly commenced: Your Honour and gentlemen of the jury, – My learned friend, with that marvellous eloquence and brilliant fancy for which he is so famous, has

presented to you in glowing language the poetry of the case. I will now proceed to give you the facts.' Seven years.[5]

Dalley was a funny man, but could also be passionately serious. On notable occasions he spoke up for the Chinese, outsiders in 19th century colonial society, and against the persecution of Jews. He was a staunch defender of a free press and of workers' rights, and a powerful advocate of religious tolerance. When Henry Parkes and others responded to the attempted assassination of Prince Alfred, Duke of Edinburgh, in Sydney in 1868 in a manner that stirred up anti-Irish and anti-Catholic feeling, Dalley was outraged. His attacks on those promoting intolerance combined calm analysis, fiery rhetoric and, in contributions to *Sydney Punch*, biting humour.

Dalley's ventures into politics were sporadic, and for years as a member of the Legislative Assembly and then the Legislative Council he made few appearances and even fewer contributions. The contrast with his highly active and productive terms as Attorney-General in John Robertson's ministries in the 1870s and his key role in the Stuart government of 1883 to 1885, including his seven months as acting Premier, could hardly be greater. Between political engagements it was back to books and writing as well as the law courts. There were idiosyncratic houses to build at Rose Bay and Manly. And, most important, there was the family. The great tragedy of his life was the death of his young wife from typhoid in 1881, leaving five young children.

On Dalley's death seven years later, *The Bulletin* described him as 'a man of many splendours, both of intellect and heart', and 'in many respects the most notable man Sydney has given birth to.'[6] The *Sydney Morning Herald* said 'his influence on the popular sentiment of the country, on the tone of public life, and on the broad character of the people' had been marked and electric; it was given to few to so 'fascinate and charm the public mind'. Noting with approval that many thousands had joined the funeral procession, it added, 'A community honours itself in honouring those whose lives and services have done the community honour.'[7]

1
Looking up

The year William Dalley was born, 1831, was a propitious one for New South Wales. The reformist Governor Richard Bourke replaced the autocratic Ralph Darling at the end of the year, an important event in its transition from remote British gaol to flourishing self-governing colony. Some of his proposals, including a mainly elected Legislative Council and a broad-based public education system, were blocked. But his six years in charge saw big advances in areas such as the fair administration of justice, press freedom and religious equality. Assisted immigration began in 1832 and grew rapidly in the second half of the decade. Numbers of convicts arriving increased too – up to 1840 when transportation ended – but as the population grew, from about 50,000 in 1831 to nearly 100,000 in 1838, the ratio of free to convict rose rapidly. And the economy boomed; revenue nearly trebled and exports more than doubled during Bourke's term.[1]

The Governor's work was appreciated – so much so that donations flooded in when admiring colonists proposed that a bronze statue be cast in England and erected in Sydney in his honour. Among the larger contributors was John Dalley, father of William; he gave £10 to the initial collection and more subsequently.[2] By early 1840 takings exceeded the £2,400 contracted cost, and the imposing statue, which stands outside the Mitchell Library, was unveiled in 1842. Dalley senior's donations are a sign that he doing very nicely in the colony.

His prospects had looked decidedly bleak two decades earlier when, in March 1818, at the age of 18, he was brought before the Dorset, southern England, assizes charged with burglary. The court found him guilty and he heard the death sentence pronounced – often the fate of minor criminals in those days. Fortunately, it was also common practice for the ultimate sentence to be commuted to transportation for life, and Dalley was among those spared. He arrived in Sydney on the *General Stuart* with about 250 fellow convicts on 31 December 1818 and was assigned to Francis Oakes of Parramatta, one of the district's earliest settlers and reputedly an 'honest, steady citizen'. Oakes engaged in farming, various business enterprises, and government work; his positions included chief constable for the Parramatta district.[3] How he employed Dalley is not recorded; the convict records give the young man's trade as 'wool comber and dyer', work that Oakes is not likely to have required of him. They also tell us that he was a Protestant, five feet eight inches tall, with a fair and ruddy complexion, brown hair and hazel eyes.

Dalley was reassigned during the 1820s to John Street of 'Woodlands', near Bathurst. This forebear of three chief justices of New South Wales[4] had immigrated to the colony in 1822 bringing merino sheep from the Henty flock in Sussex. (The Hentys, pioneers of the Western District of Victoria, came out later.) With other pastoralists, he founded the Bathurst Hunt Club in 1825 and drew up a set of rules that prescribed, among other things, a livery of scarlet frock coat with black velvet facings, buff waistcoat, white breeches and top boots for the hunt.[5] The colony's 1828 census reveals that he employed the 30-year-old Dalley as a footman – 'a male servant in livery who attends the door or the carriage, waits at table, etc'[6] – suggesting he sought to reproduce English country life in his home as well as in gentlemanly sport.

Also working for Street in 1828 was Catherine Dobbins (née Spillane), an Irish convict probably in her mid-20s.[7] She had arrived in Sydney on the *Mariner* in July 1825, having been found guilty at the Cork City assizes in April 1824 of stealing shirts and sentenced to seven years' transportation. Her four-year-old daughter, also Catherine, came out with her, and was placed in the Parramatta orphanage on arrival. The census records that Street employed the young mother – described as four feet 11¼ inches tall, brown complexion, black hair, hazel eyes, quiet disposition, Roman Catholic – as a nurse.

At the end of 1828, 10 years after arriving in the colony, John Dalley was granted his ticket-of-leave, the first step towards emancipation. Catherine received hers the following August. Less than three weeks later the pair applied, as they had to under the convict regulations, for permission to marry. This was initially refused on the ground that Catherine was already married, but the problem was somehow sorted out. Rev. John Therry, the colony's sole Catholic priest at the time looking after an exceedingly scattered flock of perhaps 15,000,[8] married John and Catherine on 12 July 1830 – John having converted to his wife's faith.[9]

The couple's first child, another John, had been born a year earlier.[10] William was second, born in the winter of 1831,[11] probably at the Dalleys' newly acquired premises in George Street North, Sydney, where John ran a clothing store. This was just back from the western shore of Sydney Cove, opposite the government stores.[12] Catherine had double cause to celebrate; the previous April she had become a free woman on the expiration of her sentence. After William's birth she wasted little time in lodging a petition for the return of her daughter, now aged about 10, from the orphanage. Dated 21 September 1831, this pointed out that she was now free and able to provide for and protect her child. The petition was successful, and young Catherine became and remained a close member of the family.[13]

Catherine senior bore five more children over the next 11 years. Only two of them survived to adulthood – Christina, born in 1839, and Richard, in 1842. James Dalley died at 14 months in 1836, another James shortly after his birth two years later, and Hannah at two years and four months in 1839. Not only infants were lost; the first-born, John, was a year ahead of William at school and, like him, an outstanding student when he died at the age of 15½ in January 1845.[14] Death was a frequent visitor to the Dalley household during William's childhood and youth.

As the family came along, the father progressed along the road to full citizen's rights. His conditional pardon – free, but required to remain in the colony – was granted in February 1833 and in June 1838 the office of the Principal Superintendent of Convicts advised that his absolute pardon was ready to collect.[15]

In the meantime, he was growing wealthy through property investments. Newspaper announcements provide glimpses of his activities. For example, in 1836 he paid £13 an acre for a little over five acres of undeveloped land on Sydney's outskirts; five years later he outlaid a much more hefty £1,750 on inner-city premises in George Street.[16] Advertisements offering rooms, houses and business premises to rent appeared frequently in the press over his name.[17] Having, apparently, come through the recession of the early 1840s unscathed, he advertised in 1844 that he had money to lend – from £1,000 to £2,000 – on freehold city property for periods of not less than two years.[18] His will, prepared in 1867, listed 17 properties in his name – mostly houses in Sydney but including a half-acre allotment at Kiama on the south coast.

Growing up in Sydney's docklands in the 1830s and '40s would have offered much stimulation to a child of William Dalley's imagination and intelligence. There was the constant coming and going of ships and characters of all sorts, linking Sydney with 'home' on the other side of the world, and with the Pacific islands and settlements up and down the coast. Convict chain gangs and their military escorts remained a frequent sight in the streets. Sydney gaol was situated just blocks south of the Dalley home in George Street, its gallows visible above the walls. Executions there were public events. The sadly depleted Aboriginal population was a reminder to those who cared to notice that British settlement, however prosperous, had come at a cost.

Admiring contemporaries have provided a few glimpses of William as a child. 'We were boys together and played on the green together,' recalled Sir George Dibbs – a colleague in the Stuart government of 1883–85 and later Premier – at the unveiling of the Dalley statue in 1897. 'Then, as afterwards at the Bar and in political life, Dalley was the idol of all… He was…full of fun and anecdote, always bright and happy.'[19] Another old friend, the lawyer Alexander Oliver, recalled forming a life-long friendship with Dalley at 'Old Taylor's' Fort Street school. He said Dalley gave Taylor, 'a good pedagogue', more to do than most of the other boys, 'being singularly averse from anything like rigid discipline'.

At that time young Dalley's parents lived in Fort-street, and young Dalley, with some of his contemporaries, used to make the Flagstaff district lively for the inhabitants. I am afraid, if the truth has to be told, that this deponent was not often missing from the roll-call when war was waged against the boys of a neighbouring school. The Hill boys were generally victorious, and their leaders, as a matter of course, generally in trouble.[20]

Then there is the tale of Dalley playing marbles with Frank Christie, later the bushranger Gardiner. A Captain Charles, neighbour of the Dalleys in George Street North, is quoted as recalling seeing 'a pleasant, fair-haired boy' and 'a bright, round-headed youngster' shooting marbles on the road.

I accidentally scuffed one of the marbles, and recollect quite well putting my hand on the fair-haired boy's head and asking him not to be vexed. He looked up and smiled, and said it was alright. He grew up to be the dark-visaged and notorious bushranger Frank Gardiner; the other boy was none other than the distinguished statesman William Bede Dalley.

This story could be true; Christie (Gardiner), aged five, arrived in Sydney with his Scottish family in November 1834. He was about two years older than Dalley. One teller of the tale, C.H. Bertie, notes that 'in the eternal fitness of things Dalley defended Gardiner at the latter's trial in May, 1864.'[21]

J.P. McGuanne provides glimpses of a slightly older Dalley, when he was a student at Sydney College and then St Mary's Seminary. 'Ever ready for fun, yet mindful of study, he induced during youth many long friendships. His pony, with a blue ribbon round its neck on prize days, would carry him skittishly to school, and race all-comers on the way home.' McGuanne added, presumably referring to his move to the Seminary, that when Dalley parted from 'his brother collegians' he quoted the lines:

Sharers of our glorious past,
Brothers, must we part at last?
Shall not we thro' good and ill
Cleave to one another still?[22]

Not yet eight years old, William Dalley entered Sydney College at the beginning of 1839, a year after his brother John. One classmate remembered him as 'ever bright, ever genial, ever and everywhere the favourite, his sunny face and cheerful talk and happy disposition…were indications of what the lad would be when arrived at man's estate'.[23]

This school, and particularly its first headmaster, William T. Cape, educated many of the colony's notable men. Dalley was one of more than 50 former pupils who gathered in June 1871 for a dinner to commemorate Cape, who had died in 1863. The purpose, in Dalley's words, was to 'honour the memory of a dead schoolmaster, to confess our obligations to his learning and fidelity, and to revive our recollections of those days when we were ourselves humble students'. The Premier and later Chief Justice, Sir James Martin, chaired proceedings and gave the main speech. Another speaker was John Robertson, five times Premier of NSW and one of Cape's first pupils at a school he began in King Street in 1829, six years before Sydney College opened. William Forster, Premier for a brief term in 1859–60, also spoke; his claim to have been 'a bit of a favourite' with Cape brought cries of 'hear, hear'. Forster remembered him as a man whose love of young people made him 'so excellent a teacher'. 'He knew every boy individually, and applied to him individually the peculiar talents he possessed. They always felt that they were under his eye…'[24]

The writer Rolf Boldrewood (real name T.A. Browne), having just been appointed police magistrate on the new Gulgong goldfield, missed the dinner. Like Dalley, he encountered Cape at Sydney College (later reincarnated as Sydney Grammar School). In an article published in 1898, he recalled cricket games in Hyde Park, learning to swim under Cape's supervision in Woolloomooloo Bay, and a 'wild romantic waste' as playground behind the school. Cape was a 'strict, occasionally severe, but invariably just and impartial ruler', Boldrewood wrote. External examiners visited twice a year to check on the students' progress; he particularly remembered one of them – the Catholic Bishop John Bede Polding, a 'gentle, dignified personage, revered by all'.[25]

Archbishop Polding.

All the Dalley children were baptised into the Catholic church, and Polding confirmed 12-year-old William at St Mary's Cathedral in August 1843; that is when he acquired the middle name Bede. Polding was only months back in the colony after an absence of nearly two and a half years on church business in England, Ireland and Rome, during which he was promoted to Archbishop. This English Benedictine missioner had taken charge of the church in Sydney in 1835, at the age of 40. In 1838 he established St Mary's Seminary, which he hoped would produce 'a native race of priests and statesmen, of lawyers and physicians, of soldiers, sailors and artists'.[26] As well as training candidates for the priesthood, it offered Catholic youths whose parents were willing and able to pay the modest fees the type of classical and commercial education offered by Sydney College.

The seminary got off to a slow start. 'The Catholics of the town do not send their children,' Polding wrote regretfully in May 1839. 'I want someone who will go amongst them and expostulate with their neglect.'[27] Cape's reputation provided a good reason for parents like the Dalleys to prefer the non-denominational Sydney College for their children's education. However, Cape departed in 1841, and the Dalley boys moved to the seminary around that time. Reports in the Catholic newspaper, *The Chronicle*, of end-of-year award ceremonies show that both John and William made their mark there.

With Polding overseas, the Vicar-General, Very Rev. Francis Murphy, presided in 1841 and 1842. In 1841 he heard young John Dalley deliver a speech 'with great good taste and correctness', and presented him with a prize for arithmetic; the following year he heard one of the boys (initial not given) perform in a 'parliamentary' debate. William started to shine in 1843, when Polding was back to present the awards. He came second in the school in elocution and took a prize for 'globes', while his brother excelled in English grammar, catechism and geometry. After the presentations, John chaired and William spoke in a debate, 'conducted with much spirit and ingenuity', on the character of Julius Caesar.

Only William appears in the awards list for 1844; probably John was already stricken with the illness that took his life early the following year.[28] As well as winning a prize for elocution, William excelled in Latin, English composition, bookkeeping and writing. For 1845, his last year at the seminary, he is listed among the top students in Latin, French, English, history, geography, mathematics and Christian doctrine. The 14-year-old carried away two prizes – 'first honour' in arithmetic and bookkeeping, and, as one would expect from his subsequent career, in elocution.[29]

Information about his life in the years immediately after school is scarce. He is said to have had a clerical job with the Burdekin family business for a time. This was established by the merchant Thomas Burdekin, who arrived from England in 1828, acquired much real estate in Sydney and other parts of the colony and died in 1844. The name lives on in Queensland's Burdekin River; the explorer Ludwig Leichhardt crossed it in April 1845 and named it in honour of Thomas's widow, Mary Ann, who had assisted the expedition.[30]

At some point William began his legal studies articled to a prominent Sydney solicitor, Frederick Wright Unwin. What further assistance he received in his preparations for the Bar after Unwin's death in October 1852 is unknown. According to a biographical note published in 1856, he spent nearly three years in the solicitor's office, and then for the next two years was 'incapacitated from pursuing any regular employment by ill-health'. During this time 'he appears to have been more or less a student, mastering Greek under his own direction, and qualifying himself in other branches of learning…'[31] In July 1856 he satisfied the examiners that he had a sufficient mastery of Greek, Latin and mathematics, as well as the law, to warrant admission to practise as a barrister.

The family maintained close connections with the church. Polding reported in July 1844 that John Dalley (senior) was a trustee of the debt-burdened St Patrick's Church in the city, and intended to place the deeds of his property, worth at least £4,000, in the bank as security for it.[32] In July 1846, 15-year-old William – doubtless the most literate member of the household – wrote to Father Therry in Hobart with the latest news. Most of the letter is about the sad drowning of a priest, Rev. Dunphy, in a river near Mudgee:

> He was compelled by duty to cross the river (on horseback), it being in a flooded state, when about half across the river the undertow threw the horse down, and as the Rev. gentleman could not disengage himself, he was drowned. A shepherd on the opposite bank saw the whole of the fatal accident but could not render the least assistance. High Mass was offered up in St Mary's Church for him on Tuesday 29th inst by His Grace the Archbishop, assisted by Right Rev. Dr Epaille, Vicar Apostolic of Western Oceania.

Other news was the Archbishop's dedication of a church at Parramatta and the dangerous illnesses of a priest and another man. 'We are all well,' he noted. William wrote to Therry again a year later to advise that the family would take care of some luggage of his. He added, 'The packet ship has just arrived bringing intelligence of the death of O'Connell.' Clearly he knew there was no need to elaborate in reporting the death of the renowned 'Liberator' of Ireland's Catholics to the veteran Irish priest.[33]

In August 1851, Dalley father and son spoke at a 'very numerous and respectable' public meeting at St Mary's Seminary called to begin fund-raising for extensions to the cathedral. John moved a motion and William seconded another one.[34] Possibly this was his first post-school public speech. What he said was not reported.

William followed his father in becoming involved in politics. John Dalley seconded the nomination of a colonial-born Catholic businessman, Daniel Egan, as a candidate in Sydney's first municipal council elections in October 1842. The following December he was listed as a supporter of William Charles Wentworth and Dr William Bland as candidates in the first Legislative Council elections. Six years earlier he had been among donors to the Australian Patriotic Association, formed by Wentworth, Bland and others to agitate for a version of self-government that did not discriminate against ex-convicts. At the municipal elections of November 1844 he stood unsuccessfully as a candidate. Despite pledging 'to do all that lies in my power to prevent heavy taxation', he secured only forty-two of the 564 votes cast in his ward.[35]

Probably the person with the biggest early formative influence on young Dalley, aside from parents, teachers and priests, was a near contemporary, Daniel Henry Deniehy. Three years Dalley's senior, the precocious Deniehy was also the son of ex-convicts. Recognising the genius of their only child, the parents took him to England, Ireland and Europe in 1843, at the age of 14, to further his education. After returning the following year he was articled to the solicitor and literary patron N.D. Stenhouse, and enjoyed the older man's friendship and support as he developed his literary interests as well as his legal skills. He was admitted as a solicitor in May 1851, and four months later delivered a series of lectures on poetry at the Sydney Mechanics' School of Arts. More lectures followed in subsequent years, including a series on modern French literature. He began submitting literary criticism to newspapers in the late 1840s.[36]

The journalist David Blair, who met Deniehy in 1851, left a vivid description of the then 22-year-old:

> He was certainly the smallest and most compact little gentleman of his years I had ever met with up till that time. He was clad in the style of a finished man of fashion – in fact, a perfect little dandy. His eyes were peculiar from extreme short-sightedness, and he wore a 'quizzing-glass,' as the single eye-glass was then popularly designated. His manners were those of a born gentleman; his laugh was clear and ringing; his spoken English, like his written English, was perfect; and he was fairly overflowing with wit, learning, and vivacity.[37]

Blair wrote that he had many rambles and discursive talks with his 'sworn friend' Deniehy before leaving Sydney a few months later. He noted elsewhere that he never met Dalley,[38] which perhaps indicates that the Dalley/Deniehy friendship had not yet been forged. Whenever it began, there is no doubt about its strength. Deniehy described Dalley as his bosom friend and companion – their connection was like that of Damon and Phythias of classical myth or Chaucer's Palamon and Arcite.[39] Dalley recalled in 1882 that it had been his 'inestimable privilege' to enjoy Deniehy's 'most intimate friendship' for years – 'to hang for hours upon the music of a speech which to my ears at all events has never fallen from the lips of any other man'.[40]

Probably Deniehy introduced Dalley into the Stenhouse literary circle, which included writers such as the poets Charles Harpur and Henry Kendall and the University of Sydney's principal and classics professor John Woolley. He may also have influenced Dalley's personal style; like Deniehy, Dalley was something of a dandy, although a more robust and handsome figure. He is said to have invariably greeted friends and acquaintances as 'old boy', 'old man' or 'old fellow'. An admiring observer of one of his court performances in the late 1860s wrote, 'It was a charming sight to see this dapper little barrister, with his well-cut coat and white waistcoat, stand up to deliver his harangue, with his hat, lavender kid gloves, and cane before him.'[41] Another writer remembered Dalley in the 1870s as 'always plump and jolly, in his dark buttoned-up frock coat, with a flower in his button-hole, his silk hat a little on one side'.[42]

Dalley watched Deniehy win renown as an orator in the early 1850s; his turn came later. Newly married and apparently doing well at the law, Deniehy addressed a large public meeting called in June 1852 to condemn proposals to resume convict transportation to NSW. 'The great cloud of caste' which 'once brooded black and thunderous over the brightest moral and social seasons of the land' had passed away, he declared. 'It would be the devilish act of the oppressors…to set it again afloat on the horizon darkening over generations yet unborn.'[43] The sentiments were similar when he joined the outcry the following year against Wentworth's proposal for a hereditary colonial peerage as part of the colony's new self-government constitution. At a packed meeting in Sydney's Victoria Theatre he coined the phrase 'bunyip aristocracy' to ridicule the proposal, and urged that the colony become 'a land where... the law no more recognises the supremacy of a class than it recognises the predominance of a religion'. There was an aristocracy 'worthy of our ambition', he said to great cheering:

> Wherever man's skill is eminent, wherever glorious manhood asserts its elevation, there is an aristocracy that confers honour on the land that possesses it. That is God's aristocracy. That is an aristocracy that will grow and expand under free institutions, and bless the land where it flourishes.[44]

Three weeks later Deniehy told a large outdoor gathering at Circular Quay that 'unjust and despotic class legislation' characterised every institution in Britain.[45] He moved to Goulburn the following year in the hope, which was not fulfilled, of benefiting his health and legal practice. Over the next two years he set out his vision for an Australian democratic republic in a long series of articles in the *Goulburn Herald*.[46]

Deniehy was the organisers' first choice to respond to the toast to 'our native land' at a gala public banquet held at Sydney's Prince of Wales Theatre on 11 March 1856 to honour Charles Gavan Duffy, who had recently arrived to settle in Australia. The 39-year-old Duffy, a prominent member of the nationalist Young Ireland movement, had narrowly escaped conviction for treason in 1848. He became a leading politician in Victoria, including serving a term as Premier, after rejecting overtures to settle in New South Wales.

Deniehy could not get to the banquet and the 24-year-old Dalley was invited to take his place. He joined a speakers' list that included Henry Parkes, rising English-born politician and proprietor of the liberal *Empire* newspaper, and the barrister Edward Butler, who had been an associate of Duffy in Ireland. Dalley praised Deniehy as one of the colony's 'most illustrious' men. And he praised Duffy, saying his presence at the banquet had brought all classes together in harmony.

He hoped 'all such paltry distinctions as had in former times been made would be by this event extinguished forever', and that all would now accept the 'utter falsity' of the idea that the circumstances of a man's birth might be 'disparaging to his success'.[47]

The speech was brief, and makes rather pedestrian reading. Nevertheless, Dalley's debut as an after-dinner speaker seems to have gone down very well, presumably because of the manner of delivery. According to a writer for the *Empire*, Duffy afterwards expressed 'a high opinion and a high hope' of the young man. He reportedly said on more than one occasion, 'If I were to stay with you [in New South Wales], I should bring out that young Australian – depend upon it, there is stuff in him!'[48]

2
Into the fray

The day after the banquet, voting began in the first elections for the New South Wales Legislative Assembly; responsible government had arrived. Not all were satisfied with the new arrangements. Some feared democracy had already advanced too far, threatening property and good order in the colony. Many of a more liberal bent disapproved of, among other things, the property or income qualification for voters,[1] the fact that country electorates would return disproportionately large numbers of members, and the non-elected Legislative Council. Duffy, fighter for radical change in Ireland, counselled acceptance in his banquet speech:

> With all its faults, I believe you have one of the safest, wisest, and most liberal constitutions in the world. I would rather live under it for the immediate present which it opens, and the certain future which it prepares, than under any system I am acquainted with on either side of the Atlantic.[2]

The key advance was that, instead of being chosen by and answerable to the Governor, appointed by the British government, ministers would be drawn from the legislature and hold office for as long as they retained the support of the elected assembly. Responsible government was introduced in Victoria, Tasmania and South Australia about the same time. The New South Wales Governor, Sir William Denison, noted in a despatch to London, 'My position, as, indeed, that of all the Governors of these colonies, is peculiar; we cease to be persons in authority…'[3] His wife professed amusement, noting in her journal that 'all the Australian colonies are in the process of receiving new constitutions, and are to have Parliaments of their own! and responsible ministers!!'[4]

After the protracted elections – voting took place in different constituencies on different days with the whole process lasting

Charles Cowper.

nearly six weeks – parliament was opened with much ceremony on 22 May. A 43-year-old merchant and landowner, Stuart Donaldson, headed the first, 'conservative', government. It lasted three and a half months before giving way to a 'liberal' group led by 49-year-old Charles Cowper, a leading player in the colony's politics since the first Legislative Council elections in 1843. Cowper's government held office for just over a month; then the 'conservatives' returned, now led by a 48-year-old businessman, Henry Parker, who had come to the colony as private secretary to Governor Sir George Gipps in 1838. His government lasted 11 months.

The terms conservative and liberal were used at the time and provide a good indication of the broad attitudes of the political players. However, the division was not sharp enough to lead to the formation of anything resembling cohesive parties that could provide stable government.[5] Denison expressed his frustration with the situation when he reported the fall of the Donaldson government to the Secretary of State for the Colonies, Henry Labouchere, in August 1856.

> I told you in my June letter that there can hardly be said to be any *political parties* in these colonies; everybody differs in opinion from his neighbour on some question or another, and is not disposed to sacrifice his opinion for party purposes. The spirit of individuality is so strong amongst people here, that they can with difficulty be persuaded to combine for any social purpose, and therefore can hardly be expected to do so for political objects.[6]

His frustration turned to anger when Cowper's government was toppled a month later. 'The main difficulty,' he told Labouchere, 'is not the absence of qualified [men] but the presence of a multiplicity of men who *conceive themselves* thoroughly qualified to direct the affairs of a great nation, to say nothing of those of a colony… Responsibility is, in fact, a name, a clap-trap, a watch-word devised by the unscrupulous as a means of deluding the unwary, meaning nothing but the right of the majority to make fools of themselves without let or hindrance.'[7]

If Dalley involved himself in the first elections, it was not in a prominent role. Instead, starting in April 1856, he contributed his oratorical skills to efforts to raise the funds needed to enable Duffy to meet the property qualification for election to Victoria's new Legislative Assembly. The funds flowed in, and the Irishman was duly elected in November 1856. 'Equality, freedom and their natural result, justice to all irrespective of creed or country', were the 'grand bases upon which statesmen should and would be compelled to govern – and no more able or devoted advocate could be engaged in this great object than C. Gavan Duffy,' Dalley told one meeting. 'His previous career was one dignified by sacrifice, toil and labours that would have won in a free country the highest guerdon a grateful people could confer. Providence had transferred his glorious and ennobling talents to a more genial clime, where they will flourish, and create new sources of human happiness…'[8] Many articles about Dalley quote Thomas Shine's observation that he was never happier than when 'wreathing the flowers of his graceful fancy round some person, or fact…'[9] This was an early example.

Admitting Dalley as a barrister was one of the first items of business for the Supreme Court on Saturday 5 July 1856, and briefs soon came his way. Cases in August 1856 included the successful defence of a young man charged with stealing a watch and appearances with senior barristers in tenancy and slander actions.[10] He reportedly caused much merriment in later years when reminiscing about how his audacious approach to advocacy in his early days at the Bar masked meagre legal knowledge.[11] The sociable Dalley also recalled spending the first £20 he earned as a barrister giving a dinner that cost £25.[12]

Probably his first entry into the political fray was in support of Charles Cowper and a colleague, Robert Campbell, at an election meeting at Sydney's Royal Hotel on 29 August. Others on the platform included Deniehy (visiting Sydney from Goulburn), the barrister Edward Butler, and Henry Parkes. In the face of concerted obstruction of its legislative program, Premier Donaldson's five-man government had resigned four days earlier in favour of Cowper's team. Campbell was his Treasurer. Under the rules of the day, newly appointed ministers had to go to the polls again to confirm their places in the Assembly.

According to Parkes's *Empire*, Dalley was 'very favourably received' when he rose to speak. He began with hyperbole, contending that 'the character of his native country was at stake' in the re-elections. Nothing, he said, would tend more to lower England's estimation of the colony than an impression that only five men could be found who were capable of ministerial office. Explaining his involvement in the campaign, he said strong objection could be taken on the grounds of his youth and inexperience, but he felt 'as deep an interest in his native country as any man breathing'. His conclusion, urging a united effort in the liberal cause, was loudly cheered (in the event, Cowper and Campbell were elected unopposed).[13]

Cowper's most controversial ministerial appointment was James Martin as Attorney-General. Born in Ireland but raised from infancy in the colony, this highly intelligent and ambitious 36-year-old solicitor had many achievements under his belt. As an outspoken journalist he had edited the daily *Australian* and weekly *Atlas* newspapers. He had been a member of the pre-responsible-government Legislative Council, and of the Council committee that drafted the colony's new constitution. However, his generally conservative political views made him an odd choice for Cowper's team. And he was not yet a barrister, a situation that in the eyes of most members of the profession disqualified him from the Attorney-General's job.

His appointment – after senior barristers approached by Cowper had refused the post – sparked an outcry. Seventeen members of the Bar signed a petition objecting to it as a violation 'of the usages of the constitution, and of the rights and privileges of the Bar.' Dalley was one of only two barristers then in practice who did not sign.[14] He had told the Cowper/Campbell re-election meeting he believed Martin would prove himself 'thoroughly qualified for the office of Attorney-General notwithstanding the prejudice which appeared to prevail against him'.[15]

The petition was presented to the Governor on 8 September. Three days later, having passed the necessary examinations, Martin was admitted to the Bar. Afterwards, reported the *Herald*, he received, 'as is customary on such occasions, the individual congratulations of his professional brethren...'[16] Martin's biographer, J.M. Bennett, notes that the petitioning barristers knew his admission was imminent, and that therefore their protest was unlikely to unseat him as Attorney-General. This being the case, 'the ingredients of personality and jealousy, hidden behind the formal terms of the petition, become obvious'.[17]

Nevertheless, the conservative forces in the Assembly had regrouped sufficiently to carry a vote of no confidence in the government. After days of rancorous debate, a close division – 26 to 23 – sealed the fate of Cowper's first administration. The Premier advised the Governor to call fresh elections, arguing that the make-up of the Assembly made strong government impossible. Denison refused, ushering in the Parker government, which took office, with Donaldson as Treasurer, on 3 October.

The political turmoil aroused passions in Sydney, whose population – city and suburbs – was now approaching 70,000.[18] An estimated 4–5,000 crowded into the Prince of Wales Theatre on the evening of 29 September for a meeting called to support the Cowper ministry, defeated but still in office. Dalley was among the speakers, moving a resolution objecting to highly 'factious and unconstitutional' behaviour by the government's opponents. The speakers struggled to be heard. According to the *Empire*,

> In the pit and other parts of the house about a hundred persons were distributed whose object evidently was to upset the proceedings; which, we are sorry to add, they succeeded in effecting. At one period of the meeting the gentlemen on the platform were placed in imminent danger, owing to a 'rush' from the pit by a number of obstructionists. The result was that the more pacific gave way, but in their retreat, they were assailed and

driven violently against the scenery and standing appointments of the stage, portions of which were materially damaged. Several blows were struck...[19]

The following evening, supporters of Parker held a meeting in the Victoria Theatre, which attracted a crowd of about 2,500. At least half were 'decidedly opposed to the objects of the meeting', the *Empire* reported. There was 'scarcely a moment's interval to the howling, hooting, yelling, hissing and other demonstrations of opposition, so that scarcely a syllable was heard of any of the speeches'. At one point, fisticuffs broke out on the stage.[20]

Presumably enjoying the political excitement, Dalley travelled to Parramatta a week later with Martin and other supporters of Cowper in the Assembly. Premier Parker was one of the two members for Parramatta; the visitors' object was to block his re-election by soliciting support for the liberal standing against him. This was William Byrnes, a Parramatta storeowner and manufacturer – and son-in-law of Francis Oakes, the man Dalley's father was assigned to when he arrived as a convict in 1818. According to the *Empire*, Dalley's 'lengthened and able' speech drew 'repeated plaudits'.[21] Speaking in Parramatta again three days later, he said Wentworth's attempt to establish a 'legal aristocracy' had been folly, but it 'would be nothing to the tyranny attempted to be established by the would-be aristocrats of the Donaldson party'. He rejected 'insinuations' that Byrnes was anti-Irish. If he thought that was the case he could not support him; the Irish had been 'missionaries of liberal opinions to the world'.[22]

Parker won the election by just twenty votes. Donaldson had less luck, losing his Sydney Hamlets seat to John Campbell, brother of Cowper's Treasurer (they were sons of the pioneer wharf owner and merchant Robert Campbell). Dalley involved himself in this contest too. Unless young men 'came forward to take a part in the public affairs of their native land, we should have no chance of progression in this country', he claimed amid cheers at an election meeting. At Campbell's victory celebration, he said voters had punished the conservatives for 'ruthlessly' assailing the Cowper ministry before it could introduce any measures. Referring to their treatment of Martin, he said night after night they had 'lifted their intellectual tomahawks against one young man who by his personal industry – by his unaided genius – made his way to the position he held in the house – to the position he now holds in society. (Loud cheers)' Another seat was found for Donaldson, who continued as Treasurer.

Shortly before Christmas Henry Parkes, on the brink of bankruptcy because of losses by the *Empire* newspaper, resigned from parliament. Who should take his place? Parkes recommended Dalley, the *Empire* advising that he

> has grown already popular with all classes of the people, not so much on account of his promising abilities, as for his high, generous spirit, and his thorough manliness of character. He is a genuine liberal in his political opinions, and is a fluent and attractive speaker. Young Australia will be gallantly represented in Mr Dalley, while the immigrant portion of the constituency will possess in his progressive mind and liberal education a not unworthy type of their national character, and no mean defence of the general interests.[23]

A public meeting at the Exchange Hotel, chaired by a 41-year-old bookseller and MP, William Piddington, considered the merits of Dalley and two other potential candidates, and opted for Dalley despite being told he was resolved not to stand. It decided there was no need to consult the young man – whose electioneering apparently had made quite an impression – before putting his name forward. The speaker who proposed this was sure Dalley would be elected; then it would be up to him 'to take his seat or to decline to represent the city'.[24] Dalley was swayed. In his message to the electors in the newspapers, he said he had been 'induced to forego my recently expressed determination of not entering upon the present contest' by the meeting's unanimous requisition. He had not envisaged seeking a seat in parliament 'for some time to come', but promised to be a diligent member if elected.[25]

While Dalley had the support of the *Empire*, his opponent, John Fairfax, naturally had the strong backing of the paper he owned, the much more prosperous *Sydney Morning Herald*. Two years earlier the *Herald* had castigated Parkes for standing for the Legislative Council;

running a newspaper was too demanding an occupation to allow time for other pursuits, and it would be undesirable for a newspaper owner to be in a position where he might be tempted to falsify the record of his own speeches![26] Memories can be short in politics and the press.

Dalley's campaign got off to a lively start with a public meeting at the Exchange Hotel, in Margaret Street in the city centre. This began indoors, but then the crowd grew too large to be accommodated so they moved outside and the speakers addressed them from an upstairs window. Martin gave a long speech in praise of Dalley, saying that, despite his youth, he surpassed Fairfax in the essential qualifications for election – education, knowledge and general ability, and, above all, independence. There used to be 'very little independence' in the colony, he said in an interesting passage on class relations. It had been 'one vast gaol' whose keepers, 'the Macarthurs and others',

> were considered men of dignity and importance; and unfortunately the natives of that day who did not belong to the Macarthur class were taught to look up to them. The very schoolmasters told their scholars when they met those men they were to lift their hats to them, and bow and scrape to them; and the servile feelings that were thus bred in the native-born of that period have grown up with them… These are not the sort of men that ought to be sent into the Legislature; but the independent natives… who have obtained their education at college and at school, who have… imbibed a spirit of independence, and who will carry it into practice in the business of life… [It] is because I believe Mr Dalley to be one of these that I now appear to support him…

Dalley, now a seasoned political campaigner, gave a long response, frequently punctuated by cheers. After repeating that he had been drawn into the contest reluctantly, he praised Parkes as one whose every act had emanated from 'the highest convictions, and the most ardent desire to benefit the country'. Then he turned to policy. He promised to seek to 'jealously guard the issue of every shilling from the public Treasury'. On occupation of the land, he said, 'We have an estate given us by the Creator for the express purpose of planting down upon it the millions and tens of millions who cannot, in other countries, earn the commonest necessaries of life.' Becoming slightly more specific, he said he favoured settling poorer people on the land but without doing any injustice to those currently in possession.

On the contentious question of primary education, he thought that, because the country was vast and the population scattered, only a national system was practicable. He would like to see one that, while universal, would permit 'the religious principle to come into operation' and 'would conciliate the heads of the various religious bodies'. His view was contrary to the Catholic church's position (favouring denominational schools), as was his support for phasing out the financial support for priests and ministers introduced by Governor Bourke, which he regretted discriminated against Jews.

He thought duty on sugar and tea should be lowered – because their main consumers were the labouring classes and a smaller tax take would encourage tea drinking and thus aid the temperance cause. He supported the spread of municipal government, and the development of railways. He wanted the electoral law changed to redress the city/country imbalance, and he would support voting by secret ballot 'if it can be made apparent to me that there is any class of people in this community who require protection in the exercise of the franchise'.

The Hyde Park hustings in 1874.

At midday on a wet and blustery Monday 29 December, around 1,500 people (according to the *Empire*; the *Herald*'s estimate was seven to eight hundred) gathered in Hyde Park for the 'nomination', the first step in the election process. The candidates, their nominators and seconders, and officials could find some shelter in the newly erected 'hustings' – the raised, wooden, open-fronted shed from which they would address the crowd. But those who had come to watch and hear were fully exposed to the elements and, unless they were in the front rows, must have had trouble catching what was said. The numbers present were a sign of the great public interest both in this contest and in the colony's new form of government. Speeches were greeted with cheers, laughter, groans and frequent interjections; it was true participatory – if men's only – democracy.

John Hubert Plunkett, who nominated Fairfax, spoke first. This 54-year-old Irish Catholic was a notable figure. As Attorney-General from 1836 up to the start of responsible government, he assiduously promoted equal treatment for all before the law, and is specially remembered for overcoming concerted opposition to secure the conviction and hanging of nine white perpetrators of the 1838 massacre of Aborigines at Myall Creek. Plunkett is not readily categorised as liberal or conservative. However, Cowper and Parkes, after combining with two others to secure their own election and his defeat in the first contest for the four-member Sydney constituency in March, were his political enemies. He subsequently won the Goulburn-based Argyle seat.

Urging votes for the 51-year-old Fairfax, Plunkett described him as a man of liberal and honest opinions. He saw Dalley as 'one of the budding hopes of the colony' and was proud to call him his friend. But he should not be standing for parliament yet; 'those who press him forward do it to make a cat's paw of him'. ('He'll beat Granny', one interjector called out; the *Herald*'s nickname dates from the paper's earliest days.)

Parkes nominated Dalley, calling him 'a worthy, able, and independent exponent of the principles which I have endeavoured to assert and carry out in public life'. Then Fairfax spoke, describing himself as an 'earnest and uncompromising friend of civil and religious liberty'. He said he had the highest opinion of Dalley, and would not have stood for election if Dalley had put his name forward first.

According to the *Empire*, Dalley's appearance at the front of the hustings was greeted with 'round after round of cheering, mingled with groans from a small body of men'. He gave a confident performance, winning over interjectors and quoting Shakespeare to praise Parkes, and Juvenal in an amusing refutation of accusations that he was too young for parliament. He called on voters to 'utterly repudiate' the 'ruthless' destruction of the Cowper government. Then he turned to policy, mostly repeating what he had said earlier but on the land issue putting forward a radical proposal:

> We must take the vast estate of this country out of the hands of those who at present hold it in possession; and we must do this not from any miserable class-feeling towards them (because hitherto, I believe, they have been the great supporters of the country), but because there are millions waiting for the change. Over the water – everywhere throughout Europe – such a change would be hailed as a blessing of the highest kind. (Cheers.) Not only should we have a population flocking in from England, Ireland and Scotland – but from France, Germany, and every part of Europe. And never until such a revision of the regulations takes place shall we have the land system of the country producing such blessings.

Winding up his speech, he said he 'thoroughly identified with the Irish, in the principles that are dearest to their hearts'. He hoped that, despite past discouragement, the native-born would soon take their rightful places in parliament. 'I would ask is there a man among those present who is a father who does not wish to see his son at some future day aspiring – and not without the best right – to the attainment of high public distinction in his own, his native land?'

If his own taste had been consulted, he added, he would 'not be here today; but would have been quietly ensconced in my chambers, poring over the first principles of black letter law'.

> During the last five years my happiness has been sufficient to prevent me desiring to add to it in any way that public distinction can increase it; but

at the same time, if you think me qualified to occupy the proud position of being one of your representatives, and you must have thought so or you would not have asked me to appear here today, it will be your duty tomorrow to justify what has been called my presumption in coming before you by placing me at the head of the poll. (Great and prolonged cheering.)

Speeches over, the returning officer called for a show of hands from the electors, which indicated a convincing win for Dalley. The next step in the process was for the losing candidate to demand a poll, which Fairfax duly did. The election was set down for nine to four the next day, when 14 polling stations would be open.[27]

Despite continuing rain, including some heavy downpours, voters turned out in large numbers. Dalley won easily – 1,998 votes to 1,493. A crowd estimated by the *Empire* at upwards of 2,000 gathered at the hustings after voting ended, and erupted with 'loud and long continued cheering' when the returning officer announced the result. The winning margin may have been even greater had the Fairfax camp not circulated a note during the day disputing Dalley's right to stand and claiming votes cast for him were null and void. Dalley said in his victory speech that this had appeared at polling stations around the time when most of his supporters were expected there. He could not object to a protest made 'in a constitutional way before a committee of the Assembly', but when it was 'introduced in order to damage my election, I think it ought to meet with severe public reprehension. (Loud cheers.)'

The ground for the protest was that Dalley was not enrolled as an elector and therefore, under the colonial constitution, not eligible to be elected. On arriving at the hustings for the declaration of the poll, Fairfax requested the returning officer to ask Dalley if he had 'any qualification' for election. Dalley's immediate response was that he would not answer 'any such impertinent enquiry'. To 'prolonged hisses' from the crowd, the returning officer then read the protest note. His announcement that he would refuse Fairfax's request to intervene, saying any protest should be made to an Assembly committee, received a much warmer reception.

Dalley's speech displayed no dampening of his spirits, or concern that the election outcome might be overturned. He suggested Plunkett had advised Fairfax on the matter and added, 'I will only remark that I presume that my honourable and learned friend did not take any fees for his advice.' Thanking the voters, he said he had observed at the polling stations that two classes had supported him – the labouring class and men of education. Education would be a priority issue for him in the Assembly; creating a 'great system of education' was essential to 'making effective that grand system of government which is coming into play in this country.'

Fairfax, who was greeted with cries of 'Sixpenn'orth of waste paper' (the *Herald* cost sixpence in 1856), made a conciliatory speech, saying he would not pursue his protest: 'I should be perfectly ashamed of myself, if – my opponent having a majority of 500 over myself – I were to take any further steps in the matter.' After the returning officer concluded proceedings, 'three vociferous cheers' were given for Dalley. Then followed a lively example of the old English practice of 'chairing' election victors.

> Mr Dalley…was laid hold of by several persons with the view of carrying him home on their shoulders. After some remonstrance…he was placed in a chair, and, amidst the cheers of the multitude, raised on the shoulders of four or five working men, carried across the park towards Market-street – the crowd cheering without interruption. The procession moved down Market-street; six gentlemen riding abreast on horseback immediately behind Mr Dalley, gave the procession a highly picturesque effect. About the middle of Market-street a native youth obtained possession of Mr Dalley's hat and tied around it a light blue ribbon – the Australian colours. This demonstration of youthful patriotism was received with prolonged cheering. At every stage of his progress the victorious candidate was greeted with enthusiastic bursts of congratulation. On the head of the procession reaching George-street, a general cheer was again raised. It was heartily taken up by the crowd that followed, and which completely filled the whole of Market-street. Amidst similar demonstrations the procession moved down George-street. When a little to the north of King-street, the chair on which Mr Dalley was seated came apart. Its occupant, however, had no sooner reached the ground than he was lifted on the shoulders of two men and carried steadily along the street…

The procession's destination was the Exchange Hotel, where Dalley had begun his campaign. As the cheering continued, he proceeded to an upstairs window to address the crowd below. After thanking them for their support and promising to work hard, he said the great interest exhibited in the contest was cause for deep satisfaction. Once a man saw that he could hope to see his sons rise to positions of honour, having received 'the education the State will soon provide for the children of the humblest among you', he would become a staunch supporter of good government. 'As far as I can', he continued,

> I shall open wide the portals of public distinction to men of the class to which I belong, that is to men who have nothing to boast of as regards their ancestry – (cheers) – but who themselves work their own way to a profession (renewed cheers), and then, if they become marked men in the community for simplicity and excellence of life – no matter how obscure they may be – they will have as grand opportunities of advancement opened for them as have been given to me.[28]

3
Assembly and Circuit

The Exchange Hotel gathering was not the end of the day's excitements; several hundred Dalley supporters next proceeded to Parliament House to witness his swearing-in. Reported the *Empire*,

> Tickets of admission were issued as quickly as they could be signed, and in a few minutes the strangers' gallery – previously empty – was filled to overflowing. We observed that several ministers and honorable members on the government side of the house expressed some surprise – if we read their countenances aright – on seeing the gallery 'rushed;' while Mr Holroyd, who was presiding at the time – the house being in committee on the Master and Servant's Act – in a stentorian voice, ordered strangers in the gallery to take off their hats. There were at the same time several hundreds of persons outside who could not obtain admission, the accommodation for strangers being fully occupied.[1]

Escorted by Cowper and Martin, Dalley entered the Assembly at 6.30 p.m., took the oath, signed the roll of members, and was warmly congratulated by various members after taking his seat on the opposition benches. Three days later, when members gathered again after the New Year's break, a surprise awaited him – a petition, presented by Plunkett, claiming his election was invalid and calling for a new poll. Fairfax had sounded as if he meant it when he said he would not pursue his election-day protest, but his supporters were not prepared to let the matter rest.

After a lengthy debate, Plunkett's motion that the petition be referred to the Assembly's elections and qualifications committee was adopted by twenty-seven votes to eleven. Dalley missed most of the discussion; he left at the Speaker's request as a matter affecting him was being considered, but not before hearing an ingenious argument in his support from Martin. The constitution provided that 'any person absolutely free…who shall be qualified and registered as a voter… shall be qualified to be elected…' That seems to mean a candidate must be a registered voter – that is, on an electoral roll. No, said Martin; the clause was 'in affirmance', not 'derogation' of common law – therefore, 'whatever rights Mr Dalley might have in common law, they were not interfered with by this clause.' It was 'an enabling and not a disqualifying clause.'[2]

The committee considering Dalley's status, chaired by one of the Hunter Valley's pioneer farmers and business entrepreneurs, Thomas Scott, met eight times between 28 January and 19 February 1857. An *Empire* reporter, Arthur Cubitt, was the key witness. He said that, on election day, he had told Dalley in the presence of Martin that he had heard he was not on the electoral roll. Dalley had replied, 'No, I know that I am not.' After Dalley had confirmed to Martin that he believed he was not on the roll, Martin had said to Cubitt, 'Never mind, don't say anything about it.' Cubitt recalled that Dalley had said, 'Here is a pretty go, Martin.' Under persistent questioning, however, the reporter insisted he could not be sure whether the references were just to the roll for Sydney or to any New South Wales electoral roll. Local record keeping made it impossible for the committee to arrange its own check of all the rolls.

Having heard Cubitt's evidence, the committee decided, by four to two, that Dalley should be called on 'to show that he is duly qualified to sit as a Member of the Legislative Assembly, by being a Registered Elector according to Law'. He declined to respond. The next day, with one member absent, a draft report was considered. This found the petition's claim had not been proved, but noted that Dalley had not shown he was on the roll anywhere and proposed laying the matter before the Assembly for further consideration. The committee removed the latter two points in votes that could not have been closer – two all, with chairman Scott deciding matters with his casting vote. One member, Samuel Gordon, apparently abstained; he and the absentee, John Oxley, had been part of the previous four-man majority.

Dalley could breathe a sigh of relief when the not proved verdict was reported to the Assembly on 19 February with no recommendation for further action. In the absence of proof that he was not on an electoral roll, he had survived by admitting nothing. The committee implicitly rejected Martin's argument that a candidate did not have to be an enrolled elector.[3]

Confirmation of Dalley's place in the Assembly came a month after Plunkett departed to become President of the Legislative Council and a week after his replacement as member for Argyle by Daniel Deniehy, a very different character. Deniehy had appealed to electors to 'let the principles so nobly sustained in the election of Mr Dalley, at Sydney, be asserted and maintained in Argyle',[4] and was returned unopposed. Shortly after taking his seat he was greeted with cheers and laughter at a public meeting on electoral reform when he noted that 'the most rabid little democrat in existence' now represented the 'respectable and conservative county of Argyle'.

Dalley also spoke at this meeting, called to support the principles of a reform bill, recently defeated in the Assembly, that had been proposed by the independent-minded squatter and writer William Forster. Putting the case for electorates with equal populations – an end to the country/city imbalance – he noted that none of the Parker government's ministers represented Sydney and claimed this showed the Premier had no interest in Sydney. He gave Deniehy – who spoke after him on a resolution calling for an end to the property/income test for electors – a warm welcome; when they heard Deniehy, he said, those at the meeting would regret that he 'had so long occupied their time. (No, no, and loud cheers.)'[5]

Three weeks earlier, Dalley had praised Henry Parkes as 'one of the greatest and purest' of the colony's public men at a meeting called to begin fund-raising for a testimonial presentation to him. Parkes aborted the project by declining the honour, an act that Dalley said reflected his 'delicacy of feeling'.

Dalley was then on the mend after an illness that had kept him out of parliament in January (bouts of illness, short and long, were to curtail his activities on many occasions throughout his life).[6] The first matter he raised on his reappearance in February was the Woodlark Island, Torres

Strait, massacre of September 1855 – the murder of a priest and four crewmen after the brig *Gazelle*, sent to resupply the Catholic mission there, was wrecked off the island. Dalley asked for all correspondence on the matter to be tabled, and said government action was imperative; if 'the natives...found they could massacre whites with impunity it would be manifestly unsafe for any vessel to go on a trading voyage to that neighbourhood.' Premier Parker agreed to table the documents, but said the matter was outside the colonial government's jurisdiction.[7]

Dalley voted with the government against a proposal from his opposition colleague John Robertson, supported by Cowper, to end mounted police patrols in the south and west of the colony as a cost-saving measure. He spoke at length in Martin's defence against 'vile persecutions' by the *Sydney Morning Herald*. And he opposed proposals to amalgamate the two branches of the legal profession – barristers and solicitors – and to eliminate the requirement that those seeking admission to the Bar pass exams in Greek and mathematics. It was 'highly necessary' that barristers should possess a high standard of general education, he said – particularly as they 'were always likely to form a considerable proportion' of members of the Assembly.[8]

When the parliamentary sitting ended, on 18 March, Dalley was in Bathurst, with Martin, for his first Circuit Court engagement. Twice a year, judges of the Supreme Court travelled to the towns on the circuit – in the 1850s, just Bathurst, Goulburn and Maitland – to hear the more serious cases. City barristers attended to defend, and sometimes to prosecute in place of the Attorney-General or Solicitor-General. The arrival of the court was quite an event. Wilfred Blacket KC recalled in his memoirs that sprucely attired mounted police escorted the judge's carriage into town. At the formal opening 'the Judge attended by the Sheriff or his Deputy appeared in his scarlet and ermine, and all men were commanded to stand up while the Queen's Proclamation against Vice and Immorality was read.'[9]

For any traveller, the journey to Bathurst over the Blue Mountains was likely to be memorable. An *Empire* reporter described a 24-hour mail coach trip in 1858. The climb from the Nepean plain was so steep that 'gentlemen' passengers were asked to help by getting out and walking. Boulders studded the road as if they had been purposely placed 'to upset the coach and break our necks'. Stops at inns during the night 'made one portion of the passengers drunk, to the annoyance of the sober portion'. On the descent from Mount Victoria, if the horses strayed 'just one foot from the proper track, nothing is more certain than that the vehicle, with its living freight, would be precipitated into the awful chasms on either side.'[10]

Justice Roger Therry, a politically conservative 56-year-old Irish Catholic who came to the colony in 1829, presided at the March 1857 sittings in Bathurst. A writer for the *Empire* who signed his piece with a capital delta – subsequent contributions signed similarly make it clear this was Dalley – witnessed part of his progress over the mountains. The judge, well muffled, sat in the back of a small carriage drawn by two horses, occasionally assisted by two or three bullocks. His unhappy-looking young associate sat beside the coachman on the box.

> The carriage is suddenly half lost in a vast pit – the brogue from within thunders to the coach-box and reverberates in the ears of the horses – but in vain. The melancholy associate leisurely descends from his place and victoriously stifles an exclamation which might shock his Honor's piety; the poor young man seizes the head of one horse, the coachman that of another; and whispering curses in the ears of both animals they induce them to make an effort, and the weight of law and learning is dragged out of the abyss. Graciously smiles the old Judge, savagely looks the associate, deeply and silently the driver damns Responsible Government.[11]

After his tiring trip, Therry declined an invitation to Bathurst's St Patrick's Day ball and supper – 'solely from an apprehension that, in my present state of health, were I out late at night, I might be prevented from performing the arduous duties of the present Circuit Court.' Dalley attended and spoke; responding to the toast to the Bench and Bar, he offered the view that 'the purest, the noblest, and the most able defenders of the civil and religious liberty of Ireland' had come from the legal profession.

In court, he appeared for the defence in robbery, rape and murder trials. Therry pronounced the death sentence at the conclusion of two of them – the murder case and one of the rape trials. The murderer's fate was uncontroversial. However, Dalley was not the only one shocked at the prospect of the teenager convicted of rape being hanged. The jury had rejected his contention that the effects on the boy of drink provided by the victim, the keeper of a sly-grog shop, would have made rape impossible, but recommended mercy on the grounds of the perpetrator's extreme youth.[12] The Executive Council – the Governor and ministers – dismissed this recommendation and other pleas and petitions, and the young man was duly executed.

The death penalty for rape had been abolished many years before in England, and when parliament met again in August Dalley immediately introduced a bill to abolish it in the colony. The second reading was carried by 19 votes to nine after a long speech in which he described the youth hanged at Bathurst as a 'poor idiot whom the woman herself had been the means of depriving of his self control by giving him liquor to cloud the little reason he had'. He rejected the argument that the fear of execution protected isolated women in the outback by deterring potential rapists. Instead, the prospect that the perpetrators would be hanged made women less likely to report attacks and, when cases did come to court, juries less likely to convict.[13]

Members of the Assembly displayed reluctance to commit themselves on the question, few turning up when the bill's clauses were to be considered in committee. An exasperated Dalley remarked that this experience had dampened any inclination he might have had to become a radical law reformer.[14] He withdrew the bill, but said he hoped the result of the second reading vote would encourage caution by the Executive Council when called on to confirm the death sentence after future rape convictions. Speaking of the 'great indifference' shown, he said that by some accident his bill had always been among the last orders of the day, 'and those gentlemen upon whom he relied to support it had generally left the Chamber when it came on for discussion'.[15]

Dalley had had a busy parliamentary break. Legal work included appearances at the Central Criminal Court for defendants on charges ranging from bank robbery to infanticide. He called Parkes 'one of the greatest of public men' at a large public meeting held as part of an effort to raise funds to save his *Empire* newspaper from collapse.[16] Shortly afterwards, he described him as a million times superior to the editor of the *Herald*, Rev. John West, who had attacked the Cowper government 'with a virulence as unexampled as it was atrocious'. This was in a long, amusing and much cheered speech at a meeting called by Cowper to report on the past parliamentary session. Dalley said he had associated himself with Cowper in the Assembly 'with the fullest conviction in the sincerity of his intentions'.[17]

A week before the resumption of parliament in August, Dalley was among prominent laymen and clergy who addressed a meeting at St Mary's Cathedral to raise funds for the proposed Catholic residential college, St John's, at Sydney University. The university had been inaugurated in 1852; two years later, government grants of up to £20,000 were offered to match funds raised by the churches to establish affiliated colleges. Justice Therry reflected the feeling of the meeting when he praised this unprecedented opportunity, given by a 'truly parental government', to promote higher education for Catholics. Donations poured in.[18]

Dalley called for scholarships to be provided so the college was open to the poor as well as the rich. In a display of his wide reading, he said that, through history, collegiate institutions had been 'designed almost exclusively for the poor'.

> From the thirteenth to the sixteenth century – from the laying of the first collegiate foundation to the last – when the sovereign genius of that mighty ecclesiastic, Wolsey, reared that splendid monument of learning – Oxford College – they were founded principally for the poor scholars who were unable to obtain a position at the University. And so in France, in these institutions the munificence of the clergy and laity had been combined in rearing the splendid college of the Sorbonne...[19]

From the start of the new parliamentary term, the Parker government's prospects of survival looked slim. It hung on after a heavy defeat on a revenue bill in late August, but an electoral bill introduced about the same time soon sealed its fate. This offered the secret ballot – an effort to appease liberal opinion – but rejected the notion of equal representation. The votes of as few as a hundred men would return a member in pastoral districts, compared with about 600 in the towns.[20]

The evening before the second reading debate was to begin more than a thousand people gathered at the Prince of Wales Theatre for a protest meeting; speakers included Dalley and Parkes. Dalley amused the crowd with a commentary on the government's antics, including an alleged statement by Parker that his ministry had been 'kept in existence in spite of himself. (Great laughter.)'[21] He then spoke at length in the Assembly debate, mainly taking the Attorney-General, John Bayley Darvall, to task for reversing his earlier commitment to universal male suffrage and, on the distribution of electorates, 'using the parrot talk of some of the country members'. The legislation was voted down 26 to 23, the government resigned, and Cowper again took the reins as Premier on 7 September.

Ten days later, Dalley set out with Martin, again Cowper's Attorney-General, for another Bathurst Circuit Court sitting. On the way – after the Blue Mountains crossing – they stopped at Hartley, centre of Martin's electorate of Cook and Westmoreland, for his unopposed re-election. Dalley gave a long speech in praise of his friend; he said he had not met him until fairly recently, but had admired him from boyhood despite holding different views on some matters. He said those who sneered when Martin was first appointed Attorney-General a year earlier now felt humiliated by his great success at the Bar. His achievement offered an example to all: 'there is not a man whom I am now addressing, although he may occupy the humblest position, who, if he adopts the proper course, may not entertain the ambition that some child of his may occupy the position which Mr Martin now occupies.'[22]

Sir Alfred Stephen.

The 55-year-old Chief Justice, Sir Alfred Stephen, presided at Bathurst this time.

Martin prosecuted in the criminal trials and Dalley appeared for various defendants. Press interest focused on two civil cases in which Dalley appeared for an attractive young woman jilted by her intended husband after aspersions were cast against her character. Some of Bathurst's most prominent people were involved, and the local paper gave the trials close to verbatim coverage, which was reprinted over a page and a half of the eight-page *Empire*. Dalley was in his element, mixing pathos and humour in lengthy appeals to the juries.

In the first case, the plaintiff, Ellen Stewart, claimed damages for defamation against Frances Wise, sister-in-law of the barrister and later Supreme Court judge Edward Wise, who had employed her as a governess. Ellen denied claims by Mrs Wise in letters to the fiancé, Henry Byrnes, and his father, and in conversations with others, that she had flirted inappropriately with a youthful relative, Charley Wise. After the jury failed to agree on whether Ellen had been defamed, the second case came on – for breach of promise by Henry when he called off the engagement. This time Dalley was successful, the jury awarding her £500 damages.

In arguing Ellen's case, he read out and commented on affectionate letters that had passed between her and Henry. In one of these, Henry mentioned a party to be held at the Wises during the March Circuit Court sittings. 'Mrs Battye [wife of the district police superintendent] must be very much annoyed that she is not able to join in the mirth at the Wises with her esteemed and venerable friend Judge Therry,' he wrote. 'He is a great admirer of hers.' Commented Dalley, 'Little did his Honor imagine…that any young gentleman…would dare to insinuate that that learned judge was otherwise employed in this town than in the discharge of his high judicial functions.' Henry also asked Ellen what she thought of Martin and Dalley; 'I am not aware she thought either of us sufficiently important to justify her in gratifying the curiosity of her admirer,' said Dalley. The reporter noted, 'During the learned counsel's commentaries on the letters, the Court was convulsed with laughter, in which the Chief Justice heartily joined.'[23]

Soon after Dalley returned to Sydney an article in praise of Stephen, clearly Dalley's work, appeared in the *Empire* over the capital delta signature. He suggested that in another era the Chief Justice might have been elected Father Abbot by the Benedictines and then canonised as Saint Alfred the Subtle. However, his expression was by no means sacerdotal; he was a man of playful moods and good temper, and looked about twenty years younger than he was. Able to skip over a groundwork of facts with 'truly Terpsichorean grace', his charges to juries in criminal cases were 'perhaps the most remarkable addresses to be heard in Australian courts'. He was 'eminently the first lawyer in this country'.[24]

Back in parliament, Dalley was active on a variety of issues. A significant contribution was the introduction of a bill removing the requirement for Sydney University students to demonstrate 'competent religious attainments' before being awarded honours or degrees. The Assembly showed no hesitation in supporting his contention that no encroachment should be tolerated upon 'the purely secular character' of the university.[25]

With William Forster, he raised complaints by Chinese miners about seizures of gold dust, worth thousands of pounds, for non-payment of export duty. The government took a hard line, saying there were no grounds for interfering with the due course of the law despite the claim of the Chinese that they were unaware of the duty. Supporting a successful motion to set up a committee to inquire into the matter, Dalley said he held that the Assembly 'was, and trusted it would ever be, the redresser of wrongs, to which any person who was injured could appeal.' When the committee was reconstituted the following year he described the Act imposing the duty as tyrannical and rejected the view that no special consideration should be given to the Chinese. Ignorant 'of our language, our laws, and our institutions', they were entitled to 'more tenderness and consideration than would be shown to British subjects who might offend in like manner,' he said. By the narrowest majority, sixteen to fifteen, the Assembly adopted the committee's recommendation that as much of the seized gold as possible be returned as an act of grace.[26]

The major political issue as 1857 drew to a close was land policy. Cowper introduced legislation on 22 October providing for auctioning of country lots with the minimum price set at five shillings an acre (more for town, suburban and agricultural land). Other provisions protected existing leaseholders but placed a time limit of five years on new leases. Few were persuaded that this was the best means of settling more people on the land, especially after John Robertson – 41-year-old bushman, squatter and 'father' of the land law eventually implemented in 1861 – stepped up promotion of his scheme for 'free selection before survey'.

Robertson detailed his plan in a letter to the *Empire* in November. It would enable people to select and take possession of portions of public land without competition or delay; all they would have to pay up-front was a quarter of the £1 per acre price.[27] Two days later Parkes, who was planning a return to politics, chaired a public meeting at which a range of speakers criticised Cowper's bill. He presided at two more such meetings over the next three weeks, the last a gathering by torchlight that attracted a crowd estimated at nearly 5,000.[28] Adding to Cowper's woes, the highly regarded Catholic priest Archdeacon John McEncroe published a letter calling the land bill 'iniquitous' and urging everyone 'who loves the peace and prosperity of this country, and the peopling of our agricultural lands' to resist its enactment by all constitutional means.[29]

Dalley voted for the bill in the Assembly, but said he felt the question was so vast that dealing with it satisfactorily required an amount of experience of the conditions of the country that he lacked. This created 'a feeling of diffidence', which he had 'never before experienced in addressing the House'.[30] He spoke briefly again after amendments drawn up by Robertson and Deniehy supporting selection before survey were introduced, saying that, on the whole, he opposed them. He favoured the settlement of small capitalists on the land, but doubted very much whether it was sound policy to encourage people with no capital to settle.[31]

Cowper withdrew the bill on 10 December after the Assembly

adopted, on the casting vote of the chairman of committees, a motion by Robertson to defer further consideration of it. The government resigned a week later, after the narrow defeat of a related bill dealing with pastoral lease assessment. Dalley was among those who voted against this. He explained later that he did so because he thought the time had come for an appeal to the country, and he had told Cowper he would oppose any more measures introduced before an election was called.[32] Governor Denison accepted Cowper's advice that the Assembly should be dissolved, so it was back to the polls.

Dalley stood with Cowper and the other sitting members, Robert Campbell and James Wilshire, for the Sydney constituency, having again been persuaded, against his initial inclination, to contest the election. The group's first public meeting, three days before Christmas, would have left them in no doubt that a battle loomed. Around 4,000 people crowded into the Prince of Wales Theatre and gave the speakers a rowdy reception. According to the *Empire*, Cowper obtained a partial hearing with much difficulty. Wilshire, after trying several times to make himself heard, gave up, and Campbell could not obtain a hearing at all. Dalley 'was at first met with determined opposition, which, however, gradually relaxed before his persevering efforts, and he at length obtained audience, and was received on the whole very favourably'.

After saying he planned to retire from parliament and had come to justify his conduct as 'their late representative', Dalley revealed that he had offered to resign his seat in favour of Parkes shortly before the land bill debate (one wonders why Parkes did not accept; he contested another seat in early December and was defeated). He praised Cowper for sacrificing his private fortune and 15 of his best years for the people's welfare, and said he intended to work 'heart and soul' for the Premier's return. He said Cowper's land bill had met the 'great cry' for a reduction in the price of land, and claimed Parkes had previously supported its '5 shillings an acre principle'. In another sign that his opinion of his first political mentor was changing for the worse, Dalley noted that Parkes had allowed a claim that his conduct in the debate had been corrupt to go uncontradicted at one of the public meetings against the bill.³³

With campaigning in full swing, Dalley set out for Melbourne at the end of the year on vacation; apparently he was serious about not standing. Back in Sydney on 7 January, he told an election meeting that he had been followed south by 'the urgent solicitations of a large number of the inhabitants of Sydney' calling on him to put his name forward. He explained later that he had been told people were wrongly interpreting his retirement as a repudiation of Cowper's policies; he had decided to enter the contest 'in order to set both himself and his friends right'.³⁴ At the 7 January meeting he mentioned another influence on his decision; he felt 'stung with injustice' after 'a gentleman he had looked upon as his friend' attacked him.³⁵

This was Frank Fowler, a young English writer who came to the colony in 1855, became part of the Stenhouse circle, and was now – with Stenhouse heading his supporters' list – standing for election for Sydney. After declaring himself in favour of progressive political reform, Fowler, according to the *Empire*, told an election meeting that 'Cowper, and to a lesser extent Dalley, had proved so dishonest, that it was necessary to have two men of average honesty [Campbell and Wilshire] to carry them in.'³⁶ Fowler despatched a one-sentence letter to the editor denying he had ever 'said Mr Dalley is 'dishonest'.' However, the paper rejected the denial, saying its reporter had taken down Fowler's words verbatim.³⁷

Dalley did not accept the denial either. He said he had been Fowler's friend since his arrival in the colony, but considered his denial even more insulting than the original assertion. Apparently Fowler did not harbour a grudge; in *Southern Lights and Shadows*, his memoir of his three years in Sydney published in 1859, he described Dalley as a 'fine, genial-hearted, smart young native'.³⁸

Three more contenders joined the contest – the Mayor of Sydney, George Thornton, the brewer Robert Tooth and a soap and candle manufacturer, William Allen. A noisy crowd estimated at 9,000 gathered around the newly re-erected hustings in Hyde Park for the nominations on 14 January. Sir Daniel Cooper, Speaker of the Legislative Assembly and the financier who had kept the *Empire* afloat for many years,[39] nominated Dalley, calling him a man of good judgement and a thorough liberal. In a spirited interaction with interjectors, Dalley reaffirmed his commitment to the Cowper government, to the principles of its land bill, and to electoral reform. He said that if the voters wished to punish the Cowper team, they should put him out 'in preference to one of your old and tried representatives'.[40]

The next day they did just that. Thornton topped the poll, followed by Tooth. Cowper scraped into the fourth spot, behind his colleague Robert Campbell. Dalley was fifth, followed by Fowler and then the other member of the Cowper group, James Wilshire. At the declaration of the poll on 18 January, Dalley said his most strenuous opposition had come from Irishmen despite the fact that no man had ever been more willing to promote their wellbeing. And all the Catholic clergy had voted against him. He did not blame them, but gloried in having stood by Cowper, even though it may have cost him election.[41]

Twenty-five years later – on 'what is to me almost a sacred anniversary' – he elaborated at another election meeting.

> Finding…my dear friend and old political leader (Sir Charles Cowper) about to be rejected, and myself to be elected in his place, I drove to every public place in the electorate, and implored my friends to save me the humiliation of being preferred to him, and to vote for the man whose talents and services were of such infinitely higher value to the country. (Cheers, and 'So you did.') I cherish the memory of that easy and delightful sacrifice as one of the proudest and tenderest recollections of my life…[42]

4
In and out of office

The loss proved a brief setback; a week later Dalley was elected the member for Cumberland Boroughs, which included Liverpool, Campbelltown and the Hawkesbury River settlements Windsor and Richmond. The news of his defeat in Sydney had reached Windsor by mail coach at 10.30 on election night. Reported the *Empire*,

> On the announcement being made to hundreds, who had eagerly surrounded the coach-office, Mr John Dawson immediately called for three cheers for Dalley as representative for the Cumberland Burroughs. This was instantly responded to with unmistakable spirit.

The gathering then moved to a nearby hotel to prepare a requisition to Dalley to stand for the electorate, 'which was forwarded to Sydney immediately'.[1]

Dalley told the two to three hundred people at the nomination at Windsor on 20 January that he had not intended to contest another seat. However, the election night events in Windsor, 'the most gratifying tribute that he could have received', had swayed him. He had to decline requisitions received, not quite so quickly, from five more constituencies – one of them Darling Downs (Queensland separated from New South Wales the following year). Placards posted around Toowoomba extolled the proposed candidate as a native-born Australian, a thorough liberal and not a squatter, and concluded with the line 'Dalley! Dalley!! Dalley!!! For ever'.[2]

He faced two opponents in Cumberland Boroughs, the conservative sitting member William Bowman and a liberal opposed to Cowper's land policy, William Redman. At the nomination, Redman observed that he had to contend not only against Dalley but also against his 'thousand and one friends', and criticised him for sticking 'hard and fast' with

Cowper. Dalley confirmed his support for the principles of Cowper's land bill, but said if anyone could show him a more equitable system he would back it. He thought 'every British subject of fair character, resident in the country for some fixed period', should have the vote. While opposing state aid for religion, he thought Governor Bourke's Act introducing it had done great good by recognising the principle that there should be no dominant church. He was a Catholic, he said, but 'would rather have his right arm cut off' than see his church dominant.³

Dalley beat Bowman easily (246 votes to 168), and Redman came a distant third. Across the colony, despite the setback in Sydney, voting generally favoured the liberals, strengthening the government's position. Parkes made his re-appearance after a close contest in the Cumberland North Riding electorate, which took in a broad area to Sydney's west and north. John Robertson's appointment as Minister for Lands and Works was the key change to Cowper's ministerial team after the elections; the proponent of free selection before survey now had the job of delivering an acceptable land policy.

The government immediately plunged into controversy with the sacking of Plunkett as chairman of the National Schools Board, a post he had filled with energy and success for 10 years. State funding for primary education was channelled through this board and the Denominational Schools Board, which oversaw schools run by the churches. Plunkett's involvement with the national system had displeased many of his fellow Catholics, clergy and lay, but his sacking – and Dalley's support for it – aroused much passion. His political supporters, including the *Herald*, railed against Cowper – and were joined by the unofficial Catholic paper, the *Freeman's Journal*. Though frowned on at the time by the hierarchy, it reflected the official view on this issue.

The dispute arose over a proposal by the national board to expand its reach by

J.H. Plunkett.

funding certain 'non-vested' schools, owned by individuals or societies. When Plunkett demanded that rules drawn up for the new scheme be gazetted, Cowper made the reasonable point that parliament's view of the plan, which would require extra funding, should be elicited first. Plunkett replied belligerently, saying his board refused to 'be guided by the individual opinion' of Cowper; then he disputed Cowper's response that the position he had stated was the government's, not just his own. Plunkett accused Cowper, who had chaired the denominational board, of having always been hostile to the national system.[4]

Plunkett gave copies of his letters to the press while the correspondence was proceeding – an 'irregular and unseemly' thing to do, Cowper complained in the letter advising that the Executive Council had decided to dismiss him. The Premier also complained of the 'highly improper' terms in which Plunkett had addressed him. Plunkett responded by resigning as President of the Legislative Council and from various other public posts, and accusing the government of instituting a 'reign of terror'.

Dalley also chose to be provocative, noting in a brief letter to the *Empire* over his capital delta signature that Plunkett had 'omitted to resign the pension he receives as ex-Attorney General'. Referring to a protest meeting planned for Hyde Park, he went on,

> It is to be regretted that the honorable gentleman has thus deprived the Rev. John West [editor of the *Herald*] and his other supporters of the excellent *materiel* for the display of their oratorical powers in proclaiming his political martyrdom in Hyde Park on Monday next, which such a self-sacrifice would have afforded.[5]

Attacks by *Freeman's Journal* on Dalley began in late February with an anonymous letter suggesting he had joined the ranks of the avowed enemies of the faith and of civil liberty.[6] After he voted with the government when Plunkett's sacking was debated in the Assembly in April, the paper predicted that certain 'sweet voices' would no longer be heard in parliament after the next elections.[7] Its Windsor correspondent took up the theme, saying Dalley's conduct was 'severely commented upon by his constituency' and predicting the disappearance of his 'sweet voice' as representative of Cumberland Boroughs.[8] A Campbelltown correspondent joined in, suggesting his 'thick and thin' support for Cowper had sprung from a desire to marry one of Cowper's daughters. 'Poor Dalley has sacrificed much in his precipitate haste to take a hop, step, and leap at once into such a social position as his hard struggling parents never dreamed of,' he wrote.[9]

In the parliamentary debate, initiated by James Macarthur, a prominent Plunkett supporter, Dalley said his opinion of Plunkett's character and services to the country was perhaps as high as that of any member. However, Plunkett had written a most offensive letter to the government and published it before the government had seen it. 'If the House sanctioned this conduct on the part of any subordinate, and allowed him to treat the Government with contempt, and moreover, to publish that contempt to the world, where would be the dignity of the Government?' He said he would be glad to see Plunkett reinstated if he withdrew the letter.[10]

Macarthur's motions condemning the government were lost, but then five liberals – including Deniehy but not Dalley – crossed the floor to pass a compromise resolution expressing the hope that steps would be taken that would allow Plunkett's reinstatement. This was an invitation to withdraw his offensive comments, but he refused to do so. Riding a wave of sympathy, he returned to the Assembly unopposed in September 1858, taking the seat Parkes had vacated at the end of August when his struggling *Empire* finally collapsed.

Undeterred by Catholic criticism, Dalley raised another contentious issue in parliament a week after the Plunkett debate. He asked Cowper whether the government intended to introduce any measure 'for assimilating the law with regard to divorce to the law of England' during the present session. Cowper said he hoped legislation could be introduced in the current or next session.[11]

England's first divorce law was enacted in 1857, and the Australian colonies followed suit with similar legislation. New South Wales, as it turned out, was last to act, not establishing its divorce court until 1873. By 1870 Dalley was an opponent of legalising divorce, winning praise from the Catholic hierarchy for a speech on the subject in the Legislative Council (chapter 12).[12] But *Freeman's* was probably right in assuming he held a different view in 1858. It noted with sorrow that 'the 'Liberal' Catholic MP, *par excellence,*' had been the first to call the Assembly's attention 'to the Propriety of introducing into the colony Lord Palmerston's anti-Christian law of Divorce'.[13] (He had another change of mind on the subject later, as Attorney-General in 1884 supporting extension of the grounds available for divorce – chapter 21.)

Dalley was in the paper's sights again in June after introducing a bill to change the rules governing the licensing of publicans. Its most contentious feature was a clause allowing Sunday trading, which, he said, was 'neither effectually prevented nor effectually carried out' under existing rules. Thundered *Freeman's*, 'The feelings of the peaceable and the religious are to be trampled upon, the happiness of families destroyed, new opportunities for disgrace and infamy offered... And all this solely to give to the publican a very slight additional means of enriching himself.' Dalley told the Assembly he would not object if a majority of members wanted hotels shut altogether on Sundays, but withdrew his bill after speakers proposed other, unacceptable, changes.[14]

Outside politics, a mixture of criminal and civil cases in Sydney kept him busy early in the year. Then it was back to Bathurst in March for the Circuit Court, this time with Justice John Dickinson in charge. This 52-year-old English-man was the original proponent of a colonial hereditary peerage, the idea taken up by Wentworth and sunk by sustained ridicule in the lead-up to responsible government. Dalley received a warm welcome to Bathurst; 'a number of the leading inhabitants' escorted him in to the town.[15]

The case that attracted most interest was a killing at the Devil's Hole gold diggings. An American miner, George Roberts, told an innkeeper that five men had attacked and robbed him in his hut and he had killed three of them. But it turned out that there was only one victim. Dalley, for the defence, suggested this man had plied Roberts with drugged liquor – hence his confusion. He also argued that Roberts had acted in defence of his property, not with malicious intent. The *Empire* was one of a number of newspapers that expressed doubts about the jury's guilty verdict and called for the death sentence to be commuted. The *Bathurst Free Press* noted the town's 'painful remembrance' of the failure of pleas to spare the teenager convicted of rape in controversial circumstances a year earlier (chapter 3), and 'rejoiced' at the news, received a few days later, of the American's reprieve.[16]

Dalley was making a name for himself as defence counsel in murder trials. Back in Sydney in early April, a young man found guilty of manslaughter rather than murder after stabbing his wife during a domestic quarrel thanked him for the 'able earnestness' of his defence.[17] Two weeks later he defended an elderly shepherd, Joseph Wilkes, whose wife and two sons had died from axe blows to the head. Charged with murdering one of the boys, Wilkes accused another shepherd of the crimes. Dalley addressed the jurors for four hours, but failed to persuade them to acquit Wilkes. Before pronouncing the death sentence, Justice Therry said he 'entirely' agreed with their guilty verdict.[18]

The condemned man continued to proclaim his innocence up to the morning set for his execution at Darlinghurst Gaol. Then at almost the last moment, as he was about to be led to the gallows, his reprieve was announced. Those in his cell at the time included four Catholic priests, Dalley and Cowper, who conveyed the letter containing the reprieve to the sheriff.[19]

That morning's events sparked a lengthy debate in parliament, with Cowper accused of cruelly delaying informing Wilkes that his sentence had been commuted to life imprisonment. Cowper acknowledged that the Executive Council had made the decision the day before, and said the announcement was delayed in case some last-minute proof of guilt emerged. The debate livened up when George Thornton, who had topped the poll at the Sydney election, said a rumour was abroad that

> Mr Dalley went to the prison, and accompanied by several persons who

must have known of the reprieve, visited the prisoner's cell, shook hands with the prisoner, who thanked him for his defence; and Mr Dalley then said, 'Good-bye, old fellow;' and prisoner, in reply, said he hoped he would meet him in Heaven. If this rumour were true, such conduct demanded the reprehension of the community.

Dalley was absent from parliament – in Bathurst again – but various members sprang to his defence. Cowper said the rumour was untrue. Peter Faucett, a conservative Catholic barrister, said no one who knew 'the kindness of disposition' that characterised Dalley would believe for an instant that he had 'sported with the feelings of any man in such a position'. Elias Weekes, an ironmonger of liberal persuasion, called Dalley one of the most kind-hearted men he had met and accused Thornton of spreading poisonous slander. A chastened Thornton said he had no intention of saying one word that could hurt Dalley's feelings.[20]

Dalley had his say in the Assembly a week later, accusing Thornton of knowing the rumour was false. He said he had accompanied Cowper to the condemned cell having been told that Wilkes wanted to thank him for his defence and shake his hand. That handshake had occurred, but he said nothing; indeed he was 'too much overcome with emotion to speak on that solemn and awful occasion'. Responding, Thornton acknowledged that he should not have used Dalley's name 'without due consideration'.[21]

The Cowper government's hold on power looked tenuous for a short time in April after the Assembly voted to oppose the despatch of Royal Artillerymen stationed in Sydney to help put down the Indian Mutiny.[22] Thornton proposed the successful resolution, which claimed removing the soldiers would leave the city defenceless. Dalley voted with the government in opposing it. He said he was sure every man would take up arms if the colony were invaded, and if a hostile vessel entered the harbour men would swim out and scuttle it. (That notion was recalled to his embarrassment in later years.[23] Though the papers did not report it at the time, he allegedly said the scuttlers could bore a hole in the ship's bottom with a gimlet.)

Dalley was among those who thought a second defeat on the artillery question a week later amounted to a censure requiring the ministry's resignation. A vote of confidence in the government, moved by Parkes and carried overwhelmingly, saved the situation. The liberals who had crossed the floor recognised that key items on their agenda, especially electoral reform, were at risk if it fell.[24]

Electoral reform – the introduction of manhood suffrage, representation according to population, and the secret ballot – was the dominant political issue for most of the rest of the year. Cowper introduced a reform bill based on these principles at the end of March, and rowdy public meetings, for and against, were held in April. Dalley and Parkes arrived together in the middle of one of these, were loudly called on to speak, but could not gain a hearing in the uproar.[25]

Conservatives predicted dire consequences from the changes. In the second reading debate in early May, Donaldson said the bill promised revolution, not reform, and if it passed he would leave the colony (he did so the following year). Dalley responded that a peaceful, bloodless, and blessed revolution was in store, and provoked much mirth when he alleged that the former Premier's declaration had brought tears to the eyes of a conservative colleague. The *Empire* commended the 'good-natured yet effective ridicule' he had poured on the 'sackcloth and ashes' brigade.[26]

The second reading vote (36 to 14) on 12 May gave overwhelming endorsement to the bill's principles. However, much hard work lay ahead in committee to secure agreement on the details – particularly the make-up of electorates. Dalley's contributions generally had a light touch. He opposed retaining the existing exclusion of clergy from the Assembly – seen as a device to keep the radical Presbyterian Rev. John Dunmore Lang out – but viewed 'with very much alarm' the possibility of 'any considerable number of clergymen' being elected.[27] He would not give the British military stationed in the colony the vote because they were not settled inhabitants. Also, they were liable 'to be influenced by a tyrannical colonel, who, if they did not vote according to his dictation, might march them off to Bondi, and so prevent them from voting'.[28]

The Assembly approved the bill, essentially intact, on 26 August. Sixty-seven electorates would return a total of 80 members, with the elections still spread out so candidates defeated in one seat could try their luck elsewhere. Dalley was part of the majority that rejected William Forster's proposal that all constituencies vote on one day.[29] The conservative-dominated Legislative Council kept the issue in suspense for another two and a half months, but finally passed the bill after the Assembly rejected its attempt to restore a property or income qualification for voters.

Four days earlier, on 8 November, the government plunged into another crisis with the departure of Martin as Attorney-General. Cowper had requested his resignation, claiming he continually failed to attend cabinet meetings and parliament, and displayed 'utter indifference to questions of government'. Martin replied that he had joined forces with Cowper because of their shared wish to remove the Donaldson and Parker governments. They had few opinions in common; for example, he did not approve of the secret ballot or universal suffrage. Now he would be free to act in accordance with his own convictions, and expected a struggle for mastery to ensue between 'the educated intellect of the country' and 'misguided ignorance'.[30]

Cowper appointed the junior legal member of cabinet, Solicitor-General Alfred Lutwyche, Attorney-General and invited Dalley to take Lutwyche's former position. Dalley's legal experience had expanded substantially during 1858, in a wide range of civil as well as criminal cases. And he had initiated law reforms in parliament, including removing the need for people to sell real estate to settle minor debts and allowing the husbands or wives of parties in civil cases to give evidence.[31] There seemed to be general acceptance that, despite his youth, he was qualified for the job. The bitter falling out of his friends and mentors Cowper and Martin placed him in a somewhat awkward position. However, after a few days' hesitation he accepted the appointment.

Accompanied by Deniehy, he returned to Windsor on 24 November for his unopposed re-election. He told the 150 people gathered at the courthouse that he had hoped to be a minister one day, but not yet, and had initially declined Cowper's offer despite the unanimous advice of his friends to accept it. Then John Robertson, one of the colony's 'most high-minded and talented' representative men, had come to see him and threatened to resign if he persisted in refusing office. As Robertson's resignation would have brought down the government, he had changed his mind.

He said he could no more have anticipated his present position than that 'five years hence he would be Lord High Admiral of England'. But it showed that high places of state were now open to young natives. Waxing lyrical, he wondered how many of his 'brave and brilliant countrymen' had laboured unrecognised 'on the banks of far off rivers – amid the deep solitudes of the forest'. But times had changed. 'Labour sedulously, speak bravely, basing all things upon the grand principles of honour as applied to public life, and the government of the country [will] rest in the hands of the youths of Australia,' he advised.[32]

Cheers from both sides of the Assembly greeted Dalley when he was sworn in again on 25 November after his re-election.[33] That was probably the high point of his brief term as Solicitor-General. Later the same evening he complained that Plunkett had 'imputed corruption to him as Solicitor-General'. Plunkett's offending remark was a claim that he had made political capital out of resolutions moved by Deniehy affirming equality of the churches in New South Wales. The resolutions were a response to the acceptance by the Secretary of State for the Colonies, Lord Stanley, of a complaint by Sydney's Anglican Bishop about the Act establishing St John's College; the Bishop objected to its recognition of the terms Archbishop and Archdiocese of Sydney as used by the Catholic Church.[34]

In the initial debate at the end of October, Plunkett and Dalley made strong speeches supporting Deniehy's resolutions. Dalley called Stanley's despatch backing the Bishop's view an act of tyranny, and said that if the resolutions did nothing more than enlighten him 'as to the state of opinion here with regard to religious freedom' they would 'effect a great and glorious purpose'.[35] He also supported a second set of resolutions that Deniehy moved in November. In both cases the motions lapsed for want of a quorum. Plunkett claimed Dalley had assured him enough members would be present the second time around for a vote; presumably his anger at seeing the chamber empty out again prompted his outburst.[36]

Dalley took advantage of a debate soon afterwards on a proposal that the Attorney-General and Solicitor-General no longer be cabinet members to try to mend relations. Both he and Plunkett supported this idea. He remarked that no Attorney-General had discharged his duties more conscientiously or with a greater sacrifice of personal interests than Plunkett.[37]

Out of parliament, good intentions turned sour at Windsor when a dispute erupted over a cup, worth £20, that Dalley donated as a prize for the Hawkesbury Regatta to be held after Christmas. He sent the cup to a publican to pass on to the regatta committee, but the publican refused to do so and won the backing of the local magistrates. Much ill feeling arose, a correspondent reported, with many townsmen 'allowing their evil passions to have full sway'. Then the regatta was a failure, with few entrants and some events uncontested. 'The cup, which has acquired so much and such singular celebrity, was unfortunately not subjected to competition,' wrote another reporter.[38]

Things did not improve in the New Year. Immediately the Assembly returned, on 4 January 1859, Martin moved that the sum voted for state aid to the churches be increased by 50 per cent. Deniehy joined Dalley and Cowper's other ministers in opposing the resolution, which was first passed and then defeated. It is ironic that Martin, from a Catholic family but no churchman, was a strong supporter of the church's position on state aid while the two young committed Catholics were equally firm opponents. Deniehy amused members with a character sketch of Martin who, he said, with 'his oracular tone' expected the house to regard every sentiment he uttered as law. Martin seemed to divide members into two categories –

> those...who in his opinion might know a thing or two, but whose

knowledge of course was not to be compared with his own colossal acquirements, [and those] whom he regarded as knowing absolutely nothing, and who ought not for a moment to question anything he said.[39]

It seems that after the debate an MP visited St Mary's Cathedral and reported that Deniehy, Dalley and another Catholic opponent of state aid, James Hart, had said some priests had told them they also opposed the additional support. The Vicar-General sent identical letters to the three, which read,

> Abbot Gregory presents his compliments to Mr [Deniehy, Dalley or Hart], and begs permission to inquire whether there is any truth in the report which represents Mr [...] as having said in the Legislative Assembly, that, having communicated with several of the Catholic clergy, he had found them entirely in favour of the measure which has just withdrawn the increase in aid of clerical stipends.
>
> And, if that report should be true, Abbot Gregory would ask as a favour, the names of the clergy who have expressed such opinions, provided, of course, that the disclosure break no express or implied engagement of secrecy.

Deniehy read his letter and subsequent correspondence with Gregory in the Assembly, saying a matter of parliamentary privilege was involved; such communications from outsiders risked interfering with freedom of debate. Both he and Hart, who spoke next, denied they had said anything about the opinions of priests on the question. Dalley then said he had been 'honoured with a similar correspondence. (Laughter.)' He refused to respond to Gregory's queries.[40]

Martin, who had no time for Deniehy (a feeling heartily reciprocated), moved in early January for a return to be laid on the table of 'all amounts paid during the last three months' to Deniehy 'for professional services rendered to the Government'. As Deniehy pointed out in the acrimonious debate that followed, this carried the implication that the government was buying his political support with fees for legal work. It turned out that the only payment he had received was 14 guineas for a job undertaken in Goulburn for the previous government two years earlier.

Indicative of the passions generated, Martin repeatedly called on the Speaker to declare expressions used by Deniehy unparliamentary and then walked out in the middle of his speech. Deniehy claimed that Martin had three motives – to retaliate against him for earlier criticisms, to insult the government, and to wound Dalley's feelings. Martin knew that 'an almost fraternal regard' existed between Dalley and himself, and the motion conveyed the impression that Dalley had improperly put 'practice and money' his way.

Dalley's response confirmed the breakdown in his relations with Martin. He said he had laughed at Martin's 'sneer' that he must have felt more astonishment than the public at being called to the office of Solicitor-General, recalling how Martin's first appointment as Attorney-General had been greeted. Noting Martin's attempt at irony in calling his speech at the start of the debate 'galvanic', he said humour was one 'of the departments of intellect' in which 'the learned gentleman' did not excel.[41]

Dalley reflected on the battles in the Assembly in his response to the toast to parliament at a dinner on 25 January commemorating the centenary of the birth of the Scottish poet Robert Burns. He noted that he was seated on one side of the chairman and the conservative John Hay on the other, and that

> in another place they were opponents – his honourable friend would permit him to say bitter opponents – attacking each other on every ground, and occasionally upon no ground at all. (Cheers and laughter.) And not over-scrupulous, when the actions of each other were blameless – in endeavouring to discover something exceptionable in each other's intentions. (Cheers and laughter.) Carrying on the war of party, in fact, without malice, yet without mercy. Tonight they were drinking wine with each other, on the best possible terms with each other, themselves, and society at large. (Cheers and laughter.)

It was good, he added, on occasions such as the dinner to be able to 'forget private or political animosities and spend an hour or two at least as Heaven intended a life to be spent'. He infinitely preferred 'this sort of thing to the public business – at all events for one night. (Loud cheers.)'[42]

Dalley's good humour quickly dissipated. Replying a week later to a letter from Parkes seeking help in finding a government job for a friend, he wrote of his 'weariness of the whole concern' and 'rare happiness… in these days'.[43] In parliament that evening he wondered aloud, during an attack on the government by a dissident liberal, how any minister could bear to hold office in the face of such abuse. He would no longer bear it, he added.[44] The next day he was in dispute again with Plunkett, claiming that the Irish veteran's hostility to the government was 'wholly unparalleled in parliamentary history'.[45]

In an estimates debate on 10 February, he remarked that responsible government had little chance if a government lacked the support of a powerful party that 'would put down crochets' on the one hand and hypocrisy in its support on the other. He then lay down on his bench, prompting Plunkett to ask the chairman of committees whether he thought such an attitude 'was a proper one for any society of gentlemen, and especially when another gentleman was putting a question to him'. Dalley responded that 'no invention of upholstery' could make a seat sufficiently comfortable for such a duty as being compelled to listen to a speech by Plunkett.[46] He resigned as Solicitor-General the next day.

5
Twank and Tiptop

One of Dalley's jobs as Solicitor-General had been to prosecute in the Central Criminal Court – a new experience for the young barrister after making his name as a defence counsel. During his three months in office he presented the Crown case at burglary, forgery, horse stealing, assault on the high seas, perjury, libel and murder trials. A newly arrived 31-year-old English barrister, Lyttleton Holyoake Bayley, appeared for the defence in the murder case, in early December 1858. The accused man, charged with murdering his wife, was acquitted. According to the *Herald*, Bayley 'made a most able and ingenious defence', which 'elicited the warmest encomiums from Mr Justice Therry'.[1]

Apparently Dalley was impressed too. A month later, Therry announced his retirement. To prevent numbers on the Supreme Court bench falling from an inadequate three to an impossible two, the government brought Samuel Milford, the judge at Moreton Bay, back to Sydney and announced that Attorney-General Lutwyche would replace him.[2] So Cowper again had to find an Attorney-General. He offered the position to Dalley, who turned it down and proposed that Bayley be appointed. Repercussions as the year progressed included a further souring of relations with Martin and the transformation of Deniehy from dear friend to bitter antagonist.

Bayley, an Eton-educated relative of John Bayley Darvall, Attorney-General in the Parker government, was admitted to the colonial Bar on 2 November 1858, shortly after arriving in Sydney with his family. He had eight years' experience as a barrister in England. Cowper announced that he would take over as Attorney-General when Lutwyche left for Moreton Bay in February and arranged a seat for him in the Legislative

Council, which he took up on 19 January 1859. A *Herald* leader three days later set the theme for the attacks to come.

> Mr Bayley is, we understand, a gentleman, respectable both in his connections and in his personal character, but scarcely known to the colonists by name. The vessel which brought him will carry back the news of his elevation to the first legal office under the Crown – that he is entrusted with the administration of colonial laws, of which he has never heard, and that he has to determine the policy of a country, the circumstances of which he must be totally unacquainted with… A thousand young briefless barristers in the English Courts will compare their own British prospects with those unfolded in the colony…[3]

Deniehy led the assault in parliament on 8 February, three days before Dalley resigned as Solicitor-General. He moved that the Assembly declare Bayley's appointment 'unsatisfactory' and insist that appointments to 'public offices of trust and power' be restricted to people who had lived in the colony long enough to establish the 'fitness and propriety' of their selection. In a long, fairly temperate speech, he elaborated on the *Herald*'s objections to Bayley. He said the government should implement the Assembly's earlier resolution calling for the posts of Attorney-General and Solicitor-General to be outside cabinet. This would make suitable candidates easier to find, he argued.

Replying, Dalley pointed out that the government had announced that the new Attorney-General would not be joining cabinet. Despite this, it had been unable to find an established Sydney barrister who was sympathetic to its policies and willing to take the job. He congratulated Deniehy on his temperate tone and language, but said finding himself and his friend 'tilting at each other' from opposite sides of the house was a circumstance he had 'certainly never expected to witness'.

Cowper also spoke, stressing the difficulty of finding candidates for the legal positions, confirming that in future they would not be cabinet posts, and praising Bayley not

Daniel Deniehy.

only as a well-credentialled lawyer but also as a gentleman by birth and education. The last point gave Deniehy an opening for his summing up; such an argument 'might be good in an old aristocratic country', he declared, but he was 'perfectly astonished' to hear it from a democratic leader 'in a country like this'. The resolution was rejected by 19 votes to 12, with Plunkett among Deniehy's supporters.[4]

Deniehy was soon at the centre of a battle outside parliament. Some prominent Catholic laymen had been engaged for months in an often-heated argument with the hierarchy over the laity's role in the church; Vicar-General Gregory was the chief target of their complaints, partly as proxy for the popular Archbishop Polding. This was the background to the disdainful reading of letters from Gregory by Deniehy, Dalley and Hart in parliament in January. When a month later Gregory proposed that a Protestant medical doctor fill the position Plunkett had resigned on the management board of the Catholic orphan school at Parramatta, passions erupted. *Freeman's Journal*, in a leader written by editor Jabez King Heydon, screamed that Gregory had committed 'treason against Holy Church and the lambs of her flock!'[5] Three days later a rowdy meeting at the Victoria Theatre appointed a 'provisional committee' to take over the job of nominating candidates for the boards of government-supported Catholic institutions such as this school.

Deniehy was the main speaker, delivering an eloquent harangue frequently interrupted by cheers. He wondered why Dalley, 'the first native Catholic minister' in the colonial government, had not been proposed for the board. There was a 'noble band of democratic young Catholics, thoroughly identified with the social, moral, and religious feelings of the country', but Gregory had 'no love for the young men of the colony'.[6]

The hierarchy responded by threatening Deniehy, Heydon and five others with excommunication unless they renounced the meeting's resolutions within eight days. All but Deniehy quickly complied. However, he was the only one for whom Polding expressed sympathy. 'We have the testimony of a priest that he has made satisfaction verbally even more fully than all the others have,' the Archbishop advised the

Vatican. 'He was disgusted at his confreres.'[7] Dalley stayed away from this fight, and from the lay agitation generally. From his speech it is clear that Deniehy still had friendly feelings towards him, but this was to change as the year wore on. Back in parliament, new issues arose related to the administration of justice, and Deniehy and Plunkett led the attack.

The first followed Cowper's replacement of Dalley as Solicitor-General by John Hargrave, a judge of the recently created District Court. Cowper chose a member of the Assembly who usually opposed the ministry, Robert Owen, to take Hargrave's place on the Bench. He told Owen that he was being considered for the judgeship, without actually offering it to him, before an expected close division in the Assembly. Owen voted with the government. Was this corruption?[8]

When Plunkett proposed that a committee be established to look into the matter, Dalley concurred despite saying he accepted Owen's assurance that no offer had been made before the vote.[9] Evidence to the committee showed it had been common knowledge that Owen was likely to go to the District Court. He said he had mentioned to two people, one of them Dalley, that he had been sounded out but not made an offer. He was confident that Dalley – who was in Bathurst with the Circuit Court and so could not be examined – had not spread the news.[10] The committee, dominated by opponents of Cowper, condemned both Owen and the Premier, but the Assembly rejected its report by 19 votes to eight.

Deniehy directed his fire at a variety of other targets, accusing the Cowper ministry in March of being 'the first responsible government to pollute the fountain of justice'. A few days later he urged the Assembly to censure Attorney-General Bayley for selecting an allegedly unknown and incompetent lawyer to prosecute at recent Circuit Court hearings in Maitland.[11] Instead, a committee was set up, chaired by Martin, which concluded that Bayley had shown 'great imprudence and want of discretion' in the matter.[12]

The next issue arose from a libel action launched by a wealthy south coast landowner, Alexander Berry, against Rev. John Dunmore

Lang. The then Attorney-General, Alfred Lutwyche, had taken over the prosecution after denying Berry permission to prosecute privately, and Lang was acquitted. Plunkett responded by introducing a bill to allow private prosecutions in such cases. Dalley opposed it, on the grounds that it related to a particular recent case and that such prosecutions were safer in the hands of Crown officers. Deniehy spoke next, saying he was astounded to hear Dalley 'make use of such sophistry'.[13]

Dalley was only recently back from Bathurst, where Chief Justice Stephen had presided at the Circuit Court. As usual, the criminal cases heard ranged from relatively minor matters to murder. Two documents that emerged from the sitting suggest there must have been moments when both Sir Alfred and Dalley found it unnecessary to concentrate on proceedings. They also confirm that the veteran judge and young barrister enjoyed each other's company, and perhaps suggest that Dalley's heavy use of tobacco at the time worried Stephen.

Wrote the Chief Justice,

EPITAPH
Here lie the Mortal Remains
(Smoke Dried)
of
WILLIAM BEDE DALLEY
a gentleman distinguished for great Energy, Patriotism and Eloquence, at the Bar and in the Senate,
But
his energy, exhausted by constant application to cigars – his Patriotism, exhibited by sacrificing himself to Foreign productions – and his Eloquence, at one time fiery, at another balmy and seductive, under the influence of consuming or consumed Tobacco, became
At length Extinguished!
Thoroughly burned up in the Furnace of his own manufacture, embalmed by the essential Oil which he had substituted for the Vital juices, and become a Receptacle for Snuff only, made by the Ashes of his own Pipe, his Pipe is now thoroughly and finally
Put out.
What remained of him evaporated,
At the early age of twenty-nine;
Curling gracefully Upwards

To
Mount Vesuvius:
On the summit of which it reposes.
Of the Residue,
The greater part is with the Tobacconists;
And the Rest lies beneath.

Dalley responded:

'RETORT COURTEOUS'
In Memory of
Sir Alfred Stephen, Knt.,
Who
Departed this Life on the 19th August, 1904; at the advanced age of 102 years.
He was a
Great Patriarch, having had nine sons and nine daughters.
He was also, in some respects, a good Judge; And he perhaps might have been a
Great Legislator,
If the Assembly had not cut short his efforts, by voting that the more a Man knows of our Laws, the less be ought to have to do with them.
He was, however, returned as
Member for the Western Districts,
In the
First Elective Upper House;
And, although he never could induce his Constituents to Prefer
Colonial Wine to Whisky,
Yet
He did some service, by compelling them to Eradicate their
Beloved Bathurst Burr.
He was not so fortunate in all his endeavours;
For, after forty-three years of writing and talking,
He
Left the Magistracy no better acquainted with
Law than he found them, and he never persuaded
One Prisoner to be altogether pleased with his
Sentence.
He was celebrated
For always doing things the most dissimilar
At the same time: – such as writing begging-letters for a College, or an Epitaph on a still Living Friend,

> While
> Summing up a Case of Assault or Cattle Stealing.
> But he was the more distinguished for dabbling in
> Architecture;
> And he amused himself, at the expense of the
> Public, by making and then unmaking so many
> Alterations in the Court House,
> That Litigants who once entered there could
> Rarely find their way out again!
> He wasted (it is said) more breath on the flute
> Than he ever did on Counsel or Jurymen;
> At last he took to
> Keeping Pigs and Poultry in this neighbourhood,
> Where
> He lived eighteen years by the sale of
> Eggs and Bacon.
> Eventually he died by over-exerting himself in a game of leap-frog
> with his great-grand-children
> Requiescat in Pace![14]

Parliament was prorogued on 9 April 1859 for the first general elections under the new manhood suffrage regime. Dalley and Deniehy threw themselves into the contest, on opposite sides. The Cowper forces received a boost during campaigning with the revival of the *Empire* newspaper under new proprietors – William Hanson, formerly Government Printer, and Samuel Bennett, a senior *Herald* employee – on 23 May. This lively paper was as consistent in its support of the government as the *Herald* was in its opposition.[15]

The contest began on 10 May with a large meeting in support of Cowper chaired by 69-year-old Dr William Bland. This political activist from the 1820s and associate of William Charles Wentworth had Dalley's father among his supporters in the 1830s and '40s (chapter 1). He launched proceedings by declaring the passing of the electoral reform Act 'the most important act of practical patriotism' in his recollection, and described Cowper as a noble, worthy and excellent Premier. Dalley spoke immediately after Cowper, saying his confidence in him remained as great as it had ever been. He regretted that Martin had defected 'on the most trifling grounds' and, no doubt with Deniehy in mind, lamented the emergence of an opposition made up of members who had been elected as supporters of Cowper's policies and had then turned on the ministry.[16]

Cowper stood for East Sydney, one of two four-member seats that had replaced the former Sydney electorate. On 17 May another crowded meeting heard Deniehy propose Plunkett as a candidate for the other one, West Sydney. According to the *Herald*, he spoke at great length, 'his speech being mostly made up of an analysis and forcible censure of the Cowper Government'. He said he had joined the opposition when he found 'there was but one active motive in the Government – that all principle was cast aside, and the keeping in office of Mr Cowper was the only object...'[17]

Dalley stood for the new Windsor electorate, and addressed a rowdy meeting at one of the town's hotels on 20 May. He said he would continue to be a 'party man' supporting Cowper; operating on 'independent principles' made government impossible. He criticised Martin on the state aid issue, and for supporting a pastoral leases assessment proposal in parliament and then advising the Governor that it was illegal ('watch all political lawyers,' he warned). He acknowledged that Bayley had been appointed on his recommendation. And he said he would never have accepted office had he anticipated being subjected to the 'humiliations and opposition' he met with, and which his successors now faced.[18]

At the nomination meeting a month later, he spoke mainly on policy. He said he now supported free selection, but would confine it to rich agricultural land – on the margins of rivers or within easy reach of markets. He would prefer a single education system that allowed the churches to provide religious teaching for their adherents to the current dual (national and denominational schools) arrangement. He doubted the colony needed a Legislative Council, nominated or elected.[19] The show of hands indicated only a narrow win over his opponent, Robert Scott Ross, a solicitor, but the vote the next day gave him a clear victory,

276 to 141. He told the cheering crowd that the contest 'had made him a better man. (Cries of 'That was all we done it for.')'. He was then 'placed in a chair, and hoisted on the shoulders of his supporters, escorted by men, women, and children to the number of five hundred, cheering vociferously, from the hustings to his committee rooms, the Fitzroy Hotel'.[20]

Deniehy's attempts to win re-election brought no such joy. Standing with Plunkett for West Sydney – a coalition, observed the *Empire*, of men whose principles had been diametrically opposite[21] – he was soundly beaten. The radical Rev. Lang topped the poll, and Plunkett took the fourth spot. Five days earlier, Cowper had topped the poll in East Sydney, followed by a returning Parkes, with Martin scraping in as number four. The parliamentary assault on the government's legal appointments had clearly not damaged its standing with Sydney voters.

At the declaration of the West Sydney poll, Deniehy said his principles were nearly the same as those of the men elected; therefore he could only account for his defeat 'on the ground of his being Catholic (Loud cries of 'No, no' and 'Shame, shame,' which lasted for nearly a minute.)'. He added that he knew dozens of constituencies were willing to accept him.[22] Putting this to the test, he stood against supporters of Cowper in three Hunter Valley electorates and lost decisively (he received only 16 votes against John Robertson's 356 in Upper Hunter). He lost a by-election for Bathurst-based East Macquarie in October but won this seat at another contest in May 1860, holding it until parliament was dissolved again the following November.[23]

Conservatives fared badly across the colony, and a banquet in honour of Cowper brought about 300 supporters to the Prince of Wales Theatre in mid-August to celebrate. Dalley made an amusing speech, with much praise for Cowper, in proposing the toast to 'the land we live in'. He said the colony was now 'blessed with the most liberal institutions of any country on earth, and blessed above all blessings with liberal electors'. Indeed, it was blessed with everything in abundance except, apparently, barristers not hostile to liberal principles and therefore willing to serve as

Crown law officers under a liberal government. But that was changing and there would soon be 'an abundance, not only for home consumption but also for exportation. (Cheers and laughter.)'[24]

While those professing liberal views formed a solid majority in the new Assembly, more than half the members were new to parliament and open to persuasion by Cowper's opponents, so the government was not necessarily secure. The *Empire* predicted in July that Henry Parkes would do his utmost to bring it down, describing him as one of those who 'can abandon principles with as much facility as they can abandon friends'[25] (similar comments were made about him on various occasions in later years). But probably not even Parkes believed he could topple Cowper within days of parliament resuming.

His ploy was to introduce a motion to repeal customs duties on tea and sugar, which contributed around £150,000 to revenue. No alternative source of funds was proposed, so the government could not accept the proposal. The Assembly did so, however, by 29 votes to 28.[26] Cowper resigned, and the Governor called on one of his former ministers but now an opponent, Terence Aubrey Murray, to form a government. After Murray's attempts to recruit a ministerial team failed, Cowper was recalled and the tea and sugar issue put to the Assembly again. This time Parkes's proposal was scuttled by 40 to 21.

Dalley spoke powerfully against the motion. If the precedent were accepted, taxes could be picked off one by one, he said. He accused Parkes, for whom he had voted in East Sydney, of having misled electors; he had not declared himself 'an antagonist of the government' until after the poll.[27]

Martin launched the next attack on the government, with a censure motion condemning its administration of justice and appointments to legal offices. In a three-hour speech, he claimed Dalley and Bayley lacked the experience and professional standing that the positions they had been appointed to required, and ranged over the other issues raised by Plunkett and Deniehy in the Assembly. If the government could not find qualified people for the top legal jobs it should resign, he said. He made considerable use of ridicule. Referring to Bayley's appointment, he imagined Dalley going to him and saying, 'in his own jocular way', 'Now, then, old fellow, I am going to have you made an Attorney-General.'

Cowper responded with spirit, as did Dalley who chose attack as the best means of defence. He rejected Martin's criticism of his failed prosecution in the murder case the previous December that brought Bayley's skills to his attention, claiming the blame lay with advice Martin had given the Crown Solicitor. He accused Martin of showing neither competence nor consistency in supporting a measure in the Assembly that he later claimed was illegal. He said that, as Solicitor-General, he had devoted all his time to the job, unlike Martin who, 'for every quarter-of-an-hour he devoted to the Government, devoted a month to himself' when he was Attorney-General. And he defended Bayley's appointment and the job he was doing; the Attorney-General's functions had not been neglected, in contrast to when Martin was in office.[28]

Martin and most of the opposition walked out when the motion came to a vote, presumably hoping to reduce numbers in the Assembly to below a quorum. The tactic failed, and the motion went down by 30 votes to one. But the government fell a week later, following the overwhelming defeat on the second reading of its education bill. This would have introduced a version of the English 'Privy Council' system under which a single board allocated funds to all schools, secular and religious, according to enrolments and other factors. Both the Catholic hierarchy and supporters of the national schools opposed the idea. Dalley was part of the 56 to eight majority against it. He and other Cowper allies wanted to see the bill changed substantially, not bring down the government. They misread the situation, and a shaky grouping led by William Forster took office.[29]

Cowper immediately resigned from the Assembly, apparently to sort out his affairs to avoid insolvency. He was re-elected for East Sydney – at the same time as one of Forster's ministers, John Black – in early November, but did not take up his seat. Dalley had campaigned for Cowper and a solicitor friend, Richard Driver, who opposed Black. He said the colony could not afford to lose Cowper's services. When parliament met again at the end of the month he said he looked forward to Forster – a man he came to admire greatly – being sent back 'to that obscurity from which he ought never to have emerged'.[30]

Dalley made some serious contributions from the opposition benches over the next months. For example, he put a convincing case that the new government had sacked a Goulburn newspaper editor as a magistrate because of his support for Cowper.[31] But he was also inclined to play the comedian. Opposing a proposal to extend an existing gun control law he spoke of its origins:

> Some six or seven years ago, a Californian, while strutting about the city, happened to drop into the Australian Club, under the impression that it was a public-house, and asked for a glass of brandy. The servants endeavoured to persuade him he had not paid his subscription, and was therefore not entitled to be served, and they tried to get him out. Finding he could get no satisfaction, the stranger resorted to the last argument, a revolver, which he presented, whereupon, the old gentlemen of the establishment fled in terror; and the measure was introduced to put down such men – that is, the old gentlemen rushed into that House [the Legislative Council], and passed the Bill.[32]

Forster's government fell in early March 1860. Dalley had resigned his seat a little less than two weeks earlier, on 26 February, having decided to visit England and Europe. Observing and commenting on all these events was Deniehy, now the star contributor to a new weekly newspaper, the *Southern Cross*, which appeared at the beginning of October 1859.

He was not impressed by Martin's attack on the Cowper government over its legal appointments. Martin was a man of callous moral nature, and his criticism of Dalley for accepting the job of Solicitor-General was unjust and ungenerous, Deniehy wrote after the censure debate. However, Dalley was a betrayer of pledges, and the 'parental fondness for this young gentleman of Mr Cowper and Mr Robertson' was worrying. Bayley's appointment as Attorney-General was generally understood to be the work of this 'Power behind the Throne – of a political Entity equally without discretion and responsibility, and like Cupid in the pleadings of the older poets, "Too young to know what conscience is".'[33]

Dalley came in for further criticism at the beginning of December. Without an atom of political principle, he gloried in being a partisan, Deniehy wrote. His attachment to Cowper was 'something like infatuation, in its riotous recklessness, its arrogance, and the utter paralysis it exhibits of every feeling not only of decency and generosity but of truth and justice'. Extraordinary luck had marked his career; 'the very highest trust the country could bestow' had been hurled into his grasp.[34]

Then, in the issues of 31 December 1859 and 7 January 1860, came 'How I Became Attorney-General of New Barataria', the article Deniehy is most famous for. In this clever satire, Bayley entertains his aristocratic friends at a London club with the story of his accession to the position of Attorney-General of New South Wales. Dalley (lightly disguised as Tiptop) is a central character, and Deniehy gives himself an important role as Twank.

The account Deniehy put in Bayley's mouth of the collapse of his friendship with Dalley is moving. 'Tiptop was born one of Nature's gentlemen – mind, manners, even the lad's voice, – a mind, indeed with so much instinctive grace and brilliancy, so much tact as, to my thinking, to manifest genius, and originally of a charming nature…' But his head had been turned by prosperity, and his passion for the aristocratic outran his attachment to principle.

> Twank, sirs, had been Tiptop's bosom friend and companion; Palemon and Arcite in Chaucer…were nothing to it… But a sense of what he chose to call betrayal of his duty, his trust and his principle on the part of Tiptop, made him…forswear in disgust that brilliant young gentleman's friendship for ever. Poor brutes! There had been some feeling, I suppose, on both sides. But it struck me that Tiptop always worshipped rising stars; and as Twank's orb, however luminous, didn't seem to go up, Tiptop got tired of believing in him. Twank, they told me, felt bitterly that Tiptop's new proceedings were anything but what Tiptop in early days had led him to believe.

There are frequent hints that Deniehy envied Dalley's popularity. He was, Bayley tells his club companions,

> a little idol, a jovial little joss, all jokes and embonpoint with hosts of

supporters. I think I see him now – there was scarcely an article of his costume, from his exquisite boot to his pepper-and-salt merino hat, that enthusiastic tradesmen had not tendered gratuitously to him…

On trips over the Blue Mountains to Bathurst men were said to fight 'for the honour of carrying [him] on their backs, or in their arms, I forget which, over what they called 'the pinches'. Others walked; Tiptop was borne.' He was 'a colonial lad of the lower classes, suddenly tossed into power and position'. Unfortunately this was before he had arrived 'at the years of discretion'; he had been 'made giddy by the fling up'.

The account attributed to Bayley of the way Dalley offered him the Attorney-Generalship provides more insight into how Deniehy saw his former friend.

> Little Tiptop came to my lodgings, springing over three steps of the staircase at a time. I think I see the stout little figure at this moment, as I saw it then under the hall-lamp. It had its pepper-and-salt merino hat on its head, its white handkerchief in one hand, its cane in the other – wide trousers, striped, à la Neuilly, and fiery tip in the mouth…
>
> He had the cheeriest of voices, the heartiest of laughs… The frankest, clearest smile in the world was always Tiptop's – the very sunshine of boyish hilarity…
>
> 'Old man,' said Tiptop…'I have something important to say to you…'

Deniehy's disappointment shines through in what happened next. Tiptop 'called upon Twank that night. Long and deep was the conversation on matters political, but no word of this scene did Tiptop breathe to him.' Twank learned of Bayley's appointment from the *Government Gazette*.

6
The other side

Dalley, 28 and unmarried, was still living with his parents. Since 1851 the family home had been in Macquarie Street – over the road from Parliament House, a short walk from St Mary's Cathedral, and within sight of the spot in Hyde Park where his statue now stands. Also at home was his 17-year-old brother Richard. His half-sister Catherine, about 40, had married 20 years earlier.[1] Christina, his 20-year-old sister, was newly married to William Greig, a merchant born in Cape Town, South Africa. Setting a precedent that both her brothers were to follow, the wedding, in June 1859, was a Church of England ceremony. It was held at Sydney's historic and fashionable St James' Church.[2]

Her father John Dalley was recorded on the marriage certificate as a witness, his situation given as gentleman. John's journey from convict lifer to high social rank and a prime Macquarie Street address illustrates what was possible in the colony for those blessed with the right combination of enterprise, intelligence and luck. In 1859 he gave evidence to a parliamentary committee on Irish female immigration as one who had employed many servants over the years. He rejected criticism of Irish orphan girls who had been brought to the colony, saying that in his experience they were good and faithful servants; 'all they wanted was to be treated kindly, and a mistress that would take a little pains in teaching them'.[3]

Writers about Dalley have made a point of his attachment to his parents. 'They were very simple, unlettered people, but he well-nigh worshipped them in private and ever delighted to honour them in public,' wrote one. Dalley is said to have taken after his mother, 'a woman of great force of character', in appearance and in 'frank openness of heart and mind'. He delighted 'to chat with her, to read to her, to repeat to her the latest gossip of the town, and to sing for her all the rollicking or pathetic little Irish ditties she had taught him, or he had picked up among his companions.'[4] A parliamentarian, John Macintosh, provided a glimpse of Dalley's relationship with his father. He often encountered father and son walking across Hyde Park to the cathedral in the morning, and

> never saw a son more fond and affectionate towards his father. He showed almost a reverence for his father. This was evident, not only from their walking together, but also from the loving and affectionate manner in which they regarded each other.[5]

Deniehy alluded to Dalley's chats with his father in 'How I Became Attorney-General of New Barataria'. The narrator Lyttleton Bayley, sceptical of Tiptop's accounts of how people received him on the road to Bathurst, observes, 'A happy man must Little Tiptop's governor have been, listening at the tea-table to his imaginative son's account of those toilsome ovations in solitary and desolate places!' A hint of envy of his former friend's popularity also colours Deniehy's comment, in *Southern Cross*, on the farewell dinner given to Dalley before his departure for England. The enthusiastic send-off was unwarranted, he wrote. Dalley had achieved no more than others could who were 'removed from the necessity of working for their livelihood'.[6]

Dalley's easy circumstances certainly did contrast with Deniehy's situation. His wife gave birth to seven children, four of whom died as infants or young children. Earning a living as a solicitor was a struggle (and his seat in parliament a hindrance – payment of members, other than ministers, did not begin until 1889). Making matters much worse, Deniehy sought release in drink, developing what became a fatal addiction to alcohol.

He was not at Dalley's farewell dinner on the evening of Thursday 23 February, and neither was that other estranged friend, James Martin. But 'a large majority' of the members of the Legislative Assembly – government as well as opposition – attended, joined by 'a considerable number of the principal citizens of Sydney'.[7] The venue was the Prince of Wales Theatre; about 250 people sat down to a 'substantial and excellent repast' at three lines of tables 'stretching from the front of the boxes to the farthest extent of the stage, the pit being boarded over for the occasion.'

> A number of flags were suspended from the walls, which, added to the gay and graceful decoration of the tables, formed a coup d'oeil at once imposing and elegant. The dress circle was occupied by a number of the lady friends of the guests… An efficient band was stationed in the upper boxes and played airs suited to the various toasts.

Proposing the toast to Dalley's health, the Mayor of Sydney, Alderman James Murphy, recalled that their guest was hardly known to the citizens of Sydney four years earlier. But his appearance at the Duffy banquet in March 1856 had revealed 'there was something in the unknown youth' and he had since established his reputation. From 'the galaxy of youth and beauty that thronged the boxes', Murphy added, it seemed that his temporary departure was 'a grief to his female friends, amongst whom he would seem to be a great favourite'. He hoped Dalley would not return with a wife, but seek her 'among the fair daughters of Australia (Cheers and laughter.)' The *Empire* reported that the toast was received with 'tumultuous applause, lasting a considerable time, and drowning the whole of the air played by the band – "Willie, we shall miss you".'

Dalley began his long, emotional and much cheered reply by saying he rarely suffered the 'nervous apprehension which characterises some public speakers', but wondered how he could justify the reception he had been given. He spoke kindly of political friends and foes, including Martin (he regretted circumstances had 'removed that individual and myself from association with each other'). He was proud of being a 'partisan' of Cowper, whose views he shared on almost all political questions. 'My definition of a party man is one who gives an honest, cheerful, straightforward support to an administration, never sacrificing his conscientious convictions on public subjects, but at the same time never starting insignificant points of difference when he should give his support.'

All those taking part in Australian politics had the 'awful responsibility' of 'laying a stone in the foundation of a new nation,' he went on.

> We have to attract to this country the elements for the building up of a vast nation, which perhaps may ultimately, in the time of Britain's danger or despondency, uphold all those glorious traditions which we have derived from British history – a nation which we may presume as the noblest inheritance – the laws – the literature – the liberty which we have received from those who have gone before us.

He said he would leave 'all my heart' in the colony, and hoped to return with a 'mind more matured'. He would be 'contemplating in older countries' the 'marvellous activity produced by the competition of great intellects'. He expected to return even more deeply conscious of the 'possibility and the desirableness of combining opposition to what I believe to be erroneous in politics with respect and generous admiration of my opponents.'

John Dunmore Lang, the fiery, politically radical and tireless – he came to the colony as a 23-year-old in 1823 – Presbyterian minister, gave the other memorable speech of the evening. He praised Dalley's 'splendid intellect' and 'fervent eloquence', and noted that until a few years earlier hardly anybody had known of his existence. He had 'stepped forth suddenly like the goddess Minerva fully armed from the head of her father Jupiter. (Cheers and laughter.)' After completing his political education in England, Scotland and Ireland, he would 'return like a knight of olden time with his panoply brighter than before, still more able to do battle for all that he believed to be right and true on this his native soil'.

Dalley left for Melbourne the following Saturday afternoon. An 'immense crowd' on the wharf cheered him 'vociferously', the *Herald* reported. 'This incident, so unexpected and so complimentary, sensibly affected Mr Dalley, and for some few minutes he was compelled to retire to a private cabin in order that he might as it were become himself again.' He and 'a numerous company' of friends and admirers steamed part way to the Heads on a vessel provided by an admiring shipowner. Then, after final handshakes, he transferred to the Melbourne steamer. The craggy 43-year-old John Robertson went with him, 'with great risk… of having an involuntary trip to Melbourne. However this gentleman managed to get back after taking a farewell which, to use his own words, "made him weep like a girl".'

The friends and admirers followed the Melbourne steamer to the Heads, 'cheering loudly and waving their hats and handkerchiefs till the vessel was shut out from view, and their valued acclamations could be no longer heard by the object of their admiration'. Among them was James Martin, who on return to the wharf said that 'within the last forty-eight hours' he had shaken hands with Dalley and their recent differences had been 'buried in forgetfulness'. Parkes and Robertson also made brief speeches in praise of the traveller.[8]

That was not the end of the accolades. An anonymous poet contributed six stanzas of advice to Dalley to the *Empire*.[9] The last three read,

> Stand on the classic ruins of old Rome,
> Still view the splendour of her glory past –
> Climb the high crags of Switzerland, and roam
> O'er the white wastes of Russia, cold and vast;
>
> And mark the varying traits of climes and men –
> How nations languish neath despotic rule –
> Compare Britannia's government; and then
> Thou'st learn a lesson in the world's great school.
>
> Thou'rt Austral's hope, and like a beacon star,
> The nation's eyes are watching thy career;
> Still be thou faithful, and howe'er so far,
> Australia hails thee with a pride sincere!

Dalley was one of nearly 600 passengers on the steamship (with auxiliary sail) *Great Britain*, which left Melbourne for Cork and Liverpool on 6 March. Designed by the renowned engineer Brunel and launched in 1843, this was the world's first screw-propelled, ocean-going, wrought-iron ship. It offered a remarkably fast passage for the time – Melbourne to Liverpool, or return, in an average of 60 days. For first-class passengers at least – Dalley was among nearly 100 on this voyage – it also offered considerable comfort. The saloon was a 'magnificent apartment', the agents advertised, and the 'sleeping state rooms' were very large, well lighted and furnished with every requisite. Cargo for England on this trip included nearly 48,000 ounces of gold.[10]

Little appears to be recorded about how Dalley occupied the three months between his arrival and his departure from Liverpool on 8 August. He was not a biographer's friend, noting in a letter to the *Herald* in 1872 that he did not keep copies of the letters he wrote and invariably tore up those he received after reading them.[11] Probably he observed with interest concerns in Britain in mid-1860 about the military ambitions of the French Emperor Napoleon III, and Lord Russell's withdrawal of a parliamentary reform bill that would have brought the country a little closer to the manhood suffrage enjoyed in New South Wales. His travels reportedly included a tour through France, Belgium, Holland, Prussia, Switzerland and Italy (but not 'the white wastes of Russia').[12]

Dalley returned to Melbourne at the end of October on the clipper *Lightning*, and was greeted by a 'numerous assemblage' when he arrived in Sydney by coastal steamer on the evening of 7 November.[13] John Robertson's government, which had succeeded Forster's the previous March, fell the same evening, defeated by one vote on a censure motion. The Governor granted a dissolution of the Legislative Assembly, and Dalley – who the *Empire* observed seemed 'greatly improved in health through his visit to Europe' – was immediately urged to stand again.

Land law had been the dominant issue during his absence. Robertson introduced his complex legislation, which after its passage in 1861 was to profoundly affect the colony's development for decades, at the end of September. A month later, a 33 to 28 vote overturned its central feature, free selection before survey. The subsequent censure vote followed the government's attempt to proceed with a supply bill.

Electioneering began immediately. A meeting of supporters of Cowper (who had been Robertson's Colonial Secretary with a seat in the

Legislative Council) decided to send a deputation to Dalley to ask if he supported free selection before survey, and if so invite him to stand with Cowper in East Sydney.[14] An article in the *Herald* (a strident opponent of Robertson's plan) on 1 November had prompted the hesitation; this quoted statements Dalley made in 1857 and 1859 on land policy. The deputation reported to another meeting two days later that his views were now 'in unison with those of Mr Robertson' but he was uncertain about standing.[15]

Dalley's announcement on 19 November declining nomination settled the issue. 'On grounds of exclusively a personal character,' he wrote, 'I shall be unable to devote to public affairs that degree of attention which the vast responsibilities of a seat in Parliament, in the present state of the country, imperatively demand.' Those grounds probably included a desire to devote more time to the law. He was busy in court from shortly after his return, successfully defended two murder charges in the Central Criminal Court over the summer, and returned to Bathurst with the Circuit Court in March.

However, he threw his support behind Cowper and his team. 'Loud and long continued applause' erupted when he told an election meeting on 2 December that he had 'no hesitation in saying publicly' that he, like Cowper, had changed his opinion on free selection. He had been 'taught by the times, taught by the people of the country', that the legislation was 'adapted to the wants of the country'. The 'great reforms carried in England' had been achieved by men who first opposed them, he added; likewise, Cowper was 'pre-eminently the man who was capable of carrying the Land Bill'.[16]

Dalley nominated Cowper from the hustings in Hyde Park three days later. He topped the poll, followed by Parkes and two more supporters of the land legislation. Martin and another opponent of the bills, the barrister Peter Faucett, were the defeated candidates. A week later, Martin and Plunkett were among the losers at the West Sydney election. Dalley was nominated for this seat against his wishes and, noting that four other free selection advocates were standing, urged electors to vote for them, not him. Most complied with his wishes; he received 215 votes. The four supporters of Robertson's legislation – headed by Rev. Lang – were elected.[17]

This pattern was repeated around the colony, and a new government took office on 10 January 1861 with Cowper as Premier and Robertson free to give his full attention to the land legislation as Lands Minister. The new Assembly passed the bills intact, and sent them to the Legislative Council on 27 March. Robertson followed them there, resigning his Assembly seat in favour of a place in the upper house. However, his persuasive powers failed to prevent the Council overturning key features of the legislation. After the Assembly immediately rejected these changes, the government persuaded Sir John Young, the recently arrived replacement for Denison as Governor, to 'swamp' the Council's conservative majority with 21 new members. Dalley was one of them.

The ploy failed. The president, former Supreme Court judge Sir William Burton, and 19 opposition colleagues resigned when the new appointments were announced, leaving the Council without a quorum. Their exit was only slightly premature; the five-year terms of the members of the first Legislative Council under responsible government were about to expire. For the government, the setback was only temporary. The new Council, presided over by William Charles Wentworth, briefly returned from England, also had a distinctly conservative complexion. But it recognised the government's mandate for the land bills, which became law in October.

Dalley was one of a large party who steamed out to greet Wentworth on the harbour on his arrival on 18 April. Earlier he had taken prominent roles in farewells to Rev. Lang, off to London to pursue a legal fight with the Presbyterian Synod of Australia in the Privy Council, and Governor Denison.

Lang left on 22 December 1860, 10 days after topping the poll in West Sydney. Dalley entertained the large crowd at a farewell gathering the night before with a lengthy speech in praise of the prelate, whom he described as 'not only the oldest, but…the bravest and the best' of the colony's public men. An unimpressed *Freeman's Journal* described Dalley as a 'young idol worshipper' and Lang as 'the most violent hater and offensive maligner' of the Catholic church.[18] Dalley was unmoved; his and Lang's mutual regard continued up to the old man's death in 1878. He was a pallbearer at the funeral.

On 21 January 1861 Dalley was the principal speaker at a meeting called to adopt an address to Denison commending his work as Governor, particularly in overseeing the start of responsible government. Denison was a conservative, he said, but in his official role had 'energetically and honestly steered clear of all personal predilection, and for that reason he is entitled to the gratitude of the people of this country'.[19]

Four months later Dalley departed for England again, in company with Henry Parkes. Their task was to encourage immigration to New South Wales, principally by delivering lectures on the colony's attractions to settlers. Parliament had voted £5,000 for the mission – to cover travelling and other expenses and two £1,000 salaries for a year.

Parkes proposed the expenditure – without putting names forward for the lecturers' jobs – in an estimates debate on 1 May. Cowper initially was non-committal, but the scheme quickly won his and the Assembly's backing and the appointments of Parkes and Dalley were announced on 14 May. It is little wonder that Cowper jumped at the idea. Parkes had been making life as difficult as possible for the government in the Assembly; the *Empire* accused him in March of 'morbid vanity' and trying to obstruct 'every liberal measure not emanating from himself'.[20] Cowper gained relief from the onslaught, and Parkes an opportunity to improve his ever-perilous financial situation. The

Henry Parkes.

Herald described 'the whole thing' as a 'job', with Parkes's appointment a 'diversion' and Dalley's a 'reward' for always being ready to serve the ministry.

Correspondence with Robertson after the appointments were gazetted provides an insight into Parkes's view of himself. He wrote,

> I notice in the *Gazette* of our appointments, that precedence has been given to the name of Mr Dalley; and I infer from this, that in any communications addressed to us jointly by the Government, the same deference will be shown to that gentleman. I presume this distinction must have been intended, as it could hardly have arisen from seniority in years, greater prominence in public life, or more intimate connection with the subject of our mission. Though this consideration, if it had been hinted at previous to my acceptance of the appointment, would have determined me in declining it, I should not now allude to the matter were it not that it may lead to some embarrassment hereafter; for instance, if we have to make joint reports to the Government, I shall decline to sign my name after Mr Dalley, unless I am instructed to do so.

Robertson replied acidly,

> I regret very much to find the view you take of the relative positions of yourself and Mr Dalley; and especially I regret the tone and temper of your observations thereupon... One of the two names necessarily appeared first, and the usual custom, in cases where it is intended that gentlemen shall hold equal positions, is to give alphabetical precedence; and as D stands before P, Mr Dalley's name would appear before yours. But there is another ground for his nominal precedence, and one that I am not disposed to overlook; it is that he has held high office in the colony, having been Solicitor General, and a member of the Cabinet, with several members of the present Government.
>
> You speak of your determination not to sign joint reports after Mr Dalley, unless specially instructed on that behalf. I have too much confidence in your good sense to suppose that you will not speedily see that a statement of that kind is unworthy of you. At any rate I feel quite sure that no difficulty will arise – that Mr Dalley will have too much regard for the important interests entrusted to him, to allow them to be impeded by refusing to you any comfort that you may desire from signing first on such occasions. I shall therefore give no order in the matter.[21]

Typically, Parkes did not retreat, and Dalley allowed him his 'comfort'. Parkes's signature appeared above Dalley's on their progress reports despatched from London, beginning in August 1861.[22]

Dalley's send-off was a low-key affair compared with the previous year's. About 40 people attended the farewell dinner in a decorated room at a hotel. A band played and songs were sung, Cowper expressed the hope that their guest would soon make his home happy by finding a wife, and Dalley returned thanks amidst continued applause.[23] Cowper and Robertson were among the large group who gathered at the wharf the following afternoon, 21 May, to see him and Parkes off for Melbourne where they were to board the *Great Britain* for the voyage to Liverpool. Dalley's 19-year-old brother Richard travelled with them, apparently intending to study medicine in England.[24]

Dalley, Richard and Parkes had about 70 companions in the *Great Britain*'s first-class saloon, and Parkes described many of them in an entertaining letter to his eldest daughter 'Menie'.[25] A Victorian squatter was a 'vain old fop', an American actress was 'a most unamiable woman', a former Belgian consul sometimes had 'to be carried away in a state of drunken insensibility by the stewards', and an Irish youth had fallen in love 'with a girl with a face just like a frog's'. Of Dalley, he observed, there were 'many points in [his] character I never knew till now, and not the best points'. His brother 'Dick Dalley' consumed his time 'between smoking & comic songs'. In her affectionate reply, Menie scolded Parkes for speculating on his companions' characters 'in most unmerciful style, you naughty father.'[26]

The traveller who most interested Dalley was the Irish actor Gustavus Vaughan Brooke, famed for his performances in *Othello*, *King Lear* and other Shakespearian tragedies. Parkes described Brooke to Menie as 'a man of a fine generous nature but I fear a very ill-regulated life'. Dalley wrote in 1885 that he often thought of the Irishman as 'the most delightful man I ever met'.[27] He told friends of the 'evenings'

The actor Gustavus Vaughan Brooke.

Brooke presented during the voyage, reading Shakespeare or a moving story by a contemporary writer. Everyone cried, he recalled, when Brooke 'did' the chapel scene from *Handy Andy – a Tale of Irish Life* by Samuel Lover – the 'sudden change from rollicking fun to tenderest pathos was so masterly, so irresistible...'[28] When news of Brooke's death in a shipwreck reached Sydney in 1866, he wrote an admiring obituary for *Freeman's*.[29]

Apart from one lapse, Dalley remained on good terms with Parkes throughout their time away. A fortnight after their arrival in Liverpool on 4 August, he wrote a cheerful letter to Parkes's wife, Clarinda, saying he had maintained 'a strict watchfulness' on her husband during the voyage and on the whole his conduct had been satisfactory.[30] The only lapse had been his failure to be 'sufficiently complimentary to a *Lady*' who, lacking in chivalry and charm, could not appreciate his devotion to his family '8000 miles away'. Clarinda was not amused, writing back that she had 'always admired his courtesy to women of whatever class...'[31] Menie told her father she had observed her 'earnest mother poring over Mr Dalley's whimsical nonsense taking it all in real downright earnest, and answering it with a face grave as a judge'.[32]

Dalley's letter to Clarinda also described 'pilgrimages' Parkes had taken him on to scenes of his youth around Birmingham. These included a visit to the 'beautiful little Church of Edgbaston, where Mr Parkes tasted once more the fluttering sensations of his bridal day by standing upon the very spot where he received your hand... In fact just now your husband is living altogether in the past – and I find considerable difficulty in calling him out of the world of early manhood into that of mature age in which he and I are to labour...' At some stage Dalley sent Clarinda a brooch; Menie reported to Parkes that it was very beautiful.[33]

Before starting their lecturing program, Parkes and Dalley visited London, where they called on shipping firms and met the Colonial Secretary, the Duke of Newcastle, who promised every assistance.[34] Dalley sent a sparkling article to the *Empire*, signed 'An Australian', about one of his visits to the Colonial Office. He encountered a venerable porter who was surely the same one upon whom 'Benjamin

Franklin looked ere the revolted colonies of America raised the banner of Independence' and who, 'with the scepticism of an essayist, or a reviewer', had 'smiled at the snowy neckcloth and religious bearing of the venerable Lang'. He expected he might still be there when, at some distant time, a future Colonial Secretary was told 'that the imperial troops have been defeated at Coogee; that the Governor is off Cape Horn on his way home; and that his Excellency the President of the Australian Republic desires the recognition of another independent state'.[35]

The pair began their lecturing program in the Midlands, Parkes speaking in Birmingham on 21 August and Dalley in nearby Coventry the following evening. Dalley reportedly provided 'a most interesting description of the colony, its immense mineral wealth, its religious, its educational, and social advantages, its extraordinary fertility of soil, and general excellence as a home for the emigrant'. He was listened to 'with the greatest attention' and awarded 'a tremendous round of applause'.[36]

Reporting progress to Robertson in late September, Parkes and Dalley said they had opened an office 'under the care of a respectable man' in London and held meetings, 'tolerably successful in point of numbers', in six counties. However, they were encountering strong opposition to emigration among the landed gentry and large employers, and in the press. Also Canada, Queensland and other colonies were competing for migrants and offering incentives that they could not match.[37]

The lecturers divided the kingdom between them, Parkes covering the west and north of England and Scotland, and Dalley southern England and Ireland. They kept in touch by mail. Writing from London in early October, Dalley told Parkes he was preparing a booklet that would present a better overview of the colony than that offered of Queensland by its immigration commissioner. He had spoken to large numbers of people who wanted information, including 'several men of capital with large families' interested in enhancing the prospects of their sons by emigrating.[38]

Reports of five of Dalley's October lectures appeared in the *Empire* in December. They were full of impressive statistics, such as the fact that

New South Wales post offices delivered nearly four million letters and more than three million newspapers in 1859. Speaking at Canterbury he noted that many families from the neighbourhood had 'found a new home…and enjoyed new hopes' in the Australian colonies. And 'two great colonists' – the Anglican Bishop Broughton and Governor Gipps – were buried in 'the great monument of the piety of former ages', Canterbury Cathedral.[39]

Parkes visited the London office in mid-November, and finding Dalley absent at the time they had agreed to meet penned him a caustic letter. In his lengthy rejoinder, Dalley objected to, among other things, Parkes's tone, 'which appears to evidence an assumption of authority which I for my own part should regret even towards a secretary'. Parkes sent an eight-page defence of his complaints, Dalley replied sticking to his guns but saying he did not wish to prolong the correspondence, and Parkes responded with a conciliatory note assuring Dalley of his 'unabated feelings of regard' for him. The storm blew over quickly. Dalley's light touch returned in a note to Parkes in mid-December describing 'the solemnity and deliberation' of proceedings during a visit to a London bank on his behalf. 'I could have managed interviews with two or three European Sovereigns more expeditiously than I have accomplished your business,' he wrote.[40]

Dalley crossed to Ireland at the end of the year, establishing his base at Dublin's Shelbourne Hotel, beside St Stephen's Green. He told Parkes in early January that after a lecture at Kilkenny hundreds of people had come to see him, including 'nearly all the tenant farmers in the immediate neighbourhood'. He had arranged visits to Carlow, Athlone and Galway, but admitted he was tiring of the task: 'You can hardly imagine how glad I shall be to get back to dear old London – and out of it – homewards as soon as duty will permit.'[41]

His next letter was more cheerful, reporting on a 'very fine meeting' at Limerick attended by many of 'the kind of people to whom our mission is mainly directed'.[42] The *Empire* reprinted a local newspaper's report of this event, held in a theatre 'crowded to inconvenience'. The city's mayor presided; also on the platform was Richard Bourke, son of the colony's Governor of that name.

The lecture followed the same lines as Dalley's earlier ones, with additions. Giving the postal statistics, he noted that he was often asked by Irish men and women in the colony 'to act as amanuensis in the composition of encouraging and consoling letters home (applause), nearly always with a comforting enclosure from the hard earnings of honest industry, to the want and misery of the old country, in seasons of distress (hear, hear, hear)'. He said the colony's government was 'entirely in the hands of the people (applause)' – with the exception of having at its head a representative of Her Majesty whose 'laborious duty' it was 'to let things take their course… (hear, hear)'. He praised Governor Bourke as the 'founder of the religious liberty of the colony' and 'one of the ablest, the most honest and the best loved representatives of royalty in Australia (hear, hear)'. Winding up, he said the Irish in the colony, 'although in the midst of all the affluence and comfort of life in this magnificent continent', were

> not forgetful of the history, and the beauty, and the misfortunes of the land of their birth and of their love (applause). In the days of famine and distress, when the cry of distress rang across the oceans which divide us, it startled the people of that distant land into a charity as active and beneficent as though they stood in the cabin of the dying peasant and saw his suffering (cheers). We sent our gold unsparingly. No spot of this island which history has consecrated, or beauty made joy for ever, but is as dear to your fellow countrymen in the New World as to yourselves (great cheering). There, with a soil open to all – with laws giving undue protection to none – with institutions which make all the distinctions of society the prizes of those who enjoy the confidence of their fellow-men, are settled tens of thousands of your fellow countrymen, enjoying the fullness of the land, and proving themselves to be as true, honest, and loyal citizens as any class of men in the British Empire (renewed cheering).[43]

7
Among bushrangers

Dalley reported to Parkes that Ireland was beautiful, but very expensive and very slow.¹ Despite those drawbacks and his homesickness, it is clear from stories he told later that his adventures among the 'quick-witted, shrewd' Irish provided treasured memories. A Dublin 'jaunting-car' driver he hired to show him the sights could not figure out where he came from. 'I don't think you're an Irishman,' he said. 'I am sure you aren't an Englishman, for you're neither stiff nor stupid, nor conceited…' Near Dublin he hired a boatman to take him to visit an Irish nobleman to whom he had a letter of introduction. 'What may you be wantin' to see th' masther for?' the man asked sternly in midstream. Taken aback, Dalley said he had a letter for him. 'Who-o-o! Is that yer game?' shouted the rower who proceeded to upset the boat, tipping Dalley out. 'His Lordship is never at home to a dirty process-server,' he called as the visitor struggled to shore.²

After the Irish trip, Dalley spent three more months in England. His letters to Parkes reported progress in distributing information to clergymen ('the ordinary advisers of the working classes') and mostly unsuccessful attempts to persuade London's press to carry news of their mission. He also described a visit to the office by William Cape, his headmaster at Sydney College, who had returned to England in 1860. He was amused by Cape's philosophising about 'the revolution in naval architecture', which was making 'the wooden walls of England' redundant.³

Dalley booked passages home for his brother – who apparently had given up thoughts of a medical career – and himself in May, choosing not to wait for the expected parliamentary vote to end his and Parkes's mission. Parkes told Clarinda in a letter home that month that he would leave after the recall arrived, probably in August. As 'hints to guide' her when Dalley called, as promised, to deliver 'anything I may have for you', he wrote a few sentences on how he saw the younger man, which are interesting in light of the later breakdown in their relations. The pair had 'not been over-friendly' in England but had not been unfriendly. They had seen much less of each other 'than you may suppose'. But Dalley would leave with his kindest wishes. 'I do not know what his feelings towards me really are, but I think they are sincerely friendly and possibly he entertains a higher opinion of me than he ever did before.'[4]

Dalley was much less reserved when he wrote to Parkes three weeks later 'to say that farewell which I found it difficult to speak last night. At the close of our relationship I am deeply sensible, my dear friend, of your uniform kindness during the whole period of our absence from home, the recollection of which at this moment almost reproaches me for leaving you.'[5] He promised to 'religiously regard' the undertaking he had given 'to endeavour…to bring about an improvement in your boy' – a reference to Parkes's 18-year-old son Robert whose behaviour, including rudeness and over-familiarity with female servants, was causing the family pain.[6] 'God bless you, my dear Parkes,' he concluded, 'and in the hope of soon welcoming you home.'

Impressed, Parkes wrote more positively about Dalley to Clarinda in June; again he showed particular interest in Dalley's opinion of him. He began by expressing 'great confidence' in the likely good effect of Dalley speaking with Robert. Some months ago, he continued,

> we were very near having a serious misunderstanding but our intercourse lately has been most friendly… I feel certain he has formed a much higher opinion of me in all respects than he ever entertained before. I explain this to you in confidence that you may speak freely to him. There is much genuine goodness in Dalley and he has a fine appreciation of goodness in others. Though not free from vices and some strange weaknesses which can hardly be called vicious, he is one of Nature's noblemen compared to some people you and I are acquainted with.[7]

Dalley left Liverpool on the *Great Britain* on 14 June, four months before Parkes departed. Ten days earlier, the Legislative Assembly in Sydney had overwhelmingly adopted a motion by Robertson to recall the lecturers (that expected news would not, of course, reach England for another two months). There was consensus that they had had virtually no success in attracting immigrants. The recently returned Rev. Lang attributed this to the current general comfort and contentment of Britons, which he said contrasted starkly with what he had seen in the 1840s and '50s.[8] The *Herald*, though still highly critical of the mission, thought it might have prompted a gradual increase in emigration of small capitalists; 'the idea of coming to New South Wales may have taken root in many households, where it had never been entertained before'.[9]

Dalley arrived back in Sydney in late August. Two months later he rejoined the Legislative Assembly, again reluctantly. His new constituency was Carcoar, south-west of Bathurst. He told the 'large and influential body of electors' who invited him to stand at a by-election that he was 'not anxious for a seat in the Assembly' and could not attend the nomination or election. But if elected, he would do everything he could 'for the welfare and interest of the district'.[10]

After being returned unopposed he held the seat until the next general elections in November 1864. He declined a new offer by Cowper of appointment as Solicitor-General and made few contributions in the Assembly over the two years. A local newspaper correspondent accused him near the end of his term of neglecting the electorate – failing to visit it or 'speak one word in our behalf'.[11] The record suggests this was fair comment.

Instead, he focused on his law practice. A police court matter soon after his return from England provided amusement for newspaper readers. A 27-year-old barrister, member of the Assembly and protégé of Parkes, William Charles Windeyer, was seeking damages from one of the Assembly's most conservative members, 42-year-old William Macleay, over an alleged breach of the peace. He claimed that after he inadvertently touched Macleay on the back as members crowded out of the chamber one evening the older man accused him loudly of being a ruffian and low blackguard. There was a time, said Dalley, appearing for Windeyer, when in a case like this the complainant would have been compelled by an unwritten but inexorable law to seek his opponent's life in mortal combat. But happily, the age of duelling had passed. Macleay was found at fault and fined 10 shillings.[12]

Dalley returned to Bathurst for more Circuit Court hearings under Chief Justice Stephen in mid-September 1862. The lawyers travelled at some risk. Frank Gardiner and some of his accomplices in the dramatic gold escort robbery near Eugowra, west of Bathurst, on 15 June had not been captured and many imitators were trying their luck at robbery under arms. Ben Hall and his gang were starting to ply their trade over an area extending from north of Bathurst to south of Yass. Dalley's electorate was at the heart of their territory. In 1863 they robbed the bank at Carcoar and, in a separate incident near the town, held up three policemen and stripped them of their weapons.

A special sitting of the Central Criminal Court in Sydney in February 1863 heard a series of armed robbery cases, which were divided among the three Supreme Court judges. The *Empire* observed that this event rivalled the inter-colonial cricket match then in progress as a popular attraction, with an eager throng besieging the doors for admission.[13]

Dalley's first appearance was to defend three men, Alexander and Charles Ross and William O'Connor, charged with stealing money and wounding a publican in an armed robbery at an inn at a small settlement, Calula, northwest of Bathurst. In what the *Empire* described as 'a long and ingenious speech', he argued that the shooting was accidental and that O'Connor, while present, had taken no part in the events. The jury found all guilty and Chief Justice Stephen sentenced them to be hanged; robbery with deliberate wounding was still a capital crime. O'Connor's sentence was subsequently commuted.

Next Dalley appeared for Charles Foley, one of two young men charged with the armed robbery of a publican at Laggan, north of Goulburn. They allegedly had made off with £75, a pair of trousers, a coat, some tobacco and other articles. As the assailants had covered their faces and placed a bag over the publican's head, Dalley was able to raise doubts about their identity. He also claimed it was extraordinary that none of the stolen goods were found on the accused when they were arrested the day after the robbery. The jury was not persuaded, and Justice Milford sentenced Foley to twelve years' gaol with hard labour.

Dalley's third client was Frank Britten, accused with two other men of bailing up a Sydney mail coach six miles out of Bathurst and stealing more than £200. The case against him was based on his being found with some of the stolen notes. Dalley argued that his behaviour when the money was identified at a bank pointed to his innocence – he did not take off as he could easily have done. Again the jury was not persuaded. Justice Edward Wise, appointed to the Supreme Court in 1860 after serving as a minister in the Parker and Forster governments, sentenced him to 15 years' hard labour.[14]

Not surprisingly, the trials of four of Gardiner's alleged accomplices in the Eugowra escort robbery, who were captured soon after the bushrangers took off with £14,000-worth of gold and cash, attracted the most attention. As shots had been fired and two policemen slightly injured, the young men – Alexander Fordyce, John Bow, Henry Manns and John McGuire – faced execution if found guilty. A fifth, Daniel Charters, escaped prosecution by turning informer.

James Martin led the defence in the initial trial before Justice Wise in early February. His powerful performance sowed sufficient doubt in jurors' minds to leave them unable to agree on a verdict.[15] The Chief Justice presided at their second trial three weeks later and, as Martin was unavailable, his assistant in the first trial, Robert Isaacs, defended the four. Three of them – Fordyce, Bow and Manns – were found guilty and sentenced to death.

Calls for clemency commenced almost immediately. The *Empire* argued at the end of February that Fordyce should be spared because the informer Charters had told the court he had not fired his gun. A few days later the Executive Council commuted his sentence to life imprisonment.[16] On 15 March six members of parliament petitioned the

Governor for clemency for Bow and Manns, primarily on the ground that it was dangerous to condemn men to death on the unsupported evidence of an accomplice. Further petitions followed, and the *Empire* again pressed the case for mercy.[17]

After the Governor decided a week later to spare Bow but not Manns – probably because gold was found on him when arrested, providing some corroboration of Charters's evidence – the agitation escalated. Martin wrote a long letter to the *Herald* claiming a series of irregularities had tainted the trials. The day before the scheduled hanging, Plunkett and others presented a petition with 14,000 signatures to the Governor. Late that evening Dalley (just back from court appearances in Bathurst and Mudgee), Martin and two other members of the Legislative Assembly called at Government House to ask that the execution be delayed pending further consideration. As it proved 'impossible to obtain an audience with his Excellency', Dalley and four others returned at 7 a.m. the next day. The Governor declined to see them, and Manns went to the gallows two hours later. It was a grotesquely botched execution; the 23-year-old – in appearance, according to the *Empire*, 'the *beau ideal* of a young Australian stockman' – took more than 15 minutes to die.[18]

In April, Dalley joined Plunkett, Martin, Archdeacon McEncroe and other prominent, mainly Irish-born, Sydney residents at a meeting to launch what turned into a successful colony-wide effort to raise funds for Dublin's monument to Daniel O'Connell, 'the Liberator'. O'Connell had been 'the champion of toleration' and 'friend of every persecuted people' even when those responsible for the oppression, as in Naples, Spain and Portugal, were fellow Catholics, he said.[19]

Shortly afterwards, he was back in court trying to thwart what he claimed was an attempt by the wealthy and powerful *Sydney Morning Herald* to crush its 'weak and almost helpless rival', the *Empire*. The smaller paper had published a letter by Rev. Lang accusing

Rev. Dr John Dunmore Lang.

the *Herald* of printing 'incessant and atrocious calumnies' against New South Wales and its representative institutions, which had been picked up and spread in England and Scotland to the colony's detriment. As well as arguing in great detail against the *Herald*'s claims, Lang characteristically launched a savage attack on its editor, Rev. West, calling him a turncoat in politics (from radical to malignant conservative) and in religion. West sought £2,000 damages for libel – not from Lang but from Hanson and Bennett, proprietors of the *Empire*.[20]

Two QCs, Darvall and Martin (he had asserted the traditional right of Attorneys-General to this distinction in 1857[21]) put West's case to Justice Wise and a jury. The more junior team of Dalley and Windeyer represented Hanson and Bennett. Dalley's long, emotional and often amusing appeal to the jury makes great reading and no doubt was wonderful theatre for those in the court. He did not defend Lang's accusations against West, but wondered why the publishers of the *Empire* should be expected to query statements made by such a well-known and eminent cleric. Then, taking a different tack, he noted that Darvall had said on West's behalf that the libel would not injure his reputation in the colony because Lang was regarded there as a maniac whose ravings were disregarded. But it would damage him in England. 'Ay, there's the rub,' said Dalley.

> It is to be precipitated at once into England among all the aristocracy – all the royal washerwomen – all the clubs. The magnates in their palatial homes are to rush out in dire dismay – the members of every club are to be set in commotion: all on account of the arrival of the *Empire* of the 21st February, containing a libel on the Rev. John West, written by John Dunmore Lang. Everyone not outside the clubs and the palatial residences are aware of the consternation that the arrival of this remarkable colonial journal creates. Stars and garters glitter and tremble. 'Have you seen it, cries a noble duke? Good God, have you seen it.' Lord Palmerston tottering up the steps of his club lifts his hands in horror, that this reverend supporter of toryism in New South Wales should have been attacked by Dr Lang…

Dalley said Lang had performed a signal service in unmasking a slanderer of the colony. Awarding West the damages he sought would probably 'at once destroy all rivalry, all competition' in the press, and nobody could foresee what evils might arise in the absence of a competitor to the *Herald*.

> Unhappy will be the country in which its legislators, its ministers of justice, its systems of education, its very ministrations of religion and of social habit, are not open to the review and, if need be, the condemnation of an enlightened Press. To deny us this liberty now, now that we know what the free expression of thought is, would be to pervert the gifts of heaven, to annihilate the fruits of that industry of thought and action which is directed for the blessing of all.

Justice Wise was not impressed by the rhetoric, in effect telling the jurors that most of Dalley's speech was irrelevant and advising them 'not to allow their minds to be biased by the insidious addresses of counsel on both sides'. It would be 'fatal to the administration of justice', he said, if they allowed their minds to be swayed by the pictures painted of possible consequences of the *Herald* being left as the sole paper. All they had to determine was whether there had been a libel and, if so, what damages should be awarded. They found for West but awarded him only £100. Hanson and Bennett announced that they would decline the many offers of financial assistance they received, except that from Lang.[22] For the time being, the *Empire* survived.

Earlier in the year the paper demonstrated its value by taking up the cause of a sane man, Robert Melville, who had been committed to Parramatta Lunatic Asylum. One of the two doctors who signed the committal papers, Dr John Scott, had been in dispute with Melville, a Maitland veterinary surgeon, storekeeper and tanner. The *Empire* began its campaign after Melville managed clandestinely to send it a letter describing his situation. He claimed to be in perfect mental health apart from the effects of having been 'detained amongst a crowd of felon maniacs for nearly a year'. After more than two months' agitation by the *Empire*, Melville was declared sane by a board of doctors and released.[23]

That was not the end of the matter; three months after Melville's release Scott announced his intention to sue the paper for libel. The case came to court, before the Chief Justice and a 12-man jury, in November 1863. Martin and Dalley represented the *Empire*'s proprietors and Darvall and Isaacs the doctor. 'The contest between the opposing counsel…has brought out the highest qualities of the New South Wales bar, and the consequent display of forensic ability has been seldom equalled,' the paper commented mid-trial.[24]

Towards the end of proceedings, which lasted two weeks, a probably exhausted Justice Stephen made the extraordinary remark that, since the jurors had heard much about the case before they entered the box, and as a result were prejudiced against Scott, he would cast his weight 'into the opposite scale'. According to the *Empire*, he did just that in his charge to the jury, displaying the 'very highest' ability as an advocate. However, all but two of the jurors were unswayed, and Scott's counsel accepted a majority verdict against his claim. 'Most deafening cheering' erupted in the crowded court when the jury's unanimous rider, that Melville's treatment at the asylum had been highly censurable and required investigation, was read.[25]

A week after the trial ended, more than a thousand people attended a public meeting in praise and support of the *Empire*. Two days later, the full Supreme Court ruled in favour of an application by Isaacs, counsel for Scott, for a retrial – on the grounds that the verdict was 'against evidence' and some medical evidence had been improperly excluded. However, Scott backed off; negotiations between the parties settled the matter, with the doctor agreeing to pay Hanson and Bennett £315, a sum well short of their costs in the case.[26]

Martin, who re-entered parliament in June 1862 as member for Orange, was the colony's Premier and Attorney-General when Dr Scott's case came to court, although presumably not at the time he accepted the *Empire*'s brief. He took office with a disparate ministry of opponents of Cowper, including Forster as Colonial Secretary, in mid-October after the Cowper government's defeat in a confidence vote on management of the colony's finances.[27] Six weeks earlier, Cowper had easily survived an attempt by Martin to censure the government over various legal matters and its failure to control bushranging. Martin attacked Cowper with venom. He said he had seen the Premier 'almost gloat' over the execution of Manns 'and snarl at honourable members who dared to lift their voices against the injustice and inhumanity of the Government'.

> But it was another proof of the truth of the saying that a weak Government was always cruel. It brought to mind the bloody scenes that were enacted during the French Revolution, when not more than two hundred desperate men ruled that great empire, through terror and bloodshed. It might be that the Government, having failed by other means to put down crime, thought that by the execution of Manns it would make a show of energy; but that act only proved how weak they were. (Hear, hear.)[28]

Dalley was absent from the Assembly for both votes. He backed the government on the first motion by arranging a 'pair' with an opponent, but was one of nine members who did not commit themselves on the confidence motion that brought Martin to power. Whether his abstention was deliberate, suggesting he was torn between his loyalty to Cowper and regard for Martin, is unclear. Possibly he was out of town, but he had been in Sydney as recently as three days before the vote when he secured the acquittal of a man charged with a tomahawk murder in the Domain.[29]

If he had lost confidence in Cowper as Premier, he had influential company. The *Empire* observed in June 1863 that the government seemed to be rapidly abandoning the 'principles of progress' it had professed.[30] A month later, after Cowper issued crime statistics shown to be misleading, the paper concluded regretfully that he now appeared 'lost to the dignity of his office'.[31] It observed in September that the government was 'tottering to its fall', and greeted Martin's ministry warmly, predicting that it would be received with general satisfaction.[32]

In a rare appearance in parliament in July, Dalley had expressed disappoint-ment with Cowper. The issue was his refusal to table papers relating to the reasons why Mahomet Cassim, one of two Indian jugglers convicted of a murder on what appeared to be flimsy evidence, had been executed and the other reprieved. Dalley said he was startled to hear the reason Cowper had given – 'because the man is dead'. That was 'the very strongest reason' for further inquiry, he said.[33] Dalley – and, as the *Empire* noted, all the other lawyers present in the Assembly[34] – voted with the majority against the government to demand production of the documents.

Dalley's presence – although he did not speak – at a re-election meeting for Martin's Treasurer, Geoffrey Eagar, was an early sign that he had switched his support to the new government.[35] He was not impressed when Cowper's son, Charles junior, stood against Martin in Orange – offering to resign as member for Carcoar and support Martin's election there if the voters of Orange rejected him. This they proceeded to do – 292 votes to 276 – but Martin did not take up Dalley's offer, instead standing successfully for Tumut, the seat young Cowper had just vacated. At a public dinner in his honour at Bathurst after his defeat in Orange, Martin acknowledged Dalley's gesture and referred to him 'in terms of high eulogium'.[36]

Dalley attended a civil service picnic with Martin and his ministers in January 1864, and a picnic given by Martin 'to those members of the Assembly who have generally supported the Government' the following September.[37] By then, after the defeat of proposed import duties and other revenue-raising measures, it was clear that this government's days were numbered. After its convincing defeat in a confidence vote in early November (Dalley voted with the government), new elections were called. Advocating free trade as opposed to Martin's protectionism, Cowper was endorsed resoundingly by the voters and took office again in February 1865. Dalley, who had appeared in parliament even less often during Martin's term than in the year before, did not seek re-election.

He remained in demand as a public speaker despite his retreat from politics. In January 1864, at a dinner for Richard Green, just back from London as gallant loser in a sculling championship on the Thames, 'deafening cheers' greeted him when he rose to toast 'the land we live in'. It seemed, he said, that in Australia there was a 'fusion of all the virtues' found in 'that little cluster of islands where our fathers first drew breath'. Australians had 'inherited the warmth of heart and generosity of the Irishman; the firmness and unflinching honesty of the Englishman, and the providence and care of the Scotchman'.[38] At the St Patrick's Day regatta on the harbour in March he observed that, while in Ireland he had been 'spellbound by the transcendent loveliness of the daughters of Erin', his 'own countrywomen in Australia combined the charms of the women of all nations'.[39]

His oratory in court continued to attract favourable notice by reporters. In September 1863 he made, according to the *Empire*, 'one of the most eloquent and feeling addresses…ever delivered within the walls of the Criminal Court' in securing the acquittal of a 19-year-old servant charged with murdering her newborn baby.[40] Three months later a jury, having been 'eloquently addressed' by Dalley, took just 10 minutes to decide that a Chinese digger charged with stealing a box of gold was not guilty.[41] In early April 1864, defending an alleged forger who was convicted on the lesser charge of uttering, Dalley 'made a most eloquent and pathetical appeal to the jury' in a speech 'replete with sound argument and divested of legal technicalities'.[42]

At the Bathurst Circuit Court a week later, Dalley put his eloquence to the service of John Vane, a young bushranger who committed a series of armed robberies with Ben Hall's gang during 1863. After his friend and companion in crime, Mickey Burke, died during a raid by the gang on the station of Gold Commissioner Henry Keightley south of Bathurst in October 1863, Vane took to wandering the bush alone. The following month the Catholic priest at Carcoar, Father Tim McCarthy, approached him at his campsite and persuaded him to surrender.

Vane pleaded guilty to three charges of robbery under arms, and then faced trial for shooting with intent to murder, which could have led to his execution. A policeman had been wounded when Vane and other members of the Hall gang attacked a coach transferring prisoners from Carcoar to Bathurst in August 1863. Addressing the jury 'at great length and in a most eloquent manner', Dalley dwelt on doubts about who fired shots during the affray and argued that the fact that Vane rode off when the shooting started showed he had no intention to wound or kill.

After 20 minutes' deliberation, the jurors found him not guilty. Perhaps Chief Justice Stephen was in a mellow mood, because during their absence he noted that some of the prisoner's relatives were in the court and assured them he would not impose the death sentence, whatever the verdict. With that threat removed, Dalley advised Vane to plead guilty to another shooting with intent charge, which related to the attack at Commissioner Keightley's station. At the sentencing hearing two days later, Dalley asked for leniency on the grounds that Vane was not yet 21, had been led astray by others, and had abandoned his criminal career and given himself up. Stephen imposed a 10 or 15 years' sentence for each offence, but 'in mercy' made them concurrent.[43]

In Sydney the following month, the trials, full of drama, of Frank Gardiner began. Gardiner, who disappeared to northern Queensland after the Eugowra gold escort robbery in 1862, was captured there in March 1864. Few doubted that he had led the Eugowra attack – Australia's largest-ever gold robbery – but Attorney-General (and Premier) Martin realised this could be difficult to prove in court. So he charged Gardiner with another capital crime – wounding a policeman, Sergeant John Middleton, with intent to murder, in July 1861. Middleton and Constable William Hosie had tracked the bushranger, wanted for an earlier mail coach robbery, to a hut in mountainous country between Goulburn and Bathurst. They took him into custody after an exchange of fire during which Middleton suffered a wrist injury, but he soon escaped – allegedly in an ambush staged by a comrade, John Peisley (who was captured, tried and hanged in early 1862).

The Central Criminal Court was 'crowded to excess' when Gardiner entered the dock on 20 May. An ill Justice Wise presided, Martin prosecuted, and Robert Isaacs and Dalley appeared for the defence. According to the *Empire*, Martin presented his case and examined witnesses in a quiet and business-like manner, Dalley followed this example, but Isaacs 'exhibited his usual unfortunate propensity for poor jokes and…for embroiling himself as much as possible with the Judge'. Justice Wise displayed 'the most painstaking attention and the strictest impartiality'. Gardiner's 'features and manner evinced great anxiety' and he paid 'the greatest attention' to every word spoken. It was clear he had the sympathy of the crowd, which was 'not so quiet as it ought to have been... The efforts of some of the constables to procure silence were so ludicrous as to cause a great deal more noise than they suppressed.'[44]

The trial lasted three days. Then, after an hour and a half's deliberation, the jury pronounced Gardiner not guilty. A 'perfect yell of delight' erupted in the court, and all the 'vociferations of the tipstaves and constables on duty' could not suppress the cheering and clapping. 'The Judge – pale as death from illness, fatigue and agitation – rose from his seat and in a voice of severity ordered the constabulary to arrest any person they saw behaving in so disgraceful and shocking a manner...' Despite the excitement, for Gardiner it was back to the cells after Martin informed the judge that another charge would be laid against him.[45]

In the event, Gardiner faced court on three more matters. Appearing before Chief Justice Stephen on 4 July, he pleaded guilty to two charges of armed robbery of gold and cash at Wombat, near the Lambing Flat diggings, in April 1862. Three days later he went on trial for wounding Constable Hosie, the second policeman involved in the events examined in the first trial; Isaacs and Dalley again defended him. This time Attorney-General Martin, presumably to lessen the risk of another acquittal, gave the court two options to consider – wounding with intent to murder (a capital crime), or with intent to do grievous bodily harm.

By finding Gardiner guilty on the second count rather than the first, the jury saved him from the gallows. The Chief Justice, however, was in no mood for leniency. After delivering a lecture on the harm Gardiner – 'the acknowledged captain of a band of robbers carrying terror and rapine through many parts of this colony' – had caused, he sentenced him to a total of 32 years' gaol with hard labour. Terms for the individual crimes ranged from seven to 15 years, but unlike the sentences he passed on John Vane three months earlier, they were to be served consecutively.[46]

8
The journalist

'How sadly is the circle that used to meet in my old library narrowed!' wrote N.D. Stenhouse in February 1864 to his friend Richard Rowe, an English writer who had spent a few years in the colony (using the pseudonym Peter Possum) from the late 1850s. Rowe, in Scotland, and Deniehy, in Melbourne since 1862, were divided from him by distance, others by death, and 'Dalley by politics!' he regretted. 'Often does the wild low wind coming from the sea at night and stirring the leaves, as I am sitting alone at my window, speak to me more thrillingly than even music can of these sad separations.'[1]

Presumably Dalley's extended absence from the 57-year-old literary patron's library at Waterview House, Balmain, was the result of a heavy work schedule rather than political differences. It is clear from a letter he sent Stenhouse at the end of 1864 that they were on friendly terms, and Stenhouse probably would have noted with pleasure that literature – or at least high-class journalism – was by then occupying much of the 33-year-old's time.

In the letter, Dalley asked the Scottish scholar if he would 'do the conductors of *Sydney Punch* and Australian literature a great service' by writing some Latin lines on the departure for England of John Woolley, Sydney University's principal and professor of classics.[2] Clearly he and the other 'conductors' of this weekly, launched in May 1864 and modelled on London's *Punch*, were aiming at an upmarket readership. George Barton (older brother of Australia's first Prime Minister, Edmund) noted in his survey *Literature in New South Wales*, published in 1866, that Dalley, 'the brightest intellect among us', had 'contributed largely' to the local *Punch*.[3] He continued to do so at least up to the late 1870s.

N.D. Stenhouse.

His early contributions included a series of satirical but admiring sketches of leading colonial figures, which reversed some of the subjects' prominent characteristics. For example, Rev. Lang's 'scrupulous avoidance of all purely controversial topics, and his exquisite discretion in treating all matters upon which difference of opinion generates a strong hostility of feeling, have saved him repeatedly from condemnation...' Cowper, Martin and Plunkett were 'reproached by the cynical (who hate all praise of virtue) for taking advantage of every opportunity to proclaim the purity of each other's motives, and the value of each other's public services.'[4]

A memoir published in 1888 recalled Dalley presiding, in 1867, at 'merry' meetings held each Friday to discuss the issue just printed and plan the next one. Among contributors who gathered around the *Punch* table – 'where law-books jostled with printer's proofs and criminal briefs rubbed shoulders with political cartoons and copies of comic verses' – were the politician, poet and essayist William Forster and the 'irritable and irritating' Solicitor-General Robert Isaacs. Professor Charles Badham, who succeeded Woolley as classics professor in April 1867, 'rolled light wit in ponderous periods like so much Greek'. Other writers present included 'the grim, sententious Stiff, an old London *Punch* man'; the 'yet untamed' George Barton; and the magazine's editor, the 'much too modest' George Ross Morton.

'Well and deftly' did Dalley 'brew' the next issue – 'almost as deftly as he did the bowl of "Badminton" in which afterwards were poured libations to its fate', the unnamed author continued.

It was not only in the fun, often fast and furious enough, of the *Punch* meetings that he was *facile princeps*, but also in the business. He had a genius for cartoons – they were almost always his, if not in the original conception, in the filling out or in the finishing touches – and as fine an instinct for 'social blocks' as a greyhound for a hare; while for the literary work, if there were subjects to be allotted, the article, whatever it might be, was almost written for the chosen contributor in the very way, if not the words, in which he was told to go and do it.[5]

Dalley also contributed to the *Sydney Times*, launched two months before *Punch*. Edited by Joseph Harpur, brother of the poet Charles, this weekly proclaimed support for two causes, Australian literature and protectionist policies.[6] Financial backers included the conservative politician and supporter of tariffs, William Macleay.[7] The paper survived just three months, and had little success in garnering public support for the import duties that Martin's government sought to introduce. Its impact on the local literary scene must also have been slight.

Dalley's contributions included an article mourning the death in December 1863 of the novelist William Makepeace Thackeray, which drew extensively on eulogies by Charles Dickens and Anthony Trollope. 'We learn,' he wrote, 'how great was his courage, how high his principle, how childlike his nature.'[8] The signature under the article, W.B.D., became familiar in later years to readers of literary pieces in the *Herald*. Dalley adopted the term 'Roundabout Paper', used by Thackeray for his contributions to Britain's *Cornhill Magazine*, as a heading for many of those articles.

In August 1864 Dalley became part-owner and editor of *Freeman's Journal*, then published twice a week. The paper became much more interesting and readable under his stewardship, and he seized the opportunity of providing a running commentary on the colony's politics. He handed the paper on in 1866, but remained a frequent contributor until shortly before his death. In 1890 the then editor, Thomas Butler, called him 'the one to whom in a literary sense it owed the most'.[9]

A leading article in October 1864 praised Cowper, as Dalley had often done before, for his 'great administrative power' and 'unwearied industry', and the many valuable reforms he had introduced. This was shortly before the defeat of Martin's government and Cowper's return to power. It was Martin's turn for praise the following January; with his powerful intellect he towered 'above ordinary mankind'.[10]

On public policy issues, *Freeman's* generally championed the liberal views Dalley had propounded as a politician. A notable exception was its support for state aid for religion, which legislation enacted in 1862 was phasing out. The paper was in favour with the Catholic hierarchy, unlike in earlier times, and Dalley apparently was prepared to defer to it on matters where there was a clear official position. An October 1864 leader argued that 'a few ill paid ministers of religion' supported by the government would be more effective in preventing and repressing crime in lawless parts of the interior than 'an army of well equipped mounted policemen'.[11]

Dalley's humour frequently found expression. For example, one leader noted that Rev. Lang, notorious for his fights with other leading lights of his church, was leaving by sea for Queensland; the voyage should be calm 'as we failed to perceive the name of any other Presbyterian minister on the passenger list'.[12] His respect for those of other religious persuasions was often on display. One article praised the 'silent bravery' and 'triumphant principle' of the Quaker Joseph Sturge who travelled to Russia in January 1854 to try to prevent the Crimean War.[13]

The paper reflected his optimistic view of humanity, and of the colony's prospects. 'The men of goodwill to whom Heaven has granted peace are every-where,' it observed at the end of 1865. And Australian progress had a 'rapidity and a steadiness' that distanced beyond competition the advances of older countries; it would be as practicable to 'stem the ocean flood and turn it from its course as to check this land of ours in its glorious career'.[14]

Freeman's published a statement of its aims shortly after Dalley took over. These included publishing 'every variety of Catholic intelligence' and 'the earliest and best intelligence of all movements for the social and political advancement' of Ireland. It would refrain from publishing anything 'calculated in any way, however slight, to disturb the harmony of our social or the equality of our political condition.'[15]

Living up to that promise, harsh words were few, except now and then for 'our senile friend' the *Sydney Morning Herald*.[16] In September 1864 Dalley penned a characteristically heartfelt response to the *Herald's* criticism of his Scottish friend John Robertson for taking on the role of president of the recently established Sydney branch of the Irish National League, which wanted self-government for Ireland.

> Many complain of his intemperance of expression – many of the extravagance of his opinions, but we have yet to learn that anyone has openly charged him, and sustained the allegation by proof, with a want of liberality in the discussion of any question in which freedom of thought, of speech and of action is involved. It may be (we only venture to hint the possibility) that he has nourished, in common with some of the noblest, the ablest, and the best loved English statesmen and writers, a sympathy for the unhappy country towards the peaceful regeneration of which he may now lend his humble assistance. It is just possible that his ears may not have been continuously closed, and his heart may have been occasionally open, to the appeals of the eloquent and suffering patriots whose Irish voices have not infrequently found echoes in English hearts; and perhaps when the opportunity presented itself of declaring his opinions, and obtaining the sympathy of his hearers, he may have seriously and sincerely availed himself of it with the honest intention of doing his best. He may have had the courage to do this, although conscious that his motives might be misunderstood, his objects misrepresented, his character assailed…[17]

Dalley did not become involved in the League. While taking a prominent role in causes such as the appeal in 1858 for funds to assist destitute peasants in County Donegal,[18] he always steered clear of local agitation on Irish political issues, presumably because of an overriding concern for the preservation of social harmony in the colony. St Patrick's Day celebrations were the usual occasion for his expressions of identification with the Irish. He chaired the lunch at the 17 March 1865 regatta, and the next day published a leader in *Freeman's* on the importance of the day to the Irish ('a gay and high-spirited race') and to Catholics. It was 'justly regarded as a day that all should solemnize' in 'this noble country, with its institutions of perfect freedom,' he wrote.[19]

Concern that those institutions were under threat seems to have coloured his initial response in *Freeman's* to legislation introduced by the

Cowper government, soon after taking office in February 1865, aimed at finally quelling the depredations of Ben Hall's gang. Under the Felons Apprehension Act, proclaimed on 8 April, declared outlaws could be shot on sight, while those convicted of harbouring outlaws faced 15 years' hard labour and confiscation of all their property. 'We have placed in the hands of imperfectly educated men, exercising authority in remote parts of the country, and not subject to any great control, powers so vast that despotic Sovereigns would hesitate to invest with such privileges their highly disciplined commanders,' *Freeman's* commented in March.[20]

Three weeks later, after Hall and his companions Johnny Gilbert and John Dunn had been outlawed under the legislation, the paper moderated its view. The government had been 'compelled to resort to an extraordinary remedy' to put down 'the evil', it observed; 'we must only hope that it will prove effectual.'[21] It proved highly effectual. Hall was shot dead on 5 May 1865 and Gilbert eight days later. Dunn was captured at the end of the year and hanged in March 1866.

Three days after the new law was proclaimed, Dalley appeared for James Dunleavy, a participant in some of the Hall gang's exploits of 1864, at the Bathurst Circuit Court. Like John Vane, Dunleavy had surrendered to a priest, this time Father Denis McGuinn. After he pleaded guilty to six charges of highway robbery, Dalley 'strongly recommended' him to the 'merciful consideration of the Court' as he was barely twenty-one, had been tempted into crime by older 'lawless scoundrels', had not committed any acts of violence in his brief criminal career, and had surrendered voluntarily.[22]

Justice Wise sentenced him to 15 years' gaol after making a speech highly critical of Rev. McGuinn. The priest had written to Premier Cowper apparently proposing that Dunleavy and another armed robber who had surrendered to him, James Burke, be given light sentences. Cowper had passed the letter on to the judge without comment. 'Such conduct on the part of a clergyman is very much at variance with the ends of justice,' Wise told the court, pointing out that the Premier could have nothing to do with sentencing. He also claimed that, 'without the intervention of the priest', the police would have taken both men.[23] *Freeman's* published two leaders criticising the judge (and the *Herald*, which had backed his comments) for the 'rebuke and disparagement… unjustly and ungratefully flung in [McGuinn's] face'.[24]

Dalley was back before Justice Wise in early May 1865, this time in the Supreme Court in Sydney representing Rev. Lang in a libel action against John and James Fairfax, publishers of the *Herald*. The offending article, published in January 1863, was a swingeing attack on the cleric, accusing him of 'indefatigable mischief'. Specifically, it charged him with 'wonderful charlatanism' in his opposition to state aid for religion. Arrested for debt in Scotland in 1840, Lang had been freed after agreeing to make over his government salary to his creditor. But on returning to the colony, according to the *Herald*, he 'then and there resigned his stipend upon conscientious scruples, stood out before the public as the representative of voluntaryism, and thus simultaneously disappointed his creditor and obtained from his congregation, in virtue of his sacrifice, new pecuniary support!'

The implication, Dalley told the court, was that Lang had 'fraudulently resigned his position as a State-paid minister' to avoid paying his debt. This was an 'utterly false and malicious' libel. Instead, Lang had remained in receipt of the salary until he arranged to satisfy the debt by mortgaging property he owned. The Fairfaxes' high-powered legal team – the Attorney-General John Darvall QC, Martin QC and Isaacs – sought to prove that Lang had given up his salary before mortgaging the property, and most of the evidence heard in the three-day trial was on this issue.

The case gave Dalley another opportunity to give full play to his oratorical skills. If the jury declared, by their verdict, that the *Herald*'s article was fair comment, then 'from the date of their doing so they might look for the retirement from public life of every man who had any regard for the preservation of his character,' he contended. Referring to praise by Darvall for the *Herald*, he said he 'blushed for his learned friend' when he heard 'that miserable, printed thing…spoken of as if it were

something that belonged to the Augustan Age of English literature...'
To a 'miserable allusion' by Darvall to Lang's poverty, Dalley responded,

> Well, during a career of forty years in this country, while a great number of persons of less intelligence, of less generosity, had realised splendid fortunes – he had not cared to make money... At a time when others were adding farm to farm, or were filling their treasuries with gold day by day, he might have been devoting his energies to introducing the starving, miserable operatives from the old countries into this glorious land; he might have been engaged in bringing out men who had since risen to positions of eminence; he might have sacrificed everything he possessed in carrying out these objects; and now at the close of his life he was to be taunted with poverty!

The Fairfaxes would have been pleased with Justice Wise's summing up. He asserted both at the beginning and near the end of his address that Lang had brought the action to avenge the success of the *Herald*'s editor, Rev. West, in his libel action against the *Empire* – over a letter by Lang – two years earlier (chapter 7). He told the jurors to bear this in mind, as well as the length of time that had elapsed between the alleged libel and Lang's launching the case. The jury found for Lang and awarded £350 damages (he had sought £5,000).[25]

Not satisfied, Martin and Isaacs, for the Fairfaxes, appealed to the full Supreme Court in September for a retrial on the ground that the verdict as it related to the state aid issue was contrary to evidence. Dalley was called on to outline Lang's case again, and elaborate in response to questioning by the three judges and Isaacs. The Chief Justice concluded that the matter should be tried again, but the majority, Wise and John Hargrave – appointed to the court by Cowper in June 1865 following the death of Justice Milford – thought the original verdict should stand. Hargrave, who proved a controversial judge, offered the view that if he had been on the jury he 'would have given Dr Lang every farthing of damages he asked for'.[26]

Dalley and his journalistic team converted *Freeman's* into a weekly from 1 July 1865 – twice the size of the previous bi-weekly and an attractive production with commentary on the news of the week rather than the usual advertisements on the front page and a range of sections inside. These included Irish Intelligence, Our Story-Teller, Ladies' Column (fashion, cookery and so on), Intercolonial News, Town News, Country News, Ecclesiastical, The Courts, Mining, Correspondence, Poet's Corner, and Gardeners' Calendar. The changes seem to have gone down well; by October more than 500 new names had been added to the paper's subscription list.[27]

No doubt sales were boosted by the main story in the first weekly issue, the destruction in a spectacular blaze on the evening of Thursday 29 June of St Mary's Cathedral. Dalley was one of those who rushed to the scene and rescued 'large quantities of robes, plate, altar furniture, paintings and missals' from a portion of the building not yet burning. His leading article on the calamity expressed concern about how the news might affect 'our dear and venerable' Archbishop Polding, who was visiting Bathurst. It also noted with gratitude 'the spontaneous and honourable sympathy in our affliction manifested by the great body of our Protestant fellow-citizens'.[28]

Fund-raising for a new cathedral (the present St Mary's) began immediately. About £3,000 was collected at a large and emotional meeting at the Prince of Wales Theatre addressed by Polding and the Governor, Sir John Young, a week after the fire. Dalley and Martin were among the biggest donors, each putting in £100. Dalley moved a resolution thanking the Sydney press for its sympathetic coverage of the disaster; an 'honest free press' was the greatest 'public virtue' a nation could possess, he proclaimed to loud cheers.

In *Freeman's*, he urged that the new cathedral be a 'really noble' structure that might take generations to build. It should 'rival in architectural beauty and grandeur the magnificent cathedrals in the old country which are so many monuments to the zeal and piety of our forefathers.'[29] The Archbishop was sympathetic to this view, but perhaps more realistic. Commissioning the architect William Wilkinson Wardell for the project in October, he asked for something 'beautiful and grand, to the extent of our power'.[30] Dalley lived to see a section of the new

St Mary's opened (in 1882); the bulk of the building was completed in 1928 but the spires were not installed until 2000.

Dalley travelled to Bathurst again in October 1865 for the Circuit Court. Daniel Deniehy had moved to the town a few months earlier, and Dalley spent some time with his ill-starred companion of former years. Less than a week later, Deniehy collapsed and died. The lawyer A.B. Piddington recorded that 'in their last conversation, when Deniehy was dragging about the streets of Bathurst, the fallen star of democratic oratory quoted bitterly' from the poet Sir Henry Taylor's 'Philip van Artevelde',

> The dog that's lame is much to blame,
> He is not fit to live.[31]

Just when Deniehy's problem with drink began is unclear, but it was established by 1860, the year he briefly (from May to November) re-entered parliament. His performances in the Assembly, which included equivocation over Robertson's land legislation, led the *Empire* to describe him as 'unstable as water'.[32] He lost his own platform for journalistic commentary when the *Southern Cross* closed in August 1860.

Deniehy spoke on 'the patriots of Ireland' at Sydney's 1861 St Patrick's Day banquet – apparently in a low voice as the first part of his speech 'was inaudible from the popping of the corks from the champagne'.[33] Reporters also had difficulty catching parts of a rambling speech he gave at a public meeting against Chinese immigration the following July. 'A lower and more debased race it would be impossible to find,' he said of the Chinese – sentiments that Dalley would have strongly rejected.[34] *Freeman's*, under Dalley's predecessor as editor, William Dolman, described the 'effusions' of the various speakers as unable 'for a moment [to] bear the test of Christian consideration, or philosophical enquiry'.[35]

Deniehy and his family moved to Melbourne in 1862 after he was appointed editor of the weekly *Victorian* newspaper, apparently at the instigation of Charles Gavan Duffy. This project seems to have begun well, but after another personal tragedy, the death of his only surviving son, Deniehy again lost control of his drinking. The journalist David Blair recalled encountering him in the street – 'a diminutive figure, shabbily clad, shuffling wearily along, barely able to keep on his feet...'[36] Stenhouse, Deniehy's mentor in the law and literature, visited him in Melbourne in April 1864; he found him apparently regaining strength after having been 'very ill', but soon afterwards heard that 'his health was again on the decline'.[37]

Deniehy returned to Sydney in mid-1864, and over the following months wrote some newspaper articles and made a few public appearances. 'Loud and continued cheering' greeted him when he attended one of the Irish National League's weekly meetings at the end of August. In a brief speech expressing confidence that Ireland would gain self-government, he praised John Robertson – earlier a target of severe criticism from him in the *Southern Cross* – as unquestionably the best man to be president of the League.[38] In April 1865 he gave a lecture on the ballad poetry of Ireland, on behalf of the League, to a large crowd at the Lyceum Theatre.[39]

Dalley was among those who renewed contact with Deniehy, and it seems that, to the extent possible under the circumstances, the old friendship resumed. Soon after coming to Sydney, Deniehy chided Dalley in a letter to his wife, who was still in Melbourne, for being 'as usual, careless and negligent' in failing to return some writings he had borrowed.[40] But on the day he left for Bathurst, apparently in a last desperate effort to beat his addiction, he was seen arm-in-arm with Dalley.[41] 'An Old Resident of Bathurst', responding in 1882 to a claim that Dalley and others had 'held aloof' when Deniehy was down on his luck, provided a glimpse of Dalley's attempts to help his friend. 'I lived in Bathurst when Mr Deniehy came to reside there,' he wrote. 'I was in daily companionship with him.'

> It was chiefly through Mr Dalley's influence that myself and a few others took a deep interest in the poor fellow. I knew from the lips of Mr Deniehy himself that the only friend who stood by him to the last was Mr Dalley. His influence with numerous Bathurst friends surrounded Mr Deniehy

with persons who tried their best to do him good. If they failed, it was not their fault, nor Mr Dalley's. I have good reason to know that up to the very last, Mr Dalley's purse was open in the same generous cause.[42]

After collapsing in the street, Deniehy died, aged 37, in Bathurst hospital during the night of 22 October 1865, the cause of death recorded as 'loss of blood and fits induced by habits of intemperance'. When he received the news two days later, Dalley wrote to Stenhouse recalling that the previous day they had spoken of 'poor dear Deniehy as one still lingering here in abject misery… I am deeply sensible how acutely you will feel this death, which had it happened but a few years since the whole of us would have regarded as a national calamity. It now comes as an event which few will deplore, even of those who reverenced his genius and pardoned his follies.' He asked Stenhouse if he would prepare 'a fitting sketch of Deniehy's life and a notice of his brilliant talents' for *Freeman's*.[43]

Sixteen lines of Latin, which appeared under the heading In Memoriam, are almost certainly Stenhouse's work, but the *Freeman's* obituary is Dalley's.[44] Deniehy 'may justly be regarded as the most brilliant of the native born inhabitants of this country,' he wrote. He recalled 'the boy lecturer' holding 'large audiences entranced' with his orations on the literatures of ancient Rome, France, Italy and England. His contributions to the press were of 'rare excellence', and in parliament he had been 'uniformly listened to with a respectful attention rarely accorded to others'. However, his political career had not been marked by the 'splendid success' expected. The 'intensity of his convictions and the irritability produced by extreme physical feebleness' had placed him in antagonism to many, and his sarcasm had widened impassably the breach with former allies.

> We abstain from pronouncing any opinion upon the justice and propriety of his course of action. His rules for the government of his own public conduct were rigorous to the last degree; and he inexorably required of others, as he himself laboriously endeavoured to exhibit in his own person, the highest consistency of conduct. Looking down upon his grave, which holds so much that was once so loved and admired – and from which

so many of the fruits of a great and honourable life were expected, his survivors will forget the bitterness of his hostility – and only remember the former triumphs of his noble intellect – ere sorrow and infirmity and disappointment had clouded, weakened and broken his genius. Few will think of the luminous spirit now gone from our midst without a tear of regret for so much power lost for ever – and of pity for a life which gave such promise of greatness – and went out in suffering – in poverty – and bitter mental distress.[45]

9
Libel and murder

Shocked by what he had seen on his Bathurst trip of the effects of the drought then gripping New South Wales, Dalley wrote to the *Empire* on his return proposing that a day 'in special prayer and humiliation before God' be observed throughout the colony. Disaster and distress appeared on every hand, he wrote; 'unless a change soon takes place, the sufferings of many will be great indeed.'[1]

Within days the colonists' prayers were answered as 'clouds driven up from the southward...abundantly watered the land'. Further drought-breaking rain followed. In a leader giving thanks the *Empire* offered some wise words, which possibly were from Dalley's pen:

> Those frequent successions of superabundant rain and parching drought which are so familiar to all who have lived a few years in Australia are, in truth, a summons for us, if we would truly colonise this noble country, to a sustained co-operation of forethought, science, industry, and capital, in overcoming the difficulties which lie in the way of one of the grandest achievements to which a community of British origin was ever called.[2]

The end of the drought provided no relief for the Cowper government; despite its success against the scourge of bushranging it was in severe trouble by late 1865. Cowper's problems included a growing budget deficit (and parliament's rejection of various proposals to cure it) and frequent ministerial resignations. In its short life, from 3 February 1865 to 21 January 1866, the government had three Treasurers, two Ministers for Lands, two Ministers for Public Works and two Attorneys-General – the second Cowper's old antagonist Plunkett. From the opposition benches, Martin and Parkes seized every opportunity to discomfort Cowper and advance their own political prospects.

Jupiter (James Martin) and Ganymede (Dalley) – from Sydney Punch.

Sydney Punch published a clever four-part 'political burlesque' in October and November 1865 representing the battle between Martin and Cowper as a contest between Jupiter, chief of the ancient gods, and Pluto, god of the underworld. Martin is Jupiter, Cowper Pluto, and Dalley Ganymede, Jupiter's adored cupbearer. Pluto believes he can triumph over Jupiter only by gaining the support of Freeman's Journal, and that requires winning back Ganymede's allegiance. On the revival of the paper under Dalley, one of the Nine Muses sings,

> From Ganymede, from heavenly Ganymede,
> The *Freeman's Journal* sprang renew'd;
> When underneath a frightful heap
> Of debt and dust it lay,
> And could not pay its way,
> His tuneful voice was heard from high,
> 'I'll make the *Freeman* pay.'
> Then quick subscribers pour'd along
> While advertisers join'd the throng,
> His power they all obey.

But Ganymede resists all the temptations offered him to change sides – a lady 'extremely wealthy, and as fair as Venus'; 'my throne, my realm'; 'hosts of slaves'; 'unbounded wealth'; and 'haughty beauties' vying for his favour. So Pluto (Cowper) is left to lament,

> Young Ganymede has sworn a dreadful oath,
> Although to swearing he's from instinct loath,
> Against my Crown to wage a bloody war,
> And make me funk who never funk'd before…
> For none like him can charm the yielding heart,
> Sway without force and dazzle without art;
> Belov'd of all, where'er his fame extends,
> The Gods and Goddesses are all his friends;
> And only he the glorious triumph knows
> Of fighting oft, yet never making foes.
> At his command, care flies the human race,
> And laughter beams o'er every happy face;
> Rejoicing mortals follow in his train,
> And hang delighted on his mirthful strain…
> And would that I, while yet the power remain'd
> Had in my Court this Prince of Wits retain'd…[3]

Dalley's 'mirthful strain' found expression in *Freeman's* leaders on political matters around this time. The characters of Chaucer's *Canterbury Tales* could hardly have been 'more ludicrously assorted' than Cowper's ministers after the reshuffle of 20 October 1865, the paper declared.[4] When a 28-year-old with no obvious qualifications for the job, Marshall Burdekin, was made Treasurer at the beginning of 1866, *Freeman's* suggested Cowper had decided to convert the *Government Gazette* (which carried the announcement) into a rival to *Sydney Punch*. 'That sensational journal anticipated the publication of *Punch* by about twelve hours – and we venture to say contained infinitely more amusing matter than the organ of humour itself.'[5]

Freeman's was highly unimpressed by Burdekin's appointment, as was Plunkett, who resigned as Attorney-General in protest. He was Treasurer for only 17 days; Parkes moved a censure motion over the appointment, which was carried easily. Martin and Parkes then combined to form a new government, which took office on 22 January 1866 with Martin as Premier and Attorney-General and Parkes in the powerful position of Colonial Secretary (responsible for, among other things, police and prisons, education, health and immigration).

Reviewing the new government, *Freeman's* noted, 'If our political life awakens fierce and inexplicable animosities, it brings about sweet and consoling reconciliations… Thus we have seen Mr Cowper embracing at one time Mr Darvall whom he had insulted and at another Mr Plunkett whom he had humiliated. Thus we now see Mr Martin enfolding Mr Parkes… The ring in which they all fought is hardly removed; we can still see the trampled grass – and the blood stains on the arena…' Nevertheless, it thought the prospects for the new team were promising; 'We shall have in exchange for little harmony of opinions great vigour in administration.'[6]

Dalley's contributions to *Freeman's* seem to have tapered off during 1866, with Richard O'Sullivan, who was appointed editor at the end of the year, taking an increasing role. O'Sullivan alienated the church hierarchy and many others with his strident Irish nationalism. A leader in March was perhaps an early sign of the change. While condemning Fenian plans for an uprising in Ireland, it said the movement was 'far from deserving the ridicule and abuse at first heaped upon it as the mere product of ruffianism and idiocy'.[7] The week before, the paper had referred – possibly they were Dalley's words – to the 'Fenian insanity'.[8]

During the summer of 1865–66 Dalley was again busy in the Central Criminal Court defending, among others, alleged murderers and rapists. An arson case in February 1866 provided a break from the routine. Edward McEncroe, a relative of the much-admired Catholic Archdeacon John McEncroe, was brought to trial for lighting the fire that destroyed St Mary's Cathedral. He had handed himself in to the police at Yass, telling them his initial intention was to burn the Archdeacon's church, St Patrick's, Church Hill, but after being ordered away and finding St Mary's unattended he had set fire to it instead. He said his friends had turned against him and he knew he would go to hell.

Sub-inspector Patrick Brennan, head of the Yass police, told the court McEncroe had asked him if he would be hanged for the crime. When he said he did not know, the prisoner had responded, 'As I won't be hanged, I think I will deny it now.' Two witnesses swore they had seen McEncroe near Jamberoo, south of Sydney, on the night of the cathedral fire, substantiating his belated denial. So the jury returned a not guilty verdict without leaving the box.[9]

Dalley's next case was even more sensational, and much more difficult. With William Windeyer, he defended Henry Louis Bertrand, 'the Mad Dentist of Wynyard Square', charged with the murder of a drunken banker, Henry Kinder, husband of Bertrand's lover. By the time the trial came on – two days after McEncroe's – newspaper readers knew much of the story, which had many twists and turns. Kinder was shot, but not fatally, and then poisoned. At the inquest, Bertrand persuaded the coroner that the deceased, beset with jealousy and money worries, had killed himself. However, subsequent suspicious acts prompted police to re-open the case. A diary and letters by Bertrand expressing his passion for Mrs Kinder were tendered as evidence at the magistrates' hearing and published in titillating detail in the newspapers. The case was sufficiently notorious to feature in an exhibition on crimes of passion at Sydney's Justice and Police Museum in 2002–03.

Dalley put forward a variety of arguments for the defence. 'The theory of the prosecution was that prisoner, having been insanely impassioned of Kinder's wife, determined to possess her, even at the cost of the husband's life; but seeing that without this sacrifice he had possessed the woman, the basis of the theory was utterly struck away,' he claimed. Referring to reported admissions by Bertrand that he had killed Kinder, he said murderers 'did not babble of their crimes'; they were 'made of sterner stuff'. If Bertrand were guilty, why had Kinder not taken any of the several opportunities available after he was shot to accuse him, Dalley wondered. And why, if Bertrand wanted Kinder to die, had he dressed the gunshot wound and sent for a doctor?[10]

Some of the jurors were persuaded and others not. As they could not reach a verdict another trial was held, eight days later. This time Dalley's 'eloquent and argumentative' three-hour address did not sway the jury, and Chief Justice Stephen sentenced Bertrand to hang. Hasty legal manoeuvring resulted in a full Supreme Court decision in favour of a third trial, but this, in due course, was overturned by the Privy

Council. Bertrand's sentence was commuted to life imprisonment and he spent 28 years behind bars before being released on condition that he leave the colony.[11]

Dalley spoke at the 1866 St Patrick's Day regatta lunch, mainly eulogising the Irish actor G.V. Brooke (chapter 6), a 'tender spirit' lost with most of his fellow passengers when the SS *London*, bound for Melbourne, foundered in the Bay of Biscay on 11 January. The following two issues of *Freeman's* paid tribute to Professor Woolley of Sydney University who, on his way back to the colony after a year's break in England, also died in the *London* disaster. Dalley's obituary lauded Woolley, a Church of England minister, for his religious tolerance and sympathetic interest in Catholic schools. Two Latin memorial poems and a lengthy review of a book of the professor's lectures were probably the work of Stenhouse, a friend of Woolley's from his arrival in Sydney in 1852.[12]

In April, Dalley travelled with the Circuit Court to Goulburn and its first sittings in Wagga Wagga. The newest Supreme Court judge, the Catholic Peter Faucett, presided; he had joined the bench in October 1865 after the death of Justice Wise. The case that attracted most press attention was a claim of cattle stealing made by one prominent Irish Catholic grazier, John Philip Sheahan, against another, Jeremiah Lehane. In his two-hour address for the defence, Dalley called the case the most extraordinary in his experience and delivered a withering commentary on the performances of Sheahan and other prosecution witnesses. The jury pronounced the defendant not guilty without leaving the box.[13]

He had less success in an appearance for David Buchanan, a colourful member of parliament, in a libel action before Chief Justice Stephen in August. Buchanan was seeking damages of £1,000 from the proprietors of the *Empire* over its commentary on a public lecture he gave in Sydney on 'The Wrongs of Ireland'. The Scotsman had gained notoriety for his fiery rhetoric, republican leanings and disorderly behaviour in the Assembly. However, he was a clever man, and after studying for the Bar in England in the late 1860s became one of the colony's most successful criminal lawyers. He was a frequent lecturer and pamphleteer; a pamphlet of 'political portraits' published in 1863 mixed harsh criticism of some – such as Martin, 'a commonplace, blustering mediocrity' – with glowing praise of others, including Dalley. 'A man might travel far before he would find so pleasant a companion,' wrote Buchanan.

> He is full of humour and anecdote, generous and genial in a remarkable degree – a perfect gentleman in all his thoughts, feelings, and actions – social, hearty, and comfortable both in appearance and practice... As a parliamentary speaker he is eloquent, sparkling, brilliant and witty. He has great command of language, a fine voice, most expressive in its intonation, and his action and delivery forcible and animated; his powers of ridicule and keen cutting satire are very great... his humour is rich and racy... I look upon Mr Dalley as by far the ablest man at the bar of this country...[14]

Martin, though Premier and Attorney-General in 1866, maintained his private legal practice and appeared for the defendants, Hanson and Bennett, in the trial. His task appeared difficult; the *Empire* had accused Buchanan of being a 'bombastic hireling' willing to promote any view for 'a few shillings or pounds' and of 'treasonable utterances' in 'denouncing the Queen's rule over Ireland'. Dalley declared that the libel 'excelled in malignity' any other of which he had heard or read. 'The most fatal enemies of true liberty' were 'unprincipled, unscrupulous and depraved journalists', he added.

If Dalley's speech had swayed the jurors towards awarding large damages, they were probably dissuaded by the Chief Justice's summing up. He made it clear he viewed the lecture itself as a greater wrong than any libel in the *Empire*'s article. He 'deeply lamented, as a member of this community', that an attempt had been made 'to inflame the passions of a section of our colonists by the raking up of past grievances that long since ought to have been forgotten' – a sentiment with which Dalley would have sympathised. That 'amongst us' should be found a man to deliver, and others to listen to, an impassioned lecture on the wrongs of Ireland was a matter for deep regret, he went on. 'For God's sake let us abstain from this; let us live in peace.' The jury found Buchanan had been libelled, and awarded damages of one farthing.[15]

Dalley returned to Goulburn with the Circuit Court in October and then accepted a variety of briefs in Sydney, mainly in the Central Criminal Court, over the summer. His defence in February 1867 of a 27-year-old butcher, William Henry Scott, accused of the axe murder and dismemberment of his wife was remembered as one of his most brilliant court appearances.[16] Not surprisingly, this was another case that excited great public interest and filled seemingly endless columns of the newspapers.

Police investigations began after a boy reported that, on a walk with his dog, he had found a human head and other body parts in a rubbish heap near Barker's woollen mill, Sussex Street. Soon afterwards, the rest of the dismembered body was found some distance away in a 'privy'. Decomposition had made the face unrecognisable, but the prosecution argued that dental features, including a missing tooth, and a wart on an arm proved that the murdered woman was Scott's missing wife, Annie. Evidence linking Scott with the crime included statements by two boys that he had asked them to help him carry a large box, which was emitting a foul odour, to a Darling Harbour wharf.

The trial, in a court 'densely crowded in every part', lasted three days; Justice Alfred Cheeke, appointed to the Supreme Court in June 1865, presided. Dalley conducted Scott's case without fee (as he did those of many impecunious criminal defendants). Addressing the jury, he stressed that the prosecution case was based on circumstantial evidence and sought to cast doubt on much of it. For instance, neighbours had heard no screams or cries, and no blood had been found in the room in which Mrs Scott was supposedly killed and dismembered. Would the murderer, 'possessed of such awful evidence of his own criminality', have asked others to help him carry the body parts to a spot where he could dispose of them? And as it was dark, could the boys Scott allegedly recruited for this task be sure he was the man with the malodorous box?

Dalley also contended that there were doubts about the identity of the body; missing teeth were common and witnesses had given conflicting evidence on the location of Mrs Scott's dental gap. He wound up his long speech with one of his more emotional perorations. He and the junior defence counsel, Patrick Healy, had had the honourable duty of 'sustaining this prisoner through the most terrible of trials', he told the jurors.

> But our responsibility, great as it undoubtedly is, sinks into comparative insignificance beside yours, for you may pronounce a judgment from which, on this side of the grave, there can be no appeal; and while the death that may be the consequence of your verdict should not shake your resolution if you are convinced of the guilt of the accused, the terrible image should be before your eyes to impress you with the deepest sense of the awful solemnity of your functions and the irreversible character of your verdict.

The jury took an hour and forty minutes to agree on a guilty verdict; then Justice Cheeke pronounced the death sentence.[17] Scott protested his innocence to the end, declaring on the scaffold a month after his conviction, 'I appear before my Maker innocent of murder'.[18]

Dalley joined his successor as *Freeman's* editor, Richard O'Sullivan, at the 1867 St Patrick's Day regatta lunch – the speeches of both urged Irish goodwill to all[19] – and then visited Goulburn and Wagga again with the Circuit Court. Back in Sydney in May he defended the proprietors of the *Bathurst Times*, Edward and Thomas Wilton, in a libel action brought in the Supreme Court by Edmund Webb, a wealthy Bathurst businessman and former mayor of the town. Appearing before Chief Justice Stephen, Webb claimed £10,000 damages over a series of hostile articles and letters.

His counsel, Sir William Manning QC, told the court the paper had been the conduit for constant personal attacks on him by his opponents. Dalley replied that the case was, 'at best, a most trumpery one, arising out of local squabbles'. He claimed that, although 'the language used was not perhaps the most choice', Webb could not have been injured by the attacks because he was known to all in the town and had great wealth and influence. A damages award would probably 'crush the defendants and their paper', which was 'not unlikely' Webb's objective.

Stephen dismissed most of Dalley's arguments in his summing up. Although judges 'did not interfere' with the award of damages by juries, he said, they might 'respectfully express' their own opinions and his was that a public man, like any other, was entitled to 'ample damages' if it was clear he had been libelled. This was so even if his position or character were such that the libel did not harm him. Presumably influenced by the Chief Justice's strongly stated view – which seems in conflict with his lack of sympathy for the politician David Buchanan in the *Empire* libel case the previous year – the jury awarded Webb £600.[20]

The Wiltons were bankrupted, and then imprisoned for failure to pay the damages (which they had no means of doing). Four months after the trial Martin joined Dalley in moving in the full Supreme Court for their discharge from gaol. Stephen agreed that they should be released but the majority, Hargrave and Faucett, said no. Sympathisers pointed out that the outcome could be life imprisonment; the Wiltons were to be held until they paid their debt, but they could not earn the money to do so while incarcerated. The law clearly needed to be changed, and this happened seven years later.[21] In the meantime, friends raised funds for the Wiltons and they were soon out of gaol and back in charge of the *Times*.[22]

Dalley's next major court appearance was for John Clarke, one of the notorious Clarke gang. Over the previous two years these bushrangers, led by John's older brother Tom, had committed numerous armed robberies and possibly seven murders in the Braidwood district.[23] Captured by police on 27 April 1867, the Clarkes, in their early and mid 20s, were tried in the Central Criminal Court before Chief Justice Stephen at the end of May. As at Frank Gardiner's trials in 1864 (chapter 7), the charge brought did not relate to one of the gang's most heinous crimes. The important points for the authorities were that prospects for conviction were good and the pair faced the death penalty.

They were accused of wounding, with intent to murder, Constable William Walsh, one of a six-man police party that tracked them to a hut where they were spending the night. Walsh received his wound, a superficial thigh injury, during an exchange of fire after the Clarkes emerged early next morning. As firing continued, the constable was sent to summon police reinforcements, who arrived about midday. Presumably concluding that their chances of escape were now hopeless, the bushrangers surrendered.

At the trial, the prosecution contended that Tom Clarke, an outlaw under the Felons Apprehension Act, had fired the shot that struck Walsh while resisting arrest. His brother had aided and abetted him, also shooting at the police, and so was equally guilty. Tom's barrister, a former District Court judge, Isidore Blake, launched the defence case. He claimed the Clarkes might not have realised the men firing at them were police because they were not in uniform. He raised doubts, supported by medical evidence, that Tom fired the shot that wounded Walsh; police crossfire could have caused the injury. And he argued that the bushrangers had not acted with murderous intent, having failed to take advantage of many opportunities to shoot the police.

Dalley, for John Clarke, insisted that it was clear his client had no murderous intent. He had walked out of the hut in the morning only to find himself 'in the midst of a perfect hail of shots which came from all sides'. At first dazed, he had then apparently thought, 'I'll just fire off a pistol and run to the house as fast as I can'. Unlike his brother, he had not stopped and fired at anybody.

Backing Blake's argument that the Clarkes may not have recognised their assailants as police, he said they were 'dressed precisely as the bushrangers were dressed, and I dare say they copied the costume of the latter in order to deceive them'. On the issue of who fired the shot that wounded Walsh, he made a case that it was probably one of the constables and noted that 'Stonewall Jackson fell by the bullet of one of his own soldiers, who would very likely have died for him if he could.' On the question of intent, he said the Clarkes seemed to have no hostile feeling towards the police, having shaken hands with them when captured.

Dalley summoned up all his oratorical skills for his conclusion. Being called on 'to pass into the secret chambers of men's minds' to discover intent 'was a dreadful responsibility', he told the jurors. He asked them to pardon him if he had spoken too long, and consider the earnestness that must animate one who feels that on what falls from his lips may hang the extinction of human life. One almost feels afraid to resume one's seat in such a case. In this atmosphere of justice – unpolluted by either the passions or prejudices of mankind; in this temple into which the exaggerations of terror, the misrepresentations of fear, the sensational horrors of journalism ought to find no entrance, you will discharge your duty as if God alone were the only witness of your conduct. The responsibility cast upon you is yours, and yours alone. No man – no number of men – can lighten it by the weight of a feather. You have no public to satisfy – no orders to obey, as you have no hope of consolation, no prospect of atonement, if you wilfully or negligently err. Under the guidance of Heaven, the fate of these prisoners is now left in your hands.

If the jurors were starting to have thoughts of acquitting one or both of the accused, Stephen's summing-up probably changed their minds. He began by defending the Felons Apprehension Act (which he had played a large part in drafting) against Dalley's description of it as a 'bloodthirsty statute' and 'disgrace to our civilisation'. It was a necessary measure against 'a series of outrages…that would disgrace any community', he said.

Stephen was convinced Tom Clarke had fired the shot that wounded Walsh. On the question of intent, he said that in law a man was presumed 'to intend the natural and probable consequences of his act', and the 'natural effect' of 'shooting at a man's body with a deadly weapon' was not in doubt. On John Clarke's culpability, he told the jury,

> If you think that the common design is established – a common design not only to resist or get away by wounding any one of the constables it may be necessary to wound, and it is done in prosecution of that design by Thomas shooting with intent to kill, then although John Clarke may not have intended the consequence of his brother's act yet he is responsible for the capital felony just as if he fired the shot himself. This is a point of law perfectly new, and no case can be found upon it in the books; but I can reason it out from the general principles I have endeavoured to explain.

Apparently persuaded by this tortuous logic, the jury found both men guilty. After delivering a speech in which he described bushrangers as 'the scum of the earth, the lowest of the low, the most wicked of the wicked', Stephen pronounced the death sentences.[24] Dalley and Blake immediately appealed to the full Supreme Court for a retrial on the ground that he had failed to inform the jurors that they could find one or both guilty of unlawful wounding, a non-capital crime. Justices Hargrave and Cheeke, who sat with the Chief Justice on the appeal, agreed that the jury should have been told this, but only Hargrave thought a retrial was warranted.[25] So the executions proceeded as planned on 25 June.

Dalley had argued that if the jury had been instructed on the alternative verdict, his client, at least, might have been spared the gallows. Few disputed that Tom Clarke, suspected of many murders, deserved his fate even if the trial was flawed, but John's situation was less clear-cut.

Tom's most cold-blooded crime seems to have been the murder of a contingent of 'specials' despatched by Colonial Secretary Parkes in September 1866, against police advice, on a mission to take the gang dead or alive. Led by a gaol warder and former policeman, John Carroll, the four men posed as surveyors and made friendly contact with the Clarkes' mother and sisters. However, the bushrangers soon saw through their disguise and on 10 January 1867 the bodies of all four, shot at close range, were found in the bush.

Two days after the Clarke trial, Dalley defended a young relative of the bushrangers, James Griffin, charged with murdering Carroll. The case against him, also heard by Stephen, depended on the evidence of two witnesses. One said Griffin had told him he had been with Tom and John Clarke and another gang member, Bill Scott, when Carroll and the other specials were killed, and Tom had shot three of them and Scott the fourth. The second witness said she had seen Griffin with three men, whom she subsequently identified as the Clarkes and Scott, near the place where the specials were killed. Being part of the group that committed the crime was sufficient for conviction; it was not necessary to have fired the fatal shot.

Dalley, at his most eloquent, accused the witnesses of perjury. Although they had made similar claims to various people, they had denied them at a police court hearing in Braidwood. Explaining the inconsistency, they made the reasonable point that the Clarkes were still at large then and they had feared for their lives. But, according to Dalley, 'this mass of perjury – of contradictions – of inconsistent statements' covered the whole case 'with thick clouds of doubt and falsehood'. Replying for the prosecution, Solicitor-General Robert Isaacs told the jury,

> Do not for a moment suppose that I insinuate that you could be misled by an eloquent address, if it were simply eloquent and nothing more. But I know the influence possessed by my learned friend, his estimable character and other numerous good qualities, and therefore it is my duty to attempt a reply.

This time, the Chief Justice was among those Dalley had persuaded. The key witnesses had admitted to perjury, he said, 'and it is perfectly possible that they have perjured themselves today'. The jury acquitted Griffin after just 20 minutes' deliberation.[26]

It was a brief reprieve. Griffin was back in the Central Criminal Court, this time before Justice Cheeke, in September charged with the murder of another of the specials, Patrick Kennagh. Dalley, for the defence, again stressed the unreliability of the witnesses. Isaacs responded in a much less friendly manner this time, saying his address 'consisted of vituperation and abuse of the witnesses, uttered in loud tones, and nothing else.' The jury found Griffin guilty, but recommended mercy 'on account of his youth and the bad associates who had led him into crime'. The judge pronounced the death sentence, but this was commuted to life imprisonment.[27]

Dalley appeared in two other Clarke-related cases between James Griffin's trials. In the first, two other members of the family, Patrick and Michael Griffin, were charged under the Felons Apprehension Act with harbouring Tom Clarke. They were acquitted after Dalley showed they had been police informers and castigated those who had placed in the dock 'men through whose instrumentality…the Clarkes had been captured'. He failed to secure the acquittal on a similar charge of an innkeeper, Mick Connell, an uncle of the Clarkes. His punishment was seven years' hard labour and forfeiture of 'your lands and all your goods' to the Crown.[28]

10
Parkes and the Irish assassin

Dalley was seldom lost for words, but the Anniversary Day (26 January) 1868 regatta luncheon on a ship on Sydney Harbour was almost such an occasion. Guest of honour was the Duke of Edinburgh, Queen Victoria's 23-year-old second son Prince Alfred, accompanied by the colony's new Governor, the Earl of Belmore. Dalley, unusually, was not listed to respond to the toast to the health of the ladies; Lord Newry of the vice-regal party undertook this task. He remarked that they were to be 'robbed of a part of their annual treat... They would not see that portly form which was wont to rise in their behalf. They would miss that tongue usually so eloquent in their praise on occasions like the present.' He spoke too soon. In response to 'numerous calls', Dalley rose and extemporised,

> The dreadful responsibility of appearing in response to this toast is always an excuse for blushes – a justification of diffidence, and an apology for failure. As everybody admits that mere human language, no matter how choice and appropriate, falls far short of the grandeur and beauty of the theme, I have always thought that no one should dare to speak on this subject but one from whose lips, like the Fairy Princess, diamonds and rubies fall in showers. But as it is somewhat difficult now-a-days to find gentlemen who speak sapphires and whisper emeralds, the melancholy being who finds himself thrust into the position that I now unhappily occupy should simply look his gratitude and, having allowed you the proper period of time for laughter at his speechless confusion, sit down. (Cheers and laughter.)[1]

Alfred, captaining the naval vessel HMS *Galatea*, had arrived at Sydney on 21 January on the third leg of the first Australian royal tour. Quite a fuss was made of his visit. The government commissioned David Jones and local hat and sword makers to prepare special uniforms for the

The triumphal arch built at Circular Quay for Alfred's reception.

Prince Alfred.

ministers to wear at his official greeting. Their blue dress coats had black velvet collars 'richly embroidered with oak leaves and palm branches in bullion'. Ostrich feathers fringed the edges of their cocked hats made of 'black silk beaver, with a gold loop and button over a black cockade'. Dress swords – rapiers in 'a black scabbard with gilt mountings, and a rich gold sword knot and tassel' – completed the ensemble.[2]

Dalley was one of the many 'friends' who joined the ministers on the first of 19 steamers that, on a wet and blustery afternoon, greeted the *Galatea* outside the Heads and escorted the royal vessel in. At noon the next, still rainy, day he was part of the large official party that gathered for the ceremonial welcome under a triumphal arch at Circular Quay modelled on ancient Rome's Arch of Drusus. The *Empire* was not impressed by the ministers' attire, observing that 'the great want of taste' they displayed 'in dressing themselves in such a way as to overshadow the Royal visitor, was the theme of general remark, and of much banter'.[3] After the welcome, a lengthy procession of marchers and dignitaries in carriages escorted the prince on a circuit of Sydney's streets, lined with cheering crowds. The next afternoon, Dalley was among the many hundreds who attended a levee, in hot sunshine, in the grounds of Government House.[4]

He had been involved in some of the organisational work for the tour. As a member of the committee appointed to arrange Sydney's public ball, he raised hackles by advising that the role of the mayor and aldermen should be kept to a minimum. It was reported, he told a planning meeting in early January, that Alfred had been 'pestered with mayors and aldermen in other colonies' and was 'now thrown into a state of consternation by the mere sight of a mayor, and whenever he was so unfortunate as to meet with one, endeavoured to make his escape'. Sydney's mayor, Charles Moore, was not amused and walked out of the meeting. Tempers subsided and the ball, held in a temporary pavilion in Hyde Park on 5 February, was reportedly 'a grand success'.

Dalley was also a member of the large committee appointed to arrange a 'public subscription picnic', to be attended by the Prince, in aid of the Sydney Sailors' Home. Opened in 1865, this dockside institution provided accommodation for sailors in port, aiming to keep them away from 'the crimping-house and grog-shop' and from 'vultures' out to rob them. The organisers hoped the picnic would help clear the home's £300 debt.[5]

Harbour steamers conveyed 2–3,000 people to the picnic ground at Clontarf, Middle Harbour, on a sunny Thursday 12 March. Prince Alfred, back from a visit to Queensland, arrived in the early afternoon, lunched with the Governor and various dignitaries, and then began a stroll with the official party among the picnickers. That was when the shot rang out that convulsed the colony.

The deranged Irish-born Catholic Henry O'Farrell thankfully failed in his attempt to assassinate the prince, who made a swift recovery. However, his act was manna from heaven for those with a taste for ferreting out alleged traitors and promoting division, and some prominent people – notably Henry Parkes – fanned the flames. Dalley was horrified by Parkes's antics and by the emergence and rapid growth of sectarian organisations such as the Protestant Political Association and Orange lodges; his responses included angry speeches and cutting articles. Relations between Dalley and Parkes quickly turned to ice, never to fully thaw.

Letters from Dalley show he had been on good terms with Parkes before Alfred's visit. In March 1866, two months after Parkes took office as Colonial Secretary, he wrote regretting that work commitments prevented him accepting an invitation to a day on the Nepean River, saying nothing would have given him greater pleasure. A series of letters sought government patronage for various people, including a publisher, a tailor and an 'accomplished and humorous' actor. Another invited Parkes to 'an elegant little feed' at a French restaurant.[6]

In June 1867, Dalley declined Parkes's invitation to join him on a 'glorious trip' to the Blue Mountains (this was before Parkes acquired his property, Faulconbridge, there). He told Parkes that his 'poor dear mother' was 'so bad that I don't like leaving home'. 'Our house is full of trouble,' he confided, 'and it would look like an indisposition to share it if I went anywhere for my own personal gratification just now.'[7] Dalley's half-sister Catherine Bainbridge – his mother's eldest child – had died the previous month. Perhaps Catherine Dalley, in her 60s, was already suffering from the heart disease that ended her life less than two years later.

The following October Dalley commented amusingly and sympathetically on a dispute that had flared between the Colonial Secretary and the Treasurer, Geoffrey Eagar. In a letter full of seafaring analogies he wondered whether Parkes could 'stick [Eagar] into the forecastle or put him under hatches somehow?' He concluded, 'Pardon my being so excessively nautical – but I am rehearsing a series of dialogues with the sailor Prince, and going in strong for Royalty and the navy.'[8]

The day after Alfred was shot some 20,000 people gathered in Hyde Park for the first of scores of 'indignation meetings' quickly called around the colony. They 'rose *en masse*, waved their hats and cheered in the most enthusiastic manner' to approve a motion that

> this meeting, impressed with a sense of the thorough and abiding loyalty of the colony of New South Wales, desires to convey to Her Majesty the Queen the undeviating devotion of the people of the colony to Her Majesty's person and throne, and their profound regret that their hospitality to her beloved son should have been disgraced by the crime of a wretch whose citizenship they repudiate.

Seeking to keep emotions in check, the organisers forbade long speeches and excluded clergymen from the speakers' list. The mover of the first resolution, Professor Badham, set a conciliatory tone, proclaiming that 'neither Irishmen, Englishmen, nor Scotchmen – Catholics nor Protestants – have any sympathy with those who make murder their profession'. Dalley, rising towards the end of the meeting 'amidst long-continued applause', called the crime 'the most awful calamity that has befallen this country' and expressed the hope that the perpetrator had no associates. 'Let us endeavour to proclaim to the world that, whilst we have in our midst one of the most villainous murderers, we have only that one.'[9]

Those inclined to believe that nests of traitors existed among the colony's Irish Catholics found ammunition in *Freeman's Journal*. Its editor, Richard O'Sullivan, maintained that, while sharing the Fenians' nationalist goals, he rejected their violent methods. The distinction was far from clear though, and the *Herald* published a potent series of quotes to back its contention that *Freeman's* had preached treason and 'inspired an assassin'.[10]

Critics of O'Sullivan's paper included the Catholic hierarchy and many prominent laymen. Three weeks before the shooting *Sydney Punch*, in an article almost certainly by Dalley, accused *Freeman's* of publishing 'senseless lying nonsense…to foment national differences, and to alienate us from each other'. As many noted, though, the paper retained a large Irish Catholic readership. The Speaker of the Legislative Assembly, William Arnold, drew cheers at a civil service meeting when he suggested Irishmen and Catholics had a special responsibility 'to come forward and deny anything approaching to sympathy not only with [O'Farrell's] act but…with the feelings of disloyalty of which it was only an open and insolent manifestation'.[11]

The police court hearing that committed O'Farrell to trial provided support for conspiracy theorists. Two policemen gave evidence that O'Farrell had declared himself a Fenian. And when asked at the end of proceedings if he had anything to say he responded, 'The task of executing the Prince was sent out to me, but I failed, and I am not very sorry that I did fail.'

Rumours soon appeared in the press that O'Farrell was one of a band of Fenian agents who had drawn lots for the task of shooting the prince, and that disclosures had been made implicating many people. Parkes, apparently undeterred by the fatal outcome of his intervention in the hunt for the Clarke bushranger gang (chapter 9), had taken personal charge of investigations. With police officers, he visited hotels where O'Farrell had stayed, conducted interviews, and took possession of diary notes written by the Irishman. Then he visited O'Farrell in Darlinghurst Gaol, accompanied by a shorthand writer who, out of sight of the prisoner, recorded their conversations. When eventually made public, O'Farrell's writings and many of his prison statements were revealed as incoherent ramblings. And it became clear that they had provided the basis for the early rumours and for some extraordinary claims Parkes made later in the year.

The government did all in its power to ferret out accomplices of O'Farrell, and sympathisers. The day after the shooting it announced a £1,000 reward for information leading to the apprehension and conviction of accomplices, and a free pardon for any who turned informant. A few days later a colonial version of Britain's Treason Felony Act was rushed through parliament, containing intimidating new clauses. Use of 'any language disrespectful' to the Queen or 'factiously' avowing not to join in 'any loyal toast or demonstration' in her honour was punishable by up to two years' gaol. And 'every person' had the power to arrest alleged offenders. If that wasn't enough, another reward, £250 for information leading to the conviction of persons meeting together for seditious and illegal purposes, was offered in April. Much finger pointing ensued, but no accomplices or sympathisers were convicted.[12]

Dalley missed much of the initial excitement, having left Sydney soon after the Hyde Park gathering for court work in Mudgee. Summoned by telegram, he arrived back in the city just in time to appear as second defence counsel at O'Farrell's trial, begun in the Central Criminal Court on 26 March, on the capital charge of wounding with intent to murder. The accused's sisters, who lived in Melbourne, had employed the 37-year-old Victorian barrister Butler Cole Aspinall – renowned for his successful defences in treason trials following the storming of the Eureka stockade in 1854 – to lead the defence.

Apparently the English-born Aspinall, a noted wit, and Dalley were old friends. A story is told of them inviting the flamboyant American actor Walter Montgomery to supper in Melbourne one evening and putting him 'on trial' for murdering the Queen's English. Dalley acted as judge and Aspinall as counsel for the Crown.

> Montgomery apparently lost his temper during the proceedings, and Dalley, in his summing-up, warned the jury that they must dismiss from their minds all they had heard in court, and rely for their verdict on what they had heard outside or read in the newspapers. Montgomery was found guilty and, on being asked if he had anything to say, made some heated remarks on the subject of the judge, the counsel for the Crown, the jury, and others who were participating in the trial. The judge replied that the 'fulsome flattery of the prisoner should not deter him from the course of justice', and proceeded forthwith to sentence the prisoner, severely admonishing him in the wittiest manner. Thus ended a remarkable evening.[13]

Justice Cheeke presided at O'Farrell's trial, which, after a brief adjournment, ran for two days, concluding on 31 March. Attorney-General (and Premier) Martin and Solicitor-General Isaacs prosecuted. Aspinall and Dalley argued that O'Farrell was insane, and therefore not guilty. One of his sisters, Caroline Allen, was their chief witness, recounting a history of 'strange and peculiar' behaviour and episodes indicative of paranoid delusions. Dalley sought unsuccessfully to strengthen the defence case by questioning her on what she had heard from others of O'Farrell's odd behaviour as well as on episodes she had witnessed. The judge rejected his contention that, as such hearsay evidence had been admitted when 18-year-old Edward Oxford was tried for the attempted assassination of Queen Victoria in 1840, it should be allowed in this trial.

Presenting the case against O'Farrell, Martin and Isaacs did not allege a conspiracy. Aspinall noted in his powerful appeal to the jury that the government had 'done all that they could to find associates in this crime', and had found none. He argued that imagining himself to be a Fenian agent was one of many signs of O'Farrell's madness. However, the jury, with clear encouragement from Justice Cheeke, rejected the insanity plea and quickly returned a guilty verdict. The judge pronounced the death sentence, and arrangements were made to carry it out just three weeks later.

Reviewing the trial in his 2002 history of the criminal law in NSW, Judge Greg Woods QC concluded that it was a miscarriage of justice on at least four grounds. Holding it so soon after the shocking event meant an impartial jury could not be obtained; the defence was not given time to obtain relevant witnesses; the Crown failed to call all relevant witnesses, notably the prison doctor; and the judge's directions 'were a virtual incitement to the jury to hang O'Farrell'. The 'most repellent feature of the whole exercise', however, was Parkes's failure to make available O'Farrell's diary notes, which were clearly 'the ravings of a lunatic'.[14] Contemporary observers made the same point. As *Freeman's* put it when the diary was eventually published, 'in the hands of Mr Aspinall, or Mr Dalley' it would have provided 'a powerful argument to establish the insanity of the prisoner'.[15]

Dalley left Sydney again shortly after the trial, this time for the Goulburn Circuit Court, presided over by Justice Faucett. He prosecuted in horse stealing, sheep stealing and wounding with intent to murder cases on the first day, in place of Solicitor-General Isaacs, who had been delayed. The next day he defended, without fee, a shepherd, William Munday, charged with the murder of his employer, John Conroy, at his home at Conroy's Gap, west of Yass. All the evidence, and his admissions, left no doubt that Munday had brutally killed Conroy, his wife, and three other men with a shear blade and axe. So, as in the O'Farrell case, insanity was the only possible defence plea.

Cross-examined by Dalley, Dr Allan Campbell of Yass, a Crown witness, said he considered Munday insane. He was delusional, believing that he was the son of the Duke of York and 'there was always someone speaking against him'. An unsettled 'expression of the eye' was another sign of his madness, the doctor thought. Dalley told the jury that Munday's 'coolness…in the presence of the awful destruction of life he had spread about him' and 'the offer he made to lift the bodies, bleeding and mangled, into the cart brought to carry them away' were further evidence of insanity. The jury was not convinced, and the judge sentenced the murderer to hang.

Six days later Dalley appeared before Justice Cheeke at the Bathurst Circuit Court, again arguing the defence of insanity. As in the O'Farrell and Munday cases, there was no dispute that the accused, William Hawkin, a shepherd, had committed the crime; he had smashed the skull and cut the throat of his hut mate, Henry Stacey. Witnesses said Hawkin had claimed to be the son of God with a commission 'to kill all scoffers'. A doctor, Andrew Ross, told the court he had diagnosed Hawkin as 'a homicidal maniac, the insanity arising out of religious monomania'. Concluding his 'very powerful', and this time successful, appeal to the jury, Dalley observed,

> It is one of the peculiar characteristics of this form of madness – religious monomania – that the very intellect which strives to fix itself continuously on the source of eternal light should become shrouded with the blackness of insanity; and, as the medical witnesses tell us, out of a desire to serve most perfectly the God of love, should spring a murderous impulse towards our fellow-creatures. Inscrutable to us is this – but we must bow reverentially before the Throne of God, and regulate our judgments of those so afflicted by the knowledge acquired by our experience, or furnished to us by the ministers of science.[16]

Dalley returned to Sydney just in time to be a player in the dramas surrounding the execution of O'Farrell on Tuesday 21 April. The day before he was to die, O'Farrell wrote a note, to be delivered to Parkes, expressing 'heartfelt sorrow' for his crime and retracting his claim that he had been one of a band of conspirators. 'I was never connected with any man or any body of men who had for their object the taking of the life of the Duke of Edinburgh,' he declared. And nobody else 'had the slightest idea of the object I had in view…'

In a statement subsequently read in parliament, Archbishop Polding, who had visited O'Farrell as he prepared for his end, reported that while the condemned man had been advised to make the declaration it was his 'free, voluntary act'. O'Farrell had written it 'in order to make some atonement for his crime' and 'for the express purpose of its being published', and in order to secure its publication had placed a duplicate 'in the hands of a confidential person'. This was the prison's Catholic chaplain, Rev. John Dwyer. He passed the copy to Dalley, who ensured it would be made public by handing it to William Macleay, a protestant MP who had accused Parkes of exciting 'an anti-Catholic feeling and cry' to make political capital for himself.

Describing the events in a letter to his former vicar-general, Abbot Gregory, Polding wrote that O'Farrell had made the duplicate because he had no confidence in Parkes. 'It is the universal belief that for his own purposes to keep up the diabolical excitement, Parkes would either have suppressed or mutilated or modified for his own ends that declaration,' he added.[17] Events in parliament on the day of the execution suggest Polding was probably right.

First, Macleay asked Parkes if he had received a communication from O'Farrell the previous day. Yes, replied Parkes, but it could not be made public yet. Another communication, 'from a source demanding the highest consideration', had come to hand at the same time, and one document could not be considered separately from the other. The government had evidence of 'a new kind of crime' that was deeply seated in the colony, he went on, and grappling with this would require all its power. Making O'Farrell's declaration public in the meantime would weaken its hand.

Macleay read his copy in parliament the next day, and Parkes came under fire even from generally sympathetic newspapers. The language he had used when refusing to table the declaration was 'calculated to excite alarm', said the *Herald*'s weekly associate, the *Sydney Mail*.[18] 'The people... do not want to be victimised by unnecessary panic.' Dalley's response, in *Punch*, was much stronger. For five weeks, 'on the *word* of...O'Farrell alone (for there is not a tittle of other evidence)', the government had been acting as if he had been part of 'a vast and murderous organisation'. Now that 'the unhappy wretch' had made 'the most formal and solemn declaration' that he acted alone, one would have thought 'any men to whom the honor and character of the country were confided' would have hastened to proclaim the innocence of the rest of the population.

What could any statement from another source have to do with O'Farrell's declaration, Dalley went on? 'And what is the nature of this 'new kind of crime' deeply seated in the colony?'

> That crime is to be found in fostering sectarian animosities – conjuring up the hatreds of rival races – invoking the damnable and meaningless antagonisms of foreign parties – making capital out of condemned cells – and transforming the gallows into a husting. Mr Punch…will be glad to have the powerful support of Mr Parkes in the stamping out of a crime like this, which, if allowed to burn into activity, will consume all that there is of truth, of goodness, of charity in this great and noble country. Meanwhile, Mr Punch would, with all the earnestness of his humanity, implore the people of this country not to be led away by any man, or body of men, into the degrading supposition that any human being in this country is, directly or indirectly, by race or religion, in heart or word spoken in sobriety, compromised by the crime for which O'Farrell has suffered.[19]

Dalley soon headed bush again. In Yass he appeared for the 22-year old son of Dr Isidore Blake, one of the town's magistrates and a prominent Catholic layman, who pleaded guilty to embezzling nearly £800 from the bank he was working for. Dalley appealed to District Court Judge James Dowling for a lenient sentence on grounds including the small salary the young man had been paid despite being given responsibility for handling very large sums of money. Blake was gaoled for two years.[20]

A month later, in Orange, Dalley secured the acquittal of a bank manager charged with embezzling £260. Next stop was Mudgee, where he appeared for one of the lesser-known bushrangers, Charles Johnson. After persuading the jury to find Johnson not guilty of shooting at a lock-up keeper with intent to disable him, he told the court his client had 'only desired to clear himself of the charge of bloodthirstiness'.[21] Johnson pleaded guilty to three charges of armed robbery and was sentenced to 14 years' hard labour.

Perhaps all the recent mental exertion and travel on rough roads – the railway did not reach Yass or cross the Blue Mountains until the 1870s – were catching up with Dalley. He was reported to be 'very seriously ill' in the second half of July, causing 'no little anxiety to his relatives and numerous friends'.[22] *Punch* articles that were clearly his work show he was back on deck in August. One, criticising strident statements by an Anglican minister and a Catholic priest, observed that 'these good men, and all of us', had much to learn 'of the gentleness, the tenderness, the forbearance, the affection of those who really had the fighting work of Christianity to do'. A week later, he mourned the death of the Irish-born Archdeacon McEncroe, 'an ecclesiastic without a particle of intolerance' who 'cherished his patriotism as a blessing instead of flinging it as a curse into the midst of society.' He also commented on Parkes's infamous 'Kiama ghost' speech.[23]

Parkes told a packed meeting of his constituents at the Kiama courthouse on 24 August that the police had been told long before Prince Alfred arrived in Sydney that 'his life would be attempted'. The government possessed evidence that would 'satisfy every unbiased independent mind in the country', but had not made it public because of its 'wise regard to the peace of society'. But if ministers continued to be 'taunted, misrepresented and vilified by a complete storm of lies' they might decide, 'in justification of ourselves', to publish it. He went on,

> I can produce evidence, attested by affidavits, which leaves no doubt on my mind that not only was the murder of the Prince planned, but that some person who was in the secret, and whose fidelity was suspected, was foully murdered before the attack was finally made upon the Prince.[24]

The speech was greeted with widespread scepticism. If the government had been forewarned of an attack on the prince, why weren't strong precautions taken? Where were the affidavits? And where was the body of the murdered Fenian (soon immortalised as the 'Kiama ghost')? Even the president of the Protestant Political Association, blacksmith and ironmonger John Davies, seemed not totally convinced. He told his organisation's weekly meeting that Parkes should make a full explanation in parliament; in the meantime he accepted that his statement, 'which had struck terror through the colony', was correct, 'coming from such a source'.[25]

It turned out that there was no warning, affidavit, or body; the eventual tabling of O'Farrell's diary notes and prison transcripts in parliament on 18 December showed these constituted the 'evidence'. Asked by Parkes in one of the gaol conversations whether he felt compelled 'by the instruction from the Fenian Government' to shoot Alfred, O'Farrell replied, 'We were under oath... I took the oath to shoot any man that did not fulfil the particular obligation which devolved on him – all did.' 'I think you said there was a band of ten?' Parkes continued. 'Yes,' said O'Farrell. The Kiama ghost story came from these lines in the diary notes: 'Woe to you England, when the glorious 'nine' carry out their programme. There was a Judas in the twelve – in our band there was a No. 3 as bad, but his horrible death will I trust be a warning to traitors.'

Dalley began his *Punch* commentary on Parkes's Kiama statement with a quote from Shakespeare's *Cymbeline*: 'Gods, what lies I have heard.' After expressing contempt for the 'astonishingly ingenious manner in which Mr Parkes continues to gratify a voracious egotism', he analysed the Kiama claims. Parkes knew, on the oaths of several persons, of a conspiracy to murder, a murder, and an attempt to murder in pursuance of the conspiracy, but nobody had been prosecuted. Not a hint of the conspiracy had been given at O'Farrell's trial, and the murder victim had been neither missed nor named. Only because they were 'vilified' would Parkes and his colleagues 'vouchsafe to inform us that they knew of murders and conspiracies'. And despite being in possession of this knowledge, they had 'chained the police, closed the tribunals, and dismissed the hangman'.

> Mr Punch has evidence before him sufficient, also, to satisfy 'every unbiased independent mind in the country.' He will not blaspheme, by saying it is 'attested by affidavits,' but it is clear and overwhelming: and it is this, that the whole statement he has quoted is a *Stupendous Hoax!!!*

11
Settling down

Parkes resigned as Colonial Secretary three weeks after the Kiama speech – not because of the outcry it caused but, ironically, in protest against Treasurer Eagar's sacking of a Catholic civil servant, William Augustine Duncan. Parkes's friendship with Duncan, the colony's collector of customs since 1859, dated back to the early 1840s when the *Chronicle*, a Catholic newspaper Duncan edited, published some of his verse.[1] His resignation came as the culmination of a string of heated disputes with Eagar, so possibly Melbourne's Catholic paper, the *Advocate*, was a little too cynical when it suggested that by resigning in support of Duncan he hoped to repair his relations with Catholics.[2] But with Parkes it is hard to be sure.

At a meeting of his constituents at Jamberoo in early October he repeated his Kiama claims, and added another piece of alleged information: 500 special constables had been sworn in to guard Alfred on his arrival in January. Within weeks Martin's government was defeated in the Assembly and John Robertson, a consistent critic of Parkes's antics, took over as Premier and Colonial Secretary. Dalley declined the Attorney-Generalship, reportedly 'on account of his health and his disinclination to re-enter upon public life'.[3]

Parliament met again on 9 December. In the next issue of *Punch* Dalley noted that Robertson had immediately 'assured the country that in no department of the Government is there the slightest trace of any record concerning the conspiracy and murder twice vouched for in the most solemn manner by Mr Parkes'. He had also revealed that Parkes's statement that 500 special constables had been sworn in was untrue. 'Mr Punch would ask the country is it possible to permit this state of things to exist?' Dalley went on. 'Is the character of the country to be slandered –

William Macleay.

its peace disturbed – its loyalty stained – and its slanderer to remain untouched?' Calling for all public business to be stopped until the issue was settled, he asked,

> Is the thing so small, which has rent this community asunder – which has made the bitterest sectarianism triumphant, and the most hateful intolerance paramount? Is it an insignificant thing that the bigot should be our master, the schemer our ruler, and that the liar should be our mouthpiece?[4]

William Macleay led the attack in parliament, demanding that all documents on the O'Farrell case be produced and an Assembly committee appointed to investigate the Kiama claims. After Robertson threatened legal action, Parkes tabled the diary notes and transcripts the following week; he also said he would cooperate in a select committee inquiry. The *Empire*'s parliamentary columnist commented that Parkes 'fell back in his seat with a look of anguish and deep sorrow' after producing the documents. 'A man with an iron heart must have softened down into pity, had he seen Mr Parkes… Even his friends began to sit a little further from him.'[5] Dalley commended the 'independent and brilliant' *Empire*, writing that for months it had been *Punch*'s sole journalistic companion in 'the good fight of reason against passion, of truth against brutal injustice'.[6]

Parkes suffered more embarrassment early in the New Year when documents were tabled revealing that he had placed on the government payroll two charlatans whose promises to expose colonial Fenians proved predictably hollow. But he was not one to retreat. The eight-man parliamentary committee, chaired by Macleay and evenly balanced between followers and critics of Parkes, finished its work in early February 1869. On Macleay's casting vote it adopted the report he wrote concluding that the evidence did not support Parkes's conspiracy claims. The four dissenting members maintained that a conspiracy had not been disproved.

The subsequent parliamentary debate was long, heated and at times vicious. As his biographer, A.W. Martin, put it, Parkes's 'triumphantly successful' tactic was to 'turn the inquiry into a personal issue and to present himself as a martyr to Catholic aggression'.[7] In a 4 a.m. vote, after many members had retired for the night, the Assembly resolved by 32 to 22 to expunge the committee's report from its records. With 'the boisterous cheers of men drunk with a miserable and ephemeral party success,' observed the *Empire*, it had sanctioned and dignified 'an act which future historians will not fail to regard as the culminating disgrace of this colony'.[8]

Punch observed these events with characteristic whimsy and anger at the political chicanery. Most likely Dalley wrote its report of a mock committee formed to 'discover a conspiracy that never existed', 'exhume a corpse that never was buried', 'listen to lies', and 'manifest Parkes as he is to the world'. This committee found 'justice has been mocked, decency outraged, and truth despised'. The only conspiracy it had been able to discover was 'one to blast the reputation of the country'.[9]

After the parliamentary whitewash the magazine published an open letter, also almost certainly Dalley's work, to Prince Alfred who was about to make another, brief, visit to the colony. 'Dear and Honoured Prince,' it began.

> You may have learnt that we have discovered that previous to your last visit a conspiracy existed in this country. It is true… The Government must have known of it before your arrival. It was a conspiracy upon the part of the entire people to show you by word and deed how profound and universal was their reverence for your illustrious mother… For this they organised! For this they conspired. With the exception of the wretched maniac whose hand struck you down – (and seems at the same time to have struck down religious liberty, tolerance, and truth in this country) – there is not one of the conspirators who would not have gladly died to save you from anguish and suffering. But, dear Prince, the crime of the creature who dishonoured us was with infamous craft fastened upon one-third of the people of the country; and from the time of your departure till your return, they have been under the ban of the bigot and the insolence of the impostor…[10]

As a gesture of support for that third of the population, the Prince wore a bunch of shamrocks in his lapel on St Patrick's Day. Apparently he felt no fear that assassins might still be lurking; his reported activities included an unescorted walk around the city one morning. He also went for rides and drives, and visited the theatre. *Punch* had expressed the hope that Alfred's return would 'be the means of re-uniting us, of driving away the clouds which lower upon us, and giving us back the frank cordiality and blessed liberality of the past'. It seems that he and the Governor, Lord Belmore, did their best in that cause; one sign was Archbishop Polding's presence among the small group of dinner guests, who also included Premier Robertson, at Government House on the prince's first evening in Sydney. (The Anglican bishop, Parkes and Martin were among the following evening's guests.)[11]

Polding appreciated Dalley's efforts to calm the storm. 'He is the principal contributor to *Punch*, and by his wit and talent has been of great service to religion during these sad times,' he told Abbot Gregory after Parkes's parliamentary victory in February. 'But Parkes, covered with infamy as he is by his conduct, still holds his place with a large party, and is sure to come into power.'[12]

Polding also described Dalley as 'a great comfort to me – so fervent, so attached to the Church'. This was a reference to the aftermath of the destruction by fire of the weatherboard building that had served as a temporary cathedral since the first St Mary's burned down in 1865. The conflagration lit up the city in the early hours of 5 January 1869 – exactly four weeks after the ceremonial laying of the foundation stone for the new St Mary's. For Polding, the loss was made worse by the destruction of relics, vestments, church plate and pictures – and his crosier and mitre – that had been rescued from the 1865 blaze.

Polding's suffering as a result of the new 'visitation' was 'infinitely more to be deplored than the loss of the building', Dalley told a meeting held the evening after the fire to start fund-raising for a new temporary cathedral. The barrister Edward Butler referred to speculation that a sectarian arsonist had lit the fire and urged Catholics, if this proved so, not to 'confound the bulk of their fellow colonists with any such person'.[13] Fortunately the coronial inquiry, which Dalley attended on Polding's behalf, found no grounds for suspicion. Witnesses he examined included a boy who slept in the building and was employed to keep it clean and to light and extinguish the gaslights. The jury observed that it seemed 'injudicious that such a responsible trust as the care of the lights in the cathedral should have been confided to a boy so young'.[14]

Dalley had his own grief to deal with soon afterwards with the death of his mother at their Macquarie Street home on 8 March. His 26-year-old brother Richard, now an articled clerk in a solicitor's office, had married in May 1868, so he was the only family member still living with his nearly 70-year-old father. It seems that John Dalley, who was to die in November 1871 of conditions described on his death certificate as 'softening of the brain' and 'paralysis', already required considerable care. Professor Badham noted in a letter to Stenhouse that Dalley could not join them on a proposed trip because he was 'the entire bondsman of his poor father'.[15]

Another upsetting death, two weeks after his mother's, was that of the editor of *Punch*, George Ross Morton. Dalley wrote in the magazine that the young humorist had been 'one of the bright spirits who inherit and bestow happiness', and had borne 'severe and protracted suffering' with 'a sweet and edifying submission'. In May he mourned John Hubert Plunkett, his old sparring partner in the Assembly but a man whose work as Attorney-General from 1836 to 1856 he had often praised. 'Great-hearted gentleman, how pathetic seems your humility by the light of our later experience of men with not half of your authority and none of your claims upon our reverence,' he wrote in *Punch*. 'Just, when to be just was to be heroic – liberal, when intolerance was mistaken for firmness – uncorrupted and incorruptible amidst great and constant temptations…'[16]

Dalley travelled to Bathurst at the end of April for the Circuit Court, but otherwise seems to have made few court appearances in the first half of 1869. At the end of May he held a watching brief at the coroner's inquest into the death of the colony's Spanish consul, Don Eduardo

San Just, who was found to have thrown himself from a window of his residence 'whilst suffering from temporary insanity'.[17] In June and July he appeared in the Water Police Court to defend two men involved in the trade in Pacific island labourers who faced charges under British anti-slavery law.

Recruitment of islanders to work on plantations in Queensland began in 1863 when the shipowner and large landholder Robert Towns employed Ross Lewin, a sandalwood trader operating in what is now Vanuatu, to obtain workers for his cotton farm near Brisbane. Lewin soon struck out on his own, advertising in 1867 that he could supply sugar growers, cotton planters and others with 'the best and most serviceable natives to be had in the islands at £7 a head'. Dalley's clients in 1869 were the captain, John C. Daggett, and 'supercargo' (the officer in charge of the 'cargo'), William Pritchard, of a schooner, the *Daphne*, that Lewin had had fitted out for the trade. Under Queensland's Polynesian Labourers Act, passed in 1868 to control recruiting and supervise conditions of employment, the *Daphne* was licensed to carry 50 islanders to the colony.

Officially, all those taken to Queensland were to be volunteers who would be employed for an agreed term and then returned home. But the potential for abuse was obviously great, not least because of the language barrier. As well as engaging in kidnapping, traders were accused of deceiving recruits about where they were being taken and for how long. Then, if islanders were returned at all, it might be to the wrong island. Various measures to stamp out such 'blackbirding' practices were introduced in the 1870s and '80s; Towns, in evidence to a royal commission held in Sydney into alleged kidnappings in 1867 and '68, had been among the advocates of tighter controls.

On her first voyage under Daggett's command, in 1868, the *Daphne* delivered the permitted 50 recruits to Brisbane. Plans changed for the second trip; twice as many islanders were taken on board and the destination became Levuka, Fiji. For Lewin and his collaborators, delivering a hundred islanders there was more profitable than taking 50 to Queensland.

Unfortunately for Daggett and Pritchard, when they reached Levuka they found the HMS *Rosario*, a Sydney-based man-of-war tasked with policing the Pacific labour trade, in the harbour. After inspecting the *Daphne*'s fittings and papers, the *Rosario*'s commander, Captain George Palmer, concluded that the schooner was engaged in 'a most irregular traffic, tending to promote and encourage the slave trade'. He deputed a naval officer to sail her, with Daggett, Pritchard and their crew, to Sydney.

Daggett's committal hearing, on a charge of having 'knowingly, wilfully, feloniously, and piratically received, conveyed, and removed… certain persons…for the purpose of their being imported…with a view to their being used and dealt with as slaves', ran for two days. Captain Palmer told the magistrates a 'special reason' that had induced him to examine the *Daphne*'s credentials closely was seeing Ross Lewin's signature on the papers: 'I heard of him at every island I was at as a man-stealer and as a kidnapper'. Members of the ship's crew insisted in their evidence, however, that the islanders had come aboard willingly and were well looked after.

The court accepted Dalley's contention that there was no evidence of the islanders being used as slaves or that Daggett had any guilty knowledge as the law required for conviction, and dismissed the charge. After a much shorter hearing, another bench of magistrates dismissed the case against Pritchard. Dalley was not involved in subsequent hearings before Chief Justice Stephen to determine whether the *Daphne* should be confiscated as a 'slaver'. Stephen concluded, in line with the magistrates' decisions, that the islanders taken to Fiji 'were not slaves in any sense of the word or intended to be dealt with as slaves'.[18]

The verdicts were a setback in the fight against blackbirding, and Captain Palmer was unimpressed. In a book he published on his return to England he accused the authorities of being lukewarm in prosecuting the cases. He had been told, he wrote, that 'so many merchants in Sydney were closely connected with, and had interest in, Queensland plantations, together with several in the New South Wales Government, that every possible delay and difficulty would be thrown in my way.'

Towns, a member of the Legislative Council, certainly had government connections. In 1869 the former (and future) Premier Charles Cowper was an employee of his company, and the current Premier, John Robertson, was a partner with him in cattle stations in Queensland's gulf country – an investment that drove him into bankruptcy in 1870.[19] The Attorney-General, Sir William Manning, had been part-owner of a property that had sought to procure islander labour.[20]

However, responding to Palmer's allegations after the book appeared, the Crown Solicitor, John Williams, argued persuasively that the *Daphne* cases had failed solely because of a lack of hard evidence. For example, Palmer had provided no information on how the islanders were recruited or whether they were detained on board against their will. The Secretary of State for the Colonies, Lord Kimberley, accepted that Williams's rejoinder and a detailed statement from Robertson exonerated the colonial government. Palmer promised to remove the offending passages if his book went into a second edition.[21]

The book contains entertaining paragraphs about Daggett's committal hearing. Palmer described it as a 'source of infinite amusement to those who came to hear it...the trial in *Pickwick* was always present to my mind';

> The ingenious brow-beating, the flashes of wit, were all new to me; and it being my first appearance in a witness-box, I must have cut a sorry figure in comparison with old Daggett, who, with long white hair and spectacles, seemed more like a missionary than master of the 'Daphne', and his appearance evidently created a marked sensation, although I thought I could detect a curious gleam in the eye of Mr Dalley, when he glanced from time to time at his interesting client... I deeply regret not being able to recollect half the ingenious nonsense that this very clever and amusing advocate talked...[22]

According to Palmer, Dalley concluded his address by proclaiming that it was 'monstrous...that English vessels, while pursuing their lawful trade, cannot sail upon these seas in peace'. The idea that they might 'at any moment be liable to capture by this Wilberforce of the

Pacific' was 'absurd and outrageous'. The magistrates, commented the naval captain, 'looked preternaturally solemn and cowed before his thundering eloquence'.

Dalley was one of nine men appointed shortly afterwards to conduct the royal commission, chaired by the colony's Auditor-General, Christopher Rolleston, into alleged kidnappings of islanders. Witnesses called to 13 hearings between July and September 1869 included shipowners, captains of trading vessels, employers of islanders, missionaries, and some islander recruits. Dalley attended only two of the hearings and was the only commissioner who did not sign the report. This presented a generally positive view of the trade and treatment of islanders and concluded that continued introduction of Polynesian labour into Queensland seemed acceptable 'under proper regulations'. The transcripts of evidence show Dalley raised concerns about the use of force in recruitment and whether islanders were returned to their home islands as promised.[23]

The murder of an Anglican missionary, Bishop John Patteson, in the Solomon Islands in September 1871, apparently as payback for the kidnapping of a group of young islanders by blackbirders, prompted a tightening of regulations. Dalley's review, in the *Herald* in 1873, of a biography of Patteson provides a further indication of his views. He noted that systematic kidnappings had 'immensely increased' the peril faced by missionaries, whose work he eulogised. And he quoted approvingly Patteson's advice that natives who killed boats' crews should not be punished unless it was clearly shown that they had not acted in 'retribution for outrages first committed by white men'.[24]

Dalley was involved in legal battles surrounding another high seas drama in the second half of 1869. In May, Denis Mackinlay, a trader, purchased a consignment of clothing worth around £2,600 from a Sydney dealer. He asked for, and was granted, generous credit after saying the clothes were to be shipped to Sweers Island in the Gulf of Carpentaria, where he expected they would be snapped up. The Queensland government representative in the gulf region was based on the island, and Mackinlay reportedly said he expected 20–30,000 diggers would soon pass through on their way to newly discovered goldfields on the mainland.

Shortly afterwards, Mackinlay was declared insolvent. He appeared in the magistrates' court in late August charged with obtaining the goods by false pretences, but was discharged after Dalley argued successfully on his behalf that the truth or falsity of his statements about the purpose of the purchases was irrelevant. Many more court appearances followed. First it was alleged that, by secretly diverting goods worth £6,000 said to be intended for Sweers Island to Auckland and Melbourne, Mackinlay had conspired with three others to defraud creditors of his insolvent estate. Dalley argued unsuccessfully at the committal hearing that the fact that Mackinlay had insured the schooner headed for Sweers Island and its cargo for £12,000 proved there was no intention to defraud.

Within days, news reached Sydney that this ship, the *Snowbird*, had burnt and sunk off Queensland's tropical coast. Her captain, Alexander Shaw, soon appeared in court charged with arson with intent to defraud the insurer. Evidence was given that he had said 'in a knowing sort of way' before sailing that the *Snowbird* would not be returning, and had ordered that two tins of kerosene be placed in his cabin and that the ship's boat be fully provisioned. Not surprisingly, he was committed for trial despite Dalley's contention that no motive for arson had been established.

All the strands came together in the Central Criminal Court in November when Mackinlay and Shaw were among six men put on trial for conspiring to defraud Mackinlay's creditors. Appearing again for Mackinlay, Dalley argued that there was no conspiracy. 'Not a scintilla' of evidence showed Shaw had set fire to the *Snowbird*, and preparing the ship's boat had simply been a wise precaution in light of the danger posed by reefs off northern Queensland, he said. The prosecutor, Edward Butler, clearly had a stronger case. He convinced the jury that scuttling the *Snowbird* was central to the alleged conspiracy, preventing discovery that the goods surreptitiously diverted were not on board. All the convicted conspirators received two-year sentences. Mackinlay was given an additional three years for fraudulent insolvency, and Shaw another two for arson.[25]

An interesting glimpse of Dalley, and his friend Premier Robertson, around this time comes from the reminiscences of an English visitor, Henry Mayers Hyndman. Then a radically inclined 27-year-old journalist, he became a Marxist activist after reading *Das Kapital* in 1880. Hyndman recalled taking morning walks and becoming quite intimate with Dalley, 'as bright and brilliant a companion as I ever met'. But 'Jack' Robertson was the man who most impressed him in Sydney. 'How a half-educated politician with no roof to his mouth, and certainly no beauty of face or form, devoid also of any great power of expression, contrived to outweigh the extraordinarily unpleasant sound of his voice, and to hold his own and dominate as Premier a by no means easily handled assembly, was a mystery to me,' he wrote. 'His influence in private was as great as in public…'[26]

Dalley's continuing involvement with the Church included taking a prominent role at meetings in April and June 1869 to raise funds for the new St Vincent's Hospital building at Darlinghurst (the Sisters of Charity had established the hospital at Potts Point in 1857). In August he spoke at a Catholic guild meeting, chaired by Archbishop Polding, which was notable for the presence of two of Robertson's ministers – Treasurer Saul Samuel and Lands Minister William Forster – demonstrating solidarity with the colony's Catholics. The following evening he was the principal lay speaker at a meeting to raise funds to cover the costs of Polding's impending visit to Rome for the first Vatican Council. Dalley praised Polding as the Catholics' 'grand protector': 'The enemies of our religious liberty are comparatively powerless while we can present to society as our representative one so noble, so free from intolerance, so just, and so good…' He feared that the Archbishop, now 74 years old, might not return.[27]

In fact, Polding returned very quickly, landing in Sydney the day before Christmas. Unwell when he reached Aden, he had left his steamer and, with his chaplain, caught the next one home. He arrived in the midst of general elections that started badly for those hoping the voters would pass a harsh judgement on Parkes and others who had stirred sectarian passions.

Seeking to make a political comeback, former Premier Charles Cowper stood in the first contest, for East Sydney, declaring that he was appalled by 'the base attempt of certain designing politicians to introduce and uphold sectarian animosities'. Parkes and Martin – now Sir James, having been knighted early in the year – were among the 10 other contestants for the four available places. Dalley urged voters to back Cowper and reject those who had 'debased and degraded the institutions of the country'.[28] Instead they placed Parkes at the top of the poll, followed by Martin and the fiery Scot, David Buchanan, recently returned to the colony. Cowper came fifth and hence missed election (he was subsequently returned for Liverpool Plains).

The winners gloated at the declaration of the poll. Parkes denied that he had traded on religious dissensions. 'But if men came to this free land, and here obeyed the bidding of other persons, who controlled them for sinister objects to serve themselves [he was clearly referring to the Catholic clergy], it would be disastrous to the liberties of the community.' Martin took up the theme, saying that priests, while protesting neutrality, had secretly made 'every effort' to influence the election; it was essential 'to put down ecclesiastical interference'. Buchanan was the most blatant, saying the main question at the election had been whether the people were to be governed by 'an ecclesiastical or civil power'. He had observed that when Cowper was Colonial Secretary there were always 'two or three priests waiting in the lobby; and at last they grew so bold as to go in without knocking. (Laughter.)'[29]

Dalley responded that evening with, according to the *Evening News*, 'as noble a burst of eloquence as ever came from the lips of man'[30] at a crowded meeting in support of Robertson, Rev. Lang and William Campbell as candidates for West Sydney. He regretted the defeat of Cowper, 'the ablest and honestest public servant' the Legislative Assembly had seen. Instead, the colony was 'damned with a Parkes and cursed with a Buchanan'. He was scathing about his former (and future) friend Martin, who had 'trampled on all honour and virtue' and in effect accused 'true Protestants' such as Robertson, Cowper and Campbell of 'Popery'.

Dalley noted that he had 'ever received the warm friendship' of Archbishop Polding, who had never interfered with him in his politics despite his identification with men 'who had no religious feeling in common with Catholics'. One of these was Lang, a man never 'accused of Popish proclivities – not even by the ignorant asses of the Protestant Political Association'. Another was Robertson; 'with what Popish conspirators he was intertwined – what dark and mysterious machinations' he could not say.

Catholics had not promoted sectarian discord, he continued. Instead, he marvelled at their patience in bearing 'every insult and contumely' that had been 'put upon themselves, their religion and their clergy'. He criticised other candidates for West Sydney including former Treasurer Eagar and the barrister William Windeyer. Doing so was 'one of the most unpleasant duties' that had devolved on him, he said; he wished to 'go through the world placidly'. But the time had come 'for speaking out boldly, and meeting insult by insult'.[31]

When he concluded, 'the entire meeting' reportedly 'rose and cheered for several minutes'. Whether his words influenced the outcome in West Sydney is debatable. An Orangeman and Protestant Political Association member, Joseph Wearne, topped the poll, but Robertson came next. Lang withdrew from the contest before the vote and Robertson's second associate, Campbell, was defeated. The other successful candidates were Windeyer, a Protestant Political Association member, and William Speer, a former Mayor of Sydney who was also an opposition supporter.

Hopes of preventing the return of Parkes and Martin to government now rested with suburban and country electorates. While displaying his usual reluctance, Dalley allowed himself to be nominated for The Lachlan, the seat Martin had held since 1864. His opponent in the contest was a Young businessman, James Watson, who was to become Treasurer in the Parkes government of 1878–82.

Dalley did not visit the electorate to seek support, or appear at the nomination meeting at Boorowa on 20 December. A prominent local pastoralist, George Eason, proposed him for election, and a storekeeper, Michael O'Neill, seconded the nomination. O'Neill said he believed there was nobody superior to Dalley in the colony, and that 'by consenting to sit if elected' he had conferred an honour on the electorate. Watson's nominator, landholder and magistrate Nicholas Besnard, agreed he was 'a fine young fellow', but thought him 'fonder of cigars and claret than of work'. Seconding Watson's nomination, John Paterson, uncle of the poet Banjo, said he expected Dalley 'would scarcely ever enter the House' if elected. His record as the reluctant member for Carcoar from 1862 to '64 gave Paterson valid grounds for this prediction.

Dalley won the show of hands at the nomination, and on election day the voters of predominantly Catholic Boorowa turned out in strength for him, giving him a 185 to 72 victory over Watson. He was also the clear winner in the smaller, strongly Catholic villages of Binalong and Jugiong. However, Watson won easily in his hometown, Young, and in nearby centres including Grenfell, Wombat and Murrumburrah. Overall, Dalley lost by 786 votes to 979.[32]

12
The dolphin and the anchor

The new year, 1870, marked the centenary of Captain Cook's arrival at Botany Bay – a milestone that speakers at the Anniversary Day regatta luncheon noted as they extolled the colony's progress. Proposing the toast to 'the day we celebrate', the Premier, Charles Cowper, declared that its relations with the mother country were 'rapidly approaching to those of an independent State'. The people of New South Wales could congratulate themselves 'on having proved worthy of belonging to the great country from which we sprang,' responded Dalley. He was glad to see they

> still cling to England, still desire to be participators in her glory and greatness. (Cheers.) When we do separate, we shall go from the arms of that mother who has reared us, with the highest possible regard for all that has been her glory and our own. (Cheers.)

He thought news of the 'quiet and thoroughly English manner' in which the colony had just passed through the 'crisis' of a general election 'at a time of considerable excitement' would be noted with hearty approval in England.[1] Robertson had retained government with a fragile Assembly majority. Then almost immediately, on 12 January, he stepped down to deal with his parlous financial situation and Cowper took over as Premier. Dalley shared the platform with Cowper, Rev. Lang and many other admirers of Robertson at a meeting called in early March to launch a testimonial fund. Robertson may have been 'imprudent and impolitic' at times, said Dalley, but 'no more straightforward, generous, or upright' politician had been seen in the colony. Contributions poured in to help the popular land law reformer out of his difficulties; more than £600 was raised in the first week and the final tally was £2,715.[2]

In June, Dalley accepted appointment to a vacancy in the Legislative Council. He took up his seat at the opening of the new parliamentary session on 11 August and, on the government's behalf, moved the resolution to adopt the address in reply to the Governor's speech. But his commitment to the political fray remained lukewarm; he declined the position of government representative in the Council. 'It suits him better to play the part of a *corps de reserve*, to come up and do battle when wanted,' commented the *Mail*. Referring in his speech to 'the serene atmosphere of this Chamber', free from the storms that raged 'elsewhere', he indicated his preference for an appointed seat in the Council to an elected spot in the Assembly. In his earlier, more radical, days he had doubted the need for a Legislative Council (chapter 5).

A major event of the Cook centenary year was the departure in August of the colony's British army garrison; apart from a continuing Royal Navy presence, defence would now be its own responsibility. Dalley said in his address-in-reply speech that he regretted that 'this portion of the connection with the mother country' was ending. But although English public opinion – whether motivated by indifference to colonial interests or by economy – was demanding the cultivation of 'self-reliance and independence', the colony's allegiance would not weaken. Repeating the sentiments of his Anniversary Day speech, he said he believed separation, if it eventually came, would be instigated by the mother country, not the colonies.[3]

Dalley's next lengthy speech in the Council was on divorce. In the Assembly in 1858 he had asked whether the government planned to follow England's example by legalising divorce, on very restricted grounds; it appeared that he supported the idea (chapter 4). Premier Cowper answered yes, but the matter was left in abeyance until March 1870 when David Buchanan introduced a bill that went further than the English Act – not only could a husband sue for divorce on account of his wife's infidelity, but the reverse also would be allowed! The Assembly quickly gave the go-ahead.

When the bill came to the Council in September Dalley tabled a petition from Archbishop Polding, and others from groups of Catholics around the colony, opposing it. He proceeded to argue that there was no public demand to allow divorce, nor were 'the best of the people of the country...loudly and generally' calling for the change. The 'venerable prelates' and clergy of both the Anglican and Catholic churches were opposed – and they, rather than politicians, were the people in contact with 'those who suffered, with those whose domestic happiness had been destroyed, with all who were in sorrow, and in trouble, and in despondency'.

He thought 'consciousness of the indissolubility of the marriage-tie' made both parties more reasonable when disputes arose – 'less inexorable in the mutual pardon of injuries – and more resolved to help, to sustain, to pity, to forgive, and to love each other'. And if divorce were allowed, why limit the grounds to adultery? 'What of the wretch who goes to his home to strike down his wife in the midst of her helpless children – to address her in language which shocks her purity – and depraves her offspring?' He noted that Hume and Gibbon, scholars 'constantly occupying themselves with those studies which would explain the degeneracy of peoples and the fall of empires', considered relaxing the marriage tie extremely undesirable.

If Buchanan's bill passed, he continued, the press would carry daily reports of the proceedings of the divorce court 'more pernicious to the morality of the nation than the most licentious publications previously in existence'. Already England was flooded with literature 'dangerous to the national morals'.

> Sensational novels, with plots and characters and accessories drawn directly from the public proceedings of the Divorce Courts...a dramatic literature – indecent – worthless and filthy – displacing the great and classic drama of the country – these are some of the signs of the times which the intelligent observers of the decay of nations have perceived and commented on in the mother country.[4]

By 10 votes to four, the Council rejected the bill. Polding, it seems, was ecstatic. A letter that he wrote or approved, signed Veritas, appeared in *Freeman's Journal* praising Dalley to the skies. 'Of all species of rhetoric, or every kind of eloquence…recorded in this country', nothing had equalled his speeches at the last elections and on the divorce bill. 'Large-hearted, benevolent, charitable', he was always ready with tongue and pen 'to repress intolerance, mockery, and insult. Hon. W.B. Dalley, how much do we not owe you?'[5]

Cowper's short-lived government resigned in December following the blocking of financial measures. Parkes, again insolvent, had just departed the Assembly. So it was Martin's turn for power again, and Robertson joined him in an unlikely coalition, but one that could be expected to command the numbers needed to allow effective government. As part of the deal between the two men, Cowper was appointed the colony's Agent-General in London.[6]

Chief Justice Stephen presided at the farewell dinner the following February. He spoke of his 30-year friendship with Cowper, which wide differences of opinion on many matters had not interrupted. Cowper also recalled old times, noting that the site of the café that was hosting the dinner 'was covered with the original forest' when he arrived in Sydney as a two-year-old in 1809. Martin, the new Premier and Attorney-General, was greeted with 'tumultuous cheering' when he rose to praise his long-time political foe. He acknowledged that his differences with Cowper had been of 'a bitter character for many years', but said he had learned that 'life is too short for one to spend it in hostility and hatred to anybody'. He noted that government and opposition members had come together in force to honour Cowper, and said no public figure was more entitled to such a demonstration of respect.

Dalley's contribution to the evening was a short speech proposing Stephen's health. He hoped the 68-year-old would long continue to preside at such functions and over the Supreme Court: 'Long may he sit, gentlemen, in banco and at banquets…serving us equally in expounding the laws and delighting us all by his capacity for the true enjoyment of life.'[7]

As usual, most of Dalley's court appearances during 1870 were in the Central Criminal Court, or the 'Tribunal of Horrors' as he was moved on at least one occasion to describe it.⁸ His clients faced trial for, among other things, infanticide, rape, bank robbery, cattle stealing, fraudulent insolvency and cardsharping. An old man charged with setting fire to a stack of wheat seems to have been as surprised as the prosecutor when Dalley's 'powerful address to the jury' secured his acquittal. After displaying 'dogged indifference' during the trial, the prisoner greeted the verdict 'with every mark of excitement and pleasurable surprise'.⁹

In November, Dalley appeared in the magistrates' court for the 31-year-old poet Henry Kendall. Recently returned to Sydney after a failed attempt to make a living from his writing in Melbourne, he was charged with presenting a forged cheque for £1. Dalley did not dispute that a case for trial had been made out, but called witnesses to show Kendall was not in his right mind when he committed the offence. One relative reported that he had constantly contradicted himself since returning from Melbourne, sobbed like a child, and said once or twice he would 'sooner be out of the world'. Another told of absent-mindedness and vacant stares. A doctor said Kendall's 'intense thirst for opium had destroyed his nervous system'. And his 'liberal use of spirits' had destroyed all desire for 'ordinary sustenance', rendering him unfit for 'any mental labour'. The witness considered that 'at the present time his mind is very shattered'.¹⁰

After being held at the 'lunatic receiving-house' at Darlinghurst Gaol for four weeks, Kendall went on trial before District Court Judge George Simpson at the Sydney Quarter Sessions. Reportedly 'so overcome' by the ordeal, he was provided with a mattress and pillow 'upon which he reclined in the dock'. Dalley secured an impressive array of witnesses to support his argument for Kendall's innocence of forging and uttering on account of his 'deranged state of mind'.

W.H. Hicks, editor of *Sydney Punch*, said Kendall had told him he had edited a comic paper in Melbourne, which he knew was not true. N.D. Stenhouse was one of two witnesses who recalled Kendall claiming he had written

Henry Kendall.

a poem in the Aeolic dialect of ancient Greek, but the poet knew no Greek. Other witnesses gave further examples of his delusions. One, the journalist and playwright Walter Cooper, said Kendall had spoken of a meeting, which never occurred, between himself, Cooper and the poet Adam Lindsay Gordon in Melbourne. Gordon, who befriended Kendall during his stay in the city, committed suicide in June 1870, and it was confirmed during the trial that Kendall also had had suicidal thoughts.

The essayist J. Sheridan Moore told the court of an occasion when Kendall spoke jocularly about Gordon's death, saying he had 'tricked them all'. Joseph Harpur recalled the poet telling him that 'if he were convinced there was a spiritual world he would go into it'. Dr Isaac Aaron, visiting surgeon at Darlinghurst Gaol, said Kendall had been found one night with a handkerchief tied around his neck. Asked why it was there, he had said he was tired of life.

Aaron, a prosecution witness, gave evidence that he had seen Kendall every day in the receiving-house and observed 'no peculiar indications that betokened insanity'. But under Dalley's cross-examination he admitted that 'the peculiarities noticed and spoken of by the witnesses for the defence were indicative of insanity at that period'. The jury took just a few minutes to decide that Kendall was not guilty on the ground of insanity. The judge ruled that he should remain in custody until 'the pleasure of the Governor is known'.[11]

Kendall was out and about again quite soon. Poems and reviews by him appeared frequently in *Freeman's Journal* between September 1871 and the end of the year. Since the departure of Richard O'Sullivan, the radical Irish nationalist, in late 1869, Thomas Butler, brother of the barrister Edward, had edited the paper and Dalley had again become a frequent contributor. According to a vignette in the paper's fiftieth anniversary issue in 1900, although it never had a 'round table' after the fashion of *Sydney Punch* 'there was many a brilliant gathering in the dingy backroom… Shy nervous Kendall has sat there amidst a bright company. The effervescent Dalley is telling a story…'[12]

Unfortunately, Kendall's recovery was brief. He was a homeless derelict for most of the next two years, his wife and children finding refuge with her family. But then, through the generosity of a central coast family who provided work and lodgings, his fortunes improved, and the Kendalls were reunited in 1876. Dalley remained a friend and supporter throughout, and the poet summoned him to his bedside when he was dying in 1882 (chapter 18).[13] Four years earlier, he published a poem titled 'William Bede Dalley'. Two of its eight stanzas read,

> He, with the faultless intuition born
> Of splendid faculties, sees things aright;
> And all his strong immeasurable scorn
> Falls, like a thunder, on the hypocrite.
>
> But for the sufferer, and the son of Shame
> On whom Remorse – a great sad burden – lies,
> His kindness glistens like a morning flame –
> Immense compassion shines within his eyes.[14]

Apart from defending in murder trials at the Bathurst Circuit Court in April and the Central Criminal Court in May, Dalley seems to have had few legal engagements in the first half of 1871. His appearances in the Legislative Council also were fairly rare. In the August 1870 to June 1871 parliamentary session he attended on just 32 of 85 sitting days,[15] mostly before the fall of the Cowper government. Possibly he was unwell again, or more likely still the 'bondsman' of his ailing father.

'Prolonged cheering' greeted him when he rose to propose the toast to 'the schools of the colony' at the dinner held on 5 June to commemorate the schoolmaster William Cape (chapter 1). He made it clear that, despite their rejection by the Catholic hierarchy, he approved of the public schools established by the Martin/Parkes government in 1866. 'We may neither have a superabundance of profound statesmen nor a superfluity of brilliant orators, nor, to borrow the French phrase, an embarrassment of any other forms of intellectual riches,' he said, 'but we have at all events not spared our revenues in the culture of our children.'

> We have adopted a system of public education of which all can avail themselves, and we have maintained it by a lavish expenditure. And we

have founded, endowed, and sustained our university, the chairs of which are filled by men whose scholarship would shed a lustre upon the stateliest homes of learning in Europe. The country has nobly done its part for the schools. Let us hope that the schools will do theirs for the country…that we, to whom such advantages of culture as are now presented were not offered, may be succeeded by those who will bring to the discharge of public duty all the learning, the experience, and refinement, which we all desire to see adorning our rulers.[16]

In August, Dalley spoke briefly at a dinner, chaired by Professor Badham, to mark the centenary of the birth of Sir Walter Scott. Proposing the toast to Australian authors and the colony's press, he remarked that the colonists had no literature to speak of in comparison with Britain, but had 'just as deep a sympathy with the literature of England. (Applause.)' Almost certainly Dalley was the author of a *Punch* article two months later welcoming the novelist Anthony Trollope to the colony and thanking him 'for all you have done, and done so well, to sweeten social intercourse, to delight, to amuse, to alleviate human suffering, to strengthen the ties that bind us to the dear old land…

> As noiselessly as the creatures of your own delightful fancy have stolen into our hearts for years and made their homes there, you have come amongst us, the brave master, the kindly magician, the eloquent teacher. The very city seems nobler when we think that you are walking its streets, and that its citizens may look upon one who has given so much happiness to millions.[17]

Trollope spent a year touring the Australian colonies and visiting a son who had a property near Forbes. He made four visits to Sydney, the longest between 16 November and 13 December 1871. In a speech in Bathurst in November he said people kept asking him: What do you think of the colony? He offered the view that Sydney was the 'loveliest spot he had ever seen in his life', and some of the gold diggings the ugliest.[18]

Dalley was among those who entertained him in Sydney and environs. 'We were all anxious to make his visit as pleasant as possible', to discharge in some way 'the debt of gratitude which every lover of pure English literature' owed him, he wrote in the *Herald* when Trollope's account of his travels was published in 1873. He found the 56-year-old completely without pretension, and a man

> who loved to ride forty or fifty miles a day – who would jump into the sea on the smallest provocation – was passionately fond of all sport, fishing, hunting, clambering over rocks only to see the fish-spearing of our aboriginals (as the writer of this notice saw him last year)'.

Trollope had lavished compliments on New South Wales, Dalley wrote. 'Our climate is perfection – our mosquitos are more musical than malignant – our snakes are abject and innocent – we have no 'sensational wild beasts' and our magpies are melancholy, not larcenous'. And Sydney harbour? He quoted a long passage from Trollope's book on the subject, beginning with an admission of inability to convey in words its unequalled beauty. A 'stout Sydney citizen' had boasted to him as they steamed toward Circular Quay one day that 'the fleets of all nations might rest securely within the protection of the harbour', Trollope recorded. Probably that was Dalley.[19]

A week before Trollope's November/December visit to Sydney, Dalley took a coastal steamer to Brisbane to appear for the proprietors of the Ipswich *Queensland Times* in a libel action brought by Queensland's opposition leader and former Premier, Charles Lilley. But the evening before the trial was to begin a telegram arrived advising that his father was dangerously ill, and he left for home the next day.[20] Sadly, he arrived the day after John Dalley died.

An 'extraordinarily large concourse' of citizens 'of all classes' joined him and his brother Richard for the solemn dirge and requiem high mass in the rebuilt temporary St Mary's Cathedral on 16 November. The Bishop of Bathurst, Matthew Quinn, presided, and then officiated at the burial at the Devonshire Street cemetery. Professor Badham was named on the death certificate as a witness to the burial – a sign of the now firmly established friendship between the Eton- and Oxford-educated classicist and Dalley, the convicts' son.[21]

Dalley chaired the 1872 Anniversary Day regatta lunch, and Badham, in 'very eloquent terms', proposed the toast to 'the day we celebrate'. Guest of honour was the Governor, Lord Belmore, who was about to return to his Irish estate after four years in the colony. Responding to the toast to his health proposed by Dalley, he thanked the colonists for having treated him very hospitably.[22]

A few days later, Belmore controversially accepted Premier Martin's advice to dissolve the parliament and call fresh elections. The Martin/Robertson government had proved almost as ineffectual as its predecessor; the issue that brought it to grief was the unsatisfactory resolution of a dispute with Victoria over border customs duties. The elections gave Parkes, back in the Assembly after receiving his discharge from the Insolvency Court in September 1871, his long-sought chance to become Premier. Remarkably, he achieved his ambition with Catholic help – thanks to an alliance with the influential layman Edward Butler, a friend from the 1850s when they had worked together on the *Empire*. Edward's brother Thomas, as editor of *Freeman's*, also assisted the cause.

From the moment the first votes were counted it became clear that Martin had erred in requesting a dissolution. Parkes topped the poll in East Sydney and Martin was rejected. Robertson just hung on in West Sydney. The pattern was repeated across the colony; Martin scrambled back in the East Macquarie electorate but three of his ministers ended up without seats.

On 11 March, when most results were in, a long letter from Parkes, signed 'An Elector', appeared in the *Herald*. He estimated that the government would have the support of less than a third of the members of the Assembly and gloated that 'the result has in no respect surprised me'.[23] Martin, as 'Another Elector', disputed his figures in the next day's paper and claimed 'Mr Parkes is not yet on the threshold of power'.[24] Parkes shot back, accusing Martin of trying to neutralise 'the verdict of the ballot box'.[25] Then William Forster, the nominal leader of the opposition, joined the fray as 'Third Party', diverting the correspondence to a more philosophical path.

He objected to the 'mechanical analysis' of voting intentions engaged in by Parkes and Martin, and called on members of the Assembly to judge all issues on their merits even if this might sometimes require acting contrary to previously stated intentions.[26] Parkes responded that such a doctrine, which he claimed condoned repudiation of political promises, was 'fatal to the efficiency and purity of government'.[27]

Dalley, as 'W.B.D.', now joined in, taking aim at 'the eminent moral teacher', Parkes, over his debts (amounting to more than £35,000, compared with assets of less than £12,000, when his estate was sequestrated in October 1870[28]). The same rule should apply to a promise of paying as to a promise of voting, he wrote. And Parkes had misrepresented Forster, who had not suggested that political promises need not be taken seriously. For Parkes to offer Forster moral guidance, Dalley contended, presented 'that whimsical incongruity' so happily expressed in the Japanese proverb 'the anchor teaching the dolphin how to swim'.[29]

Forster defended himself in further letters, but the main, increasingly bitter, argument was now between Parkes and Dalley. Parkes accused Dalley of 'watery reasoning and tinsel scurrility'; his 'effusion' was like 'certain specimens of fungi, which present some glitter to the eye, but which are unpleasant to touch, and of which nothing can be made'. Referring to the proverb Dalley quoted, he thought 'Dolphins' would be a suitable name for 'the small party of exquisites' who sat 'in judgement on the judgement of the electors'. A good 'anchor' might be 'of more value to the ship's safety'.[30]

Replying, Dalley professed to wonder what he had done to spark Parkes's 'manifest vexation'. All he had maintained was that a promise to pay was at least as binding as a political promise; 'one could not be commercially infamous and politically illustrious'. Then he became even more personal.

> I once in early life enjoyed the intimate (and to me somewhat expensive) acquaintance of a great public moralist, who on all questions of political relationship and legislative action maintained dogmas of which the inflexible severity appalled me at the first till I took refuge in scepticism, and held them to be considerably alloyed by imposture. Before my infidel period that distinguished person used to absorb a great deal of my time,

and of other spare matters, for which as a philosopher he was not bound to take any account; nor did he take it... Of course 'An Elector' will regard this as an imaginary sketch. I give him my assurance as a gentleman that I am in possession of a curious little volume which will prove the contrary...[31]

Parkes returned to the dolphin theme in his reply, saying he had lighted on a new variety that, 'when slightly wounded, gives out a piteous wail not unlike the shriek of a whipped child'. It was true, he went on, that Dalley and he had been friends, and he would not object to a history of the friendship being published. Their estrangement was, in fact, relatively recent, dating from 'the execution of a celebrated prisoner' [O'Farrell]. Since then Dalley had 'seized upon all convenient occasions to cast his abuse upon me, and on all those occasions I have yielded to the recollection of former friendship, and have remained silent'. But no attack could have been more wanton and unprovoked than his latest.

> If...it is permissible for him publicly to refer to transactions between professed friends, a dozen years ago...it may be prudent for him to consider whether others, who have never yet descended to any similar mode of warfare, will not feel justified in resorting to means of reprisal rather unpleasant to himself... When this 'gentleman' informs the public of his 'possession of a curious little volume,' relating to 'An Elector', has he forgotten the many detached records of which I am the possessor, bearing date years subsequent to any transaction to which he can possibly refer, and some of them teeming with expressions of 'W.B.D.'s' *'sense of the value and sincerity of my friendship?'*[32]

The *Herald* let Dalley have the last word. Parkes had always kept his correspondence, he wrote, 'in obedience to a profound sense of public duty' to produce old letters 'for the confusion and humiliation of those who presumed to look upon him as not quite immaculate. In this quality, as in many others, I did not regard him as an object worthy of imitation.' He thought a history of their friendship would be of little public interest, but feared he might emerge

> with rather a damaged reputation for commercial shrewdness; and should possibly forfeit the good opinion of those simple, honest trading people in whose interest I have endeavoured to show that to pay one's debts, to keep

one's word, to be mindful of one's pecuniary obligations in every way, are at least duties as imperative as to preserve one's political consistency, and redeem one's hustings' pledges.³³

Dalley attended the opening of parliament on 1 May. Martin, recognising that his government lacked the numbers to continue, had already submitted his resignation. Forster, as opposition leader, was called on first to form a new administration and recruited Dalley, Macleay and two others to take office with him. However, he soon found he could not put together a full team of ministers and handed back his commission. Parkes, turned to next, had no such difficulty and became Premier and Colonial Secretary on 14 May. Edward Butler was his Attorney-General.

Other ministers included two who had served under Robertson and Cowper between 1868 and 1870, but Robertson, in a letter to the *Herald*, objected strongly to the elevation of the 'unscrupulous' Parkes. He wondered whether Butler approved of, among other things, 'his un-English and dastardly conduct in cross-examining a prisoner while awaiting in gaol trial on a capital charge, and, without letting that prisoner know it, placing a shorthand writer behind the door, to take down his carelessly spoken words'.³⁴

Robertson spoke briefly in support of a political unknown, James Jones, who stood against Parkes when he faced the electors again at the end of May. But it was Dalley's speech that made this lopsided contest memorable. 'I have come here this evening,' he told voters crowded into Sydney's Masonic Hall, 'to denounce the candidature of the Premier of the country, and to declare his occupation of the office a disgrace and a national humiliation.'

His attack focused on the 'absolute and unqualified falsehoods' Parkes had uttered during the O'Farrell affair – statements that had 'alarmed and convulsed the country' and 'split up into sections a community that had existed in peace and harmony so long'. He said Attorney-General Butler had persistently denounced Parkes as an 'arch-plotter against the peace of the country'. The 'dishonest and scandalous alliance' he had now entered into with Parkes was 'infinitely the most odious and least pardonable' political combination yet witnessed in the colony, and Catholics would soon come to regret their support for it.

> Mr Parkes will succeed; and, in all probability, will have a great triumph… Irish Roman Catholics, who, yesterday, regarded him with unspeakable horror, will on Wednesday lift him to power. But their day of remorse will come.

Dalley referred briefly to Parkes's 'gigantic genius for indebtedness', suggesting it was unsafe to have a man with his 'natural talents for the procurement of other people's money' in 'a post so eminent, with powers so large'. Concluding his speech – which, as he predicted, did not stop Parkes winning easily – he thanked the meeting's organisers for giving him the opportunity to get off his chest things he had wanted to say from the moment he heard of the ministry's formation. 'I never wish to say an unkind word of any living creature,' he continued,

> but there are characters so repulsive as to make silence upon the part of honest men a crime, and combinations too infamous to make toleration anything but treason against truth. Such a character, and such a combination, are now before you.[35]

13
A married man

On 5 June 1872, shortly before his 41st birthday, Dalley married 29-year-old Eleanor Jane Long at St John's Church of England, Darlinghurst. She was a sister of 39-year-old Lady Isabella Martin, wife of Dalley's good friend (again), Sir James Martin. A year earlier Eleanor's younger sister, Selina, had also married well – to George Cheeke, a nephew of Justice Alfred Cheeke of the Supreme Court.

Dalley's sister, Christina Greig, who lived in Melbourne, arrived three days before the wedding on the mail steamer *Nubia*, which also brought the colony's new Governor, Sir Hercules Robinson, and his wife, three children and eight servants to Sydney.[1] William Long, Eleanor's father, presumably gave the bride away. He was an ex-convict who had done even better in business than John Dalley. With his wife Isabella, née Walford, and family he lived in a fine house that still stands, 'Tusculum', at Potts Point. His principal business was a wine and spirits shop in George Street, and he owned much prime Sydney real estate. When he died in November 1876 the value of his 'goods' was estimated for probate at £100,000.

Those recorded as witnesses to the marriage were Professor Badham and Dalley's three new brothers-in-law – Martin, George Cheeke and Eleanor's 31-year-old brother William A. Long. Admitted as a barrister in 1862, Long was a member of the Legislative Assembly from 1875 to 1880, Treasurer in the Robertson government of August to December 1877, and later a Legislative Councillor. However, he made little mark as a lawyer or politician – much more as a Melbourne-Cup-winning racehorse owner.

Eleanor has been described as combining good sense with a large-hearted good nature and placid kindliness of manner.[2] Those were

'Clairvaux', Rose Bay.

qualities that would have helped her cope with Dalley's frequent entertaining – the best food and wine and much talk into the night – and with the five children born between March 1873 and May 1880. Little information has come to light about her or the marriage, but it is clear that she and the family were very important to Dalley. He was devastated when she died of typhoid in January 1881 – eight months after the birth of their fifth child, Mary – at their home, 'Clairvaux', overlooking the harbour at Rose Bay. This large, romantic house, whose distinctive features included a freestanding, three-storey castellated stone tower, had been built to his design. Although the family had moved in little more than a year earlier, he and the children left immediately; it is said he could not bear to set foot in it again.[3] Dalley wrote later that his life had been 'consecrated' to Eleanor.[4] The writer Frank Myers recalled him reflecting on his career late one evening: 'There is nothing in it, old boy... I have gone some way, you may go farther; God knows! But the little house, the little wife, the little child. There's nothing else...'[5]

The marriage moved some of his friends to verse. Badham wrote a poem of four stanzas and a celebratory sonnet, which read,

> This day, dear friend, hath Love at thy behest
> Built thee a home, wherein thy heart may dwell;

And hath performed his ministry so well,
And in his work thy very wish exprest,
That Love himself desires no other rest
But thy continual inmate will abide;
Where he shall hover round thee and thy bride,
And ever blessing both, of both be blest.
A thousand lamps shall make that dwelling bright,
Lit from the thousand hearths which thou hast cheered;
But chief from that wherein thy soul was reared
To thoughts of gentleness, and deeds of grace;
When fed by daily-duteous hands the light
Beamed on thy Father's venerable face.

Inspired by Badham's effort, William Forster also wrote a sonnet, in a book presented to Dalley after the wedding. The journalist Frank Hutchinson chose the same poetic form for his contribution, written after he read Badham's and Forster's work in the *Herald*.[6]

After their marriage in Eleanor's church, the couple retained their separate religious affiliations. The Catholic hierarchy frowned on mixed marriages – a position reinforced by the provincial council of bishops in Melbourne in April 1869 – and Dalley's connection with his church was apparently strained for some time. One indication is that he was not among the laymen taking prominent roles in the welcome for the new Coadjutor Archbishop, Roger Bede Vaughan, who arrived from England in December 1873.[7] Relations seem to have returned to normal by the mid '70s. There is no doubting his religious feeling; 'Clairvaux' was named after the Cistercian abbey founded by St Bernard in 1151, a figure of the Blessed Virgin stood guard by the porch, and upstairs was a small chapel.[8] And his practical support for the church continued; a fundraising meeting for the new cathedral in August 1873 was told he had promised £30 a year.[9]

William and Eleanor began their married life in the old Dalley home in Macquarie Street, which William had inherited, along with other Sydney real estate, from his father. Their first child, the second William Bede Dalley, was born there on 23 March 1873. By 1 January 1875, when their second child, Eleanor, was born, they were renting a large house, 'Tivoli' (now the site of Kambala girls' school), at Rose Bay. They were still there when the second son, John Bede, was born on 5 October 1876.

The next move, in late 1877, was to 'Greycliffe', on the Wentworth estate at Vaucluse. As thanks for packing the family china so well that nothing broke in transit, Dalley is said to have given the maid who did the job, Annie O'Brien, a small brass holy water fount. The young Irishwoman, according to the same family recollection, considered Dalley a 'very fine man'. She told of his befriending the Aborigines living on nearby Shark Beach – taking large pots of stew to them and listening with great interest to the stories they told. And when the Aboriginal 'chief' and his wife had disagreements, they came to the house seeking his adjudication.[10]

This story meshes with the recollections of a contemporary journalist, J.T. Donovan, who wrote of Dalley being regarded as a friend by many Aborigines, always being 'good and kind' to them, and describing one old man as 'the most perfect type of Nature's gentlemen' he had met.[11] The Dalleys' fourth child, Charles, was born at 'Greycliffe' on 19 July 1878. Dalley bought the four and a half acres on which 'Clairvaux' was to be built in October 1877, and the family moved in to the new house about two years later.[12]

The joy of the marriage on 5 June 1872 was followed swiftly by family tragedy; Dalley's 30-year-old brother Richard died just 10 days later of 'prostration', leaving a young wife and two small children. Though never in the public spotlight, it seems he was a talented young man. 'I can well remember attending Dalley's maiden lecture on 'Shakespearean Characters' with his brother in the chair,' wrote a journalist in 1901. 'It was a great success, and proved young Dalley to be as gifted a lecturer as he was an accomplished musician.'[13] Christina Greig stayed in Sydney after the wedding to be with her dying brother, returning to Melbourne four days after the funeral.[14]

Dalley did not reappear in the Legislative Council before the parliamentary session ended on 13 August. His first venture back to the

Central Criminal Court seems to have been a few days later, to defend a young woman charged with infanticide. Sad cases of unmarried women concealing pregnancies and births – some going to the length of killing their newborn babies – were all too common. In this case the doctor who examined the child's body gave evidence that he had been born alive and strangled. But the jury, no doubt influenced by Dalley's oratory, was sympathetic to the mother's plight and found her guilty only of concealment of birth. Justice Cheeke sentenced her to six months' gaol.[15]

Also in August, the first of many lengthy articles that Dalley was to write for the Herald on literary topics appeared. He had noted the death of William Thackeray in the *Sydney Times* in 1864 (chapter 8); the new article was a review of a tribute to the novelist by an American, William B. Reed, in *Blackwood's Magazine*. Reed wrote about Thackeray's love of the United States displayed during lecturing tours in the 1850s. 'What a picture [Reed] gives us of a great hearted, clear brained, pure souled English gentleman,' wrote Dalley in characteristic style. He noted that Anthony Trollope, who had left Sydney recently, had 'enjoyed, perhaps, more than any living man', the friendship of 'the great satirist'. Trollope was now on his way 'to the country of Lowell and of Longfellow, of Oliver Wendell Holmes and Ralph Waldo Emerson, to bear himself in such a great company as worthily as his dear, dear master'.[16]

The *Herald*, still edited by Rev. John West, had been the target of many scornful mentions by Dalley in *Freeman's* and *Punch* over the years and West himself had come in for pointed criticism. Presumably the 63-year-old editor did not bear a grudge against his paper's erudite new contributor. *Freeman's* professed amazement and amusement at seeing Dalley's article appear in the *Herald*. 'What on earth…has come over our venerable friend in her declining days,' it wondered? 'Has she lost her spectacles, and mistaking a paper on light literature for a letter on the Superannuation Act, published the wrong contribution?' It commented approvingly on Dalley's 'quick sympathies with all that is good and graceful and sweet and beautiful in humanity', but suggested he had been lazy in applying his 'great gifts'. He should try to emulate

Thackeray's industry: 'No inglorious ease for this man, with the world, as it were, at his feet; no dallying with the golden hours whose worth he knew so well; only work, honest, brave work, while the day lasted.'[17]

The southern railway reached Goulburn in May 1869, and shortly afterwards the famous 'zigzag' on the western escarpment of the Blue Mountains was completed, placing the western line's terminus an easy coach ride from Bathurst. These developments made it possible for Dalley to make court appearances in Goulburn, Sydney and Bathurst in one particularly busy week in late October 1872. He failed to avert murder convictions at the Goulburn and Bathurst Circuit Courts, but convinced Sydney's Water Police Court that the case against three men charged with assault on the high seas was compromised by the way evidence had been taken.[18]

In November he appeared in the Central Criminal Court for two men charged with manslaughter. They and the victim, John Reynolds, had been part of a group planning celebrations for the launch of a new punt on the Manning River near Taree; the idea was to 'fire off' two boxes of gunpowder to mark the event. The three decided, however, to set off one of the boxes the evening before, and Reynolds died in the explosion. Dalley had no difficulty convincing the jury that this was a sad misadventure rather than a crime.[19]

A week later he appeared for one of five youths on trial for their lives in a gang rape case. A sixth member of the group testified against the others. This young man and the victim, a young servant from Woolloomooloo, gave evidence that the youths had forced her into a boat and rowed her across the harbour before some raped her while others abetted the crime. Defending his client, allegedly one of the accomplices, Dalley urged the jury to disregard the evidence of the 'ruffian' male informant, but said he accepted that a gross outrage had been committed and believed every word of the victim's testimony. Three of the five, including Dalley's client, were found guilty and sentenced to death; the sentences were commuted to 12 years' hard labour.[20]

Dalley attended the re-opening of the Legislative Council at the beginning of November but made few further appearances before resigning his seat ten months later. He neither spoke nor voted when David Buchanan's divorce bill was considered again. The member who moved the second reading, Robert Owen, noted that the Assembly had passed it five times with large majorities. Perhaps Dalley accepted that the time for resistance had passed. It is also possible that his Council speech on the subject in 1870 (chapter 12) had been more that of an advocate for his church's position than an expression of strongly held opinions of his own; his later support for extension of the allowable grounds for divorce (chapter 21) supports this view. The Council passed the bill, with amendments, in February 1873. Dalley was not among the large contingent of barristers present when the new divorce court, presided over by Justice Hargrave of the Supreme Court, was formally opened the following July.

The early months of 1873 – the last of Eleanor's first pregnancy – seem to have passed in a fairly leisurely fashion. On 8 February Dalley joined Martin and many others at a picnic, hosted by John Robertson, for delegates to the intercolonial conference on communications and trade then in progress in Sydney. The venue was the picturesque grounds of 'Greycliffe', Vaucluse. Dalley's tasks, as well as proposing toasts to the ladies and Rev. Lang, included providing fish from the harbour for the luncheon. Commanding 'Mr John Cuthbert's magnificent new steam launch', he set out from Circular Quay 'with fishermen and fishing-nets' at an early hour to contribute to the 'plentiful supply of beautiful fish' offered to the guests.[21]

He wrote three more lengthy articles for the *Herald* in February and March – the pieces noted earlier on the murdered Bishop Patteson (chapter 11) and Anthony Trollope (chapter 12), and a review of *Wanderings in Spain* by Augustus J.C. Hare. Spain, as described by this 'delightful author', was a land that taught 'the hot and fevered visitors from the great centres of life and ambition and high intellectual competition' the sweetness of silence and repose, wrote Dalley. 'The brain-whirling rapidity of life elsewhere – the sleepless exertion – the express train speed of human action – all these give place in this country to a steady well-sustained and picturesque indolence…' Visitors should be prepared for hotels even worse than Australia's remote bush taverns and roads 'nearly all as bad as that between Wallerawang and Mudgee'. But they would find 'kindly, generous hospitality…freely poured out' for them.[22]

A sad event in February was the death at 66 of N.D. Stenhouse. After the funeral, conducted by Rev. Lang, Dalley joined Professor Badham in initiating a public appeal to help the family, who had been left in financial difficulty. Chairing the meeting called to launch the appeal, he delivered a heartfelt tribute to the mentor he had shared with Deniehy, Kendall and many others with literary aspirations and interests. Knowing Stenhouse intimately had been one of the 'great intellectual privileges' of his life, he said.

> In return for his rare scholarship – in acknowledgment of his great treasures of learning, poured out for my edification with all the munificence of his noble nature, I had no tribute to offer but my admiration and gratitude. And these sufficed… It would be an impertinent egotism for me to state this, but for my knowledge that my case and my experience were those of many of my fellow countrymen and fellow-colonists, who found in him the wisest of advisers, the fairest of critics, the most patient of hearers, and the tenderest and truest of friends. To lift the veil of his charities would be to reveal a sympathy with genius which neither the depravity of the subject could lessen nor ingratitude weaken, nor repeated trials and disappointment extinguish…[23]

Soon after the safe arrival of William Bede jnr on 23 March, Dalley headed south for Circuit Court appearances. One was the defence at Yass – still not reached by the railway but added to the Supreme Court judges' circuit in 1872 – of a man charged with murder after a fatal axe fight in the bush. The jury found him guilty of manslaughter.[24]

Back in Sydney, Dalley was elected unopposed in mid-April, no doubt with Badham's support, to the university Senate spot vacated by Stenhouse. On 6 May, with most of Sydney's prominent men, he attended the funeral of William Charles Wentworth at St Andrew's Cathedral and joined the procession escorting the remains to the vault at Vaucluse. Wentworth, who died in England in March 1872, had asked that his body be brought to Sydney. Martin delivered the eulogy at the tomb. A memorial poem by Badham appeared in that morning's *Herald*.[25]

A few days later a British sailing vessel, the *Rifleman*, entered Sydney harbour carrying the body of its captain, James Longmuir, preserved in spirits and his alleged killer, the ship's steward Wilhelm Krauss, under lock and key. The murder was the most sensational to come before the Central Criminal Court for some years. Dalley, assisted by a rising young barrister, John Henry Want, undertook Krauss's defence without fee.

With a crew of 22 and three passengers, the 700-ton *Rifleman* was off South America en route from London to Sydney when the crime occurred. In the early morning dark, according to crew members' evidence, Krauss told chief officer George Morgan, who was on watch, that Captain Longmuir wanted to see him. Krauss followed Morgan to the captain's cabin, and hit him on the head from behind with a long iron bolt. Then, as the two men grappled, Krauss produced a pistol and shot and wounded the boatswain, who had come to see what was going on. More crewmen arrived and overpowered Krauss. The body of the captain was then found; he had been struck on the head and strangled. Other evidence suggested Krauss had tried to poison all on board with adulterated liquor.

Dalley did not dispute the crew's account of events, but sought to prove Krauss was insane and therefore not guilty. When the case first came to court he won a two-week adjournment due to what he denounced as a flagrant and cruel interference with the administration of justice. The *Empire* had made fun of his invitation to doctors to visit Krauss in gaol and examine his mental state; 'Wanted, medical gentlemen well up on the subject of manias of all kinds, and especially the medical mania. Apply to Messrs Dalley and Want', its paragraph began.

Three doctors responded to Dalley's call, and gave evidence that Krauss was insane. The prosecution also called medical witnesses, one of whom agreed he was probably insane. The other, the visiting surgeon at Darlinghurst gaol, Dr Aaron, said he believed Krauss was acting. When Aaron gave evidence in Henry Kendall's trial in 1870 Dalley's cross-examination persuaded him to reverse his initial contention that the poet was sane (chapter 12), and this time he again wavered under persistent questioning. Dalley then called the governor of the gaol, who acknowledged that about 20 prisoners Aaron had reported were feigning insanity had later been confirmed as 'lunatics'.

However, Dalley's efforts, culminating in a lengthy address to the jury in which he detailed many precedents for a verdict of not guilty on the ground of insanity and begged mercy for one whose brain was 'poisoned with disease', were to no avail. Encouraged by Justice Hargrave's summing-up, the jury took just 15 minutes to agree on a guilty verdict. Krauss was hanged four weeks later.[26]

This trial may have been the occasion of the story of the crumpled peroration, told in later years. It was Dalley's custom, the Sydney *Law Chronicle* recalled in 1895, to 'prepare with great care' the concluding passage of his address to the jury in 'heavy criminal cases' (his peroration at the trial of the bushrangers Clarke in 1867 – chapter 9 – is a good example). This time,

> Dalley had written out his peroration on a sheet of foolscap, and, just as he was beginning his address to the jury, handed the document to his junior with the following injunction: 'Here, Want; when I come to the words 'In the name of Almighty God,' hand me this peroration.' The great orator proceeded with his address, and his junior sat ready with the document. After speaking for about an hour and a half, Dalley came to the cue. Mr Want, who meantime had been hanging on the music of Dalley's eloquence, oblivious of everything else around him, had unconsciously twisted the peroration into all sorts of shapes, and quite forgot the cue. Dalley went on – 'And now, gentlemen, in the name of Almighty God – (sotto voce, 'Want!') – Gentlemen, in the name of Almighty God – (sotto voce, 'Want! Want!!') – Gentlemen, in the name of Almighty God – ('Want, where the —'s the peroration?').[27]

Dalley's other cases at the mid-year Central Criminal Court sittings included a failed defence of the proprietor of the *Gulgong Guardian* in a criminal libel action brought by the local police magistrate and gold commissioner Thomas A. Browne, better known as the author Rolf Boldrewood. The paper had accused Browne, in language that Dalley acknowledged was 'not altogether commendable as a specimen of literature', of corruption. Dalley reportedly 'enlarged upon the necessity for a free and unfettered press' in an address to the jury of 'great length' and 'great eloquence'. But again Justice Hargrave set the scene for a guilty verdict, advising the jurors that freedom of the press was not to be taken as an apology for licence. The *Guardian*'s proprietor, another Thomas Browne, was sentenced to six months' gaol.[28]

The 70-year-old Chief Justice, Sir Alfred Stephen, submitted his resignation on 12 June 1873. Presumably he was being playful when he nominated 5 November, Guy Fawkes Day, as the date it would take effect. Like the leader of the 1605 plot to blow up the British parliament, one of the two obvious candidates to succeed him, Attorney-General Butler, was a Catholic, and the other, Sir James Martin, was from a Catholic family.

To general praise for the choice, Premier Parkes announced on 11 November that Martin had been appointed. A political masterstroke one might think, as Martin was the leader of the opposition in the Assembly as well as a highly respected barrister. Instead the events surrounding the appointment weakened the government, setting it on the path to defeat. They also showed Dalley had been prescient when he predicted 18 months earlier that Irish Catholics would come to regret the part they had played in lifting Parkes to power (chapter 12).

Sir James Martin.

In line with an English convention that the Attorney-General had first claim to any judicial vacancy that occurred during his term, Parkes had told Butler – who, like Martin, had won a high reputation at the Bar – that the job would be his if he wanted it. But as the date of Stephen's departure drew near, sectarian opposition to Butler's elevation grew, not least among Protestant politicians.

In a censure debate in the Assembly on 30 October the government appeared headed for defeat; then, as one member put it, 'a marvellous change' occurred. Apparently Parkes had made it known to the relevant dissidents that he had changed his mind and the Catholic Butler would not be Chief Justice.

Announcing his resignation as Attorney-General in parliament on the day Martin's appointment was made known, Butler tabled letters that had passed between him and Parkes including the one, dated 5 November, in which Parkes told him he would not receive the appointment. This was a particularly nasty composition. Parkes denied that religious considerations had influenced him, claiming instead that day by day he had become increasingly aware of well-founded objections to Butler among lawyers and 'the great majority of the community, including all classes'. His explanation was generally seen as hollow, and Butler won praise for his dignified response. *Freeman's* commented, not surprisingly, that Butler had been rejected 'simply and solely' for being Catholic. Butler declared that he felt no personal hostility to his former friend, but nothing more 'than the common courtesies of life' could ever again pass between them.[29]

Dalley, who no doubt welcomed Martin's elevation, commented obliquely on these events when nominating Robertson as a candidate for West Sydney at the December 1874 general elections. The crowd at the hustings cheered when, in an obvious comparison with Parkes, he said Robertson was not 'one of those happily rare heroic characters who would offer up upon the altar of public duty their dearest friends as a sacrifice.'[30]

Presumably either out of town or unwell, Dalley did not attend Stephen's farewell by the Bench and Bar on 25 September 1873 or Martin's formal installation as Chief Justice on 22 November. However, he was one of many prominent men who spoke in praise of Stephen at a public meeting held in December to initiate a testimonial presentation. 'For half a lifetime,' said Dalley,

> he has held our highest office, upon which, exalted as it is, he has rather conferred dignity than derived it from his place. (Cheers.) Day by day,

with inimitable patience, with surpassing industry, and with an amiability which no impertinence could disturb and no insolence diminish, he has borne himself as an enlightened, able and impartial magistrate. (Cheers.) And in a society such as ours, where from various causes we have not on all sides those restraining and refining influences which are the privilege of old communities, the example of such a life is of incalculable value.[31]

The following May, Dalley wrote to the *Herald* urging that Stephen be granted a retiring allowance matching his former annual salary, £2,600, rather than the £1,400 provided. He praised Stephen's services to the law and community, and calculated that by remaining on the Bench for 34 years he had saved the colony up to £35,000. That was the amount that would have been due in benefits if both he and his successor had retired, as they were entitled to do, after just 15 years' service. Dalley wrote that he was speaking out after waiting, 'somewhat impatiently I admit', for testimonies from others 'who enjoyed more of his intimacy, and had larger opportunities of observing his daily life in the Courts'. The government was persuaded; Parkes's Minister for Justice, George Wigram Allen, used Dalley's arguments when he moved in the Assembly in November that Stephen be awarded a £7,000 gratuity. However, the plan was narrowly voted down.[32]

Dalley submitted his letter to the *Herald* after Circuit Court visits to Mudgee and Maitland in April 1874. By the time he returned to Sydney a new issue – one on which he and Stephen held opposed views – was dominating political discussion. This was the decision by the Governor, Sir Hercules Robinson, to allow the bushranger Frank Gardiner – sentenced by Stephen to 32 years' gaol in 1864 (chapter 7) – to go free provided he left Australia.

More than 400 people signed a petition got up by two sisters of Gardiner in late 1871 seeking his release. Grounds advanced for clemency included his honest work as a store- and innkeeper between his escape to Queensland after the Eugowra gold robbery in 1862 and arrest two years later, good behaviour in prison and declining health.

Five attachments gave the petition added weight. In the first, Dalley and a solicitor friend, Richard Driver, recommended it to the Governor's 'merciful consideration, the more especially from the desire to reform evidenced by the prisoner before capture, and his conduct since his incarceration'. They trusted His Excellency 'may be pleased, under all the circumstances of the case, to deem the period of the sentence already expired sufficient for the ends of justice.' In the second, William Forster and another member of parliament, Richard Hill, noted Gardiner's good conduct during an attempted mass breakout from Darlinghurst Gaol as a factor that should operate in his favour. The other attachments were by a physician who considered Gardiner had 'completely recovered from his evil ways', another MP who was 'fully convinced' he regretted his wrongs, and a magistrate who had had first-hand experience of his 'civil and obliging' conduct in Queensland.

Soon after taking office in May 1872, Premier Parkes referred the petition and attachments to the Sheriff, Harold Maclean, who advised that, in consider-ing reduced sentences, it should be noted that 10 years with exile was equivalent to 15 years followed by unconditional release. The documents then went to the newly arrived Governor Robinson, who, in Parkes's view, had sole responsibility for decisions on pardons for prisoners.[33] Robinson asked for a report from Chief Justice Stephen, who wrote that he 'dare not incur the responsibility of advising any mitigation in this case', remembering the nature of Gardiner's 'past character and his crimes'.

In early December 1872 Robinson informed Parkes of his decision that, if Gardiner's conduct remained good, he should be pardoned after 10 years' imprisonment (in mid-1874) on condition that he leave the country. Gardiner's sisters were officially informed of the decision a few days later. Not satisfied, one of them, Archina Griffiths, submitted another petition in early 1874 seeking unconditional release for her brother. Again Dalley – this time one of nine signatories to attachments – added his support to the plea. Robinson rejected it.[34]

The decision to commute Gardiner's sentence does not seem to have become public knowledge until March 1874.[35] Lively debates ensued in parliament, culminating in a tied vote on a motion by the member for Bathurst, Edward Combes, disapproving of the release of Gardiner and other prisoners also about to be freed (including Bow and Fordyce, accomplices of Gardiner at Eugowra). The Speaker's casting vote saved the government from defeat. Robinson then persuaded a reluctant Parkes that he should be given the opportunity to explain his decision publicly, which he did in a long minute tabled in the Assembly on 25 June, the last sitting day of the session.[36]

Escorted by two policemen, Gardiner left Sydney for Newcastle by steamer on 20 July on the first stage of his journey to exile in California.[37] The controversy, however, had not ended; when Parliament resumed in November Combes seized on the Governor's minute to resume his attack. He moved a resolution condemning the document and regretting that Robinson had been advised to communicate his thoughts to the Assembly. Combes particularly objected to the statement that an 'unreasonable and unjust clamour' had been raised against Gardiner's release. It was highly undesirable that the records of the House should be converted into a 'means of conveying censure or reproof to our constituents', his resolution contended. And if the reproof was aimed at the debate in the Assembly, 'then it is in spirit and effect a breach of the constitutional privileges of Parliament'.[38]

Again the government was saved from defeat by the casting vote of the Speaker. But with general elections nearly due anyway – the parliamentary term had been changed from five years to three – Parkes took the vote as a censure and asked the Governor for a dissolution. This was granted, and the contest began in December.

14
Robertson's Attorney-General

Poetry is not a form of expression that Dalley was noted for, but he turned his hand to the craft at the end of 1874. Boys of the Catholic secondary school, Lyndhurst College, read a prologue by Dalley and epilogue by Badham as part of their performance of *Hidden Gem*, a play by Cardinal Wiseman, the first Archbishop of Westminster, at the school's break-up ceremony. This tells the story of Alexius, the 'heaven-directed' only son of a wealthy Roman senator, who left his father's house to lead the life of a poor pilgrim and years later returned as a stranger and beggar. After his early death, a 'voice heard though all the churches in the city proclaimed him a saint'.

Dalley's prologue, read 'in a masterly style' by Master Thomas Fitzpatrick of Bathurst, comprised 30 rhyming couplets, including

> Like some peculiar star, one boyish face
> Sweetly salutes us through the dizzy space;
> The senatorial child, content to be
> An outcast for the babe of Galilee…
> What the ambition of this noble boy?
> And how did he his few fleet years employ?
> By charity, by thought, by studious pain
> He purged his boyish heart from passion's bane,
> To love the humble, reverence the pure,
> Cherish the meek, and seek in paths obscure
> The sore and stricken whom the proud despise;
> To kiss the tears from suffering's sad eyes.
> To stand beneath the world's contempt and ban,
> Courteous to churls, to roaring beasts a man.[1]

Dalley seems to have missed the performance, perhaps because he was busy electioneering. The day before, he nominated his friend John

Robertson, standing again for West Sydney, in his inimitable style. He knew, reported the *Herald*,

> that for the extremely fastidious, Mr Robertson's language was sometimes too forcible – for the exceptionally bitter his conduct was occasionally marked too much by generosity. Mr Robertson sometimes said more than he meant, and the sight of a discomfited opponent disarmed his indignation… They might easily find a more pretentious man – with infinitely nobler sentiments and a much more exalted standard; but they would have some difficulty in finding a more sterling friend or a more generous enemy…[2]

Robertson topped the poll; a few days earlier Parkes had received similarly strong support at the East Sydney election. Which of them would have the numbers to govern was not clear when Sir Hercules Robinson opened parliament at the end of January 1875. A motion by Robertson to incorporate the gist of Edward Combes's resolution criticising Robinson's minute on the Gardiner affair (chapter 13) in the address-in-reply to the Governor's speech settled the issue. The Assembly carried it by 33 votes to 28, and Parkes and his ministers resigned.

Deeply offended, the Governor sent a message of complaint to the Assembly and commissioned Sir William Manning, a member of the Legislative Council, to form a government. 'I determined upon marking my sense of the impropriety of the course taken by the House, by selecting a middleman to form a ministry,' he told the Earl of Carnarvon, Secretary of State for the Colonies. His ploy failed; after fruitless attempts to recruit a ministerial team, Manning advised Robinson to send for Robertson, and he reluctantly did so. Robinson's despatch to London noted as an 'illustration…of the hollowness and insincerity of the Gardiner commotion' that Dalley and Forster, who had petitioned for the bushranger's early release, were among the new ministers. Dalley had accepted Robertson's offer of the Attorney-Generalship after Edward Butler declined it and Forster was the new Treasurer.

The Governor offered some sceptical but pertinent comments on the colonial political scene. It must be borne in mind, he wrote, that

The Robertson ministry, 1875: Premier Robertson at top; John Docker centre; clockwise from top William Forster, John Burns, Thomas Garrett, John Lucas, Dalley, and John Lackey.

parties here are not divided, as they are at home, by any differences of opinion as regards matters of principle or policy... When therefore a ministry has been for some time in office, and has necessarily disappointed or offended a certain number of its original supporters, it becomes weak, and on the first favourable opportunity the seceders can, without sacrificing any political opinion, walk across the House and put out the Government. A new ministry is then formed, differing only from the last in its 'personnel', and the effect upon the business of the country is simply that a few weeks' delay is caused by the re-election of Ministers, the disadvantage of which is sometimes supposed to be counterbalanced by the vigour of the new hands.[3]

Dalley's parliamentary career to date suggested to some that little vigour could be expected from him in his new role. Instead, he threw himself into the Attorney-General's job, becoming a key member of Robertson's cabinet. *Freeman's* observed at the beginning of 1876 that he had 'surprised everybody by his capacity for business'.[4]

Dalley took his new seat in the Legislative Council – he had resigned from it 17 months earlier – on 9 February. A week later he was busy in the Central Criminal Court filling the unfamiliar role of prosecutor (he prosecuted at each of the court's quarterly sittings while he was Attorney-General). Preparing legal opinions was an important part of the job, and his work was widely applauded. A large volume published in 1877 contains the more than three hundred opinions he wrote during the government's two-year life.[5]

One of the first concerned a serious problem that had arisen under Robertson's land laws of 1861; by taking up blocks in the names of their children, free selectors could acquire much larger portions of grazing runs than the legislators had intended. The wealthy politician Sir John O'Shanassy, three times Premier of Victoria, was one squatter who felt the impact. In 1873 William Joachim, on behalf of himself and eight children, selected 2,880 acres of the 44,500 acres leased by O'Shanassy in the Riverina.[6] O'Shanassy objected strenuously. The colonial courts had consistently upheld the right of minors to select, but he won approval to take his case for ejecting the young Joachims to the Privy Council.

This potentially posed a very expensive difficulty for the government. If the Privy Council found selection by minors illegal, large demands for compensation would follow. Robertson and his Lands Minister, Thomas Garrett, raised the possibility of the government intervening in the case in support of the Joachims. Dalley squashed this idea, advising 'unhesitatingly' that it 'ought not to identify itself with either party to this appeal'. Instead, he favoured seeking leave for counsel for the government to appear to present 'the whole case in as exhaustive a manner as possible'. Failing that, it might, even-handedly, furnish both sides with all the information it could.[7]

The Privy Council rejected the government's application to appear, and in March 1876 found in favour of the Joachims.[8] By then the government had acted to both pre-empt an adverse decision and solve the initial problem. Legislation passed in August 1875 ratified existing selections by minors and set sixteen years as the minimum age for those selecting land in future.

Another of Dalley's early legal opinions formed part of the sorry tale of the sacking of Johann Krefft, curator of Sydney's Australian Museum for the previous 10 years and a major contributor to knowledge of Australia's fauna.[9] The museum's trustees dismissed Krefft in 1874 after he was accused of drunkenness and other failings. He disputed their power to take this action and barricaded himself inside the building. Dalley's opinion, of March 1875, confirmed the trustees' power of dismissal.[10] However, Justice Cheeke of the Supreme Court took the opposite view and awarded Krefft damages after he was forcibly ejected from the museum. The Executive Council confirmed his dismissal in July 1876, but legal battles continued.

In April 1875 Dalley prepared a bill to increase the number of Supreme Court judges from four to five and raise their salaries. In an explanatory letter, he noted that the colony's population had increased by more than 40 per cent since 1865 and the number of practising barristers had nearly doubled, from 38 to 63. The judges were now required to hold Circuit Court hearings twice a year in 12 regional centres. The workload had increased greatly but the number of judges had stayed the same, and they were paid much less than successful barristers earned.

Dalley attached correspondence with Sir Alfred Stephen and Sir William Manning, whom he had invited to preside at two towns each during the coming Circuit Court round to ease the strain on the three available judges (the fourth, Justice Cheeke, was on extended sick leave). Both were glad to help. 'I think it my duty, while sufficient health and strength remain, to place my services at the disposal of the Government, on any emergency' wrote the 72-year-old Sir Alfred. Sir William told Dalley in his acceptance letter that there was nobody 'within reach of the office you hold, in whose sincere and single desire to use its privileges and powers for the public good greater confidence could be felt'.[11]

The hardships of the Supreme Court judges attracted little sympathy in the Assembly. When the bill came to a vote in June a mere 27 members were present and only 10 gave their support.[12] Recalling the defeat in 1883 in a speech promoting another bill (this time successful) to raise judges' salaries, Dalley described it as 'a great misfortune' and 'a great injustice'.[13] By then, Cheeke had died, Hargrave had retired in poor health and Sir James Martin's health was breaking down. Stephen, 10 years retired, was still well and active.

On 18 May the barque *Chevert*, commanded by William Macleay, notable as a patron of science as well as for confronting Parkes during the Fenian scare of 1868, left Sydney for New Guinea on a private voyage of scientific exploration. Dalley and Anthony Trollope, on a return visit to the colony, were among more than 200 guests at a farewell luncheon earlier in the day on a steamer anchored in Vaucluse Bay. Responding to the toast to the ladies, the 43-year-old Dalley observed to 'great laughter and cheers' that while he had reached the period of life 'when one becomes conscious that youth is fled' he aspired to be of the 'privileged company' who defied 'age and ridicule, wrinkles and sneers' and preserved their 'gaiety of heart'.[14]

The *Chevert*'s departure coincided with renewed calls – similar proposals had been made in the 1860s – for Britain to annex eastern New Guinea (the Dutch already claimed the west). The government was caught up in the enthusiasm, Robertson arguing in a minute to the Governor that Britain should also take possession of the arc of islands from New Ireland to the New Hebrides (Vanuatu). As well as protecting the Torres Strait shipping route, this would allow a 'great evil', the unlawful traffic in islander labour, to be extinguished, he wrote.[15] Robinson was unimpressed, reporting sceptically to Lord Carnarvon on both the annexation agitation and Macleay's mission.[16]

Macleay had spoken in favour of annexation at his farewell luncheon, but returned in September with a dim view of prospects for colonising New Guinea.[17] Feeling vindicated, Robinson reported to Lord Carnarvon that the expedition had achieved no 'noteworthy result', fully bearing out his previously expressed opinion 'as to the unsuitability of New Guinea as a field for European colonization'.[18] Colonial interest in annexation subsided until the early 1880s, when Dalley was prominent among those seeking to cool the clamour (chapter 20).

Trollope left for home at the end of August after a farewell picnic attended by Robertson, Martin, Dalley and another 20 or so leading colonists near the site of today's Warragamba Dam. A special early morning train took the party to the Nepean River, where they boarded a steam launch that had been sent from Sydney with rowing boats and men to crew them. After breakfasting about three miles upstream, they proceeded to the confluence of the Nepean and Warragamba, where they transferred to the boats. Next stop was the site selected for lunch, where the servants and hampers were landed. Then they 'ascended the Warragamba as far as the boats could go' and admired 'the magnificent scenery of the upper portion of the river' before heading back. After a long lunch and speeches – 'I feel that I am in the midst of old and dear friends,' Trollope remarked – they reboarded the boats, arrived at the launch as the sun set and travelled home in the dark.[19]

Parliament had risen in early August after an acrimonious six-months session whose principal achievement was passing Garrett's legislation ending free selection by minors and dealing with other problems in the operation of the land laws. Always on the lookout for opportunities to score points against the government, Parkes attacked Treasurer Forster in June over his decision, supported by a legal opinion from Dalley, to move some government funds from the Bank of New South Wales to other banks. The next target was Garrett, a protégé of Robertson with a colourful past as a newspaper owner, mining speculator and Orangeman.[20] Parkes seized on a claim, which Garrett strenuously denied, that he had accepted payment for finding a man a government job.

A luncheon in honour of the ministry at Clontarf in mid-August was notable for Robertson's declaration of support for votes for women and Dalley's emotional defence of Garrett (and, by implication, criticism of Parkes).[21] Dalley returned to the subject a week later at a dinner given to Garrett by constituents at Picton, south of Sydney. He was glad to see that most members of the Assembly – an institution he now believed he had entered far too young – had treated the allegations against the Lands Minister with 'noble scorn and manly detestation'. It was vital, he believed, to guard public men from 'slander and rash censure', not merely out of a sense of justice.

> Let it once be understood that when a man accepts the responsibilities and undertakes the laborious duties of a Minister of the Crown, he is straightway to be made the victim of every foul slander which filthy fingers can collect, and forthwith the inspiring temptations, the ennobling fascinations of high public service, which at the same time exalt the office and purify the holder of it, disappear. (Loud cheers.) For what young man, jealous of honour, would risk the peace of mind, and that personal dignity which is an attribute of genius wherever it is found, by entering into an arena where patriotism is rewarded by slander, and where the most triumphant in the emulations of public life is the most audacious and the most unscrupulous?[22]

Towards the end of the parliamentary break the new cable link with London brought news of the much-regretted death, on 19 October, of Charles Cowper (since 1871, Sir Charles). Forster succeeded him as Agent-General, and was replaced as Treasurer first by Robertson and then, from February 1876, by the future Premier Alexander Stuart. Dalley was in Parkes's sights when members re-assembled in November. All sound principle had been breached with the appointment the previous March of Sir Alfred Stephen and Sir William Manning as temporary judges, he proclaimed. They were members of the Legislative Council and therefore 'political judges'. Robertson treated the proposition with the scorn it deserved and Parkes, presumably realising that he would get little support, did not propose a censure motion on the issue.[23]

Keeping the Circuit Courts going had become a recurring problem for the overstretched Supreme Court, and for Dalley. Three barristers accepted temporary appointments to preside in seven towns in April 1876. Only two of the judges, Martin and Faucett, were then up to the task; Hargrave was ill and Cheeke had died in March.[24] Dalley declined the opportunity to succeed Cheeke, recommending appointment of the well-credentialed Manning. The 63-year-old, a former acting Supreme Court judge (in 1848–49) and Attorney-General, was sworn in on 4 May. Dalley chaired a Bar dinner for him a week later.[25] In his invitation to the new judge, sent uncomfortably close to the occasion, he apologised that 'I sometimes forget my pleasures as well as my duties' being 'so overwhelmed with work'. He hoped 'our dear friends the Peers' (the members of the Legislative Council) would let him get away at 6.30 on the evening.[26]

Frequently on his feet in the Council, Dalley delivered one of his more passionate speeches in December 1875 in favour of a bill introduced by the barrister, later Chief Justice, Frederick Darley abolishing verdicts of *felo de se* – essentially wilful murder of oneself – at suicide inquests. Up to 1823 'the law subjected the suicide to the ignominy of being buried in a highway with a stake driven through the body', he reminded members. Then private interment between the hours of 9 p.m. and midnight was substituted. The colony had already left the British law behind, allowing Christian burial and not requiring forfeiture of the suicide's property. But the stigma of a *felo de se* verdict remained and was a 'scandal to our civilisation' and out of harmony 'with the growing humanity of the age'.[27]

Primary education was the big political issue in early 1876. Through legislation introduced in February, Robertson sought to replace the five-man council and secretariat that oversaw government-funded schools with a minister for education and government department. Other provisions aimed to make it easier to establish new public schools. Denominational schooling, on the other hand, was to be discouraged; funding would continue for existing schools but there would be no money for new ones.

The Catholic Church was the chief advocate of denominational schools. But they also had prominent Anglican supporters, including the Treasurer, Alexander Stuart, who joined the government in February only on condition that he could oppose the proposed funding freeze.[28] Professor Badham, ordained an Anglican priest in 1848, expressed his support for the schools in a long and entertaining letter to Dalley on primary education, subsequently published as a pamphlet. His main point was the importance of teaching pupils to think rather than stacking their minds with 'facts'.[29]

Although Dalley seems to have been happy with the legislation, a claim by William Pigott, a solicitor, that he 'was in the hands of the priesthood' drew loud cheers at a NSW Public School League rally in March (the league advocated free, secular, compulsory schooling).[30] Dalley sent an amusing response to the *Herald*. 'Gentlemen who propose to themselves the sublime duty of devoting their oratory and dedicating their lives to the holy labour of public education should not scandalize the little ones by telling stories,' he began. The Catholic 'priesthood' had opposed his election to the Assembly. Now they were even 'louder (and I will pay them the small compliment of saying incomparably more eloquent) than Mr Pigott in their condemnation' of the schools bill.[31]

Opposed by supporters of denominational schools on the one hand and advocates of a purely secular system on the other, the bill came close to defeat at its second reading in mid-March. It was killed off a week later in committee.

Little of consequence was achieved during the remaining five months of the parliamentary sitting. In the Council, Dalley agreed with Sir Alfred Stephen that consolidation and amendment of the criminal law were needed urgently;[32] he attempted the task in the government's dying days at the end of 1876 (chapter 15) but legislation did not pass for another seven years. He urged members 'not to succumb to the wearying, unwavering, torturing pertinacity of egotistical and self-sufficient persons' seeking piecemeal changes to electorates rather than a comprehensive electoral redistribution.[33] He rejected criticism of the Executive Council's decision not to commute a death sentence for murder: 'if capital punishment were to be retained in this country there never was a case which so clearly called for its exercise.'[34] And he praised the colony's magistrates as 'as good, as honest, and as trustworthy a body of men as existed in any community' in a speech supporting legislation to give them power to deal with contempt in their courts.[35]

Parliament was prorogued on 22 August. Four weeks later, Dalley, Robertson, Works Minister John Lackey and other dignitaries set off at midnight on the government steamer *Ajax* on the short journey to Kiama, where a new man-made harbour, Robertson Basin, was to be declared open. They arrived off the town at 6 a.m., and as the official welcome was set for 9 occupied three hours with 'a little schnapper fishing' and breakfast. Then, accompanied by another steamer, the *Ajax* 'steamed beautifully' into the basin to a greeting of 'lusty' cheers.

Constructed from local bluestone and concrete, Robertson Basin provided safe anchorage for coastal traders; it now protects the town's fishing and recreational craft. At the opening ceremony, Lackey was cheered when he explained that it was being named after the Premier, whose first government had accepted tenders for the work in 1860, 'at the request of the inhabitants of this district'. At the banquet in the evening, Robertson thanked the locals for their warm welcome, noted that ministers 'were not used to flattery' and referred to his 'many struggles' to have the basin built. Then he handed the speechmaking task to his 'eloquent friend' Dalley, who had Kiama's former member, Parkes, on his mind.

He made fun of a recent particularly pompous speech by Parkes in which he claimed to be in correspondence with 'leading men of Europe' – a task he undertook as a duty that would assist him in the performance of his public functions and benefit the country. Nobody in the current government could match this, said Dalley; none was 'in receipt of any kind of letter from any foreign nobleman, distinguished statesman or exalted personage of any kind in the mother country'. But there was no great difficulty in opening up such a correspondence. 'You have only to write a letter, and by the obligation of their nobility, although they may regard you (as they probably will) as an unmitigated bore, they will answer your letter... With a sheet of letter-paper, an envelope, a threepenny stamp, and a little assurance, you can secure the autograph and pretend to the friendship of the chief of one of the great governing classes of the empire. (Laughter.)'

Naturally he also had something to say about the Kiama ghost. This was his first visit to the town, despite the fact that

> at the smallest sacrifice of time and money I might at any time in a few hours have passed out of the real world of flesh and blood and human passions into this land of shades and sepulchres. (Laughter and cheers.) Gentlemen, now that I have seen this beautiful country I am more than ever convinced that it is haunted ground – that it is a place of enchantments. (Cheers.) But it is haunted by the spirit of beauty, and its enchantments are those of the most perfect loveliness of nature. (Cheers.) Not to be associated with that dismal and dilapidated old Fenian spirit – (laughter) – who was once conjured up in your midst, and who was sent upon a melancholy political mission to be forever pursued with inextinguishable laughter – (laughter and cheers) – but to be the home of all sweet and generous spirits, who brighten and ennoble and make joyous our human life...

Living politicians, even 'fair, honest, liberal' ones, were 'scarcely in harmony with this tranquil beauty', he added. Ghostly politicians, 'coming out of their graves to sow dissentions, inspire suspicions, and make us all hate one another', should be banished eternally 'from this lovely place'.[36]

15
Three more governments

At a function in Wollongong the night after the Kiama banquet, Robertson apologised for the absence of 'his brilliant friend' Dalley, who had been called home urgently because of illness in the family.[1] Presumably the summons followed a worsening in the condition of his father-in-law William Long, who had been suffering for months from a swollen blood vessel in one of his legs. He died at the age of 79 on 18 October 1876. Another reason for Dalley to be at home with his wife was the impending birth of their third child, John Bede, who arrived safely on 5 October.

Robertson and Dalley, this time with Lands Minister Garrett, steamed south again on 12 November and were entertained lavishly at a 'public breakfast' at Tathra and a banquet at Bega. In their speeches they pointed to the prosperity of the area as a demonstration of the success of free selection. 'I know of no purer source of happiness than that which Mr Robertson has enjoyed since yesterday in the contemplation of the numbers of happy homes...which have been planted in your midst by his statesmanship,' said Dalley at Bega. 'These are among the great pleasures of a patriotic life, the taste of which amply compensates for obloquy, misrepresentation, and unsparing abuse.'[2]

Dalley also used his Bega speech to have the last word in a dispute he had ignited with Michael Fitzpatrick, a fellow Catholic who retired as head of the lands department in 1869 and was now a member of the Assembly. In his speech at Kiama in September, Dalley used colourful language to criticise Fitzpatrick over a failed no-confidence vote he initiated. The thought that its success might have resulted in this 'subordinate and pensioned member of the old system' [the 59-year-old Fitzpatrick joined the civil service before responsible government] becoming Premier was 'altogether too grotesque and intolerable', he said.

Fitzpatrick replied at a meeting of his constituents in Yass, taking strongest exception to Dalley calling him 'subordinate'. He described his humble origins, gave a detailed account of his career – which, he said, compared favourably with that of 'the rotund person of William Bede Dalley' – and claimed Dalley had asserted 'the hideous principle' that only a man 'born with a silver spoon in his mouth' could serve the colony creditably.[3]

Dalley responded that by 'subordinate' he had meant only politically insignificant; otherwise there was no backtracking. 'I do not think that there is a man, woman or child in this community who could believe me, of all men, capable of sneering at the humbleness, the obscurity, or the poverty of any human being,' he said. Cherishing and preserving the friendship of 'many men of humbler station than Mr Fitzpatrick ever occupied' had been one of the greatest pleasures of his life. But there were some men

> on such unspeakably good terms with themselves that they remind one of the man in 'Balzac,' who, whenever he heard his name pronounced, always took his hat off for that august appellation. (Roars of laughter.) This morbid sensibility to criticism (which very often co-exists with a great capacity for offensiveness) led this gentleman to indulge in language of which I trust he will repent at his leisure.

Parliament met again on 12 December, and Dalley immediately obtained leave to introduce a very large bill to consolidate and amend the criminal law. This already had a history, being based on a draft drawn up by a law reform commission appointed in 1870.[4] The commission's chairman, Sir Alfred Stephen, was its main proponent and author. He told his fellow Legislative Councillors that, as a judge, he had kept a book by his side for 30 years in which he noted difficulties in administering the existing law.[5] Edward Butler, in 1872–73, was the first Attorney-General to seek to have the bill enacted. George Innes, his replacement for the remaining year of the Parkes government, made another abortive attempt. According to the judge and legal historian Greg Woods, the modern criminal law of New South Wales is substantially based on the legislation eventually passed.[6]

In his first reading speech on 22 December, Dalley said the bill repealed and re-enacted in a condensed form more than 50 colonial statutes, and embodied provisions of British Acts going back as far as the time of King Edward VI (1547–53). A major aim was to make it much easier for judges to ascertain what sentences they could legally impose. Currently they faced great difficulty in 'even discovering the law as to punishments in the existing confusion caused by the number and variety of enactments having reference to the most ordinary offences.'

Dalley paid tribute to Stephen's contribution. Through his experience, learning, industry and unselfishness, order had been created out of great disorder. The bill would make the criminal law simpler and more intelligible, and in harmony with 'the legislation of the Empire and the increasing humanity and wisdom of the age'.[7] Being able to put it forward was 'one of the fortunate accidents of my position', he said in his second reading speech the following month.

> Save that I have spared no labour to make it intelligible, I can claim no share in its construction… I honesty believe that this bill will, if it becomes the law of the land, tend to the more effectual prevention and punishment of crime – will increase the reverence of the people for the administration of public justice – will protect in the fullest sense the best interests of society – and will uphold the empire of order based upon law – 'Whose sceptre angels kiss and furies dread.'[8]

Examination of the bill's detail in committee in the Council began in February 1877 and continued, on and off, for nearly five months. Most clauses passed unaltered, but amendments were agreed to provisions relating to, among other things, bigamy, setting fire to crops, and obstruction of railways. A move to abolish the death sentence for rape was easily defeated in May. Dalley had changed his mind on the matter; he introduced an abolition bill in the Assembly in 1857 (chapter 3), but now thought 'the atrocity of the outrage and the circumstances of the country perfectly justified the retention of the highest penalty known to the law'.[9] (This was a question that he continued to think about; he had another change of mind in 1879 – chapter 16.)

The Council ended its deliberations on 13 June and sent the bill to the Assembly. By then, unfortunately for the prospects of criminal law reform, Robertson's government had fallen and its successor, led by Parkes, was heading for defeat. Three more governments came and went, and intermittent consideration of the bill continued, before Dalley resumed the Attorney-Generalship in 1883 and brought the saga to a successful conclusion (chapter 19).

The Robertson ministry's slide to defeat began in January 1877 when Lands Minister Garrett came under renewed attack. His resignation, following an admission that a drinking spree in Melbourne had left him unaware of where he was for four or five days, saved the government from defeat in a confidence vote in early February. But later in the month a supply bill was voted down and the government suffered heavy defeats on a proposed electoral redistribution and a motion condemning its failure to table all papers relating to the release from gaol the previous year of a bushranger, Larry Cummins. One of the missing papers was a minute by Dalley; its omission, claimed Parkes, awakened 'the most serious and damaging suspicions'.[10]

The mover of this motion, Stephen Brown, a solicitor, claimed that after Governor Robinson approved Cummins's release the Minister for Justice, Joseph Docker, sought an opinion from Dalley on the decision. In a detailed personal explanation in the Council, Dalley denied that any such 'unpardonable interference with the constitutional prerogative of the head of the Executive' had been proposed. He had not given, or been asked to give, an opinion on the exercise of the prerogative of mercy in the Cummins case, or any other.

Instead, his opinion had been requested on a tricky legal question. Could prisoners whose death sentences were commuted to terms of 'hard labour on the roads or other public works', or those originally sentenced to that form of punishment, instead be held, and required to labour, within the walls of a gaol? The Governor had offered the view that this was illegal. If so, advised Dalley, this would be fatal to the reputations of 'so many of our most eminent lawyers, Judges and Governors' who, over decades, had endorsed such a variation. But, 'after mature consideration', he was convinced that what had been done was perfectly legal.[11]

Smallpox made a brief but alarming appearance in Sydney at the beginning of 1877. In the Council, Dalley observed that 'some sacrifice of the ordinary personal liberty' was necessary 'for the good of society generally' in such situations, and undertook to review the relevant laws.[12]

He took a conservative view in a debate initiated by Thomas Holt, a wealthy philanthropist who had been Treasurer in the first 'responsible' government in 1856, on treatment of the accused in criminal trials. Holt argued that they should be placed in the dock only when concern for security demanded it, and have the option of sitting or standing. Dalley thought placing prisoners in the dock was necessary to prevent escapes. And judges always allowed them to sit if standing would cause suffering; in his 'very long experience in the criminal courts' he had never seen 'any indifference to suffering or want of sensibility on the part of judges or others engaged in the administration of justice'.[13]

A week later, he joined Holt in supporting a 'trades union protection bill' designed to give unions legal standing to take action against theft by their employees. Dalley said he had 'very strong opinions as to the rights of labourers to control the terms on which they parted with their labour, just as employers would bind themselves to only give certain terms for that labour'.[14]

The government fell on 6 March when a resolution moved by Parkes condemning it for remaining in office after its recent defeats in the Assembly was carried by 31 votes to 28. The Governor granted Robertson's request for a dissolution, but with a proviso – he might reconsider his decision if parliament failed to vote supply for the election period. His minute, read in the Assembly, asserted that there was no doubt supply would be granted in similar circumstances in England.

Much debate ensued in parliament and the press as to whether this amounted to a 'conditional dissolution'. Dalley made a long speech in the

Council arguing that there could be no such thing, and refusal of supply would constitute a 'grave crisis' of a kind not experienced in England since 1784. But it seems he was not persuaded by his own rhetoric; his speech ended with a prediction that ministers' seats in the Council would soon be vacated.[15] Supply was not forthcoming, the Governor reconsidered, and Parkes became Premier on 22 March.

Six days earlier, Archbishop Polding had died at the age of 82. Presumably because he expected the end was near, Dalley found time at the start of the month to write an article for *Sydney Punch* in praise of his spiritual mentor. 'To have dwelt for forty-two years in the midst of a society made up of infinitely diversified faiths and religious opinions, as the head of a Church which claims 'through earth and heaven to bind and to unbind,' and to have lived through controversies and jealousies and sectarian bitternesses without provoking an angry thought or an ungenerous suspicion, is a wondrous achievement,' it began.[16]

A stream of prominent colonists – Catholic and Protestant, clerical and lay – visited Polding as he drifted in and out of consciousness during his final week. The fiery Presbyterian Rev. Lang came after the archbishop mentioned to Premier Robertson that he would like to see him. 'No one but God and those two saints knows what passed between them, but when he came out there were tears on the dear old Doctor's face,' Robertson recalled later.[17] Polding was fully conscious when Dalley visited five days before he died; 'the interview between him and Mr Dalley, who has always reverenced him with a filial affection, was a most pathetic one,' reported *Freeman's*. Dalley was subsequently 'in daily attendance at his Grace's bedside'.[18]

Crowds many rows deep lined Sydney's streets for the funeral procession on 19 March. Fifteen thousand representatives of Catholic societies and schools marched ahead of the hearse, and 276 carriages followed. Dalley rode in the third carriage with Robertson, Treasurer Stuart and the Crown Solicitor.[19] He wrote another short piece for the next *Punch*:

> The lips that were never opened but in prayer for peace and goodwill are closed – the hands that were only raised for benedictions are for ever still…

Some one has said that a poet's heart is large enough to hold two nations. Of this good old Archbishop it would not be an extravagance to say that his heart was large enough to hold humanity itself...[20]

With Parkes due to face the electors again after taking office, a public meeting on 25 March decided – on the recommendation of William Hezlett, a businessman who had been a Protestant Political Association activist – to ask Dalley to stand against him.[21] Dalley declined with thanks, telling a deputation he was glad of the 'period of repose' that the change of government allowed. He added that his 'political hostility' to Parkes was 'not today any more or less intense than it has been since I voluntarily withdrew myself from all public action with him, and did my best to weaken his influence and discredit his authority in public affairs'. But he had 'no special or individual interest' in permitting himself to be made the instrument of Parkes's 'chastisement', and did not seek political office.

Every one in the country knows that I sought to evade the acceptance of [the Attorney-General's] office with as much earnestness and industry as are usually exhibited in attaining it: and although I laboriously, and I may be permitted to say faithfully, discharged its duties for more than two years, I left it with a feeling of gladness that my loyalty to my friend, Mr Robertson, and my colleagues required no further proofs than I had already given them.[22]

The friends Dalley and Robertson depicted by the Illustrated Sydney News as 'champion complimentary sentimental duettists' in a Georgian Minstrel show.

Dalley remained active in the Legislative Council. He opposed a move in May to allow the University of Sydney to follow the practice of Oxford and Cambridge and award Master of Arts degrees to BA graduates without an exam. It would be a misfortune if 'we educated the public to look with indifference upon the higher degrees of our university, or diminished the ardour of the students in the pursuit of knowledge', he said. The Council followed the Assembly in backing the measure, but then the Assembly changed its mind and the bill lapsed.[23]

The following month he spoke at length in defence of William Forster, the colony's Agent-General in London since 1876, who had been sent a letter of admonishment by Premier Parkes. Forster had implied in a letter to a magazine that Parkes's free-trade credentials were less pure than often claimed. And he had given a speech throwing cold water on prospects for federation and criticising a speech by Governor Robinson that took a more positive view.

Parkes's relations with Forster were probably as cool as those with Dalley. So, however justified his complaints may have been, the rebuke had a personal edge. He accused Forster of, among other things, 'indulging' in 'political utterances' and using unbecoming and disrespectful language in his comments on the Governor's speech. Robertson moved a resolution in the Assembly regretting the letter's 'tone and spirit', which was defeated by just two votes. In the Council, a motion declaring the letter 'wholly uncalled for' and requesting its withdrawal was carried by 13 votes to five.[24]

Dalley contended that, if the office of Agent-General was to have any value, its occupant must have full liberty to discuss colonial policy and imperial policies affecting the colony. On the federation issue, Forster had a duty to correct the erroneous view in some English circles that public opinion was in favour. 'Is there any evidence that from one end of the colony to the other a fractional part of the community have the slightest curiosity to hear the subject discussed?' he asked. Defending Forster as the right man for the job, he put more rhetorical questions:

> Is it desirable that this distinguished office should be regarded as one that ought only to be occupied by a man of high character, of large and

varied public experience, of the fine sensitiveness to unfair criticism which characterises, or which ought to characterise, a gentleman? Is it to the manifest advantage of the public that the colony should be represented in the capital of the empire by a high-spirited man, who would regard such interference with his liberty of speech and action as this as an unspeakable impertinence and an insupportable piece of official insolence? Is the office to be one of the prizes which a free Government can confer upon its leading citizens; one of the few distinctions in our gift by which we reward service to the State, recognise culture, and secure the representation of our intelligence and refinement in the place where all of us have the noble ambition to be seen in the best light? If this is to be so, then it becomes a duty on our part to stamp such a communication as this with our unqualified condemnation.[25]

The Parkes government resigned in August and Robertson returned as Premier, with Dalley again Attorney-General. The change of Premiers was a swapping of knights; both Parkes and Robertson had been appointed Knight Commanders of St Michael and St George (KCMG) – an order created in 1869 to recognise 'those who have achieved distinction in the colonies' – in June.[26] An odd dispute brought Sir Henry's brief government to an end: did the phrase 'five miles square' in Garrett's land legislation of 1875 really mean 'twenty five square miles'? Dalley was a key player in the argument.

The motion, moved by Garrett, that sank the government declared an opinion on the question prepared by Parkes's Attorney-General, William Windeyer, incorrect and directed that it not be acted on.[27] The relevant clause of the Act allowed holders of pastoral leases to provisionally purchase areas – from 40 to 640 acres – on which they intended to make improvements, preventing free selection there. But there was a confusing proviso; the land bought could be no more than 'one square mile [640 acres] within each block of five miles square out of each lease or a proportionate quantity out of any holding of less area'.

Garrett, as Lands Minister, had requested an opinion from Attorney-General Dalley in September 1876 on whether this meant lessees whose holdings lacked a block literally five miles square were prevented from making such purchases. Dalley's response had a Delphic tone, essentially spelling out the clause in slightly different words. If the answer to

Garrett's question were yes, opportunities to purchase would be much less than allowed by a more liberal interpretation. Critics pointed out, among other things, that the reference to areas smaller than 640 acres said nothing about their shape; therefore, surely, five miles square meant twenty-five square miles in any configuration. Windeyer took this view. Squatters, naturally, favoured a liberal interpretation and selectors a restrictive one, making the issue politically potent.

Dalley addressed it in a very long letter (five and a half columns) to the *Herald* in September 1877. He quoted many authorities in support of the view that the ordinary meaning of words applied, so five miles square meant exactly that. He thought, but was not sure beyond doubt, that the legislators meant the same geometric interpretation to apply also to smaller blocks.[28] The *Herald*'s commentary was to the point:

> It is pleasant to see Mr Dalley drawn out. He is always worth reading, because even when he has a bad case he is so ingenious and plausible, and if he is not too much worried by the difficulties of the situation he is pretty sure to be entertaining. When he has a good case, he delights in gently worrying his opponent; and though he cannot indulge that sportive vein when his difficulties are too serious, still he can manage to surround his discussions with a display of learning and a flow of rhetoric that adorn the subject, even though they do not illustrate it, and may even obscure it. The critics can always forgive the defects of his logic for the pleasure afforded by his rhetoric, while for those who are not critical it is very fine and wonderfully convincing.[29]

A test case came to the Supreme Court the following March. The majority, Justices Hargrave and Faucett, accepted that 'five miles square' meant a square block and so concluded that an application to purchase 640 acres of a lease that was large enough but the wrong shape must be rejected. Chief Justice Martin dissented, noting the 'manifest absurdity' of the clause if taken literally. 'Nothing…could be more ridiculous than to suppose that a man with 15,999 acres [an acre less than 25 square miles] of any shape could get nearly 640 acres; while a person holding 20,000 acres, out of which he could not get a block five miles square, was to get nothing.' The Privy Council agreed with Martin when the case went there on appeal in 1879.[30]

Robertson's government was defeated within days of parliament reassembling in September after the ministerial elections. The leader of a new 'third party' in the Assembly, James Farnell, who had been Lands Minister in the Parkes ministry of 1872–75, led the assault by immediately tabling a no-confidence motion. But before this could be debated the government lost a vote that would have allowed it to introduce a supply bill. Robertson asked for a dissolution, the Governor again said he would agree only if supply were voted, this was impossible, so the ministers tendered their resignations.

Instead of calling on Farnell, the man who had precipitated Robertson's fall, the Governor invited Alexander Stuart, and then Stephen Brown, to form a government. After both failed, he at last called general elections. The voters made it clear they wanted change; first Parkes was defeated in East Sydney and then Robertson in West Sydney. Parkes, typically, drew consolation in his defeat from the fact that many great men had suffered similar reversals. 'I remembered that Sir Robert Peel, that Lord Macaulay, that Edmund Burke, that John Bright, that Richard Cobden, and Mr Gladstone had been rejected by constituencies, and I knew that, unless I had a singular immunity from the fortunes of public men in the English nation, sooner or later rejection might come to me,' he told voters.[31] He and Robertson were returned for other constituencies.

When parliament resumed on 27 November Farnell immediately moved another motion of no confidence in Robertson's government, which was carried by one vote a week later. Parkes received the Governor's summons, but failed to form a ministry. Farnell, generally seen as an unlikely leader, was then called, and commissioned as Premier on 18 December. He took the lands portfolio; Michael Fitzpatrick, Dalley's sparring partner a year earlier, was the new Colonial Secretary. Despite facing both the knighted veterans, Parkes and Robertson, across the despatch box, Farnell's team managed to retain government – although achieving little – for just over a year.

Sir Alfred Stephen had words of praise for Dalley's work as Attorney-

General when parliament met again in January 1878. The occasion was a debate in the Legislative Council on whether he had been right to instigate the reprimand of magistrates who acquitted a husband and wife charged with savagely beating their four-year-old daughter. Dalley said the assault was a 'scandal and reproach to our civilisation' and a grievous error had been made in not committing the couple for trial. Stephen defended the magistrates, but added that 'in every case he had known or heard of' Dalley had acted 'with singular ability, very great judgment and promptitude, and with every desire to do justice to the community and to vindicate the position of his high office'.[32]

Catholic bishops from Queensland, Victoria, South Australia, Western Australia, New Caledonia and country New South Wales were in Sydney in January for the ceremonial investing of Polding's successor, Archbishop Vaughan, with the pallium, the vestment symbolising his authority. All gathered again three days afterwards at St John's College at the university, where Dalley was among the speakers at a library opening. He quoted approvingly the views of the renowned priest and writer John Henry Newman, 'one of the greatest of living Englishmen', on the vital role of universities in cultivating young minds and developing gentlemanly character. And he praised his friend Professor Badham as

> one of the very first scholars of Europe, one of the truest friends of education, and one of the kindliest men in the world, who is at any time accessible (like your library) to the humblest student, seeking to improve his mind.[33]

The university's Chancellor, 77-year-old Sir Edward Deas Thomson, announced his retirement at a Senate meeting two months later. Dalley, who had been a fairly regular participant in the monthly meetings since his election as a Fellow five years earlier, seconded the motion expressing the Senate's regret. At the next meeting, on 3 April, he joined Arthur Renwick, a medical doctor later to turn politician, in nominating Sir James Martin as Deas Thomson's successor. The Government Astronomer, Henry Russell, nominated Martin's newest Supreme Court colleague, Sir William Manning, for the position. Both candidates were

Fellows of long standing, Martin having been elected to the Senate in 1858 and Manning three years later.

Martin had distinguished supporters in the contest: Badham, Deas Thomson and Justice Faucett, as well as Renwick and Dalley. But Manning had the numbers, attracting seven votes including those of the prominent conservatives William Macleay, Sir William Macarthur and Sir John Hay, and the university's other professors, John Smith and Theodore Gurney.

At a special meeting a week later, a 'distressed' Manning announced that Martin had resigned from the Senate 'on account apparently of my election', and Dalley had followed suit. He said he had 'not sought this place or its honour' and had 'discouraged the wish to the few who have spoken to me on the subject'.[34] Which raises the question: why did he allow his name to be put forward? Probably Martin aspired to the post principally as a further demonstration that, though of humble birth, he had reached the highest social rank. By also resigning, Dalley joined him in protesting at the slight.

The Governor, Sir Hercules Robinson, son of an admiral, was one who had never recognised Martin's standing. He angered the Chief Justice by declining to follow precedent and appoint him Administrator during an absence from the colony in late 1874. The following year the two men engaged in a heated dispute, in letters published in the press, over Robinson's contention that Martin had concurred in the early release of Frank Gardiner.[35] In a despatch to Lord Carnarvon in July 1875 Robinson accused Martin of 'unparalleled impropriety', which, if New South Wales were a Crown colony, would have led to his sacking.[36]

Relations had not thawed by 1878, and it seems that the Governor used his influence against Martin in the election of the new Chancellor. Writing to Macarthur before the vote, Badham reported that Robinson had spoken to him on the subject and 'is not so indifferent in this matter as one has a right to expect'. He added that it would be 'a very hard thing for us' if, by rejecting Martin, 'we are to turn a useful champion into at least a stranger if not a foe, because a gentleman who is here today and gone tomorrow does not like to meet him'.[37]

Possibly there was an element of truth in another theory advanced by *Freeman's Journal*. It thought an anti-Catholic feeling had shown itself since the death of Polding, who was a Senate Fellow from 1856. In December 1877 ten Fellows including Martin, Dalley, Badham and Manning invited Archbishop Vaughan to nominate for a Senate vacancy. However, another candidate, Sir George Wigram Allen, Speaker of the Legislative Assembly, came forward and Vaughan declined to enter a contest for the position.[38] *Freeman's* saw a parallel between the response to Vaughan's candidature and the rejection of Martin, who was born and raised a Catholic. The Fellows had demonstrated that they 'prefer mediocrity, which by comparison is contemptible, to a Catholic of the mildest type, however distinguished'.[39]

Badham appears to have made his own protest at the university's annual 'commemoration' in June, presided over by the Governor. He attended, but did not deliver an oration as in previous years. There was 'an air of unmistakable gloom and disappointment about the whole proceedings', *Freeman's* observed. 'There was all the difference in the celebration between the severest form of Calvinistic service and Pontifical High Mass with Mozart's music.' What was the reason for Badham's 'significant silence'? Possibly he conceived the university 'to have been materially weakened by the preference as Chancellor of a man of eminent respectability and mediocrity to one of unquestionable power of the first class', the paper conjectured. Or 'he may have felt bitterly' the departure of Dalley, 'one whom he has uniformly honoured with the most devoted friendship'.[40]

16
Political battles and a busy pen

Dalley emerged from his terms as Attorney-General a QC, but from now on made infrequent court appearances. He gave more time to speech making in the Legislative Council on issues he considered important, oratory in support of the Church, and his literary interests. Periods of intense activity were punctuated more often than before by episodes of illness. One in June 1878 caused serious concern, but towards the end of the month he was reported to have recovered sufficiently to take 'riding and boating exercise'.[1] The following February he told a correspondent he had been very ill and 'unhappily am very slowly mending'.[2]

In the Council, one of his first speeches of 1878 was a call for action against the 'wanton cruelty' being inflicted on sea birds around Sydney. Anyone acquainted with their 'various places of resort' knew they were 'the objects of the sport of cockney sportsmen…constantly occupied in the shooting at and maiming of these beautiful creatures', he said. Recently he had seen several wounded birds, shot days previously, 'dying, slowly starved, in pain, and exposed to the assaults of their unharmed companions'. He noted a practical reason to protect sea birds; they provided 'the best of all warnings to seamen when in proximity of land in thick weather'.[3]

In May he denounced an electoral reform bill passed by the Assembly that would have increased its membership from 73 to 115. The legislation proposed by the Farnell government provided for a smaller increase, but dozens of amendments had been made as members sought advantage for their districts. The result, said Dalley, was a 'radically defective measure' that did not, as intended, remove inequalities between electorates. For example, Parramatta would have 600 voters and Paddington 2,500. There was also a major problem with any enlargement of the Assembly; it would 'multiply...the number of trading politicians – the hunters of public office – the men who coerce feeble administrations – who waste public time by advertising their political activity in Parliament, and public money by securing needless and expensive public works for their electorates.' The Council agreed, rejecting the bill by 14 votes to eight.[4]

Later in the month he made a powerful speech opposing what he considered dangerously 'loose and ill-considered' legislation on parliamentary privilege passed by the Assembly. The Council threw this bill out too, but the battle was to resume, with much intensity, the following year. Dalley saw it as a fight for 'popular liberty', especially freedom of the press.[5]

Rev. John Dunmore Lang died, aged 78, on 8 August 1878, in his 56th year as a minister in the colony. Tens of thousands turned out for his state funeral two days later. Lang had earned notoriety for his attacks on 'popery' and 'Romish superstition', but his friendships with Dalley and some other liberal-minded Catholics, notably Very Rev. Dr John Forrest of St John's College, showed a more attractive side to his character. So did his support for the colony's Chinese. A 'large number of the Chinese residents of the city' took their place at the front of the mile-long funeral procession, and Dalley was one of the four pallbearers – two others were Robertson and Parkes – who walked beside the hearse.[6]

In November, a notorious excommunicated Canadian Catholic priest, Charles Chiniquy, visited the colony to lecture on 'the dark mysteries of idolatry, immorality, degrading slavery' and so on concealed behind the walls of 'that Modern Babylon', Rome. He had the support of the *Protestant Standard* newspaper and attracted large crowds; sectarianism remained alive and strong. Dalley took him on in characteristic style – a combination of humour and eloquent disdain – in *Freeman's* and *Punch*.

The *Punch* articles presented mock speeches. In the last, Chiniquy shocks his audience by revealing that in some monastic orders 'the guilty creatures' rise at midnight not for prayer and meditation but to 'commence their orgies'. A photograph of every 'lovely novice' is sent to the General of the Jesuits for submission to the Pope. 'In their accursed palace at Rome the pictures of millions of these youthful, deluded, and lovely beings tapestry the walls and fill the cellars and presses and bookcases of the brethren.' Chiniquy concludes his speech:

> And now, brothers and sisters, I have done. You know the glorious objects of my mission. They are twofold – To insult the two hundreds of millions of people who belong to the Roman faith, amongst whom I lived for half a century, and to carry back to Canada as many dollars, barrels of salt pork, quantities of molasses, and other things necessary to the maintenance of holy religion as I can procure. It is true that I have accomplished nothing among you, except to gratify the intolerant, the malignant, and the vulgar; but I have done my best...[7]

The Farnell government fell in December following the heavy defeat of a lands bill. Governor Robinson called on Robertson to form a new administration, and Dalley again accepted the post of Attorney-General. However, the recall was brief. Lacking sufficient support, Robertson handed back his commission and resigned from the Assembly, prompting Dalley to pen an open letter to 'Dearest and Best Beloved Jack' in *Punch*. 'You were never younger, never abler, never more influential,' he wrote; his place was in parliament.[8] Robertson soon joined Dalley in the Legislative Council – as what would have been unthinkable a year earlier, the representative in the upper house of a Parkes/Robertson coalition government. After two decades as antagonists the knights had discovered, during their joint spell on the opposition benches, that they could cooperate.

The postponed issue of parliamentary privilege was near the top of the agenda when parliament resumed in January 1879. Dalley vigorously opposed the new government's proposal to give the Assembly and Council essentially the same 'privileges, immunities and powers' as the British House of Commons. Many of those powers, 'arrogantly claimed in times not remote', were 'flagrant violations of personal liberty', he said. In Britain the 'growing force of a trained public opinion' and 'the forbearance, the temper, and the decency' dominant in recent times had seen 'these extraordinary and atrocious powers' fall into disuse. But 'could we, in this young country, in our infant legislatures, with our politics into which personal elements so largely and so necessarily enter, expect that we should exhibit all these high qualities?'[9]

The bill returned to the Council in March after the Assembly rejected its main amendment, which restricted application of the claimed powers to acts done, or words spoken or written, in parliament. In no mood to retreat, Dalley told the story of the imprisonment of the then publisher of the *Argus*, Hugh George, by Victoria's Legislative Assembly in 1866, soon after it adopted the privileges and powers of the House of Commons. George had been summoned to the bar of the Assembly to answer for statements contained in his 'great and ably conducted' paper, denied the right to be heard in defence of the statements, and locked in a damp cell in Parliament House for three weeks. Dalley said he was keen for the Council and Assembly to maintain harmonious relations, but 'shrank from the sacrifice of popular liberty for even so desirable an object'.[10]

In the Assembly, after the Council stood firm, a ministerial colleague of Dalley's in the Robertson government of 1875–77, John Lucas, accused him of having become a creature of the *Herald*. Dalley had once seen things differently, Lucas recalled, describing the paper's then editor, Rev. John West, as 'this hoary-headed ruffian' and advising members that they had the power to bring him 'on his knees' to the bar of the house.[11] Making a personal explanation in the Council, Dalley admitted that, 20 years earlier, in the 'intemperate heat of youth', he had used some such language. His behaviour then stood as a warning against giving parliament the extraordinary powers now sought. He had apologised to West.[12]

Dalley made two more speeches on the subject before the government withdrew the bill in mid-May.[13] By then, after the rejection of more legislation, the debate had broadened into an argument over the Council's right to thwart the wishes of the popularly elected Assembly. The second bill blocked would have increased the number of Supreme Court judges from four to five – a change Dalley had advocated strongly four years earlier (chapter 14). The problem with the new bill was a clause making attorneys, as well as barristers, eligible for appointment.

Dalley contended that it would be dangerous to appoint men who had chosen to remain solicitors and therefore not taken the opportunity to show, by appearing as advocates in the highest court, that they possessed various qualities required in judges. These included 'quickness of apprehension, clearness of statement, readiness in dealing with the various departments of law, and, above all, the daily familiarity with intellectual contests maintained with temper and courtesy'. The Council agreed, insisting by a large majority that the clause be removed. The Assembly refused, so the bill was lost.[14]

The bill whose rejection caused the most fuss sought to 'regulate and restrict' entry of Chinese into the colony. The number any ship could bring in would depend on its tonnage – no more than one for every 10 tons. Ships' masters were to pay Customs £10 for each person landed; failure to comply would result in forfeiture of the vessel. And Chinese entering the colony by land were to pay, or have paid for them, the same sum.

An upsurge in anti-Chinese sentiment in the second half of 1878 prompted the legislation. At a large meeting called by the Trades and Labour Council in July, the main speaker, Thomas White, urged 'working men' to unite 'to put down Chinese labour in every form'. The crowd applauded when he advised that 'if they came against a Chinaman on the footpath, it was their bounden duty to shove him off it'.[15] An increase in reported assaults followed – mainly people being pelted with stones or, in one case, a piece of filthy meat. The *Mail* commented that the inflammatory language had had its intended effect on the perpetrators, the 'loafers and larrikins' who congregated on Sydney's street corners.[16]

Matters took a serious turn for the worse in late November when seamen employed by the Australasian Steam Navigation Company began a strike in protest against the employment of Chinese on its coastal steamers. An estimated ten thousand people attended a demonstration in Hyde Park on 4 December. Afterwards a mob of some 2,000 headed to the Chinese district around Lower George Street where they hurled stones at houses and tried to set fire to a cabinetmaker's premises. The police reportedly 'laid into them unmercifully with whips, and staves, and sticks, chasing them up George-street…' Many other assaults were reported, including one in which a man was struck on the head with a heavy hammer and severely injured.[17]

A compromise settlement that reduced the numbers of Chinese employed on steamers ended the strike in early January 1879. Parkes introduced his legislation to restrict immigration at the end of the month and it passed easily through the Assembly in March. In the Council, Dalley made a long speech arguing that there was no need for the bill, but saying he would vote for the second reading because, in the face of the public demand for action, resistance would make 'more intense and unreasonable an already embittered popular sentiment'. He would seek changes in committee to ensure the legislation did 'not dishonour us as a civilized community'.

Dismissing claims that Chinese were swamping the colony, he produced statistics showing numbers had actually fallen by nearly half, to fewer than 10,000, over the past 18 years. On their character and behaviour, he quoted police reports from around the colony, which generally read 'more like a panegyric than a condemnation'. And he doubted that the legislation would achieve its intended effect. A vessel of 2,000 tons could still bring in 200 Chinese, and the 'iniquitous' poll tax would not stop large employers hiring them. The tax would simply be deducted from their wages.[18]

The *Mail* called Dalley's speech a masterly oration and, in the Legislative Council, Professor Smith observed that, after the 'brilliancy' of his denunciation of the bill, it almost took one's breath away to hear that he would vote for it.[19] He was one of only five members who did so.

The issue of execution for rape came to the fore again in mid-1879 after the Executive Council first rejected, and then acceded to, calls from around the colony for the death sentences passed on three young men in April to be commuted. Supporting a private member's bill to make murder the only capital crime, Dalley said the recent events made abolition of the death penalty for rape 'indispensable'. The convicted youths had been saved by the 'unmistakable expression of public feeling'; under these circumstances another execution for rape could not take place 'without shocking the community'.

He argued that abolition deserved support for other reasons as well. It would make guilty verdicts in rape trials more likely as juries would not shrink from the consequences, and it was in harmony with the 'sentiments of humanity and tenderness of human life' that were 'the highest characteristics of the age'.[20] The bill was lost, and the death penalty for rape remained on the books after Dalley eventually secured passage of the Criminal Law Amendment Act in 1883.

The clash of the two houses of parliament came to a head in July after the government withdrew new land legislation following amendments by the Council. The bill proposed halving to 10 shillings an acre the value of the improvements selectors were required to make on their land; this would apply to past as well as future selections. The result, thundered Dalley, would be to punish honesty and offer 'a premium to evasion'. Those who had violated the law by not spending the agreed sum would escape sanction, while honest selectors would see the value of their holdings fall.[21] The Council overwhelmingly accepted this argument, removing the retrospective provision.

With his main legislation blocked and parliament about to take a three-months break, Parkes responded angrily. Carefully prepared and considered measures had been 'cast to the winds, almost without consideration whatever, when they get into another place', he complained. He moved a string of resolutions deprecating the nominated Council's behaviour and advocated its replacement with an elected body. The last resolution implied that, in the meantime, the government should be free to swamp the Council with its supporters; it maintained that appointments were a matter purely for 'Her Majesty's ministers'.[22]

Dalley responded with a notable speech subsequently published as a pamphlet. He observed that most members of the upper house had a long history of popular support as members of the Assembly, gave a detailed defence of the actions taken on the contentious bills, and pointed to the strong support in the press for what had been done. He reminded members of Parkes's love of sensation and his habit of seeing

> a crisis as the normal condition of a politician of lofty genius – dwelling in a certain loneliness of grandeur, remote from the ordinary temptations and daily difficulties of common men. It was soothing to his soul that mysterious forces should be brought into play to counteract the schemes of his noble ambition. And so creatures of gloom and mystery, spiritual agencies, and all the delicate fancies of a dreamy nature have from time to time played no inconsiderable part in his statecraft.

He said his friend Robertson was a quite different character, who 'looked upon any enemy who could not meet him in a fair combat as utterly contemptible; dealt with facts, and detested false sentiments'. He hoped the colony would not, 'at the insolent dictation of any man', sweep away a legislative body that had 'more than once frustrated a policy of arrogance and selfishness – stood between men who prated of freedom and yet feared it, and has not scrupled to exercise its powers on the side of justice when it might have easily obtained an inglorious popularity by its inaction'.[23]

Dalley had more to say about the political scene and, by implication, Parkes in an article in the *Herald* in May on sayings and proverbs. Confucius had observed of 'a statesman of expediency' that 'When out of office his sole object is to attain it; and when he has attained it, his only anxiety is to keep it. In his unprincipled dread of losing his place he will readily go all lengths.' Chinese who visited the colony would have their faith in 'the universal applicability' of the great philosopher's reflections confirmed 'by experience of our institutions and the contemplation of our political system', wrote Dalley. China – 'a nation of proverbial philosophers, concerning whom it was lately proposed that we should guard against the perils of their acuteness and humour by requiring them to pay us ten pounds a head on their landing in our country' – was probably the world's greatest source of 'maxims of practical wisdom'.[24]

Away from politics, Dalley gave a lecture in early February on 'Spanish cathedral-builders' in aid of the St Mary's Cathedral building

Archbishop Vaughan.

fund. He told a fundraising meeting chaired by Archbishop Vaughan in September 1877 that he had been reading about the cathedral built by the canons of Seville of 'distant ages', a magnificent 'monument of their folly'. Their 'sublime foolishness' was difficult to emulate, he said then, but those engaged in building cathedrals 'ought at all events to make the attempt'.[25]

The archbishop invited Dalley to expand on the theme; the resulting talk, which reportedly kept the audience 'crowded in every part' of the hall in a 'pleasant humour',[26] was a romantic tour of the glories of Florence and Constantinople as well as Spain. He noted that 'the mad monks' of Seville had embarked on their 'sublime insanity' in the time of Columbus and St Ignatius Loyola – 'an age for lofty enterprise, for noble conception, daring adventure, romantic achievement, sublime self-sacrifice'. The cathedral they built was 'one of those great achievements of soul and art before which all men feel humble and grateful'. Those building St Mary's were undertaking a 'much humbler work – in an altogether different age', he conceded.

> But it will be to your spirit's gain to pause and think awhile of these men who thought so little of themselves and so much of posterity. You may ask why did they raise these wondrous piles of beauty towards Heaven… Did they know that tens of thousands of broken spirits – hearts stricken with great sorrows – minds disturbed and distracted, would in the shadows of this vast temple – amidst its gorgeous gloom – at the foot of its altars of jasper, and beneath these masterpieces of human genius in painting upon its lofty walls – find that peace and repose which the world could not give them. For the influence of these temples upon great souls is a marvellous thing. They preach with a persuasiveness and a grandeur of language which no human tongue can emulate, and their eloquence softens hearts which no voice, however tenderly pleading, could reach.[27]

Henry Kendall was one of those inspired, quickly writing a poem, 'On a Spanish Cathedral', which he dedicated to Dalley. It provides, as the following extract shows, a glimpse of his own spiritual searching:

> The music, the colour, the gleam,
> Of their mighty Cathedral will be
> Hereafter a luminous dream
> Of the Heaven I never may see.
> To a spirit that suffers and seeks
> For the calm of a competent creed,
> This Temple, whose majesty speaks,
> Becomes a religion indeed.[28]

Among Kendall's other works of early 1879 was a cantata to be sung at the opening of the Sydney International Exhibition in September. It seems Dalley helped secure the commission. He told the editor of *Freeman's*, Thomas Butler, in early March that he had just delivered the piece to the exhibition's executive commissioner, Patrick Jennings, praised its 'great beauty and power' to him, and advised that he was unlikely to get anything 'so good from any other quarter'.[29] Jennings was not sure, reporting to Dalley in June that he had arranged for several people, including Sir Alfred Stephen, Chief Justice Martin, Professor Badham and Archbishop Vaughan, to read it. He considered the first two of its four parts 'very fine', but hoped Kendall would 'not feel angry' if the third and fourth parts were removed.[30] Some changes were agreed, but the much-cheered performance on the great day, by 700 singers, eight pianists and a 50-piece orchestra, had four parts.[31]

Dalley's critical skills were called on early in the year to choose the winner of a literary competition run by the *Mail*. The paper offered £100, and publication, to the author of the best tale – a story suited to serialisation in weekly parts – submitted by a colonial author. It received more than sixty entries, employed an unnamed 'thoroughly competent literary authority' to whittle these down to three, and then called on Dalley to make the final adjudication. He was, wrote the *Mail*, a 'gentleman of acknowledged literary ability whose name and reputation…would be the surest guarantee that the most meritorious work would be selected'.

The chosen piece, 'Luke Mivers' Harvest' by N. Walter Swan, a Victorian journalist, is a morality tale about a squatter, Mivers, whose ill-gotten wealth wins him little happiness. Dalley declared it a 'very powerful and original story' providing 'very masterly' pictures of Australian scenery and sketches of colonial society. His only criticism was Swan's 'want of self-restraint' at times: 'A noble imaginative faculty is not always under the control of a sober judgment'.[32]

In April, Dalley published a lengthy article in the *Herald* celebrating Pope Leo XIII's appointment of 78-year-old John Henry Newman as a Cardinal. He included passages from a wide range of Newman's writings, aiming, he wrote, to convey some idea of this 'very remarkable' former Anglican, long regarded as 'intellectually the most distinguished member of the Roman Catholic Church'.[33]

The following month William Archer, an English-born Catholic convert temporarily in Sydney following a purge of senior civil servants by the Victorian government, suggested to Dalley and other prominent laymen that the colony's Catholics organise a testimonial to Newman. Dalley thought it an excellent idea, but told Archer he felt restrained in participating 'by the personal consideration of my unworthiness'.

> My feeling about John Henry Newman is of a devotional character. If I ever saw him I should fall upon my knees before him. I hardly ever think of him as a being of this world. No priest of the Catholic Church of whom I have ever read so affects me by his life and works.[34]

Despite his reticence, Dalley took the main public role in the movement. A meeting of lay Catholics in June decided, on his suggestion, that Newman should be sent a salver of 'pure Australian gold' bearing a suitable Latin inscription. In July, he reported that work was under way, and the salver's decorations would include portraits of the Pope, Newman and St Philip Neri, founder of the Congregation of the Oratorians of which Newman was 'so distinguished a member'. Six incidents in the life of the saint would be depicted, while another portion of the salver would contain 'some beautiful delineations' of Australian flora.[35]

Dalley recruited Professor Badham to write the Latin inscription (he told Archer Badham would 'lovingly' do this 'in the best Latin in the world'[36]), and read out a translation at the testimonial committee's next meeting in August. The classicist's text extolled Newman's genius and his labours in leading men 'into the light and tranquillity of the City of God'.[37] In the meantime, more than twice the sum needed had been collected. In a letter to the Duke of Norfolk, who was to make the presentation, Archer said 'shillings and even pence' had flowed in from all parts of the colony. 'Many of these modest contributions came not only from poor people in scattered townships, but from struggling selectors, wood-splitters, fishermen; from folk that toil in the remote bush, in wild woods, and on lonely coasts remote from the capital'.[38]

At the presentation, in London in May 1880, Newman described the salver as 'singularly artistic'.[39] Earlier, after learning of plans for the testimonial, he had written to Dalley to express his gratitude. The salver would 'abide' in the Birmingham Oratory after him, 'to be preserved with care, and shown with pride as a memorial both of your good opinion of its founder and of his good fortune'. He added that he had said Mass for Dalley's 'friend…who was intending so zealously to co-operate with you in my favour'.[40]

This was Edward Butler, who died aged about 55, on his feet in the Supreme Court, on 9 June 1879. Dalley told the first Newman testimonial meeting four days later that Butler had discussed the plan with him the day before he died and been keen to lend his support. Dalley was a pallbearer at the funeral; any strain in relations following Butler's political association with Parkes in 1872 had been forgotten. The eulogy Dalley delivered in the Legislative Council to his friend and fellow member is a notable example of his oratory. Butler, he said, was a colonist

> whose career in this country is eminently deserving of the attention of those who desire to fashion the generous youth of our times upon noble and affecting and unobtrusive examples. From the humblest beginnings – by mere force of a pure character – a clear and powerful intelligence, and an indomitable spirit he reached a very high, if not the highest, place in a profession in which a signal success can only be achieved by patience, by labour, by courage, and by intellectual power; and he did

this not only without inspiring envy of his good fortune among his less successful competitors, but with the full enjoyment of their sympathy with his advancement, their admiration of his growing power, and their conviction that his good fortune ennobled their profession. In the midst of that good fortune he was unchanged – the same simple, earnest, homely, compassionate man, who entered upon an arduous career with meekness and with hope, and who was neither cast down by disappointment nor lifted up by an unlooked-for success. He will be missed in his profession whenever the occasion arises for a great argument to be sustained by much legal learning, to be ordered by the culture and experience of a laborious life, and to be enforced by the impassioned eloquence of a sincere nature and of a vigorous intellect. And in this Chamber we shall always deplore his absence when subjects of discussion are before us which are above the mere vulgarities and idle purposes of party politics, and involve the consideration of matters in the determination of which the whole country is profoundly interested.[41]

Dalley was also prominent in obsequies for 79-year-old Sir Edward Deas Thomson, Colonial Secretary in the 20 years before responsible government and Chancellor of the university from 1865 to 1878, who died a month later. He accompanied the 'chief mourner' representing the family, William Macleay, in the funeral procession, and again spoke in the Legislative Council. A number of lessons could be learned from the life of 'our most distinguished colonist', he said. These were 'the winning grace of simplicity, the nobleness of labour [and] the true courtesy of taking any place to which a man may be called – high or low – in which he may be useful to his fellow creatures.'[42]

17
Dark times

Dalley caught the train to 'Numantia', Sir James Martin's retreat in the Blue Mountains, shortly after the 20 August Newman testimonial committee meeting. Possibly this was the family's temporary home while construction of 'Clairvaux' was in its last stages. Members of the Martin family visited from Sydney while Dalley was in residence; their movements, and visits by Sir Alfred Stephen from his nearby holiday home, 'Alphington', are recorded in a diary kept by Lady Stephen. Dalley returned Stephen's calls, on one occasion visiting 'Alphington' 'for a minute with his eldest boy' and on another dropping in 'with fresh eggs and lemons'.[1]

On Dalley's mind as he enjoyed the brisk air and peace was a new outburst of sectarian rancour prompted by a highly provocative pastoral letter on education issued by Vaughan and the colony's three other Catholic bishops at the end of July. Dalley was hardly being prescient when he remarked at the Newman meeting that Catholics could expect to be 'exposed to a storm of misrepresentation and insult – to be the sport of the fanatic and the capital of the political adventurer'.[2]

The bishops denounced public schools as 'seed-plots of future immorality, infidelity and lawlessness, being calculated to debase the standard of human excellence, and to corrupt the political, social, and individual life of future citizens'. Parents with children at the schools were exhorted to remove them and examine their 'religious instincts and moral condition'. If, as could be expected, they found 'faith and morals weakened, and the germs of lawlessness apparent', they should, 'with great anxiety', do all they could 'to redeem the time and to remedy the evil'.[3]

Concerns about the denominational schools system, the government-funded alternative to public schools, seem to have played a large part in prompting the bishops' outburst. Catholics had always been exhorted to avoid public schools, but increasing numbers of their children were attending them as the denominational system declined. The church complained that the Council of Education, which managed both systems, was prejudiced against denominational schools and had too much say in what they taught. And it seemed things would only get worse. Most of the other colonies had already ended, or signalled an end to, state aid for denominational schools. The Robertson government's abortive legislation of 1876 (chapter 14) was a step in the same direction, and Parkes remarked in June 1879 that whenever the education question was reopened it would not be 'in favour of denominational schools'.[4]

By contrast, the church was making considerable progress in establishing schools outside the denominational system and so free from the Council's control. One aim of the pastoral undoubtedly was to boost support among the faithful for these. At least two of the bishops expressed confidence that, when calm returned, the government would concede that as Catholics paid taxes like everybody else their schools should, in justice, receive public funding. If that eventuated, the expected demise of the denominational system would be unmixed good news.[5]

Away from the action but following the outcry against the bishops in the newspapers, Dalley reached the view in early September that 'the time is drawing near when the laity will have to speak'. He wrote to William Archer asking,

> What think you of an address to the Catholics on the present situation, preparing them for a fair consideration of the question? It would require much thought and the thing would have to be done very skilfully. But I have an idea that it could be done so as to be of great service… It would of course be largely characterised by the language of protest against the ferocity of the assault upon Catholicism which we are witnessing… It should be full of information so as to be of practical use to such members of Parliament (alas! a miserable minority) who love fair play, and it should be a manual on the subject for use at elections. Then in order to make it acceptable its tone should be in the highest degree fair and (I use the word advisedly) liberal.[6]

Dalley asked Archer to seek the views of Jennings and other prominent laymen on the matter. He did not say he was volunteering to prepare the address, but probably that was assumed by those consulted. He soon got down to work; later letters to Archer asked for copies of speeches he wanted to quote and for various statistics.[7] He delivered the result, some 18,000 words, in a packed St Francis's Hall, Haymarket, on the evening of 15 October. Archbishop Vaughan, presumably pleased with the lay initiative, presided. Also on the platform were others, including Sir John Robertson, who strongly opposed the pastoral's sentiments; they shared Dalley's concern for denominational harmony.

Dalley began by urging Catholics to respond calmly to the 'blind fury' of their enemies, denying them 'the luxury of supposing that they have been able in our regard to "freeze the genial current of the soul"'. Then he detailed progress in establishing Catholic schools in Sydney and the country dioceses, and made the case for their receiving a 'fair share' of state funds. He offered precedents from France and Germany, and said England's leading statesmen and intellectuals had accepted that 'the State is not justified in disregarding the conscientious difficulties of large bodies of citizens in the arrangements for the diffusion of public education'. The solution adopted there was to recognise the contribution of church schools to the nation's secular culture – by teaching reading, writing, arithmetic and so on – through 'payment by results'.

He hoped that, when the issue was settled in the colony, those responsible would

> rise above the level of sect or party into the clear atmosphere of statesmanship – of that catholic statesmanship which, contemplating mankind as it exists – with its prejudices, its follies, and, if you will have it, its superstitions also – wisely struggles, not for a perfection which is humanly unattainable, but for as near an approximation to it as our most imperfect nature will permit. Let us hope that no scheme of public policy, professing to accomplish the higher enlightenment of the people, will be disfigured and rendered ineffective by a contemptuous disregard of the conscientious convictions of any section of the community.[8]

Thanking Dalley after he sat down amid a 'prolonged burst of applause', the archbishop said all Catholics, lay and clergy, should 'take a lesson from the urbanity, the gentlemanliness, the fairness, the logic, and the overwhelming power' he had displayed.[9] *Freeman's* commented that it would be 'strange, indeed' if, through the 'force and felicity' of his speech and the array of facts and authorities presented, he had 'not completely turned the secularist flank'. Published as a pamphlet, the talk was in great demand. *Freeman's* reported in mid-November that a sixth printing was under way; orders noted a week later included more than 2,000 copies for Bishop Lanigan of Goulburn.[10]

The government, however, was unmoved. Parkes introduced his Public Instruction Bill – creating a ministry to take charge of schools, making education compulsory for children between the ages of six and 14, and ending, on a date to be set, funding for denominational schools – in early November. The legislation won overwhelming support in parliament. At the third reading in the Assembly at the end of February 1880, 42 voted for and only six against. A young Catholic barrister, John Dillon, was among the supporters and the former Colonial Secretary, Michael Fitzpatrick, abstained.

Dalley had acknowledged during a debate in the Legislative Council soon after the bill was introduced into the Assembly that a diversity of views on the issue existed even in his church. Under discussion was a motion, which the Council rejected, to set up an inquiry to determine whether public schools were indeed having the dire effects claimed by the bishops. Dalley observed that some who gave evidence would be convinced that the schools were 'admirably designed to promote morality, to cherish belief, and to support authority'. Others 'equally conscientious and equally capable of judging' would claim they induced 'contempt of religious restraint', cultivated disbelief and promoted disrespect for authority. He said these 'utterly irreconcilable witnesses' could come from any of the churches because all included people who took both views.[11] He gave no indication that he had reversed the favourable view of public schools he expressed in 1871 (chapter 12).

On the bishops' choice of words, he observed that 'the language of churchmen of all denominations' was tinged 'with a colouring too rich and gorgeous for the ordinary daily arena of human intercourse – empurpling the commonest circumstance'. He added that he thought he had seen 'in some quarters a passion on the part of the enemies of these distinguished ecclesiastics to rival them in this respect' – implying that the bishops had been as provocative as their fiercest critics.

Probably Dalley was seeking to further calm passions when he contributed 'A Roundabout Paper on Education' to the *Herald* in January. Readers would have been surprised to find he made no mention of the current controversy. Instead he discussed the 'unspeakable importance' of the education given to junior officers of the British navy and speculated about Shakespeare's schooling. He also had something to say on a topic he discussed with his old headmaster, W.T. Cape, in London in 1862 (chapter 7), the relative merits of wooden and ironclad warships.[12]

Dalley presented petitions against the education bill in the Legislative Council in December and January, and stated his views in the second reading debate in early March. Like his October address, this speech was the product of much preparation; he reportedly rose 'with quires of manuscript in his hands, the table specially arranged for his accommodation, and upon his face the light of the brilliant periods he was about to deliver'.[13]

He thought it deplorable that legislation on so important a question had been introduced at a time when the public mind was in an 'inflamed state'. Reiterating the need for governments to avoid trampling on religious convictions, he quoted a passage from a speech by Parkes in 1872 forcefully expressing the same view. He also read extensive extracts from three addresses by Archbishop Polding – claimed by supporters of the bill to have been much more reasonable than his successor – to show he had shared Vaughan's view that public schools were 'an evil' as far as the Catholic Church was concerned.

Dalley reached full oratorical flight in responding to statements by proponents of the legislation that it was a response to the bishops' criticism of public schools. No precedent existed, he said, for introducing such a measure 'because of the insolence – if you will – of the ungovernable arrogance – if you deem it – of the supreme contempt for all considerations of compromise and moderation – if you so regard it – of certain prelates'. The effect of doing so would be to

> punish, not them, for they are childless, but the fathers and mothers of thousands of little children bred up in a religion which invests with all sorts of supernatural terrors and pains and influences disobedience to spiritual authority... But the ludicrous aspect of the situation is heightened, and the thing becomes sublimely grotesque, when you consider that, in order to repress the arrogance of the Roman Catholic hierarchy and to humble their dangerous pretensions, you destroy the Church of England schools... Though Dr Barker [Sydney's Anglican bishop] fulminated no pastorals, brandished no crozier in your faces, reared no mitred front against your liberties, yet he and his clergy, his schoolmasters, and people, are to suffer the same penalty as if they went to confession, loved the Jesuits, heard mass regularly, and hated the Government.

If the legislation passed, he said, Catholics would maintain their schools at their own cost but feel a 'daily and hourly sense of wrong'. No 'political sophistry' could hide the fact that they would end up paying 'for the education of your children and of their own'. The result, particularly if Catholic education proved inferior to that provided by the 'richly-endowed public schools', might be to generate 'all kinds of angry and dangerous feeling towards authority'. He expected the bill would pass, in defiance of the example of the 'mother country' where 'the wisest and best of public men' had put aside personal prejudices, and religious and party antagonisms, to insist on justice for all.[14] It did so in March 1880, and 31 December 1882 was fixed as the day when support for denominational schools would end.

With the success of its education bill apparently assured, the government was determined at the end of 1879 also to have its way on land law. Less than six months after the Legislative Council rejected its proposal to halve the value of the improvements required of free selectors, it introduced a slightly altered bill seeking the same outcome. Again the legislation would have retrospective effect, so the argument against it was as compelling as before, said Dalley in the second reading debate in the Council. But this time he would vote for it, because the government had shown 'the strongest determination' to carry the measure 'without alteration, and without delay'. He believed that 'in all sustained contests with the elective branch', the Council must, sooner or later, give way. The majority accepted his argument and the bill passed.[15]

A week before Christmas he spoke at length in support of a proposal from William Macleay for the establishment of a royal commission to inquire into the 'state and prospects' of the colony's fisheries. Fish were 'one of the most wholesome, abundant, and delicious' forms of food, he said, but already some fishing grounds, particularly near Sydney, had become impoverished. This was hardly surprising given the 'indiscriminate destruction, by means of line and net, of the young of the very best fishes which has been going on for so long a time'. Dalley was a member of a 14-man commission, chaired by Macleay, appointed the following month. Its report, including recommendations aimed at conserving fish stocks, was tabled in parliament in May 1880.[16]

In March, Dalley took a central role in another heated argument over the respective roles of the Legislative Council and Assembly. This began when the Council amended a stamp duty bill to remove any possibility that it could act retrospectively. At the strident urging of Parkes, who claimed the Council could not alter money bills, the Assembly laid that bill aside and sent an identical replacement to the Council. The Council again insisted on its amendment, the Assembly rejected it, and so the bill lapsed.

Dalley made two long and two short speeches on the issue. He insisted that the colony's constitution was perfectly clear in giving equal powers to the Assembly and Council, with one exception – money bills had to originate in the Assembly. The Council's most valuable function was the 'calm and deliberate revision of what comes before it', he said. It should always act moderately to avoid providing 'an excuse for the abandonment of public business or an attempt to complicate the relations between the two houses'.[17]

Dalley did not remain in the Council for the final three months of the long parliamentary session, which saw an easing of tensions between the two houses. Increasingly unwell, he resigned his seat at the beginning of April. The decision had been painful, he told Sir Alfred Stephen in his reply to the 77-year-old's letter of regret, but 'absolutely necessary in the interests of my family and of my own repose'.

> For months I have been conscious that an honest discharge of my duties was incompatible not only with any hopes of improving health but with the preservation of so much (or properly speaking so little) strength as I at present possess. And on two or three occasions I was on the point of withdrawing myself from excitement and peril, and was only restrained by a feeling that it was hardly the time to retire from the front and ask for such leisure.[18]

Parkes was another who felt moved to write, recalling good times from earlier years. Dalley replied in kind, saying 'it would be impossible for me to cherish any other sentiment than one of thankfulness for your sympathetic letter…'

> I too, like yourself, have a keen and consoling remembrance of times when you and I enjoyed other relations than those in which circumstance and conviction have more recently placed us towards each other. I shall not willingly permit this recollection to be tarnished and shall I trust always think of you, however we may be fated to differ from each other, as one whose friendship it was my privilege to possess when I was accumulating the first honours of my life; and to retain through many vicissitudes and experiences.

He told Parkes he had 'sadly felt for some time that I was unequal to even the mild strain of public life to which I was physically and mentally subjecting myself, and I could measure my increasing unfitness by each successive effort. Under these circumstances my duty to my family pointed to my home and repose as the humble and only present objects of life.'[19]

Robertson was among those who offered kind words in the Council; he said he had always had 'a high respect – I will say, a great affection' for Dalley and hoped his absence would prove temporary.[20] The press also was full of praise, and regret at his departure. The *Herald* said Dalley's carefully prepared speeches contrasted with the glib utterances usually heard in parliament.[21] Melbourne's *Australasian* commented that nobody in any Australian parliament could match his combination of 'wit, and brilliancy, and keen argument, and telling eloquence'.[22]

Freeman's described him as 'the protector of the weak against injustice, the advocate of popular liberty against the dark designs of unprincipled Ministers'. For the church, the void created by his retirement was 'simply irreparable', it added.

> His lecture and speeches on the education question have passed into household words. They tell us in every line, not only how just and holy our cause is, but how true and loyal a Catholic their author is. They have gone like seed upon the waters, to bear their fruit in due season; and when the hearts of our enemies are softened, and they learn at last that that cannot be right which is not just, the next generation will acknowledge the deep debt of gratitude they owe to William Bede Dalley.[23]

Eleanor gave birth to the Dalleys' fifth child, Mary, at 'Clairvaux' on 19 May. The happy event came at a difficult time; not only was her husband seriously ill but the family of her sister, Lady Isabella Martin, was wracked with grief and turmoil. The Martins' 16-year-old daughter Eleanor died of typhoid at 'Numantia' in February. Lady Isabella apparently attributed the disease to germs inhaled from a polluted Rushcutters Bay during trips between the Martins' Potts Point home, 'Clarens', and 'Clairvaux'. She and Sir James – on leave from the Supreme Court with a heart condition since March 1879 – had been in conflict over her view that 'Clarens' was an unhealthy place to live and his plan to build a stone mansion at 'Numantia'. Her departure alone on a visit to Melbourne in August 1880 signalled a deeper breakdown of their marriage. A still-ailing Martin returned to work the same month after the government refused a further extension of his leave.[24]

Dalley reappeared in public in June, speaking at the laying of the foundation stone of a Franciscan church and school at Randwick. Archbishop Vaughan told the gathering that plans for eight or nine new Catholic schools in Sydney had been initiated since the Public Instruction

Act took effect. Dalley observed that the new education system could not command the title 'national' while 'its operation on a large section of the community is simply to stimulate the foundation of independent schools, to foster the growth of establishments which are altogether dissociated from the State...' He contrasted the spirit of Saint Francis, founder of the Franciscans, with the tone of the colony's 'education controversy':

> The saint who went singing through the Umbrian mountains, praising God for all things – for the sun which shone above, the day, the night, his *mother* the earth, his *sister* the moon, for the winds which blew in his face, for the pure precious water, and for the jocund fire (the epithets are his own), for the flowers under his feet, and the stars above his head – saluting and blessing all creatures, animate or inanimate, as his brothers and sisters – presents to us a picture in which it would be difficult to trace the lineaments of your modern educational reformer.[25]

Less than four months later he spoke at the opening of the building, and noted that many more similar 'modest, but convenient' structures would soon spring up. 'Its walls seem to have risen by enchantment,' he said. 'But we know that it is the magic of pure charity, of thorough earnestness, and of victorious self-denial.'[26]

Also making progress was St Mary's Cathedral. Vaughan told the building committee's annual meeting the day after the Randwick school opening that it would be the last held in the temporary cathedral; next year's would be in the first section of the 'real' cathedral, 'just before the permanent cement is put down for the floor'. Dalley again spoke in praise of the great European cathedral builders, noting that Cologne Cathedral had been completed recently after six centuries' labour. He said Sydney's Catholics also were engaged in a great work, 'with a magnificence in proportion to our humble circumstances and to our obscure place'.[27]

Dalley accepted a legal brief in December, representing John Dibbs, brother of the future Premier George Dibbs, in the divorce court. To end his marriage, John was seeking to prove that his wife had committed adultery with a bank clerk. George was assiduous in gathering evidence, allegedly to the extent of paying witnesses. He was in gaol when the case was heard, having refused to pay the fine imposed after being found guilty of slandering the solicitor representing Mrs Dibbs. Dalley defended George's activities in his long address to the jury; 'was it not evident,' he asked, 'that that interference was the result of a deep conviction that his unfortunate brother was not equal to the terrible task imposed upon him?' The jurors could not reach agreement on whether adultery had occurred.[28]

Henry Kendall's well-received poetry collection *Songs from the Mountains* appeared at the end of the year. Dalley had written to him in September saying he would 'esteem it a privilege to have a small share in assisting you to give to the world your little book' and placing an order for seven copies (perhaps one each for his wife, five children and himself). Writing again in December, he offered no sympathy with Kendall over the publisher's removal of 'The Song of Ninian Melville', a satirical attack on a populist politician, from the book. This described Melville as, among other things, a 'straight descendant from Professor Huxley's ape'.

'Though entertaining the most sovereign contempt for the subject of your satire and enjoying heartily the humour of your lines, I am of course aware that they were unquestionably libellous,' Dalley wrote.

> Personally I very much regretted the insertion of the Melville thing as a disfigurement of the volume, and am glad for your reputation that it is out of the book. There are too many fine and noble and successful pieces in your volume to permit under any circumstances the publication of anything no matter how brilliant about so contemptible a person.[29]

Dalley told Kendall he had sent a review of the book to the *Herald*. Including lengthy extracts from poems that he particularly liked, this appeared on 12 January 1881.[30] He found 'both power and beauty of a rare order, imaginative tenderness, emotional fervour, and an easy command of rich and forcible English' in Kendall's poetry. However, the review was not all praise. In some poems, Kendall's 'vivid and highly creative imagination' was not 'under the empire of a sober judgement'; their 'poetical beauty' was marred by the 'absence of a just restraint of sensuousness and fervour'.

Poems such as 'Jim the Splitter' demonstrated Kendall's powers as a humorist, Dalley wrote. Others, 'which manifestly owe their origin to circumstances of domestic sorrow', contained much genuine pathos; 'the veil of home affliction is tenderly and delicately uplifted by the graceful and trembling hands of one who has suffered.' Dalley included the opening stanzas of one such poem, 'Araluen', in the review. This was a tribute to Kendall's first-born child, whose death as an infant was apparently one of the events that precipitated his breakdown in 1870 (chapter 12).

The day after Christmas 1880, Dalley spoke at another school opening, at Darlinghurst. He praised Archbishop Vaughan for his 'unfaltering energy and unceasing activity' in establishing Catholic schools and listed more than a dozen that had opened recently. He also offered Vaughan the gathering's 'deepest and tenderest' sympathy on the recent death of his father. 'You have become in a few years so much a part of our daily life that we are unable to divest ourselves of a share in anything that affects your peace; and thus your domestic affliction becomes a sorrow as wide as your people are scattered,' he said.[31]

A month later it was Vaughan's turn to offer his sympathy. Eleanor Dalley contracted typhoid early in the new year and died at 'Clairvaux', at the age of 38, on 17 January 1881. She was interred in the Long family vault at St Jude's Church of England, Randwick, the next day. Only family attended the funeral.

Dalley had intended to address a fundraising meeting for the cathedral on the evening of 17 January. Vaughan told the gathering the organisers considered calling it off when they heard of Eleanor's death earlier in the day, but thought Dalley would want them to 'continue their labours' to build 'a great monument to the love of God'. He was sure every Catholic, in fact everyone 'with a heart beating in his breast' who knew Dalley, shared his deep grief.[32]

18
In praise of troubled genius

The Bulletin, the smart Sydney weekly launched to immediate success by J.F. Archibald and John Haynes in January 1880, published an engraving of Dalley on its front page five weeks after Eleanor's death. The accompanying eulogistic article praised his intellect, oratory and 'unqualified love of his native land', and even more warmly the 'tenderness of his nature – his frankness and generosity'. Referring to his recent 'bitter affliction', it expressed the hope that he would 'emerge from the gloom of his sorrow, to do good service again for the country, which was the first passion of his soul, and will probably be the last'.[1]

Dalley apparently had no intention of shutting himself away, even contem-plating speaking at the opening of a Jesuit primary school at North Sydney just six days after Eleanor died. Father Kennedy, the priest in charge, told the gathering, 'In the midst of his affliction and sorrow Mr Dalley told me that if possible he would be here to speak in support of Catholic education… But his sorrow has been too great for him; and I am sure that we, having a grateful remembrance of the services he has rendered to our religion, will readily excuse his absence and sympathise with him in his affliction.'[2]

He lost little time in putting pen to paper again. A long, scathing, review of *Endymion*, the last novel by Lord Beaconsfield (Benjamin Disraeli), appeared in the *Herald* on 15 February. To the author of the *Bulletin* article, it confirmed that Dalley ranked 'amongst the most subtle and refined critics of the age'.

The review took Beaconsfield to task for the novel's 'pitiful and malignant attack' on William Thackeray, a man with 'a marked sensibility to all forms of human suffering – a quick, and eager, and irrepressible sympathy – a spiritual tenderness, and a woman's compassion for all suffering, all poverty and misery.' Just as bad was its depiction of children. While Thackeray had portrayed them with delicacy, affection, intense sympathy and 'manifest reverence for the sacredness of childhood', Beaconsfield's eight-year-old hero and heroine were haughty, disdainful and supercilious. Could anything be 'more revolting', Dalley wondered, than an ex-Prime Minister of England leaving this 'kind of teaching concerning holy childhood' as a literary legacy?[3]

'Clairvaux' was sold a month after Eleanor died. Dalley, the children and servants had moved to a house bequeathed by his father, 30 Upper Fort Street – near one of his childhood haunts, Flagstaff Hill. Their next home, from late 1881, was a rented property, 'Bay View', in the harbour- and seaside village of Manly. Dalley purchased real estate at Bilgola, near Pittwater, in June 1881, and early the following year bought a 125-acre property, 'Rockmoor', at Sutton Forest in the southern highlands. This became the family home for most of 1882. His next purchase, in December 1882, was a house on a prominent hill at Manly that he transformed into the stone edifice 'Marinella', fondly remembered as 'Dalley's Castle'.[4] Describing Manly in July 1884, the *Mail* noted, 'The castle set upon the hill is the abode of the grand seignior of the village, Mr Dalley. It dominates the little town; its occupant is fitted to rule a

'Marinella' ('Dalley's Castle'), Manly, in 1887.

larger town.'⁵ Among its quaint features were a square tower, from the top of which one could see miles up and down the coast, and a small chapel with stained glass windows and a fireplace.⁶

Shortly after moving to Upper Fort Street, Dalley was one of the journalists, lawyers, politicians and others who established Sydney's Athenaeum Club. Its Castlereagh Street premises, opened in May, quickly became a favoured haunt of writers and thinkers; some literary, artistic or scientific qualification was required for membership.⁷ Dalley, a founding vice-president, spoke at various functions there over the next few years. The idea for such a 'literary, scientific and artistic club' had been around for some time; a group including Dalley, Professor Badham, N.D Stenhouse and the editor of *Sydney Punch*, W.H. Hicks, met in February 1870 to discuss establishing such an institution. Nothing came of it then – perhaps Sydney was still too small.⁸

In April, Dalley accepted a government appointment, to a six-man fisheries commission set up to implement the recommendations of the previous year's royal commission. William Macleay, chairman of the royal commission, presided. Its activities included hands-on investigations; for example, in January 1882 commissioners took to the harbour to test a new trawling system. Dalley resigned when the family moved to Sutton Forest three months later.⁹

The first cases in a frightening epidemic of smallpox were diagnosed in Sydney in June 1881. By the time it was brought under control early the following year more than 150 people had been infected and 41 had died. Many more, identified as possible carriers, had been isolated in their homes or at the North Head quarantine station.¹⁰ Perhaps fear for his children's health was a factor in Dalley's decision to move from Flagstaff Hill – near the Rocks, a centre of infection – to Manly and his purchase of the Sutton Forest property.

Chinese immigrants, who had recently been arriving in greater numbers than usual, were popularly blamed for introducing the disease (it is by no means certain that they were responsible; more than 600 people died of smallpox in London in the first quarter of 1881¹¹). The inevitable result was an upsurge in anti-Chinese rhetoric and abuse, which were already at a high pitch.

The 36-year-old MP Ninian Melville, subject of Henry Kendall's satire and Dalley's disdain (chapter 17), was the principal rabble-rouser at a 'densely crowded' meeting in May 1880 protesting at the arrival of a shipload of Chinese.[12] Sporadic agitation continued until some two thousand more landed the following April; their greeting was a demand for government action from a crowd that filled 'every foot of space' of the Masonic Hall, with 'some hundreds' unable to gain entry.[13] A month later an estimated 10,000 people attended an anti-Chinese demonstration in the Domain.[14] When smallpox appeared in June, responses included boycotts of Chinese shopkeepers, increasingly vicious name-calling and stone throwing by Sydney's 'larrikins', and forcible ejections from tramcars, buses and steamers.[15]

Premier Parkes responded in July by introducing new legislation to restrict Chinese immigration. This was essentially the same as the bill rejected by the Legislative Council in 1879 (chapter 16) – limiting the numbers ships could bring in and imposing a poll tax – except for two harsh new clauses. One required that all arriving vessels with Chinese on board be held in quarantine; the other prevented them acquiring or holding real estate. Despite adverse press comment – the *Mail* condemned the quarantine clause as 'monstrous'[16] – the bill passed quickly through the Assembly. When it came to the Legislative Council at the beginning of August, members accepted a petition from 'certain Chinese merchants' requesting permission for their case to be put at the bar of the house by legal counsel.

Dalley, at his persuasive best, appeared for the merchants a week later. He produced an array of facts and figures to show the Chinese were a law-abiding section of the community making important economic contributions and there was no possibility of their 'swamping' the colony. Barring Chinese from acquiring real estate was a perverse notion, he thought; a man whose 'self-denial, industry, and conquest of all difficulties' had enabled him to become a freeholder was unlikely to 'become a bad citizen'. He believed the proposal to 'quarantine ships without reference to disease' was unparalleled in European legislation. Never before had the power that governments necessarily possessed to restrict the spread of disease been 'avowedly employed to prevent the peaceful intercourse of nations'. He noted that there was 'no satisfactory evidence whatever' that Chinese had brought smallpox to the colony.

Referring to the recurring anti-Chinese agitation, he said he doubted that any other portion of the community would have 'borne itself with such pathetic and unresisting calmness in the midst of open wrong and scandalous forgetfulness of the dictates of human pity'.

> Their patience has been subjected to a sharp test, both by actual infliction upon them of cowardly injury and by the absence of that generous and noble sympathy which it should have been our pride as it was our duty to extend to them. And it may be said without extravagance that they have already suffered more from the cruelty of cowardice and prejudice than they will be called upon to endure even under the provisions of the most hostile legislation.[17]

When debate on the bill began in the Council a week later, Sir John Robertson suggested Dalley had changed his mind on the issue, noting that he had voted for the 1879 bill to restrict Chinese immigration. (This was not entirely fair; Dalley was highly critical of that bill but thought some measure was needed to assuage public opinion and hoped an acceptable outcome could be reached in committee.) Robertson conceded that it might have been unjust to juxtapose Dalley's view as a member of the Council with his speech as an advocate for the Chinese merchants.

> But it is impossible for me, after my long association with Mr Dalley, with the great respect I have for him – with the love, indeed, which I have for him – to think of him only as an advocate of the Chinese. I cannot help remembering that he is one of our best and foremost public men, and I cannot help now taking this opportunity to express my extreme regret that he ever withdrew from this Chamber. *Honorable Members*: Hear, hear.[18]

The Council made major amendments to the bill, which the Assembly duly rejected. Compromise was eventually reached, and the legislation took effect at the end of the year without the quarantine and real estate clauses, the provisions Dalley – and most members of the Council – considered most objectionable.

In late August Robertson chaired and Dalley spoke at a well-attended public meeting to raise funds to assist the Jews of southern Russia, then suffering vicious persecution. 'We had thought that the persecution of peoples was but a gloomy historical memory,' Dalley said, but instead found it 'as fresh and vigorous today as in the fifteenth century'.

> Who shall presume to estimate the extent of the debt of restitution which we owe to the Jewish people for all our atrocious national cruelties of former and not very remote ages? We cannot read of them, think of them, glance at the pictures of them, without sentiments of indignation, and without noble resolutions to make amends to a patient, suffering, and most richly gifted people for centuries of wrong inflicted upon them by ignorance and barbarism.

He noted that the colony's Jews responded promptly and gladly 'to the calls of our public Christian charities'. Now Christians had the privilege of offering practical sympathy to Jews in their affliction, 'of doing that work which, in the language of the Talmud, bears interest in this world, and the capital remaineth in the world to come. (Loud and prolonged applause.)' An impressive sum, nearly £1,000, was collected at the meeting.[19]

Dalley found time for a good deal of writing in the second half of 1881. A 'Roundabout Paper' in the *Mail* linked the 'transcendent genius' Jonathan Swift with Lord Belmore, former Governor of New South Wales, as men wrongly denied degrees by Trinity College, Dublin.[20] Another unflatteringly compared the Minister for Justice, Sir George Innes, who had indignantly reprimanded a constable who blocked his passage, with Lorenzo the Magnificent of Florence.[21] The next in the series reported on an obituary in the *Times* of London that, in contrast to the paper's usual 'severely accurate' notices of the newly dead, told of 'the tenderness, the gentleness, the pity of the great life closed'.[22]

A longer article in the *Mail* discussed a book about Walter Savage Landor, a writer of 'unrivalled powers and supreme culture' but with very few friends and abundant enemies. Landor had a 'sovereign contempt for his contemporaries', Dalley wrote. 'And yet when his great heart was touched by pity or suffering, when those whom he loved were either rudely or ungratefully treated, or wounded in life's struggles, or withdrawn from them, a cry of the soul escapes him that strangely thrills and troubles the hearer.' He noted Landor's praise for Caroline Chisholm's work for female immigrants to New South Wales – her 'humanity and sacrifice and tenderness won the admiration of the haughty solitary' – and quoted a poem by him predicting that future historians would record that 'Under God's guidance by His Chisholm's hand' a 'potent empire' had been established in the colony.[23]

Dalley contributed the opening article in the first issue of the *Sydney University Review*, a literary magazine edited by a friend, the lawyer and journalist Alexander Oliver, which appeared in November. Titled 'A Plea for Horace Walpole', this contended that the 18th-century writer, son of a prime minister, deserved much more respect than many critics accorded him. Lord Beaconsfield's view that Walpole's literary tastes and performances were 'as artificial as the style and ornament of the house he inhabited' was 'utterly absurd', Dalley wrote. Walpole had transformed his villa at Twickenham into a pseudo-Gothic showplace with cloisters, turrets, and battlements;[24] possibly his architectural efforts inspired the design of 'Clairvaux' and 'Marinella'.

Dalley wrote admiringly that Walpole's sympathies were with the workers rather than the privileged classes: 'His never-failing consciousness of the hollowness of fashionable life, the insignificance of its aims and concerns, might be illustrated by a thousand passages.' And he had an 'absolute contempt for the pride, pomp, and circumstance of glorious war… The deaths of war-loving kings are the subjects of his sincerest congratulations.' Dalley suspected that 'some of our colonial democrats who cherish so fierce and absorbing an ambition to become members of knightly orders' would be amazed to learn that when Walpole became Earl of Orford he 'humorously lamented that "he was called names in his old age"' and sought to avoid making use of the title.[25]

On 17 October, Dalley was the principal speaker at the first meeting held in the unfinished first section of the new St Mary's Cathedral. The night was 'black and cold and wet', but an estimated five thousand people turned out for the historic event, the last annual meeting of the fundraising committee before the cathedral's planned opening in 1882. Gas standards and 'a flaming illumination at the rear of the platform' lit up the 'splendid edifice', and by 8 p.m. when proceedings began 'every seat had an occupant, every inch of standing ground was packed, every pillar had a fringe of humanity clinging about its sides, and every narrowest projection was made a coign of vantage for ease to weary limbs'.

Archbishop Vaughan introduced Dalley as a link, 'so far as the laity are concerned', between the past and present – between his 'great and venerable predecessor', Archbishop Polding, and his 'humble self'. 'No more gracious task could be placed in more gracious hands,' he added. Dalley, greeted with 'hearty cheering', took up Vaughan's theme. He recalled how, after the destruction of the old cathedral, Polding had 'stood trembling with that emotion which evidenced his love of all old associations – and yet with that composure which proved the stability of his faith – and with that confident security in the generosity of his own people and the friendliness of the community which it was his privilege – as it has been Your Grace's – to enjoy'.

Dalley's oration 'thrilled with eloquence and fervour and poetic beauty', wrote the *Mail*'s reporter. The 'twisted traceries and misty masses of multi-tudinous pinnacle and diademed tower' of the great European cathedrals were monuments to their builders, he said. In the future, 'although our very names have been forgotten', St Mary's would be seen similarly as a memorial 'to the sacrifice and fidelity' of those who built it. He praised Vaughan for having 'inspired and sustained the enthusiasm' for the cause. In 'the oblivion of individual effort however noble, and in the crumbling into dust of the history of human labours however great', his name would be 'the last to disappear from the eyes of those who kneel in this place in far-distant times. (Loud and prolonged cheering.)'[26]

A week before Christmas, Dalley spoke at another important Catholic event, the first prize-giving ceremony at the Jesuit secondary school, St Ignatius' College, Riverview. He praised the Jesuits' work as missionaries and teachers, and told the story of a Jesuit-educated Irishman Rev. Francis Sylvester Mahony, better known as the writer 'Father Prout'. A 'rare scholar', 'delightful humorist' and 'above all, a brave, sincere, tender-hearted gentleman', Mahony had been a 'dear and honoured friend' of Thackeray, Dickens and other literary figures, Dalley said. A man of 'perfectly Quixotic tolerance', his life showed that 'the pupils of the Jesuits can be not less liberal than brilliant, and that the education of the order does not restrain the growth of the strongest human sympathies.'[27]

Possibly on Dalley's mind was a recent example of Catholic intolerance, the denial of the presence of a priest – whether by Vaughan or somebody lower in the hierarchy is unclear – at the burial of the former Colonial Secretary Michael Fitzpatrick on 12 December. Widely attributed to Fitzpatrick's failure to support the church's position on the education legislation of 1879, this caused an outcry in the press and parliament. In an attempt to repair the damage, a requiem mass for Fitzpatrick and a burial service at the grave were conducted ten days later.[28]

Dalley reportedly was 'one of the first and foremost' to make his disapproval known 'in the press and elsewhere'.[29] He may have been the author of an article in *Freeman's* that claimed the rites of Christian burial 'should never have been refused' and Catholics had a right to a clear explanation of what had happened 'for they have suffered deeply in their interests as well as in their feelings'.[30] These were strong words for a paper that seldom offered even a hint of criticism of the hierarchy.

Around this time, a newspaper war of sorts was in progress between *Freeman's* and a short-lived 'official' Catholic paper, the *Express*. In a letter to his father after its launch in January 1880, Vaughan said he had started a paper 'of my own in which I salt and pepper (red pepper) my opponents more freely than if I had to put my name'.[31] According to a story told later in *Freeman's*, Vaughan mentioned to Dalley that he objected to the established Catholic paper because it was 'too Irish and supported Home Rule'.

> His Grace...somehow got the idea that W.B.D. was a Tory of the English Cawtholic type... Not being under any bond of secrecy, and indignant at the attempt to undermine the journal that for thirty years had done all the fighting for Catholics and Irishmen in New South Wales, Dalley lost no time in communicating what Dr Vaughan had said to the Freeman office. Oddly enough, the Very Rev. Dr Gillet (the Archbishop's private secretary) called at the Freeman office a day or two after with a message from the Archbishop. 'His Grace,' said Dr Gillet, 'asked me to call in a friendly way to assure you that he has the kindliest feeling towards the Freeman.' Editor Butler smiled.[32]

Dalley was clearly the author of a *Freeman's* article in October 1881 contrasting its political outlook 'of moderation, of friendliness, and of patriotism' with the *Express*'s 'extravagance, hostility, and folly'.[33] The sniping escalated early the following year after an *Express* article gave credence to the 'Donation of Constantine', a document purportedly granting the Pope temporal dominion over the Western Roman Empire but long accepted to be a forgery.

W.A. Duncan, the pioneer Catholic newspaper editor (chapter 11), recog-nised as an authority on church history, exposed the error in *Freeman's*. The *Express* responded by admitting it had probably been wrong but then lashed out at its competitor for, among other things, 'attacking the Catholic Religion and its teachers', 'posing before the public as a bad copy of the lowest Orange organ', and ingratitude. 'The thought,' it observed, 'that we have been hitherto warming a changeling in our bosom, which after feeding upon us turns round and stabs us, is not a pleasant one.'

Dalley had his say in the next *Freeman's*. He derided the notion that the paper that for so long had 'upheld as far as a Catholic journal could the interests of religion in this colony' had 'derived warmth and nourishment from the bosom of the *Express*'. Rather, the *Express* had been established 'as a protest against our existence' and sought 'nothing short of our suppression'. He accused the new paper of 'insulting the first Catholic scholar of Australia' – a reference to Duncan that must have stung the scholarly Vaughan. Even more provocatively, he accused the *Express* of 'a cautious and cowardly silence' in the face of base and persistent slanders directed against Bishop James O'Quinn of Brisbane, who died in August 1881.[34] Vaughan had been engaged for years in surreptitious efforts to discredit O'Quinn, and the Irish bishops of country New South Wales, in the eyes of the Vatican.[35]

The first meeting in the new cathedral, in October 1881, seems to have been the last occasion on which Dalley and Vaughan appeared in public together. Apparently confirming a breakdown in their relations, Dalley is not mentioned in reports of fund-raising for a testimonial to mark the archbishop's departure on a reporting visit to Rome in April 1883, or of the ceremonial farewell. Vaughan died of a heart condition, at the age of 49, in England the following August. It seems Dalley regretted the rift; he is reported to have said later of the erudite and imposing English prelate that he was 'an ascetic at home, but a Prince of the Church abroad, and nobody understood him'.[36]

Dalley reappeared in the Central Criminal Court in February 1882. After failing to win an acquittal in a high-profile forgery case, he represented a disgraced former minister in the Parkes/Robertson government, Ezekiel Baker, and two others on trial for conspiracy. The three were trustees of the Milburn Creek mining company, which developed a copper deposit near Carcoar in the mid-1870s. Title to the land was disputed, and after the Supreme Court ruled against the company in 1877 the trustees successfully sought compensation from the government. A subsequent inquiry upheld claims that Baker, now Minister for Mines, and the others had fraudulently appropriated a large part of the compensation. Baker was then expelled from parliament.

Dalley's address to the jury rejecting the charge that the three had conspired to defraud the company's shareholders was long (it filled five columns of the *Herald*) and closely argued. He said their labours for the company fully justified the payments they had received, there had been no attempt at concealment, and no shareholder had complained of the way the compensation was distributed. He sought to appeal only to 'reason and justice', he told the jurors, having 'condescended to no arts to snatch a verdict from their compassion'. They failed to agree on a verdict, and the case was dropped. Parliament rescinded its censure of Baker in 1883 and he was re-elected the following year.[37]

At the end of February Dalley spoke at a meeting in Manly to raise funds for the village's Catholic priest; he mentioned that he was shortly to 'terminate his visit' to this 'beautiful place', a reference to the family's impending move to Sutton Forest.[38] His next major engagement was as the much-cheered chairman and main speaker at a memorable St Patrick's Day banquet at the Town Hall.

Dalley's toast to the Queen was unconventional, praising her as the first monarch for centuries to confer an honour on a Jew and for the 'immense expansion of the principle of religious liberty' that had occurred during her reign. His major speech, proposing the toast to 'the day we celebrate', also broke with tradition, not offering the usual praise for Irishmen who, despite their country's trials, had risen to posts of distinction. More deserving of honour, he said, was the

> sad yet...majestic procession of men of genius vibrating with the noble indignation which springs from a holy patriotism and a deep-seated consciousness of cruelty triumphant, liberty pierced and prostrate, suffering unavenged, and the world indifferent. They pass before your eyes bearing with them every title to the admiration, the reverence, the love, and the astonishment of mankind – the tenderness of poetry – the supremacy of golden eloquence – the rarest gifts of imagination – the magical touches of unrivalled humour, and greater and holier than all, the consecration of the soul which flows from a spirit of perfect sacrifice.

This set the scene for his eulogy to Daniel Deniehy, which was greeted with 'a perfect storm of applause'. None had surpassed Deniehy's love of Ireland, said Dalley, and he 'might have easily occupied the highest places among the most gifted and honoured of modern Irishmen'. But, unhappily, 'the poverty of his fortune' meant only the colony, 'a stage altogether unworthy of his power', had witnessed his genius, and he had left behind nobody 'who could presume even to measure the proportions of his intellect'.

Dalley said it had been his 'inestimable privilege' to enjoy for years Deniehy's intimate friendship, to hang for hours 'upon the music' of his speech.

> I ask Irishmen, from a sense of gratitude for his tenderness to their country, and Australians from a proud remembrance that he was their countryman, to cherish the memory today and forever of incomparably the most gifted Irish-Australian of our history – Daniel Henry Deniehy. (Long and continued cheering.) If on such occasions as this you honour and cherish such noble memories, you build up by your tenderness the most enduring monument, you preserve fresh for your children the finest examples of culture and devotion, you soften the asperities of life, you discourage imposture 'in the corrupted currents of this world' – (hear, hear) – and you do your best to refine, to elevate, and to purify society.[39]

In early May, Dalley chaired a dinner at the Athenaeum Club for Archibald Forbes, an English war correspondent who had reported conflicts in Europe, Afghanistan, Burma and South Africa. 'Free peoples' demanded the fullest and earliest information about wars their countries were engaged in, he told the gathering, and Forbes was one of the most fearless and honoured of the 'cavaliers of the Press' who provided it. He added – in a comment first borne out just three years later with his despatch of the Sudan contingent – that Australians, though far from the fields of contention, could not expect to continue immune from involvement in war.

> [As] our prosperity increases and we are bound more and more closely day by day to the glorious empire to which we owe our foundation, our literature, our refinement, our very existence – (loud cheers) – we incur graver responsibilities, and should be prepared to play our part in cooperating with her alike for the protection of our own homes, and the jealous guardianship of her vast imperial glory. (Cheers.)[40]

Letters from Dalley show the family moved to 'Rockmoor', Sutton Forest, before the Forbes dinner. He wrote to George Ranken, a former Queensland pastoralist who had settled in Sydney, in April praising a story he had written about outback life.[41] A letter to Jacob Clarke, a

Sydney publisher of music and seller of books and fine art, in early May thanked him for a consignment of little pictures that were 'much admired by the small art critics for whose delight they were got'.[42] Dalley remained out of the public eye for nearly three months, until the sad death at the age of 43 of Henry Kendall on 1 August.

A telegram from Kendall's wife Charlotte to 'Rockmoor' on Saturday 29 July brought the news that her husband was gravely ill and would like to see Dalley.[43] He travelled to Sydney to visit the poet the following Monday, the day before his death. Dalley told Alexander Oliver later that Kendall had been concerned that his memory be protected. He did not mind how posterity regarded his poetry, but wanted his friend to 'try and prevent the cruel and the malignant from staining his poor life, to the dishonour of his little ones'.[44]

Dalley wasted no time in writing a lengthy tribute to Kendall for the *Mail*. Completed two days after he died, this contrasted the troubled poet with the 'comfortable, prosperous, eminently respectable people who have happily been saved from the agonising sensibilities of genius'. Like the opium-dependent Samuel Taylor Coleridge, whose 'sanctity' was 'as genuine as his genius', he had experienced 'the curse' of a 'dominating imaginative faculty'. He was a modest man, conscious that he had not achieved his poetic aspirations. But he had made his mark; there was not a home in the colony, however humble or distant, that 'some of his pieces have not reached and brightened'.[45]

A more considered piece appeared in the December issue of the *Sydney University Review*. That 'the sweet singer who left us…so quickly and so sadly' had been 'so lovingly lamented' was an auspicious sign for 'our dawning national life', Dalley wrote. While the colony's 'material environment' was 'in almost necessary antagonism to the world of imagination', Kendall had 'softened sympathetic hearts with his sweet and melancholy confidences'. He was not one 'to whom was entrusted the message of joy – to sing of summer in full-throated ease'. But his work would continue to be read admiringly by those whose lives had been 'touched and tempered by a fine natural pity, by sorrow or disappointment'.[46]

19
He's back

Dalley visited Sydney three weeks after Kendall's death to chair a public meeting at the School of Arts to raise funds for his widow Charlotte and the children. A good crowd turned out to hear speeches by Professor Badham and two future Prime Ministers of Australia, Edmund Barton and George Reid, as well as Dalley. 'Our work is a very humble but a sacred one,' said Dalley. 'It is to provide for the human necessities of some who have a two-fold title to our affectionate compassion and interest – their utter helplessness, and their kinship with a man to whose genius we confess our obligations.'[1]

The response was disappointing. Only about £100 was collected at this meeting and the final total, after a series of fund-raising events, just exceeded £1,000. Extra help came in the form of a temporary free place for Kendall's eldest son, Frederick, at the King's School, Parramatta, and a government job that Dalley procured for Charlotte.[2]

Dalley wrote to her in July 1885 saying he had had the pleasure of seeing both Frederick and a good report from his school, and remarking on the 14-year-old's 'marvellous likeness to his poor dear father'.[3] When, around this time, King's began requiring its £52 a year fee for Frederick's schooling, Dalley and others chipped in to pay it. He advised Charlotte in September 1886 to impress upon her son 'the necessity of renewed exertions so that he may be enabled to be a prize taker at the end of the year.' Frederick rose to the challenge, winning a scholarship to the university in 1888.[4] But he did not take it up; it seems his inclinations were more practical than of the mind. With a reference from Dalley, who recommended obtaining another from 'dear old Sir John Robertson', he found employment in the engineering department of the government works office.[5]

At the end of September 1882 Dalley wrote to the dealer Jacob Clarke asking for some small framed photographs or chromolithographs, to the value of £5, for the walls of a room just built at 'Rockmoor' for his two- and seven-year-old daughters.[6] This suggests he had not yet contemplated returning to Sydney and a more active public life. Indulging his literary interests, he wrote a long, emotional review of a new book about the essayist and critic Charles Lamb for the *Sydney University Review* around this time. 'I think I know more of Charles Lamb than Mr Alfred Ainger [the book's author] does, though he has done his work very conscientiously,' Dalley told the editor, Alexander Oliver, in his letter offering a contribution. 'But if after this Parkesian egotism you perhaps, justly enough, infer that so self-satisfied a gentleman will be hardly a suitable reviewer, I shall take up any other subject…'[7] Oliver gave him the go-ahead to write about Lamb, whom he described as a man of 'saintly sweetness and compassion – loving the abject, the neglected, and all held in the world's contempt'.[8]

What persuaded Dalley to end his semi-exile in the country shortly afterwards is unclear. Possibly a gushing open letter to him in *Freeman's* in mid-October had an effect. This praised, among other things, his 'copious eloquence ever kept in subordination to close reasoning' and his 'so delicate, so manly' patronage of Australian men of letters. On the other side of the ledger, his 'habits of self-seclusion' had disappointed his admirers, who regarded his 'evident dislike to Parliamentary life' as a fault.[9]

A visit to Sydney at the end of October was probably the decisive event. Dalley was among the speakers – others included Parkes and Robertson – at a public meeting to begin fundraising for a monument to Rev. John Dunmore Lang (the statue, at Wynyard Square, was unveiled in 1891). He praised Lang's 'unceasing, untiring exertion' and his many contributions 'so lavishly and unselfishly' made to 'the civilisation which we enjoy'. Earlier in the day his political friend William Forster, a man he had come to admire greatly, died at the age of 64. Dalley described Forster in *Freeman's* as 'the boldest, frankest, least selfish, and most

Alexander Stuart.

honourable man who has taken part in our public life'. His indifference to the distinctions and rewards of office 'would have been comprehensible in one who regarded public employment as irksome and disagreeable'. But in his case it was the product of a 'lofty ideal of public duty'.[10]

Dalley's words contain at least a hint of self-criticism for his retreat from public life. Encouraging thoughts of a return, the days of the Parkes/Robertson government appeared numbered. And he was a friend and admirer of 58-year-old Alexander Stuart, the Scottish-born businessman turned politician who now led the opposition. Like Dalley, Stuart was a close friend of Sir John Robertson. However, he thought Robertson's land laws needed a drastic overhaul to, among other things, calm the growing tension between squatters and selectors. When Robertson introduced a bill in October to consolidate the existing law and deal with abuses, Stuart argued persuasively that more fundamental change was needed. Robertson's bill was defeated in the Assembly at the second reading in mid-November, and new elections called.

Back at 'Bay View', Manly, Dalley wrote a very friendly letter to Stuart – beginning 'My Dear Old Boy' – just before the vote on the land bill. He praised his speech on the bill and, foreshadowing a change of government, added, 'of course you are prepared for the consequences.' He expected to see Stuart 'many times before you are called upon to ship your crew and sign articles'. He wished he could take a bunk on the vessel, 'but the voyage is too long for me. I can give you all I have to give by advice and my prayers'.[11] It seems that Stuart had already sounded Dalley out about joining him in government.

Dalley appears to have taken little part in the election campaign, perhaps because of renewed illness. He had to miss, 'much to his regret', a lecture on Dante given by Professor Badham on 25 November in aid of the Kendall fund.[12] However, a piece in *Freeman's* celebrating the defeat a few days later of Parkes, 'the old mystery-monger', at East Sydney (he was subsequently elected for Tenterfield) looks very much like his work.[13] One of those elected for East Sydney, a fiery Catholic supporter of Stuart, John McElhone, credited Dalley with writing 'every word' of his address to the electors of Upper Hunter, where he was also returned.[14] The elections were a resounding success for Stuart; three ministers, besides Parkes, were defeated.

In December, Dalley bought the Manly property on which he was to build his 'castle', chaired a second talk by Badham on Dante, and prepared an erudite and lively lecture on the political philosopher and orator Edmund Burke. Hundreds crowded into Sydney's School of Arts hall four days after Christmas for this event, which was also in aid of the Kendall fund. Only Dalley could have brought out such numbers on a hot summer night, wrote an admiring commentator, 'Hawkeye', in the *Mail*. His position as a public man was 'as unique as it is certainly enviable'. While others might be admired or respected, he was 'both that and loved'.

Badham chaired the meeting; seeing him with Dalley offered a glimpse of a friendship of 'two rare congenial natures', 'Hawkeye' went on. When Dalley rose to speak, the audience 'rejoiced to see the merry face as beaming, the blue Irish eyes as bright, and to hear the well-known voice after the first few sentences as clear almost and resonant as of old.'

Dalley traversed notable events in Burke's life, and spoke of his 'heart passionate for freedom, justice and beneficence'. He said one could not study 'his lofty and kindly genius without feeling refreshed and strengthened both for the real work of social life and the discharge of public duty.' This provided the cue for Stuart, who moved the vote of thanks at the end of the talk. He hoped Dalley would 'recognise in his hero of tonight a powerful voice calling upon him to follow in his footsteps' and take the place in public life 'for which his great talents so eminently fit him.' Stuart added,

> Methinks that, if the eighty years which have gone by since Edmund Burke passed away could unroll themselves, and the great orator appear upon this platform tonight, he would be heard and seen pointing the way, and urging his able panegyrist to devote himself, even though the personal sacrifice might be great, to the upholding in this great country of the purity and honour of parliamentary life, and the consecrating of all the powers of his mind to saving it from the degradation which, alas! there are on all sides too many influences at work in effecting.[15]

Presumably Dalley was already contemplating joining Stuart in government. Parkes and his ministers resigned soon after parliament reassembled on 3 January 1883 and Stuart took office two days later. Dalley, reappointed to the Legislative Council, was the new Attorney-General and government representative in the upper house. At the opening of parliament on 17 January, 'Hawkeye' observed 80-year-old Sir Alfred Stephen and Dalley together; Stephen, with a red ribbon in his buttonhole, was 'the youngest-looking man in the room' and Dalley, sporting a red rose, 'the happiest'.[16]

Three days later, Dalley appeared at a re-election meeting for the new Minister for Works, Henry Copeland, a mining entrepreneur from Yorkshire. According to 'Hawkeye', when he entered the hall 'the vast crowd rose as one man, and ringing cheer upon cheer testified to the hold their old representative and champion in many a battle still has on their hearts, and their delight at seeing him once more in the van.'

He did not let them down, provoking much laughter during the amusing start to his talk and then prolonged cheering as he delivered his serious message. This was that Copeland's opponent, Dr Arthur Renwick, Mines Minister in the previous government, had behaved scandalously in stating that he and his then colleagues, except Robertson, had never really supported the land bill that the general election was fought over. Renwick had covered 'his colleagues with dishonour, and himself with infamy', Dalley declared. And he did not believe him, because

> I cannot and I will not believe that my friend Sir John Robertson would have been a party to such a proceeding. He is a courageous, outspoken,

generous man. (Cheers.) He has true Parliamentary instincts. He has a right conception of public duty. This question is the question of his life. His place in history is fixed by it forever. I am asked to believe that he knowingly and falsely came down to Parliament with a bill which he knew his colleagues held in abhorrence and would be glad to see mutilated by Parliament. I refuse to believe it. (Cheers.) For this would have been a piece of unworthy conduct, to which his life itself gives the lie.

Renwick's supporters ran a vicious campaign, claiming Copeland wanted to flood the colony with Chinese and distributing 'large pictorial placards' showing him welcoming the arrival of thousands. It seems Dalley's speech had a larger impact; Copeland won more than twice as many votes as his opponent.[17]

However, Copeland's career in the Stuart government was brief. Eight weeks after his re-election he responded to the toast to the ministry at Sydney's St Patrick's Day dinner. Unfortunately he made a drunken fool of himself and rambled on in the face of calls to sit down, even failing to take the hint when the band struck up. Dalley, who was not there, reportedly was incensed, declaring that if Copeland did not resign he would. The minister departed, but not gracefully, blaming the press for his downfall.[18]

As he did as Robertson's Attorney-General in the 1870s, Dalley threw himself into the job. His first major task was securing enactment of the Criminal Law Amendment Bill, Sir Alfred Stephen's great work of legal consolidation first put to parliament in 1872 (chapter 15). In his second reading speech in the Legislative Council on 25 January he urged that it be passed as quickly as possible. Every clause had been considered carefully over the years and delay could result in political exigencies again preventing its passage. All credit for 'the care, the labour, and the learning' that had gone into it belonged to Sir Alfred, he said, and no measure was 'more sorely needed'.[19]

Debate on the bill's clauses in committee proceeded quickly. A proposed amendment permitting people without legal qualifications to appear for defendants in country courts was withdrawn after Dalley warned against letting 'bush lawyers' loose. Provisions allowing whipping as a punishment for 'larrikin' behaviour prompted an emotional debate. Boys aged from 10 to 13 could face up to 18 lashes, and youths up to 20, for offences including assault, indecent exposure, vandalism and cruelty to animals. Did this signal a return to the floggings of the convict era, wondered 77-year-old Edward Flood, who recalled seeing 'a man flogged at a cart's tail from George Street to the gaol, a distance of about half a mile, blood pouring down his back all the way'.

Dalley suggested a better comparison was with the corporal punishment that some of England's 'kind, impartial, noble, and forbearing' statesman had experienced at their public schools. 'I would never countenance any kind of cruelty to any human being,' he said, but something had to be done to stop larrikins recklessly setting 'public law and public decency at defiance'. He felt strongly on the issue, at one point asking Flood whether,

> when those brutal youngsters who during the time of the persecution of the Chinese here treated those unfortunate wretches with every kind of cruelty, he would not gladly have had them dragged up and punished with the utmost severity for their brutal conduct towards inoffensive creatures who were not even able to speak our language? I myself on Christmas morning saw two of those ruffians brutally ill-treating a Chinaman, and I felt the strongest indignation that any human being should be subjected to such treatment. I felt how fortunate it would be for the vindication of our humanity before the civilised world if we could have the offenders dragged up and flogged much more severely than this clause would allow us to flog them.

Dalley made two concessions, agreeing that whipping was not appropriate for boys and youths convicted of disturbing a 'lawful assemblage' by yelling, hooting or other offensive conduct, or behaving in a riotous or disorderly manner in a public place.[20] The Council sent the bill, with minimal amendments, to the Legislative Assembly on 7 February. More amendments were made there, including changes to the larrikin provisions that effectively ruled out whipping as a punishment.[21]

Some of the Assembly's habitual obstructionists did their best to block the bill. Cleverest was Adolphus George Taylor, a feisty 25-year-old journalist who, as debate on the bill drew to a close, claimed it was a 'money bill' because one of its clauses provided for payment of expenses to witnesses. Under the constitution, money bills could not originate, as this bill had done, in the upper house. So if it were one, it must lapse.

The Chairman of Committees, Angus Cameron, thought Taylor's point valid, which meant a ruling was required from the Speaker, Edmund Barton. In the meantime, Stuart sought an opinion from Dalley, who advised – sceptics said predictably – that the bill was not caught under the constitutional provision because any payments to witnesses would have to be specifically provided for in an appropriation Act. At this point Parkes, probably even more predictably, joined the fray in support of Taylor. He claimed that by requesting an opinion from the Attorney-General on the rights of the Legislative Assembly the ministry had perpetrated 'an unprecedented scandal in parliamentary government'. Dalley held, by contrast, that the Attorney-General had 'the undoubted right…to give any opinion, which his colleagues invite him to give, on any question of public importance on which they desire to have his advice.'

Barton's opinion on the constitutional issue coincided with Dalley's, allowing the bill to proceed to its third reading in the Assembly on 11 April. In the Council, members accepted the argument of both Dalley and Stephen that, while some of the Assembly's amendments were imperfect, they should be accepted so the bill could pass without further delay.[22] It did so on 17 April and 'this great legal reform', as Dalley described it, took effect nine days later.[23]

Passage of the Inscribed Stock Bill in March was a less notable achievement, but won Dalley much praise as a parliamentary performer. Intended to improve management of the colony's debt by allowing the government to convert debentures into registered securities, the bill passed easily through the Assembly but ran into stiff opposition in the Council. Dalley demonstrated a mastery of the topic – which he said he had 'spared no labour' in acquiring 'though the task is foreign to my tastes and employments' – and prevailed after days of often-heated debate.[24] He presented 'such a front to his antagonist as to destroy every barrier erected against him', commented the Treasurer, George Dibbs.[25] Praising Dalley at a banquet a year after the event, the future Chief Justice Frederick Darley said there was no subject, however uninteresting, that he did not 'throw a glamour over. We all remember that Inscribed Stock Bill. (Hear, hear.)'[26]

The parliamentary session, which ran until the beginning of May, was unusually productive. One bill that passed quickly sought to deal with a major new concern, the rabbit plague that was threatening the wool industry by destroying sheep pasture. After a release near Geelong in 1859, 'wild-type' rabbits had multiplied and spread at a dramatic rate, and crossed the Murray River into New South Wales in the late 1870s. Arguing for the proposed new control measures, Dalley told the Legislative Council in March that more than a fifth of the colony was already infested. 'It is evident,' he said, 'that our staple industry is in danger of being destroyed by this pest. I could hardly have conceived the possibility of such a state of things.' The new law provided for the appointment of inspectors charged with destroying rabbits or ordering their destruction. Funds raised by a levy would reimburse landholders for control work they undertook.[27]

Dalley had been a proponent of introducing animals and plants from the 'old world', joining Sydney's Acclimatisation Society in 1864 and supporting the cause in *Freeman's Journal*. 'It is hardly possible,' he wrote in May 1865, 'to conceive a nobler employment than that of multiplying the forms and varieties of animal life, and introducing into vast and untilled wastes those plants which in other and not so highly favoured countries have furnished food to millions.'[28] Two decades on, he knew better. He proposed in April 1885, when it was clear the new measures were having little effect on rabbit populations, that the colonies jointly offer a large reward to 'the discoverer of any method of extermination which will be effective, and at the same time innoxious'. New South Wales was prepared to put up £10,000, but Victoria rejected the idea.[29]

Three bills that passed with little opposition in April implemented Dalley's long-held desire to increase the salaries and pensions of the colony's judges (chapters 13 and 14). While 'no advocate of a lavish expenditure of public money for any purpose', he thought it ridiculous that judges earned far less than the barristers practising in their courts. Chief Justice Martin's salary, to rise from £2,600 to £3,500, was 'absurdly inadequate'. His speech supporting increased pensions for retired judges included a long and glowing account of Sir Alfred Stephen's contributions to construction of the colony's laws over more than 40 years, culminating in the Criminal Law Amendment Act.[30]

Another important piece of legislation sought to clarify and remove anomalies from the colony's liquor licensing regime. Comments by Dalley during the Legislative Council debate provide some interesting insights into his view of the world. Teetotalism was 'about the most despicable type of fanaticism', he said. He favoured licensed railway refreshment rooms; long journeys necessitated, 'if anything can do so, support by means of spirits'. He was not worried that ready availability of liquor might lead to more railway accidents: 'In approaching a dangerous part of a line an engine-driver is so habitually careful that even if partially intoxicated his vigilance in approaching those dangerous parts would be exercised.'[31]

Dalley described the United States as 'the greatest of English-speaking communities' in a speech in April commending a recently arranged faster postal link with San Francisco. Its 60 million people had 'been cradled in our literature, shared the glory of the noblest parts of our history [and] grown up under our laws', he said. 'Our sympathies of race, literature, and kinship of institutions must necessarily be deeper and wider than with any other people in the world.'[32]

Another matter he addressed in April was the carvings, not yet complete, decorating the Pitt Street frontage of Sydney's new General Post Office. These works by an Italian sculptor, Tommaso Sani, were intended to portray arts, sciences and customs of the day. Instead, they disfigured a fine building and 'make us a laughing-stock of other countries', complained the barrister Frederick Darley. A 'gross caricature of some judge' represented the law, he said, and a postman handing

Two of the offending carvings: the postal scene with 'simpering barmaid' on the right.

a packet 'to what appears to be a simpering barmaid' depicted postal communication.

Dalley was inclined to agree, but said it was not the Council's job 'to constitute itself a committee of the beautiful and the aesthetic'. He undertook to have the carvings examined by people competent to judge.[33] The three selected, two trustees of the colony's National Gallery and the architect of St Mary's Cathedral, William Wardell, pronounced the carvings unsuitable, but nothing was done. When Darley raised the matter again three years later, Dalley offered the view that they conveyed 'the lowest possible idea of our taste'.[34] By a narrow majority the Council decided not to advise their removal, and they are still there.

Less than four weeks after parliament was prorogued on 2 May, members were recalled, on Dalley's advice, for a special session to cancel the effect of a Supreme Court decision. The court had ruled, after a fatal collision between a steam tram and a horse and cart in Elizabeth Street, that existing law did not allow steam-powered tramways. The potential consequences were drastic. Every day, nearly 18,000 people travelled on the trams, which linked the city with suburbs as far out as Coogee and Waverley. The system had developed rapidly since the first steam motors were imported three years earlier. Reversion to horse power was not practicable; as the *Mail* commented, it would result in Elizabeth Street, the heart of the network, being 'occupied by a force of cavalry'.[35]

The title of the bill introduced when members gathered on 29 May – 'A Bill to declare Legal the employment of Steam Motors on Tramways…' – stated its purpose succinctly. Speaking in the Legislative Council, Dalley said he wanted it distinctly understood that he would 'not attempt to argue against the judgment of the Supreme Court'. However, he implied that he thought the judges were wrong, saying nobody had doubted when the legislation establishing the system was debated in 1880 that steam was to be the motive power. Despite critical speeches by some members, including a 68-year-old who favoured a return to horse-drawn trams, the bill passed easily.[36] To 'have the law determined by the highest appellate tribunal', Dalley launched a Privy Council appeal against the Supreme Court ruling. News of its success reached Sydney in July 1884, prompting the *Mail* to comment, 'The outcome of the affair shows that the law of the Attorney-General was sounder than that of the Judges, and that is a matter of some consequence.'[37]

Dalley was nearly as busy outside parliament as inside. He was one of only five mourners at the funeral of Mary Deniehy, mother of Daniel, on 12 February.[38] In April he wrote a long article for the *Herald* in praise of Edward Broadhurst QC, one of the colony's earliest and most successful barristers, who had just died.[39] In June he gave the oration at the unveiling by the Governor, Lord Augustus Loftus, of the statue in Macquarie Place of Thomas Sutcliffe Mort, the wool marketing, marine engineering and refrigerated meat trade pioneer, who died in 1878. Mort was a speculator in 'schemes of gigantic benevolence', said Dalley. Always sympathising with those who 'laboured with and for him and for society', his democratic sympathies were shown in deeds, not speeches.[40]

Dalley spoke at a Trade Defence Association luncheon at Clontarf in February and at a picnic in May organised by the colony's Linnaean Society to honour its benefactor William Macleay.[41] In April he chaired the Athenaeum Club's first 'annual house dinner'. Proposing the toast to parliament, he joked that the Legislative Council was a paradise for reporters; 'our atmosphere is so deliciously tranquil…we almost invariably disperse at the dinner hours'. In his toast to the 'liberal professions', he described newspapers as guardians of liberties, providing 'protection alike from the dangers of intolerance and the insolence of faction'.[42]

Demonstrating his commitment to a free and forthright press, Dalley undertook the defence, with Darley, in a libel action against the *Herald* in June. The paper had published a lengthy exposé of a supposed training college for destitute boys, which showed the inmates were poorly treated and received no useful instruction. Government inspectors reached similar conclusions and removed the boys. Nevertheless, the institution's owner, George Anderson, claimed he had been libelled and sought £2,000 damages from the *Herald*'s proprietors, John Fairfax and Sons.

In an emotional two-hour address to the jury, Dalley praised the *Herald* for its careful reporting and the important public duty it had performed. He warned, amid quickly suppressed applause from the large crowd of spectators, that a guilty verdict would mean that in future no 'crying wrong' would be redressed because 'the only voice that can appeal to the public conscience' had been stifled. The judge, Sir George Innes, appointed to the Supreme Court by Parkes in 1881, saw things differently, advising the jurors that Anderson was entitled to damages if they found any of the *Herald*'s allegations unsubstantiated. They concluded that he had been libelled and awarded him £450.[43]

An unimpressed Dalley announced in July that he was examining possible changes to the law to discourage 'legal speculation' in the form of actions for libel against papers engaged only in 'the right duties of their office for the protection of the public'.[44] In a speech in August, he described producing 'a great newspaper' as among 'the highest public duties' a man could perform. 'His difficulties are greater than those of the statesman, his services to society not less…'[45]

Darley, for Fairfax, applied for a retrial of the Anderson case in August, on the ground, among others, that Justice Innes had misdirected the jury. Chief Justice Martin joined Innes in saying no, despite agreeing that the *Herald* had discharged a public duty and rendered a public service in publishing its report. The third judge who heard the application, Justice Faucett, favoured a new trial. Martin took the opportunity to condemn criticism of Innes's summing-up published in the *Herald* and its evening associate, the *Echo*, saying it probably amounted to contempt of court. With Faucett and Justice William Windeyer, also appointed to the court in 1881, he decided four weeks later that this was indeed the case, and fined Fairfax a further £250.[46]

Dalley responded when parliament met again in October by introducing a bill to amend the law of contempt. He cited the views of two leading English Law Lords to support his proposal that the Attorney-General, rather than the offended judges, be made responsible for initiating prosecutions against newspapers for contempt of court, and that juries, rather than the judges, determine guilt or innocence. He thought it a 'monstrous' anomaly that under the existing law 'the injured party not only summons and prosecutes but exclusively judges and punishes'.[47]

Sir Alfred Stephen opposed the changes, and as the second reading debate wore on it became clear that the Legislative Council would reject them despite strong support from Darley; it did so by 19 votes to 14. A large crowd gathered for Dalley's final plea for support. 'Never before, perhaps, was he in better form,' commented the *Mail*. 'With vehement expression and vigorous action, he was all that is expected in a great orator addressing himself to a great subject.' When he finished amid cheers, it was 'to the evident relief of his opponents', whose faces had revealed their 'agitation and anxiety' as he assailed their arguments.[48]

Dalley said he had accepted Fairfax's brief in the Anderson case reluctantly – he normally declined all professional engagements – but also with pride, believing that the *Herald* had performed 'one of the most valuable public services which men could undertake'. Much of his speech was a ringing rejection of the notion that, because the existing contempt regime had existed for a long time, it must be just. He described barbarities inflicted by England's old Court of Chancery on men, women and children accused of contempt, and said opponents of his bill had employed 'language which has in all ages been used to arrest reform…and to sanction every kind of brutal and cowardly wrong'. He accepted the blame if the government, in putting the bill forward, had erred in trusting 'too much to the character, the courage, the patriotism' of the Legislative Council: 'I thought I knew the temper of the House…'[49]

20
The 'Dining-out Administration'

Dalley's view of his fellow Legislative Councillors had been rosier when he accompanied Stuart on a meet-the-people tour south of Sydney in July. Most might have passed the prime of life, he told a banquet audience in Wollongong, but age should not be measured by years but by 'maturity of thought, freshness of interest in all human affairs, and survival of sympathy with good causes'. Judged by this test, they constituted 'as youthful, hopeful and courageous a branch of the Legislature as ever existed', he said.

> To me these noble old men always seem as the flowers at Llanthony did to Landor, and of which he said: 'They always meet one in the same place at the same season; and years have no more effect on their placid countenances than on so many of the most favoured gods.' (Cheers.)[1]

Stuart seems to have enjoyed himself as much as Dalley as the pair travelled from settlement to settlement, from one feast to the next. 'Hawkeye' of the *Mail* commented that the Premier, a normally sedate Scotchman, could have been mistaken for the 'most warm-blooded, rollicking' Irishman. 'As for the silver-tongued one himself, if delicious fun and fancy, sparkling wit, and the rarest eloquence grew wild in Illawarra air, he could hardly have been happier or his hearers have more 'revelled in sweets'.' He was 'at his very best, and a best of that kind is as seldom equalled, unhappily, as it is heard.'[2]

Dalley joined Stuart in spelling out the government's plans for the next parliamentary session, including land law reform, but the portions of his speeches greeted with most cheers extolled the beauty and agricultural richness of the region and the hospitality of their hosts. He joked at Kiama that he feared the impending arrival of the railway could result

Attorney-General Dalley, 1883.

in 'the thousands of gallons of pure milk and all the farmyard treasures of the district' being whisked away to Sydney. So instead of 'this plenteous board, these delicacies, this repose, this generous hospitality', visiting ministers might have to settle for 'flavourless and scalding tea, or boiling soup, or indigestible pastry' from a railway refreshment room.[3]

At their last lunch stop, Dalley observed that having just eaten 'abundantly' he and Stuart faced a banquet at Nowra in an hour and a half. There he intended visiting 'the most experienced chemist' to procure 'those mixtures which should form for several days the only needed and beneficial provision for a party stricken down by an unexampled visitation of hospitality. (Roars of laughter.)' He remarked at the banquet that 'it would be infinitely pleasanter, and perhaps safer' to 'stay with you' than return to Sydney and face their political foes. 'But they have to be met… with that courage which belongs to honest conviction, and with that courtesy which ought to disarm violence. (Cheers.)'[4]

But not yet. Dalley and some of his ministerial colleagues visited the Hunter district in August for more banquets and speeches. At West Maitland, he told an enthusiastic audience that the libel law needed to be changed to ensure newspapers could unmask 'public imposture' without facing ruinous damages.[5] He did not go on to attempt this reform, probably concluding after the defeat of his proposed changes to the law of contempt in November (chapter 19) that the cause was hopeless. An apparent change in judicial attitudes, which saw Fairfax acquitted of libel in September 1884 after another *Herald* exposé, may also have influenced him.[6]

Professor Badham.

Back in Sydney, he was one of 150 men, ranging from politicians and judges to young University of Sydney graduates, who attended a banquet at the Town Hall on 21 August to mark the 70th birthday of Professor Badham. 'There were twenty-two courses', the barrister Albert Piddington, then a newly graduated 20-year-old, recalled in his memoirs, 'and, with Dalley in the confidence of the caterers, the wines came on in orthodox order and profusion.'[7]

Proposing the toast to Badham, Dalley spoke of his 'buoyancy of nature, which we have been unable in sixteen years to impair' and his 'inordinate and utterly irrepressible ambition to cultivate us all'. He added that Badham's intimate friendship had been 'one of the choicest blessings' of his life. Badham responded with an eloquent plea for literary culture. 'Depend on it,' he said, 'if you want the young to learn all that is sacred in duty and all that is great in man, and how much happiness depends upon a little self-denial and self-restraint, you must make them study literature.' On his friendship with Dalley, he remarked that it had 'sweetened and aromatised my life from beginning to end'.[8]

Badham died the following February. Dalley accompanied Badham's sons in the funeral procession from the university to ferries waiting at Fort Macquarie, and stood with them at the head of the grave during the burial service at St Thomas's Church of England cemetery, North Sydney.[9] Piddington recorded that Dalley was 'visibly weighed down by ill-health' at the banquet, and at the funeral 'his sensitive face was refined into a more engaging humanity than that of the dashing man-about-town of his earlier photographs'; his appearance suggested a 'consciousness of approaching fate'.[10] If so, it seems he was determined to make the most of the time that remained.

The week after the Badham dinner he took the mail train south with Stuart and Dibbs for another meet-the-people visit. He joked at the banquet at Wagga Wagga that 'for some weeks we have entitled ourselves to be demerited (I make a present of the phrase to our opponents) as a dining-out Administration.' But ministers had been working very hard, and 'more than once I have felt myself so unequal to the strain upon my health and poor qualities, that I have suggested to [Stuart] the desirableness of letting me retire in peace'. Much of their effort had gone into ensuring that those with conflicting interests under the existing land law were dealt with justly – that the new arrangements would produce no 'victims'.

> The cannon ball kind of reform, to borrow the fine language of Schiller, which flies direct and rapid, shattering what it reaches, may recommend itself to the violent and unscrupulous; but this military vigour and directness have no part in political sagacity and justice, and we are neither sufficiently bold nor sufficiently unprincipled to attempt it. We may alienate some by our audacity, but we shall justify the desertion of no supporters by our injustice.

Dalley noted that his 'dear old friend' Sir John Robertson had rejected criticism by some that the government had been too slow in finalising its land legislation. Robertson was the one from whom, 'except on private and personal grounds', ministers were entitled to the least consideration because it was 'the policy of his life' that they were 'pledged to alter in material respects'. But he was 'a politician of rare generosity'.

> It is a distinction and a pleasure that we are about to meet, in the great battle soon to be fought, an enemy who will carry into the engagement valour and the skill of an old soldier, and the gallantry and grace of a gentleman. Next to the honour of defeating such a man is the consolation of being conquered by him, and, gentlemen, it is no small gain I think to the public life of this country that we enter upon the struggle now about to take place with such feelings as these towards each other. To impart a sentiment of chivalry to our public conduct is to discourage the men who trade upon mere vulgarities, to attract the sensitive and the high-minded, and to make the great prizes of public life the objects of the legitimate ambition of the best men of the community…[11]

Dalley's speech moved 'Hawkeye' to comment that 'if the 'dining-out Administration' does nothing else for the country, it will at least have done one great service in the admirable after-dinner, so to speak, course of lectures on the true spirit of public life and public men by its most distinguished member.'[12] At the next feast, a banquet in honour of the two representatives of the St Leonard's constituency, Treasurer Dibbs and Bernhardt Holtermann, much praise was offered to Dalley, and to Stuart for persuading him to re-enter public life. Stuart responded by recounting how he had recruited his 'dear friend'. On many occasions he had told him what a great loss it was to the country that he did not take 'the prominent position to which his brilliant talents and his rhetorical power entitled him'.

> And I remember him saying to me, 'My dear boy' – for he generally calls me so – (laughter, and hear, hear) – 'I will never go into public life except as your Attorney-General.' I think the words were spoken partly in jest, when the time he referred to was to him like the Greek Kalends, a very remote period which he little anticipated would arrive. But when the opportunity was afforded to me to recall to his mind the promise he had given me, even though it were in jest, I was enabled to press it home with double power upon him, and he did that which his chivalrous nature would under any circumstances prompt him to do, and he said, 'I cannot see you in a difficulty, if you think my services are of any use to you, I will place them at your command.' (Cheers.) I can only look with pleasure and pride, and the country looks I am sure with satisfaction, at this brilliant ornament to our Legislature. (Cheers.)

Speaking next, Dalley chose not to comment on Stuart's account and counselled caution in expectations of the government. 'Of our determination to do all that we are able and permitted to do, I am sure you entertain no doubt,' he said. 'Of our capacity to accomplish what we desire, I dare say there are some amongst us humble enough to regard ourselves with as little extravagant competence as our enemies feel in us.'

> I have always thought, gentlemen, that there was an affecting tenderness as well as a delicate humour in the prayer of that venerable minister of the Canongate, who invariably, previous to the meeting of the General Assembly, humbly implored Almighty God that the assembly might be so guided as 'no to do any harm.' And if we professed to have any recognised form of parliamentary devotion, I should strongly recommend the adoption of this beautiful little prayer…[13]

In the last week of September, Stuart, Dalley and three more ministers visited Newcastle for, as the *Freeman's* columnist 'The Flaneur' described it, the final performance by 'the Stuart Comedy Company...of that most successful farce entitled the "Dining-out Administration".' Dalley spoke again on the vital role of the press, and took the opportunity to scotch a report that he was to be made a baronet, 'by means of what was called a "confidential despatch," and an address signed by distinguished citizens.' He said he had no ambition 'for the kind of distinctions which have been somewhat indiscriminately conferred of late', and 'could not accept such distinctions under any conceivable circumstance'. His only ambition was to be 'a humble member of the community, giving whatever poor service I can offer to my country, and feeling abundantly rewarded by the only honour which I hope to carry to the grave – the love of my countrymen. (Prolonged cheering.)'[14]

Two more engagements remained before parliament resumed on 9 October. First was Sydney's Eight-Hour Day banquet on 1 October, at which Dalley was the main speaker. A working man, he said, should not 'be daily withdrawn for too long' from his home, should return 'not depressed and exhausted by excessive hours of labour', and should have the time and means to, if he wished, 'enlarge his knowledge, to exercise and strengthen his faculties, to find a new delight in human life, and by degrees to fit himself for higher duties and more responsible employments'.[15] A 'parliamentary picnic' in the National Park south of Sydney (now the Royal National Park), established four years earlier by Robertson, occupied the following weekend. This was Dalley's idea – a far cry from the usual banquet for government supporters held in the parliamentary refreshment room on the eve of the resumption.

All members of both houses were invited and about 45 came despite inclement weather. They included some opposition supporters, most notably Robertson. Marquees had been erected to supplement the facilities of the park's 'permanent encampment'. Proceedings began on the Saturday morning with a boat trip six miles up Port Hacking River, followed by a dinner that seems to have occupied most of the afternoon.

Dalley began the speechmaking with a toast to 'our old and dear friend' Robertson. He likened the picnic to an occasion, described by Thackeray, when during the reign of Queen Anne the soldiers of 'two great rival armies came down to the little stream which divided their picuets and exchanged their brandy flasks and their tobacco pouches on the evening before they were to meet in bloody battle'. Replying with a toast to 'our hosts', Robertson described Stuart and Dalley as his 'old and faithful friends…friends of my lifetime – of their lifetime is the proper way to put it, for I knew Mr Dalley when he was a boy. I am glad to drink their health.'

Many speeches followed. Then, according to the *Herald*'s reporter, the evening passed quickly with card playing, singing and recitations, and in some cases 'a quiet weed and a chat'. The next morning's pre-breakfast activities included swimming and rifle shooting at suspended bottles. After another trip up the river, and return in a downpour, proceedings ended with luncheon and a sentimental speech by Dalley. 'I devoutly and fervently wish that we could keep you here,' he said.

> You may rely on it that this is the very spot where the great question that we are about to try and settle could be viewed with more fullness, discussed with more friendliness, and decided with more justice and public advantage than anywhere else in the whole world… Gentlemen, we shall do something towards it if we carry away from this place, and into the debate, the spirit that for the last two days has prevailed amongst us here. (Cheers.)[16]

The often-bitter parliamentary consideration of the government's Crown Lands Bill, which began the following week and dragged on for a year, belied that hope. The bill was 'exceedingly comprehensive', commented the *Mail*, and the job of preparing it must have been 'herculean', as would be the task of examining it thoroughly.[17] Stuart had foreshadowed important features – including giving pastoral leaseholders security of tenure on half of their runs while the other half remained open for selection – before he took government. A controversial report commissioned from George Ranken, a former pastoralist, writer (chapter 18) and long-time critic of the old land laws, and Augustus Morris, a pastoralist, on the state of the public lands provided data that assisted the drafting process. Ranken and Morris damned the existing system, claiming its faults included opening 'a door for the entrance of every phase of abuse and fraud'.

The second reading debate in the Assembly began on 7 November with a speech of nearly five hours by the Lands Minister, former Premier James Farnell. It concluded five weeks later with an overwhelming vote in favour – 76 to 16. However, in a sign of things to come, the bill's opponents managed to drag the final sitting out to an eye-glazing 36 hours. Fearing that it might continue through a second night, Treasurer Dibbs arranged for bedding from the government stores to be placed in the Legislative Council chamber for the benefit of exhausted Assembly members. In response to strident complaints from some Legislative Councillors, Dalley joked that 'it is something complimentary to the sweet peacefulness and tranquillity of this Chamber that it should have been selected as a place of calm and repose by spirits who are popularly supposed not to appreciate these enjoyments too highly'. But he assured them the episode would not be repeated.[18]

The Legislative Council's main business in the last months of 1883 was Dalley's failed contempt of court bill (chapter 19); because of the drawn-out discussion in committee in the Assembly, the lands bill would not reach the upper house until August 1884. Dalley's first major speech of the session was a long and often amusing response to criticism of the government's financial management.[19] He was in even better form than in the previous session, commented 'The Flaneur' of *Freeman's*.[20] But there was no denying that drought and a bigger than expected reduction in revenue from land sales had begun to erode the government's healthy budgetary position. As government leader in the Council, Dalley also presented the case successfully for legislation to coordinate Sydney's fire brigades and, with a feisty attack on the government's critics, secured passage of a supply bill.[21]

Dalley the humorist was on display at a dinner held at Manly in late October for the directors of the Port Jackson Steamboat Company, which had upgraded its ferry service to the growing settlement. Proposing the toast to 'Our Village', he extolled Manly as a place of weekend refreshment for 'the toiling masses' from 'the crowded thoroughfares of the city and suburbs' and as a restorative for people of 'the interior' during 'the most oppressive season of the year'. Then, probably with tongue not entirely in cheek, he took the opposite tack to earlier speakers who had looked forward to the progress that faster and more frequent ferries and an envisaged tram service would bring. 'You are aware that, in the festivities of older times, there was always an element introduced to qualify excessive complacency and to repress a too great exuberance of self-satisfaction,' he said.

> The death's head at an Egyptian banquet was a wise institution to make men think when they were under the dominion of excessive happiness. (Laughter.) I know this in not an agreeable role to assume, but I feel compelled, however inconsistent it is with my former appearances at banquets, to appear in this character, as they say in the sensational playbills, for this night only. (Laughter and cheers.)

Further laughter greeted his prediction that the improved ferry connection would result in the 'influx of a large population', which would 'change the face of our simple life, invade and occupy all our lovely spots, disturb the repose which is one of the chief charms of life in this secluded spot, and alter our whole simple manner of living.' His call for those present to bind themselves together to resist 'such an oppression' as the proposed tramway brought 'roars of laughter'. He concluded by telling the story of an old man he had 'chanced to meet in one of the bays in our harbour' 10 years earlier. Born and raised in Sydney, this man had not returned to the city for more than 20 years. He told Dalley, 'I stopped in the place as long as I could, but when I found that they were going to cut up and build over the old Barrack-square, I thought it was time to get out of the place...'[22]

In November, Dalley was among those who greeted and entertained 36-year-old Lord Archibald Rosebery, who was on a tour of the colonies after resigning a Home Office ministry in Gladstone's government.

Unlike many British Liberals of the time, Rosebery was a committed imperialist. 'There is no need for any nation, however great, leaving the British Empire,' he declared in a speech in Adelaide in January 1884, 'because the British Empire is a commonwealth of nations.'[23] This is credited as the first use of the term British 'Commonwealth'.

Dalley was one of the party – others included Governor Loftus, Premier Stuart and Professor Badham – who accompanied Rosebery and his wife on an excursion by steam yacht up the Hawkesbury River at the end of November.[24] Two weeks later, he proposed the toast to 'the Imperial Legislature and Imperial Connection' at a dinner for Rosebery hosted by the Speaker, Edmund Barton. The British parliament was 'one of the great sheltering bulwarks of the world between civilisation and barbarism,' he proclaimed. As for the empire, the colonies, as participants in its glories, were ready to share its obligations.

Rosebery responded with a call for federation of the colonies, saying it would enable 'a fair and manly and frank communication of views between Australia and the mother country'. The 'broad voice of united Australia' would command more respect than 'the dispersed voice of different colonies, which may be supposed to represent their narrow interests and individual jealousies'. He predicted that the Intercolonial Convention, just held in Sydney, would come to be seen as a major event in Australia's history.[25]

Premiers or their equivalent of all the Australian colonies, New Zealand and Fiji, supported by senior ministers, spent 10 days discussing three issues – proposals for British annexation of eastern New Guinea and various Pacific islands, concerns about French convict settlements in the Pacific, and a limited federal arrangement. Queensland's unauthorised annexation of the half of New Guinea not claimed by the Dutch was the event that sparked the meeting; on the orders of the colony's Premier, Thomas McIlwraith, the police magistrate based at Thursday Island 'took possession' of the territory in the Queen's name on 4 April. McIlwraith had the strong support of the Premier of Victoria, James Service, who cabled London two months later urging British annexation of the rest of unclaimed Melanesia. In early July, soon after news arrived that Britain had repudiated Queensland's unilateral action, Service pushed resolutions through both houses of the Victorian parliament calling for the annexation of eastern New Guinea, the New Hebrides and the other islands between New Guinea and Fiji.[26]

New South Wales, despite being the colony with by far the largest trade with the Pacific islands, gave only lukewarm support to the annexation calls. Nevertheless, Service persuaded Stuart to host the convention; he chose Dalley and Dibbs as his fellow delegates.

Draft resolutions submitted by Service used strong language to demand action from Britain: it would be 'disastrous' if the islands fell into foreign hands, and the Imperial government should 'at once' annex them or at least establish protectorates to secure them from foreign occupation. Dalley's was a voice for moderation. Any representations to London should display an understanding of Britain's 'place amongst the nations' and avoid creating difficulties for her, he argued. Delegates should bear two questions in mind: what was absolutely essential to Australasian security and independence; and what, in the interests of humanity, might declarations of protectorates over the islands accomplish?

He thought England would decline to annex the islands for the mere purpose of holding them 'as fortresses against occupation by any foreign power'. And foreign powers, particularly those with interests in the islands, could not be expected to 'calmly regard and permit' the appropriation of 'such vast tracts' by a power that had no immediate plans for colonisation but claimed the land simply to prevent others appropriating it. If the islands were placed under British jurisdiction, the Australasian colonies would have to bear the cost, he predicted. Would they 'be prepared to undertake so indefinite and possibly so enormous an expenditure?'[27]

The resolutions eventually adopted began with a sweeping declaration that 'further acquisition of dominion in the Pacific, south of the equator, by any foreign power would be highly detrimental to the safety and wellbeing of the British possessions in Australasia, and injurious to the interests of the empire'. However, beyond calling for action to incorporate eastern New Guinea – and, if negotiations with France made it possible, the New Hebrides – into the empire, they offered no advice on how the foreigners should be kept out.

The British government was urged to use 'every means in its power' to stop France proceeding with plans to transport 'large numbers of relapsed criminals' to its possessions in the Pacific, an action that would be 'disastrous to the interests of Australasia and the Pacific islands'. And approval was given to a draft bill to set up a Federal Council of Australasia to deal, initially, with relations with the Pacific islands, preventing 'the influx of criminals' (reflecting concern about absconding French convicts), management of pearl and beche-de-mer fisheries, and extra-territorial legal issues. Colonies would be able to refer additional powers to it.

On receiving the resolutions, Britain's Secretary of State for the Colonies, Lord Derby, observed that some were 'mild enough'. But he ridiculed the proposal to keep foreign powers out of the south Pacific as equivalent to the 'Monroe doctrine' under which the United States in 1823 claimed a pre-eminent role in the Western Hemisphere. The notion that 'Australia cannot be secure if any other power is allowed to establish itself between the Australian coast and South America' was 'mere raving', he contended.[28]

This 'raving' apparently at least hastened Germany's decision, announced in December 1884, to annex northeastern New Guinea. Derby had concluded earlier in the year, after Bismark publicly rejected the Australasian 'Monroe doctrine', that the New Guinea question was urgent. The British government decided in August to declare a protectorate over the whole of the eastern half of the island, but a few days later, deferring to German objections, restricted the area claimed to the south-east.[29]

Dalley's refusal to join in the outcry that greeted the news of Germany's foothold in New Guinea brought him much criticism (chapter 22). However, his low-key assessment of the significance of the convention seems to have reflected the predominant view in New South Wales. Speaking in the Legislative Council the week before Christmas 1883 he said the New South Wales government would have preferred it were called a conference, and had agreed to take part only on the united urging of the other colonies.

Nevertheless, he considered a British presence in New Guinea vital, as foreign domination of Torres Strait could be disastrous in the event of a European war. And it would be impossible to exaggerate the dangers of the French proposal to crowd 'their worst class of criminals into the islands of the Pacific'. He claimed the New South Wales delegates had succeeded in their aim of securing moderately worded resolutions that would facilitate action by the imperial government while avoiding embarrassment with any foreign power.

On the federal issue, he had little doubt that Britain desired 'the complete confederation of these Australasian colonies', but was certain that, 'at the present moment', such a project would 'be entirely premature'. However, he strongly supported the proposed Federal Council and hoped the New South Wales parliament would take the 'wise, unselfish, patriotic' course of backing it. Whether or not it did, he believed 'the other Australasian colonies have quite made up their minds to take this first step towards federation'.[30]

In a major speech in July 1884, Dalley spoke approvingly of a proposal advanced without success by Parkes in 1881 for a federal body, with limited powers, that would pave the way to 'a complete federal organisation'.[31] The following October, after the lands legislation had finally passed, the New South Wales parliament considered the outcomes of the convention. Asking the Legislative Council to approve the resolutions on New Guinea, the French convicts and the Federal Council, Dalley noted the steps taken recently to establish a New Guinea protectorate and expressed confidence that British diplomacy would influence French penal policy favourably.

He revealed that New South Wales had refused to join Victoria in a new push for a British protectorate over 'all unappropriated islands in the Pacific'. Indeed, he believed there was 'not a little to be said against discouraging a foreign occupation of those islands'. The growth of colonies 'planted by French or German enterprise, and fostered and maintained by their governments', would benefit the Australian colonies commercially because they would be their principal suppliers. Also, the foreign colonisers would have to deploy naval and military forces to their new territories, which would help maintain peace. 'Why is England herself the power whose policy is pre-eminently one of peace,' he asked?

> Simply because she has interests everywhere which require her to divide her care and her resources in protecting those interests… Nations cannot pursue at the same time a great warlike and a great colonial policy.

On the Federal Council, he noted that all the other Australian colonies had already given their approval. He thought it would be 'deeply to be regretted' if New South Wales stood outside the inauguration of 'so great, so imposing, so essentially beneficial a union'.

> By its age, its resources, its history, it is entitled to the leading place in any movement of a national character. The opportunity is now afforded of its occupying that place. The first liberal statesmen of England are as anxious as the most patriotic colonists that this union of the colonies should be immediate and complete. They wish for it in the best interests of the colonies and of the mother country…[32]

The Legislative Council adopted the resolutions by thirteen votes to nine, but the Assembly, with many members absent, rejected them 22 to 21. The Federal Council, comprising two representatives of each participating self-governing colony and one each from the Crown colonies of Western Australia and Fiji, held its first meeting in Hobart in early 1886. It continued to meet, usually every second year, up to 1899, the eve of federation. New South Wales never joined.

21
The land war won

Dalley recovered sufficiently from another bout of illness at the start of 1884 to take his seat when the Legislative Council met again in mid-January.[1] A call by a pastoralist member, George Cox, for repeal of the Act of 1677, inherited from Britain, 'for the Better Observance of the Lord's-day, commonly called Sunday' was the first matter debated. Reports of the convictions of a Chinese market gardener for watering his vegetables, and of a boy for selling newspapers, on a Sunday prompted Cox's motion. He noted various absurdities in the Act, including a provision that 'if a person travelling on Sunday is robbed he shall have no redress because he was doing an illegal act'.

Responding, Dalley agreed that the Act was in some respects 'inapplicable to the circumstances of the colony', and thought police and magistrates should show more discretion than had been demonstrated in the cases Cox raised. However, he opposed the motion because no other law prevented Sunday becoming 'a day of ordinary labour'. While not regarding 'with much favour either Calvinistic Sabbaths or continental Sundays', he thought 'any interference with this day of repose and bodily and mental restoration' for the labouring classes would be 'the most signal misfortune'. A large majority of the Councillors agreed.[2]

Possibly the fact that Dalley had some difficult legal issues on his plate at the time explains his failure to act on Sunday observance anomalies. Most urgent was a new problem raised by A.G. Taylor, the clever obstructionist who came uncomfortably close to aborting criminal law reform nine months earlier with his claim that the historic legislation was a money bill and therefore should not have been introduced in the Legislative Council (chapter 19). Taylor discovered two legal flaws in

Stuart's appointment of George Reid as Minister for Public Instruction (and Parkes's appointment of Francis Suttor to the same post in the previous government). The colony's constitution provided that only five ministers, in addition to designated officeholders including the Colonial Secretary and Treasurer, could be members of the Assembly, but there were six. And the position of Minister for Public Instruction had not been gazetted as required.

Taylor dropped his bombshell in early December 1883. The Assembly's elections and qualifications committee, to which the matter was referred, concluded reluctantly that Suttor and Reid had been invalidly re-elected after their appointment as ministers. While the committee was considering the question, Dalley prepared a lengthy opinion reassuring the government that, whether or not the elections were valid, the ministers had acted with legal authority during their time in office. Another opinion rejected legal doubts raised about the gazettal of other ministerial positions.[3]

Dalley's bill to prevent a similar problem arising again and validate the elections of Suttor and Reid passed easily through the Assembly in late January, but had a more difficult passage through the Council. This was despite removal of the retrospective clauses after both men agreed to recontest their seats. Feeling the pressure, Dalley indicated again that he was on the brink of retiring as Attorney-General, saying he could not carry on much longer in the absence of 'entirely new and enlarged provisions for the Crown Law Department. I cannot but for a short time, perhaps a very short time, longer bear the strain of the responsibility to which I am at present subjected.'[4] The *Mail* expressed the hope that this 'very brilliant comet' had not yet 'burned himself out' – a hope that, for the time being, was fulfilled.[5]

When Reid faced the electors at the end of February the opposition had a strong issue to campaign on, a property tax proposed by the government. Its candidate was a wealthy property-owner, Sydney Burdekin, younger brother of Marshall Burdekin whose appointment as Treasurer precipitated the collapse of the Cowper government in

1866 (chapter 9). Dalley was in fine form on the hustings, ridiculing claims that the tax would hurt the poor. Men who had 'accumulated enormous fortunes, built miles of terraces, and never manifested any womanish tenderness towards the poor and suffering' had suddenly become the deepest sympathisers with the 'poor and starving men who owned extensive properties', he said to laughter and cheers. 'Never was there such a miracle of flinty-hearted men transformed into weeping humanitarians and hysterical philanthropists.'[6] It was a close contest; Reid's loss by 40 votes was a blow to the government.

Dalley introduced complex legislation in late January to reform the colony's bankruptcy law, fulfilling a commitment made the previous July to 'try and make the law of insolvency more conducive to the protection of the creditor and less of a lucrative enterprise to the bankrupt'.[7] Typically, he took 'the earliest opportunity of disowning any personal claims to the merit of its authorship', but it is clear from his second reading speech that he had put much effort into crafting it from information and ideas gleaned from many sources. He observed that it had been said of Jonathan Swift

> that he had never been known to take a single point from any writer, ancient or modern; and, although that statement was not literally true, his claims to marvellous originality have been invariably recognised. Of this bill perhaps the exact opposite may truthfully be said. It is, as it stands, not characterised by any originality whatever...and yet I venture to submit that this is its highest recommendation.[8]

One important source was a set of recommendations written by Sir Alfred Stephen in 1871, which also formed much of the basis of a bankruptcy bill prepared by Edward Butler shortly before he resigned as Parkes's Attorney-General in 1873. Despite the widespread view that the existing law had long allowed unscrupulous traders to enrich themselves by avoiding responsibility to their creditors, Dalley, like Butler, failed to secure enactment of his bill. Reform was eventually achieved in 1887.

He narrowly secured another important reform – allowing judges to impose shorter sentences than the minimums prescribed under the new consolidated criminal law in cases where there were strong extenuating circumstances. The amending bill passed by just one vote in the Legislative Council; it almost certainly would have gone down had he not recruited a reluctant Stephen, principal author of the Criminal Law Amendment Act, to prepare it. That 'he should have induced his venerable learned friend…actually to draw the bill, undoing his own handiwork, is really one of the most remarkable proofs of his persuasive powers that even he has ever given us,' commented the Mail.[9]

Dalley acted after the press highlighted a string of cases in which judges were forced by the law to impose sentences, in his words, 'grotesquely disproportionate to the offence'. An instance in which a man was sentenced to three years' gaol for, in a fit of temper, striking and killing a calf that was eating his horses' feed prompted him to comment that there was 'not a member of this House who under similar circumstances might not commit the same offence.' Before voting for the bill, Stephen made a long speech arguing that undue leniency by the courts was fostering crime in the colony. While agreeing that much crime might have arisen from inadequate sentences imposed early in criminals' careers, Dalley said he considered too severe punishment 'a still greater source of danger'.[10]

Another valuable legislative achievement was a set of changes to the Matrimonial Causes Act to remedy problems that had shown up since divorce was legalised 11 years earlier. As originally drafted, the amending bill extended the grounds for divorce with provisions relating to violence and desertion. Dalley expressed strong support for these, but dropped them after concluding that leaving them in the bill would jeopardise the urgently needed procedural reforms.[11] Eight more years passed before similar provisions were enacted.

Despite his heavy ministerial workload, Dalley still sometimes prosecuted in the Central Criminal Court. His failure in March to secure the conviction of five young men charged with murdering a prostitute was greeted with cheers in the court. 'A more repulsive crowd of faces even those grim walls never looked upon,' commented the Mail, 'and as the hoarse throats sent up their ghastly cheer, it seemed as a very chorus of fiends rejoicing over the defeat of baffled law and justice'.[12] The paper praised his 'great courage and resource' after a win shortly afterwards in the trial of a man accused of sexually assaulting an unconscious drunken woman, who died shortly afterwards. Finding himself apparently blocked in one line of legal attack, he had 'boldly struck out a fresh one and followed it to a successful result, which, of all his many services to the country, is certainly not the least'.[13]

A family matter demanded some of Dalley's attention around this time. His sister, Christina Greig, and her children came to Sydney in straitened circumstances after her husband fell into insolvency and fled Melbourne in early March. A private detective gave evidence to an insolvency court hearing that William Greig had indicated to the hansom cab driver who drove him from their Toorak home to the city that he would not be returning to Melbourne. But a letter he left with the managing clerk of his merchants' firm promised he would return and pay his creditors; it stated he was travelling to his birthplace, the Cape of Good Hope, 'to consult friends'.[14] He did come back, and the family returned to Toorak.

Dalley presided at two banquets in the first week of April in honour of men about to visit England. Guest at the first 'large and brilliant gathering' was John Woods, a prominent businessman whose enterprises included the Port Jackson Steamboat Company, operator of the ferry service to Manly. His career, said Dalley, showed what a man with 'a love of labour, an independent spirit, and a determination to better his fortunes by unsparing industry' could achieve in the colony.[15] The second banquet was for the barrister (and future Chief Justice) Frederick Darley. Dalley praised the 'sense of duty and patriotism' that had seen him 'patiently investigating all public business' and 'correcting, amending and aiding legislation' night after night in the Legislative Council for many years despite occupying 'the first place in his profession' and being 'overwhelmed with professional engagements'.[16]

A few days earlier, he had referred to the rarity of his own appearances as a barrister in recent years in a new debate in the Council on the perennial question of whether solicitors should be allowed to appear as advocates in the Supreme Court. 'Occasionally, very rarely, I have of late years appeared, always with reluctance, in some important cases,' he said. 'I have been compelled, as many attorneys know, to decline numberless professional engagements.' As a result, he claimed, he was personally disinterested in the outcome of the Council's debate, and so could address the issue 'in a more thoroughly impartial frame of mind'.

Supporting the status quo, he said the tasks of the solicitor 'who collects, arranges and prepares the materials of legal proceedings' and the barrister who argued the cases were 'wholly and essentially different'. Very rarely would 'the faculties, the qualities necessary to the discharge of both duties' be found in one person. As far as he was concerned, barristers were in no way superior to solicitors: 'I...recognise no superiority but that of intellect and refinement and virtue.' And with 'one great exception', the men 'of the finest sensibility, the choicest and fullest culture, and the highest intellectual power' he had known were solicitors, he said, clearly referring to Badham (the exception), Stenhouse and Deniehy. 'No man who has ever occupied a place at the bar of this country' could for an instant be compared with them 'in genius, in variety of knowledge, in perfect taste.'[17] The Council overwhelmingly accepted his view.

The issue arose again the following month after the Assembly voted to allow solicitors to appear as advocates in the divorce court. Dalley was prepared to reluctantly accept this proposal, but the Council rejected it by 15 votes to eight.[18]

With his second son, seven-year-old John Bede, and a neighbour, Major-General Sir Edward Strickland, Dalley travelled by government launch from Manly to St Ignatius' College, Riverview, on the first Monday in May for a celebration of the feast day of the college's principal, Father Joseph Dalton. Strickland, prominent as a Catholic layman since retiring to Sydney in 1881 after a distinguished career in the British army, was on the speakers' list with Dalley. A posting to Sydney in the early 1840s apparently had left him with happy memories of the colony. Cardinal Patrick Moran, in his history of the Catholic Church in Australasia, recorded that the then young soldier had 'received some kindness' from Archbishop Polding, and 'wept with joy' on encountering him again in 1865 on Malta (the archbishop was on his way to Rome).[19]

In his speech to the gathered pupils, Strickland contrasted the 'cheering scene' at Riverview with the 'extreme severity' of the regime he had experienced at the English Jesuit college, Stonyhurst, in the 1830s. Dalley, who was 'greeted with loud and hearty cheering', extolled the 'inestimable service' that teachers provided and exhorted the Riverview boys to recognise that 'your advantages here are great, both intellectual and spiritual, and your responsibilities are proportionately large'.

> You owe much to your parents, much to your teachers, much to yourselves; but more to your country. From such an institution as this we may look for young men who will serve society by cultured intelligence, by a noble liberality of thought, by an entire unselfishness; who will adorn our public life by a boldness of speech and action, tempered by a perfect courtesy; who, while maintaining their own opinions with unshaken courage, will respect the honest convictions of, and carry themselves with a chivalrous politeness towards, even their bitterest opponents. (Cheers.)[20]

In the Legislative Council the following week, Dalley was among those who took umbrage at a complaint by a voluble Irish Catholic member of the Assembly, Daniel O'Connor, that the Council neglected its business 'owing to the physical incapacity of many of the members'. O'Connor's outburst followed the Council's failure, due to the lack of a quorum, to deal with a bill he had put forward to extend the vote in municipal elections to non-ratepayers. Dalley contended that the Council performed its work efficiently, in contrast to the Assembly where 'the transaction of public business is subordinated to the embarrassment of opponents, to the interposition of meaningless difficulties in the way of legislation, and to the bringing about of a state of confusion in public affairs'. With O'Connor clearly in mind, he said it was intolerable that the Council should be 'exposed to vulgar ridicule whenever any small ambition is foiled or ridiculous vanity rebuked by its action'.[21]

O'Connor saw red, and replied with an attack on Dalley that all but one of Sydney's newspapers – and the official record, Hansard – judged too shocking to publish in full. Only the *Daily Telegraph*, launched in 1879, recorded his breaking the taboo on allusions to the convict ancestry of prominent figures. Dalley was one of those people about whose ancestry it would be best if 'funeral palls' were 'dropped to shield them from the penetrating eye', he suggested.

He called Dalley a 'well-dressed fop' and accused him of vanity for giving copies of his speeches to the press. Whenever 'great public questions' agitated the public mind, he retired 'to 'our little village' or to some obscure place along the line [presumably a reference to Sutton Forest] to enjoy wealth which he had never earned…' Like Sir Joseph Porter, First Lord of the Admiralty in Gilbert and Sullivan's *HMS Pinafore*, he went below 'when the wind of popular excitement blows with hurricane force'. But in fine weather, when everything was 'clear and straightforward and easy', he emerged and gathered 'the loaves and fishes of office'.[22]

Dalley did not respond publicly. Confronted by a hail of criticism, O'Connor apologised profusely. He wished he could withdraw 'anything that I have uttered…outside the legitimate order of debate' and hoped 'the recording angel might drop a tear and wipe it out forever'. That 'high official' was unlikely to respond sympathetically, thought *Freeman's*: 'There are some offences so rank that no tears, no penance can purge them…'[23]

While debate on the land legislation ground on in the Assembly, the Council discussed a range of other issues. Questioned on the collapse of the Oriental Bank, a London-based institution with operations in the colony, Dalley offered reassurance that the Sydney Savings Bank, relied on by 'the great body of the working-classes', was safe.[24] He gave three lengthy speeches explaining the Executive Council's rejection of pleas to commute the death sentence of a Frenchman, Joseph Cordini, convicted of murdering a hawker in the Riverina. Through the press and in letters to the French consul in Sydney, Cordini's solicitor and defence counsel had mounted a case for clemency that rested partly on alleged popular prejudice against France due to its policy of sending convicts to the Pacific. They convinced the consul that there had been irregularities in the trial, but Dalley described their claims as 'a tissue of misrepresentations' and went into great detail in refuting them. He had the strong support of Sir Alfred Stephen, who thought the lawyers' actions scandalous.[25]

With widespread rain in April offering hope that the colony was emerging from drought, Dalley observed during debate on a bill to regulate construction of dams that 'the peculiar circumstances of this country render the permanent storage of water one of the most difficult labours of a wise statesmanship'.[26] Supporting legislation regulating the collection and farming of oysters, he noted that these delicacies, not long ago 'cheap, abundant, and easily procured', had become 'costly, scarce, and difficult to obtain'.[27] He vehemently opposed a private member's bill to prohibit the employment of women in bars to protect their morals. Limitations on women's employment were already excessive and unfair, he said. And, contrary to the assertions of 'a fanatic' recently in Sydney lecturing on temperance, most barmaids were decent and respectable. He condemned the 'cruel fanaticism of those who invariably associate vice with anything which they oppose on what they deem to be a principle of moral conduct'. The bill was rejected by just one vote.[28]

Debate on a supply bill in July brought another demonstration of the oratorical skill Dalley could bring to discussion of a subject that, in his words, was 'of a nature somewhat foreign to my ordinary occupations'. His most persistent antagonist on budgetary matters, William Piddington, a 69-year-old bookseller who had been Treasurer in two Parkes governments, chided him for 'burning the midnight oil, not in studying finance, but in studying the abstruse matters dealt with by Puffendorf, Grotius and Coke upon Littleton'. Dalley responded by wondering whether Piddington performed his calculations with 'that mysterious instrument which the Chinese employed', the 'Suan Pan'.

> It is said that in their hands [arithmetical operations] may be conducted with much rapidity and with perfect accuracy; but in other hands, while the machine may be used with immense facility for addition, it is not at all to be depended on for subtraction, and no rule can be discovered for

employing it with accuracy in division. This would exactly explain my honourable friend's mode of treating questions of finance.

Piddington claimed the government had used loan funds to pay interest on its debt – an accusation that Dalley failed to address – and was rapidly running down its reserves, with spending for the year likely to exceed revenue by nearly a million pounds. Dalley painted a much rosier picture, claiming revenue was perfectly satisfactory. 'The real ground for astonishment and gratification,' he said, 'is that, considering the almost unexampled depression of valuable interests owing to the protracted and widespread drought, so great and so assured a prosperity is found to exist.'[29] Experience over the next 18 months was to prove Piddington's gloom more soundly based than Dalley's optimism.

In the Legislative Assembly, the lands bill, steered patiently through a grinding clause-by-clause examination by Lands Minister Farnell, reached its third reading at the end of July. After various obstructive tactics had been employed to delay the vote, and a 33-hour sitting, the legislation passed easily, by 65 to 30, on 7 August. In a last attempt to block it, opponents sought unsuccessfully to have the votes of landholder members disallowed on the ground that they had a personal interest in the outcome.[30]

Dalley introduced the bill into the Legislative Council five days later, commenting that no question had been 'more profoundly studied, or more searchingly investigated' and urging members to deal with it expeditiously.[31] The next day he delivered his second-reading speech, an hour-and-a-half performance that the *Mail* described as 'really remarkable even for him' and demonstrating 'easy mastery of the question in all its bearings'. A 'brilliant audience' packed the Council's gallery for the speech; 'let no one doubt the power...of Mr Dalley's oratory, the mere expectation of which can fill even the Upper House as the fame of a world-wide 'star' a theatre, and, better still, which does not, after all, as famous 'stars' often do, disappoint the expectation.'[32]

He began by noting that, despite extensive sales under Robertson's land laws, some 160 million of the 200 million acres of 'public estate' remained unalienated; dealing with this 'magnificent territory' in a way that protected existing interests, offered fresh fields for enterprise and promoted general prosperity was a matter of vital importance. He said Robertson, the object of 'a universal public feeling of regard and pride', had implemented an 'utterly revolutionary' scheme to settle families on the land, and it had worked well in areas with suitable soil, climate and access to markets.

But things were different in the interior, especially after changes to the law in 1875 allowed selectors to excise areas as large as 2,560 acres from pastoral leases to run stock. Naturally they chose the choicest portions, meeting the 'bitterest hostility' from the squatters and sparking 'a struggle between these two classes which resulted in a train of evils with which we are all familiar'. These included massive debts taken on by landholders to buy land to 'protect themselves', and frauds 'not infrequently' perpetrated to 'save themselves from absolute ruin'.

Describing the new legislation, he spelled out plans to divide the colony into eastern, central and western divisions, and the different conditions for leases and land purchases that would apply in each. Competition between squatters and selectors would be managed by dividing existing pastoral leases into two equal portions, with the squatters having security of tenure over one and the other open to selection and a new form of tenure, homestead leases. Local land boards would deal with compliance issues and disputes, and 'bring into the full light of day public matters that have hitherto been arranged in the ante-rooms of ministers'.[33]

The Council accepted the bill at the second reading without a vote, but it became clear during the debate that Dalley would have a fight on his hands to prevent major amendments favouring squatters, and a clash with the Assembly that could lead to loss of the bill. He appealed to members to recognise that it was a compromise, 'as all practical legislation concerning great subjects, vested and widely scattered interests, and conflicting themes, must necessarily be'.[34] While generally putting his case calmly during the four weeks of debate in committee, frustration sometimes burst through; he rejected one proposal with the remark that 'the absurdity of the honourable gentleman's figures is only equalled by the absurdity of his statements with reference to the operation of the measure'.[35]

His pleas to avoid changes that could lead the Assembly to lay the bill aside were generally heeded. He reminded members that, despite serious illness, he had come to the Council 'night after night' in early 1880 – 'at great inconvenience, and even danger to my life' – 'to protect the rights of this Chamber' (chapter 17). He did not dispute the constitutional right of the Council to make any amendments, including ones with financial implications, to legislation, but the Assembly had made clear that it took a different view. 'If, after the other Chamber has been 12 months maturing it, and the whole country has been so long waiting for it, the bill should from any cause fall through now, it will be nothing short of a public calamity,' he said.[36]

Dalley let his guard drop at one point, accepting an amendment that would have reduced the revenue obtained from western division pastoral lease rents. Recognising the danger, he apologised to members a few days later and asked them to rescind the change, which they proceeded to do without a vote.[37] Not all were happy with his approach. In the third reading debate on 24 September, George Cox accused him of treating members 'like children rather than as men who had met to discuss a very great question'. 'Perhaps in my anxiety concerning the passage of a measure of such unspeakable importance I may have inadvertently on some occasions used language liable to misconception,' he conceded. The Council approved the amended bill by 23 votes to six.[38]

His concern about the Assembly's response proved well founded. When the bill returned to the lower house, the Speaker, Edmund Barton, pronounced that some of the Council's amendments interfered with the 'privileges' of the Assembly as they could affect government revenue. He told members they had two choices: lay the bill aside or reject those amendments. In recent times, he added, the majority of precedents favoured laying it aside.

Opponents of the bill, and the Assembly's perennial obstructionists, jumped at the apparent invitation to kill it. Parkes spoke first, contending in typical style that the bill's importance was 'as nothing compared with the proper and constitutional conduct of business'. Stuart, doubtless after a briefing from Dalley, presented a range of British and colonial precedents in support of his argument that the Council's actions were unexceptionable and its amendments should be considered. He noted that previous land bills had also been amended in the Council, and that Parkes had earlier argued against the position he was supporting now.

After Stuart prevailed by 56 votes to 17, the clever A.G. Taylor raised three technical objections to debate proceeding, one of which Barton considered presented some difficulty. Another obstructionist raised an issue that also caused him 'some hesitation', but he decided against blocking consideration of the amendments in committee.[39] The Assembly proceeded to accept some and reject others; then, on 14 October, the Council accepted the bill as it now stood. The new Crown Lands Act came into force on 1 January 1885.

In a long speech in the Council on the day the bill finally passed, Dalley took aim at Parkes, Taylor and like-minded colleagues who used the term 'unconstitutional' as a 'party instrument', 'not to enlighten but to utterly confuse public opinion'. The powers of the two houses were defined by the constitution, which did not recognise the 'privileges' claimed by the Assembly, he said. He never doubted the Council's right to make any of the amendments proposed by members, but felt an overriding concern to 'defeat the machinations' of those whose sole ambition was to destroy the bill. 'I felt again and again almost ashamed to make the demands upon the consideration of honourable members for concessions [that] I felt to be essential to the safety of the bill.'[40]

Dalley made this speech as Acting Premier and Colonial Secretary. The strain of a long and difficult parliamentary session had left Stuart looking worn and haggard for some time, and the near loss of the land legislation at the final hurdle was probably the last straw. On 7 October, five days after the Assembly's belated go-ahead to the bill, he suffered a stroke that paralysed his left side. With Stuart confined to a sick room set up at the Colonial Secretary's Office and initially under doctors' orders to see only his family and Dalley, Cabinet decided on 9 October that Dalley should take charge.[41] Stuart's mind and speech remained unaffected, but physical improvement came slowly. He moved from the city to Parramatta in mid-November, and then travelled to Tasmania in December to begin five months' convalescence away from the colony, mainly with his brother, an Anglican bishop, in New Zealand.[42]

Parliament remained in session for the rest of October. The Legislative Council's main business was finalising another of the government's notable achievements, the Civil Service Act, whose aims included ensuring appointments and promotions were based on merit and seniority rather than patronage. Despite heated opposition from a few members – which prompted a frustrated Dalley to observe that he was 'only here now under a sense of duty' and would willingly surrender his position – the bill passed easily.[43]

22

In charge

Stuart's condition had ceased to be cause for apprehension, Dalley was pleased to inform the Legislative Council on 19 November during a brief sitting called to pass an appropriation bill. The next day he wrote to the Premier – beginning 'My Dear Old Boy' – from the Colonial Secretary's Office to assure him 'everything is going on pretty well'. Apart from occasional visits to the Central Criminal Court at Darlinghurst 'to open some important case', he was spending his days in the office.

> The old Governor kept me the other night till I just heard the first shriek of the Manly steamer at 5 minutes after 11 and had just time to catch her. He talks much of you – and both he and dear old Lady Augustus (who is a saint) were very affectionate in the expression of their sympathies. There was an 'At Home' at Govt House last night to which I did not go, preferring to be snugly in bed at 7 o'clock. I get up at ½ past 4, Miller gets me a cup of tea at 5. I walk about till the steamer starts and get here soon after ½ past 7 – remain till I go to the Criminal Court – return here then and clear your table.[1]

Cases Dalley took to the court's November sittings included an 'exceptionally brutal' attempted rape at Junee. Originally listed for hearing at Wagga Wagga during 1885, he arranged for it to be heard quickly in Sydney, believing 'cases of this kind should be dealt with at once, both in the interests of the persons outraged and of society'.[2] In early December he led the prosecution of William Webb, editor of the *Campbelltown Herald*, for criminally libelling Sir Henry Parkes. Webb's suggestion that Parkes had left the colony to evade his creditors (he returned in August 1884 after 13 months away, mainly in England) was one alleged libel. The others were claims that he had sold a ministerial place in his last government for £500 and attempted a swindle involving a proposal for a bridge over the harbour.

On the Manly ferry, the no smoking sign ignored – an Illustrated Sydney News sketch.

There was much irony in Dalley, who had publicly castigated Parkes for his 'gigantic genius for indebtedness' and talent for procuring other people's money (chapter 12), now defending him against such accusations. He told the jurors they should concern themselves only with the specific allegations in the offending article. The public actions of public men were open to unrestricted 'fair and legitimate criticism', he contended. But when a man who 'had given his nights and days' to public service was 'represented as corrupt and infamous', the State had a duty to 'call upon his assailants to prove the truth of their charges, or to incur the penalty of their vituperation'. If such charges could be laid with impunity, how, he wondered, could 'men of frankness, of sensibility, of gentleness, of public virtue' be expected to come forward to serve the public?

For the defence, John Want, a future Attorney-General who had appeared frequently in criminal cases as Dalley's junior, argued that the jury should take a broad view of Parkes's commercial record in considering whether he had been libelled. Sir Alfred Stephen was among the witnesses called to impugn that record; he confirmed that he had concluded in a court judgment that Parkes had tendered a cheque he knew would be dishonoured. The jury failed to agree on a verdict, so the case lapsed.[3]

Again in serious financial difficulties, Parkes resigned from parliament a month before the trial. *Freeman's* commented that, if his character had been damned by Webb's article, the defence evidence had 'doubly damned' it and his public career was probably at last at an end.[4] A month earlier the paper had been less certain, observing that he had made many 'descents into the tomb of political life' over the years but had always risen again.

> No one believes that if tomorrow the exigencies of public affairs (which may be interpreted to mean the faintest possible prospect of a return to power) required the resurrection of the departed that he would not be forthcoming in his grave clothes at a moment's notice.[5]

This prediction was borne out, to Dalley's discomfort, just months later. In December 1884, however, he felt sympathy for Parkes, who had sent him a thank you note. 'I am naturally gratified that you should have expressed your satisfaction with my performance of a public duty which, although suffering from pain, I cheerfully undertook to vindicate the public character of the country,' Dalley replied.

> You will have perceived from the press how grossly I have been attacked for an act which had I not performed I should have deserved to be stigmatised as unworthy, in the office which I hold, of public confidence. With you I deeply sympathise. But I lament more that the gravity of the issue which I endeavoured to raise is so imperfectly appreciated by those who ought to be the guardians of the character of great public servants.[6]

The pain that afflicted Dalley in early December was probably the product of gout, named as the cause of an absence from the Legislative Council three months later.[7] He wrote to Commodore James Erskine, based in Sydney as head of the Royal Navy's Australian station, the day before the trial regretting that illness had prevented him offering immediate personal congratulations on the success of his

Raising the flag over the New Guinea protectorate.

just-completed mission to Port Moresby. Erskine had proclaimed the New Guinea protectorate on 6 November with assurances to the chiefs and others gathered for the flag-raising that Britain's intentions were wholly benevolent.[8] Dalley, ever the romantic imperialist, was moved by Erskine's reported speech, telling him,

> You have in a way, as far as I know, quite unprecedented in the assertion of Imperial authority made it at the same time a manifestation of beneficent protection to the helpless – and aroused no susceptibility and inspired no suspicions. I think you ought to be prouder of your achievement than of any bloody victory no matter how glorious, and to crown your works Heaven gave you the opportunity to prove to the savage what the power he had seen displayed meant for his peace and security.

He told Erskine he had arranged for the Government Printer's Office to produce an illustrated 'brief official narrative' of the voyage. One copy, which he would ask the Governor to dispatch, was to be 'got up regally for the Queen'. Dalley wrote to Erskine again on 27 December, after Germany's annexation of north-eastern New Guinea and the New South Wales government's decision to reject a call by Victorian Premier James Service for an immediate joint protest by the Australian colonies to the British government. He joked that he had implored the Governor to cable Lord Derby, Secretary of State for the Colonies, in cipher requesting that he 'annex Service and establish a protectorate over the Colonial Secretary's Office'.[9]

Dalley had two weighty legal matters to consider during December, both of which were eventually settled in the Privy Council. First was a dispute with the Bank of New South Wales, which held the contract to conduct the government's banking business, including negotiating loans in London. Under the agreement, the government could transfer the loans task to the Bank of England; if it did so, the Bank of New South Wales had the right to seek revision of the other provisions. But it could not, Dalley advised in an opinion dated 6 December, unilaterally declare the whole contract inoperative, the course it took when the government moved its loans business to the British bank in the second half of 1884.

The colonial bank registered its displeasure by raising the interest rate on government overdrafts by three percentage points and refusing to transfer £1.2 million of government funds from London to Sydney.[10] Treasurer Dibbs, with Dalley's endorsement, responded by shifting all the government's banking business to other institutions. The dispute moved to the courts, and in November 1885 the Supreme Court ruled the bank's retaliatory actions legal as its contract with the government had ended when it requested revision; it did not remain in effect, as Dalley had advised, until agreement was reached. Ordered to pay more than £55,000, the government appealed to the Privy Council, which in December 1887 overturned the decision. 'The view taken by the Privy Council is very much that taken by Mr Dalley,' the *Herald* noted.[11]

His opinion on the second issue did not receive similar endorsement; instead, the final court of appeal vindicated another of the disruptive A.G. Taylor's legal ploys. After being suspended from the Legislative Assembly for a week in April 1884, Taylor reappeared twice in the chamber and was escorted out by the Sergeant-at-Arms. Claiming the suspension and removals were illegal, he took Speaker Barton to the Supreme Court and won, the judges ruling that a member could not be suspended beyond the day of his offence. In his recommendation for a Privy Council appeal, Dalley expressed confidence that precedent supported the Assembly's power to suspend a member for as long as it deemed necessary to uphold order. Taylor travelled to London to argue his case, and the Privy Council ruled in February 1886 in his favour.[12]

Three days before Christmas Dalley spoke at a meeting to raise funds for the widow and children of Professor Badham, a monument at his grave, and a university scholarship in his name. Badham's 'enduring monument' had 'already been built up by the first European scholars of his day', he said to loud cheers. 'There by his scholarship – here by his sacrifices and services to education – there amongst critics and here amongst humble scholars – there by his books and here by his life – he has built up a monument which will endure forever.' Edmund Barton, acknowledging the contributions of the speakers who preceded him, noted the 'practical wisdom and cultivated speech' of Sir James Martin and Sir Patrick Jennings and 'the oratory, inspiring so much enthusiasm', of Dalley.[13]

The Bulletin's depiction of the ministry after the land legislation finally passed. Stuart rests in the back of the ambulance wagon; Dalley is at the front. Farnell is carrying his very large bill.

He was in good form again the next evening at a large banquet at the Town Hall given by 'the citizens of Sydney' to honour the ministry. He described as 'historically accurate' a *Bulletin* cartoon showing ministers returning from the parliamentary battle not 'with the air of splendid conquerors, with anything of the pride, pomp, and circumstance of glorious war', but in an ambulance wagon 'in which a few shattered soldiers were seated'. Stuart was one, Dalley another.

Praising Stuart, who had been 'stricken down by excessive and unparalleled labour', he said 'no more clear-sighted, laborious, single-minded, self-sacrificing man' had ever served his fellow citizens. Of the opposition, he commented that, 'if patriotism is to be measured by unsleeping vigilance, by unrivalled ingenuity, by exhaustless resources' it was 'a body animated by the strongest patriotic principles and convictions.' But he had no right to complain, being

> a member of a Chamber which believes that the public business is best transacted by men who are in their beds at reasonable hours – ('hear, hear;' and laughter) – and which, indeed, prefers generally the transaction of public affairs in time to permit its venerable members to go home to dinner. (Laughter.) I was not therefore subjected to those experiences, so familiar to my colleagues, of working through the night and seeing the sun rise upon their Parliamentary labours – of using the Legislative Chamber as a hall of debate and as a dormitory – (laughter) – of being lulled to sleep by some sweet voices and rudely awakened by others not musical. (Renewed laughter.)

He again praised his 'old and dear and honoured' friend Sir John Robertson, the 'legitimate' leader of the opposition, who, though 'not inferior in both intellectual and physical activity to his party', was 'unquestionably their superior in consideration of others'. Robertson had declined an invitation to the banquet in a letter in which he described the ministers as 'old friends of mine, for whom I have the greatest respect and kindly regard' and whose 'very good health' he was always glad to drink.

Dalley said he looked forward to 'many happy, peaceful months' – with 'no more midnight attacks, no more work in the trenches, no need for surgeons, hospital nurses or ambulances (Laughter and cheers.)' –

preparing for a 'great winter' parliamentary campaign.[14] With a shift to seafaring analogies, he expanded on the theme in a banquet speech at Maitland three weeks later. Ministers were experiencing 'that delicious feeling of intoxication which springs from the consciousness of a long and deserved holiday', he said.

> We have been on such a dreary journey, so long tempest-tossed, so rarely seeing land, and having, when we did catch sight of it, only glimpses of reef and perils, that now the anchor is down, the sails furled, and the freight discharged, we are due for a long run ashore. (Hear, hear.)

After this light start came a long and vigorous defence of the government's decision to reject Victoria's proposal for a joint protest against Germany's New Guinea venture. It was hard to decide which was greater – the impudence or the absurdity of the proposal, he said. Germany had an undoubted right to annex the territory and, as 'the first Empire of arts and arms of the world', should be welcomed in the region. 'Friends, co-partners in civilisation and, certainly, to take a more commercial view, customers of these Australian colonies, why should we object to them?'[15]

He had more to say on the subject at a banquet at Nundle, near Tamworth, two days later. While binding itself 'closer and closer to the mighty Empire', the colony should 'welcome all who are engaged in the great work of civilisation', he said. He ridiculed the Pacific 'Monroe doctrine' proposal endorsed by the 1883 Intercolonial Convention (chapter 20), saying it was absurd to suppose that 'we are in the dispensations of heaven the fee-simple proprietors of all the unappropriated islands scattered over these seas…'

> We know that we can never, in all probability, occupy them. We know that we have before us on this magnificent continent half a century of work of civilisation in order to enable it to be the home of the tens of millions who occupy it. We know that we should welcome every civilising agency – every form of industry and culture – every kind of help, material and intellectual – which would aid us in this mighty work. In these days, when the dream of the philanthropist should become the labour of the statesman, and distinctions of race should be merged in the great work of bettering

the condition of the whole human family, we are asked to place ourselves in antagonism to the first and noblest and grandest powers of civilisation.[16]

Critics of Dalley's internationalism organised a public meeting that attracted a large crowd – but, apart from Sir Henry Parkes, no high-profile speakers – to the Town Hall on 4 February 1885. Parkes's 'startling resurrection from the grave which he had so carefully and deliberately dug for himself only a few weeks ago, was absolutely essential to invest the meeting with any interest whatever', commented a cynical *Evening News*.[17] Parkes lamented that the British flag did not fly over the whole of New Guinea and nearby islands and criticised London's 'great apathy and unconcern to the real interests of Australasia'.[18]

Playing down the significance of the meeting, the Governor, Lord Loftus, reported to Lord Derby that it had been 'attended by a noisy crowd and conducted in a disorderly manner' and, with the exception of Parkes, 'no influential public man was present'.[19] He wrote in an earlier despatch that he had advised Dalley not to yield to 'the impetuous ardour' of the Victorian Premier and join in the proposed protest to London over Germany's move into New Guinea.[20] It is doubtful that Dalley – who had developed a close relationship with the 67-year-old former diplomat, to the extent of writing speeches for him[21] – required much persuasion.

Lord Loftus.

Loftus's despatches did not tell the British government only what it wanted to hear. Writing at the end of December 1884, he observed that 'great disappointment is felt at the acquisition by Germany of any portion of New Guinea', and 'serious consequences' could arise if the colonists, 'however loyal', should 'be impressed with an idea that their interests have been sacrificed'. Long before this advice arrived by mail, Derby received a telegram Loftus sent on 2 January 1885 complaining that the colony was being kept in the dark on important matters. The New South Wales government had no desire to embarrass the imperial government, he wrote, 'but there is deep feeling of dissatisfaction that no information as to what has been done as to New Guinea is afforded to Govt here which is being exposed to daily attacks and censure for inactivity'.[22] Four days later Dalley telegraphed the colony's Agent-General in London, Saul Samuel, requesting without delay 'result of the communications between Imperial and German governments' and 'precise intelligence of all that is now comprehended within the Protectorate of New Guinea'.[23]

The focus of complaint soon shifted to a request, conveyed in instructions issued to the newly appointed special commissioner for British New Guinea, Major-General Peter Scratchley, that the colonies meet all costs of the protectorate. Scratchley was a familiar figure in Sydney. With Sir William Jervois, later Governor of South Australia, he was sent to the colonies in 1877 to advise on their defences. Then he oversaw the development of defence works and forces, mainly volunteer, in each colony.

New South Wales offered Scratchley the use of the *Wolverene*, a corvette provided by Britain in 1882 for the colony's naval brigade, to establish his Port Moresby post. As had become the pattern, London's response was slow to come; the news that the colonies were expected to fully fund the protectorate arrived first, prompting a strongly worded telegram from Dalley to Samuel.

> Have read instructions to General Scratchley and am unable to discover in what way his jurisdiction as Commissioner is to be exercised. This Government cannot undertake to commit itself to an increased contribution until it is made fully aware of what the Imperial Government propose. It was never contemplated that the burden of maintaining the Protectorate should be exclusively borne by Australian Colonies. On being fully informed concerning mode by which jurisdiction is to be exercised this Government will re-consider situation with desire to act in the matter with liberality and effectiveness.[24]

No reply to the offer of the *Wolverene* had been received when he telegraphed again two weeks later to say its rejection would leave Scratchley seriously embarrassed. 'This government made the offer as the only means of surmounting a serious difficulty, and General Scratchley is deeply impressed with this conviction,' wrote Dalley. 'If any difficulties are placed in the way of the acceptance of the offer, this government will not concern itself in the matter any further.'[25]

If the imperial government's casual approach to colonial concerns risked giving rise to ill feeling, as Loftus warned again in a despatch to Derby at the beginning of February,[26] one decision suggested that regional defence remained a high priority. This was the appointment, for the first time, of an admiral to head the Sydney naval station. Rear Admiral George Tryon arrived on 22 January and took up residence at Admiralty House, Kirribilli, which the New South Wales government had bought for him. A man of 'frank, cheery, genial manners' with a 'love of hospitality', he became a great friend of Dalley's, his biographer recorded.[27] Tryon described Dalley in a letter to the First Lord of the Admiralty, Lord Northbrook, in May 1885 as 'a very interesting person to work with – clever, impulsive and eloquent, generous and kind hearted – he grasps a thing at once and I like him much'.[28]

Tryon and Scratchley joined Dalley and, among others, Queensland Premier Samuel Griffith, Sir James Martin and Sir Alfred Stephen on a sightseeing trip to the Blue Mountains on 2 February;[29] no doubt New Guinea was among matters discussed. Tryon formed a cynical view of Scratchley's intentions. 'It is very doubtful if he ever means to go to New Guinea, or if he does he means to come back very soon', he observed in his letter to Northbrook. Scratchley

General 'Chinese' Gordon.

eventually took up residence at Port Moresby in late August. He died of malaria three months later.³⁰

Probably also discussed on the Blue Mountains journey was the sorry situation of the popular hero General Charles ('Chinese') Gordon, under siege at Khartoum, Sudan, since early the previous year. News of Khartoum's capture by forces of the Arab insurgent, the Mahdi, reached Sydney four days later. Another five days passed before confirmation arrived that the seemingly invincible Gordon had been killed during the night of 25–26 January, two days before a rescue mission sent up the Nile from Cairo reached the overrun fortress.

Grief and anger swept Britain and the colonies, unassuaged by the fact that Gordon's recklessness had probably sealed his fate. Sudan in 1885 was theoretically a colony of Egypt, whose rulers answered to Britain. After the Mahdi's crushing defeat of an Egyptian force in late 1883, Prime Minister Gladstone ordered a British withdrawal, except for a garrison at Suakin, Sudan's Red Sea port. Under press and political pressure, he then commissioned Gordon to visit Sudan and provide advice to the government. Rather than inspect and report, Gordon resolved to suppress the insurgency, and was trapped with his troops at Khartoum.

Again pressed to act, Gladstone reluctantly agreed in August 1884 to send the unsuccessful rescue mission, led by General Lord Garnet Wolseley, up the Nile. Earlier in the year, with similar reluctance, he had sent four thousand troops to Suakin to take on the forces of an ally of the Mahdi, Osman Digna, who had seized control of most of eastern Sudan. This force, under Major-General Sir Gerald Graham, had some successes against Osman's guerrillas, but was then mostly withdrawn after being denied permission to launch a relief mission to Khartoum by striking southwest across the desert to the Nile.³¹

Sydney's evening papers carried the news of Gordon's death on Wednesday 11 February 1885. The next morning a letter to the editor by Dalley's Manly friend Sir Edward Strickland appeared in the *Herald*. 'It is in the first moments of grief and indignation on hearing the news that 'Gordon was dead,' that the idea flashed across me that Australia should at once give expression to her deep sorrow at the loss of this great commander and *preux chevalier*…[by] tendering to our mother country substantial aid in the time of need,' he wrote. He proposed that a regiment of a thousand men be raised to aid British troops 'already engaged in bitter war both in North and South Africa' or to travel to England to replace 'drilled battalions sent out to reinforce their comrades in the field'.

He wrote admiringly of the foe – 'the warlike, brave Saracens, led by the Mahdi' and 'the hardy Boer, a deadly shot and an excellent soldier'. Harking back to the Crusades, he advised of the 'Saracens' that, 'if not crushed now, by force of arms, they may easily become as formidable as their renowned ancestors of old'.

> It therefore well becomes every Christian people to aid in the great task now undertaken by England single-handed, and to no Christian people is this a more sacred duty than to the children of old England. Every Christian-born subject feels to-day that he has lost a friend in Gordon, therefore all Christendom will ring with praises of the gallantry of Australia in losing not a moment in tendering aid in the hour of need for the maintenance of the integrity of our nation and the ascendency of Christianity.[32]

It seems Strickland was not exaggerating when he wrote that the idea for a New South Wales contingent came to him immediately he heard of Gordon's death. He apparently called on Dalley with his proposal soon after the papers carrying the news hit the streets. According to a story told later by a colleague of Andrew Garran, editor of the *Herald*, the Acting Premier initially was non-committal. 'My dear boy,' he advised the 63-year-old, 'take it to the *Herald*, and hear what they think of it.' Garran published Strickland's letter without comment the next morning. His leader commending the proposal appeared the following day, with news that the government had wasted no time in acting on it.[33]

Dalley declared at a banquet for Lord Rosebery in 1883 that the colonies, as participants in the glories of the British Empire, were ready to share its obligations (chapter 20). Eighteen months earlier he spoke of responsibilities that went with sharing Britain's 'vast imperial glory'; Australians, though far from the fields of contention, could not expect to continue immune from involvement in war (chapter 18). A golden opportunity, he apparently decided, had now arisen to live up to these sentiments.

Presumably after catching the first steamer from Manly and arriving at the office around 7.30, Dalley set a cracking pace in turning Strickland's proposal into reality. News that morning that the British government had ordered General Graham back to Suakin, with ambitious plans to defeat Osman Digna and then take on the Mahdi at Khartoum, strengthened the case for immediate action. It also removed any doubt that Sudan should be the colonial contingent's destination.

Dalley first called in Colonel John Richardson, commander of the colony's military forces, and artillery commander Colonel Charles Roberts for a briefing on what assistance could be offered. They told him that two batteries of artillery and a battalion of effective and well-disciplined infantry could be made available quickly. Then he received assurances from the manager of the Orient shipping line that transport could be provided to Suakin without delay. Next he wrote a cabinet minute proposing that 'two batteries of field artillery properly horsed and 500 infantry' be offered, to land at Suakin within 30 days of receipt of the order for embarkation. Ministers then in Sydney gathered to approve the offer, and Dalley advised Governor Loftus of the decision in a minute that said it testified 'to the readiness of this colony to give instant and practical help to the Empire in an emergency'. After this good morning's work, the offer was telegraphed about midday to Agent-General Samuel in London.

Loftus also cabled London, recommending to Lord Derby that Britain accept the contingent and advising that 'refusal will be deeply felt in the colony'. Samuel waited on Derby and Lord Hartington, Secretary of State for War, with his cable, and Dalley received a preliminary reply at 8.30 the next morning, Friday 13 February. 'Your offer greatly appreciated, and will be at once considered,' Samuel wrote. 'Operations in the Soudan [as it was then spelt] expected will have to be deferred, as getting late in season.' This sounded like a prelude to rejection, or possibly an invitation to withdraw the offer. Derby, it was revealed later, favoured acceptance and Hartington rejection.[34] The British government took its time to reach a decision.

Dalley left by train for Galong, north-west of Yass, on the Friday evening with a party of about a dozen including Treasurer Dibbs and Mines Minister Joseph Abbott. Arriving around 6 a.m. Saturday, they were met by their host for the weekend, John Nagle Ryan of 'Galong Castle'.[35] At a dinner in nearby Boorowa that evening Dalley extolled Ryan's unmatched hospitality, which 'we escaped miraculously with our lives to-day' and would again encounter, 'and I trust…survive, on our way back tomorrow'.[36]

Dalley's performance at this dinner moved Dibbs to remark that 'a more brilliant or more powerful effort of oratory they had never before been treated to'; there was no sign that the excitements and exertion of the past few days, the overnight train trip and Ryan's hospitality had worn him down. Mostly the speech was a vigorous defence of his view that other European powers should be welcomed in the South Seas. He rejected accusations that his position was cowardly, but admitted to being 'dreadfully afraid of excitable and frothy Britons when they begin to be really dangerous to the peace of the world by their ravings'. He said they were living at a time when nations were 'drawing closer to each other' and 'men are filled with shame at the folly of past national differences'. Any policy that sought to 'shut out…the light of any knowledge but our own' was 'unworthy of our civilisation and a disgrace to our humanity'.

He concluded with a brief reference to the Sudan offer. It would, he said,

> proclaim to the world our preparedness to share in the perils as we have shared in the glories of the Empire, to discharge in part the heavy debt which we owe to our parent, and testify that in moments of danger we are ready from the most distant dependencies to send whatever substantial help we can afford… It is our sacrifice, our enthusiasm, and conception of the true duties of citizenship in our necessarily limited way, which will speak to the world of the fertility and grandeur of the Empire, the members of which, however dispersed, are one in sympathy, purpose, and in sentiment…[37]

The visitors left Boorowa at 11.15 next morning – Dalley and the other Catholics in the party having attended mass – and called first at Frederick Hume's nearby station, 'Tarengo'. A messenger with a telegram from Samuel advising that the offer had been accepted caught up with them there, at which point 'Mr C. Huenerbein,[38] who happened to be at the piano, at once struck up *Rule Britannia* amid scenes of wild enthusiasm'. Celebrations, including a toast captured in a sketch by one of the men present, continued when they returned to Galong Castle for luncheon. Presumably tired but happy, they boarded a special train at Galong at 5.30 and arrived in Sydney shortly after midnight.[39]

The Galong toast. Dalley is the short man on host John Ryan's right at the head of the table.

23

To Sudan

The eminent English historian James Froude arrived in Sydney at the start of a brief visit on 12 February 1885, the day Dalley offered the Sudan contingent. At stops as his train from Albury approached Sydney 'boys appeared on the platforms with baskets of grapes and newspapers', he recorded. 'From the latter, New South Wales appeared to be wholly occupied with the Soudan business, the death of Gordon, and the discredit of our poor country at home.'

Froude was a proponent of a strong and united empire, and what he saw on the trip pleased him. The offer, and the anxious wait for an answer, 'confirmed all the impressions which I had formed of the colonists' true disposition', he wrote. He thought much would turn on the answer; a 'refusal would be especially pleasing to those who wished ill to the English connection'.

Lodged at Sydney's patrician Australian Club, he found the reading room after breakfast 'full of gentlemen in eager and anxious conversation' on the matter; the prevailing tone was one of 'warm approval' of the offer and hope that it would be accepted. When news of the acceptance arrived, the 'enthusiasm was irresistible'. However, he acknowledged that there were dissentients with valid arguments, both at the club and outside.

> I listened for a quarter of an hour to an orator haranguing a crowd in the public park. He spoke well, and I was glad that I had not to answer him… The crowd listened, and here and there, especially when the speaker dwelt upon the right of all people to manage their own affairs, there were murmurs of approval; but the immense majority were indifferent or hostile.[1]

Samuel's cable breaking the exciting news said Her Majesty's

Government had accepted the offer 'with much satisfaction', on the understanding that 'force must be placed absolutely under orders of General commanding as to the duties upon which it will be employed'. Only one of the two offered artillery batteries was accepted. As published in the press, the message went on, 'If your Government prefer the immediate despatch of your contingent, the War Office does not desire to delay it.' Samuel had actually written,

> I am to inform you, in strict confidence, that plans of General not fully formed, but may probably involve placing troops in summer quarters after short Campaign from Suakin; if after this knowledge your Government prefer immediate despatch of contingent, War Office does not desire to delay it.

The confidential lines, which would have provided extra ammunition for critics had they known of them, implied the troops might have little to do. Why was the offer accepted? *Freeman's* commented perceptively that it 'must have been received with a paternal smile in the first instance; but a moment's reflection was enough to show that it was really a golden opportunity for attaching the colonies to the Empire, removing the sense of irritation occasioned by the vacillating and unsatisfactory conduct of affairs at the Colonial Office, and possibly promoting the cause of Imperial Federation'. The *Bulletin*, after observing that the contingent could have no effect on the Sudan war, made a similar point. Dalley's offer had provided an unexpected opportunity to soothe the feelings of colonists 'sore over the German Pacific annexations'.[2]

While *Freeman's* viewed the Sudan adventure sceptically and the *Bulletin*, in clever cartoons as much as commentary, ridiculed it, Sydney's daily papers offered largely uncritical support. Britain's rejection of troop offers made almost immediately by Victoria, Queensland and South Australia did not dampen the initial enthusiasm. Messages from Lord Wolseley, who looked forward 'with pride to the honour of having Australian troops under my command in the field', and Queen Victoria, who expressed 'warm and grateful feelings at the proffered aid', helped sustain it.

Men rushed to enlist, offers of all sorts of provisions – including ten chests of tea from the prominent Chinese merchant Quong Tart – poured in, and some of the colony's wealthy volunteered to contribute large sums of money (the proprietors of the *Herald* and the *Evening News* each offered £1,000 a year).³ 'The rush of feeling was curious and interesting to witness,' commented Froude. 'The only question with me was if it would last'.⁴

He was taken to meet Dalley.

> We found the acting-Premier in a spacious lofty room, the windows all open, himself at his table in his shirt-sleeves; secretaries about him busy writing; officers, civil and military, waiting instructions, and the Premier himself, the coolest-looking object in the apartment, giving out his instructions with an easy unembarrassed manner, as if organizing expeditions had been the occupation of his life. Several minutes passed before he could attend to us, and I used them in looking closely at a man who was making, perhaps, an epoch in Colonial history. Mr Dalley was a short, thickset man of fifty or thereabouts [he was fifty-three], with strong neck, large head, a clear steady eye, and firmly shaped mouth and chin. The face was good-humoured, open, and generous. When he laughed it was heartily, without a trait of malice. The directions which I heard him giving were quiet but distinct, no words wasted, but the thing meant clearly said.

Froude was accorded a brief interview – he had a longer meeting with Dalley at a less busy time later – and came away thinking, 'There…is a man whom it is worth while to have come all this way to see.' Dalley arranged for him to be taken around the harbour – 'the loveliest of all salt-water lakes' – in the government steam launch. Calling at Manly, he was shown over Dalley's residence. 'It was a castle half-finished; built in pieces, a room completed here, a turret there, with the intervals to be filled up at leisure. The exterior of the mansion was picturesque in its way, or promised to become so. The interior jarred a little on my bigoted Protestantism, for the walls of the living rooms were covered either with fresco paintings or pictures and engravings, all of a neo-Catholic complexion.'⁵

Preparations proceeded so quickly that Dalley was able to name the contin-gent's departure date, Tuesday 3 March, within days of returning from Galong.⁶ At the end of the first week, an estimated twelve thousand people gathered in Sydney's largest hall, the Exhibition Building, for a meeting to endorse the project and raise funds to assist soldiers' families. The first speaker, Chief Justice Sir James Martin, announced to 'long continued applause' that around £30,000 had been subscribed already (the final total was more than £40,000).

He predicted that in times to come the story of the Sudan contingent would be told 'by many a fireside throughout the wide lands of Australia'; their children and children's children would 'look back with pride upon the action of their fathers…' He also responded to critics of the propriety of his appearing at the meeting. It had been suggested, he said, that the Supreme Court might have to rule on the legality of spending made ahead of parliamentary approval. This was not an issue, he claimed. Urgent need sometimes required such spending; 'only the other day when [British] troops were sent off on the receipt of the news of General Gordon's death to the Soudan, no vote was obtained for defraying the cost, but the expenditure was incurred in the anticipation of the sanction of Parliament'.⁷

Martin's colleague Justice Faucett took a different view, observing in court on the day before the troops departed that 'the Governor, before enlisting any force, military or naval, must have the authority of Parliament'.⁸ Sir Henry Parkes, the most prominent critic of the Sudan enterprise, also made much of the claimed unconstitutionality of the government's action.

He wasted no time in launching his attack. The first of a series of letters to the *Herald* appeared two days after the contingent was offered (the day before its acceptance). He also tried to exert influence behind the scenes, cabling Lord Derby a week later saying the offer had been made 'in the absence of the Premier and without the sanction of parliament, and a strong feeling was increasing daily'. Derby sought advice from Loftus, who sent a reassuring reply.⁹

Parkes's letters became increasingly strident. Ministers had committed 'a great political crime' in making the offer, he wrote in late February. They had already stripped 'all dignity from government by running over the country in twos and threes to village banquets'. In characteristic style, he boasted 'it is true I have never been an Acting Colonial Secretary, but I have held that high office by direct appointment for more than 10 long years, and in seasons of immense difficulty, not without some little credit both here and in England.'[10]

A letter in late March sought to show Dalley had a much worse record than himself in leaving and returning to public life when it suited him. 'The difference between him and me,' he wrote, 'is really that, while I often manage to run my head against a stone wall in battling for what I believe to be a principle, he generally contrives to reappear in Parliament when the emoluments of office are at his fingers' ends without any trouble to himself.'[11]

Another of Dalley's after-dinner speeches had prompted this outburst. With preparations for the troops' departure well in hand, he and three ministerial colleagues travelled by special train to Orange on 26 February. A 'large assembly of the principal residents of the town and district', and a band playing *The British Grenadiers*, greeted them at the station. At the banquet in the evening he presented an ambitious (and impossible) vision of future water conservation works that would 'prevent any suffering to man or animal' when drought struck again. Then he turned to Sudan. 'Any man in my place would have done all that I did,' he contended. 'It was a simple act of duty…'

> There were those who thought that the colonies of England were her weaknesses; that in great struggles the nation would feel them as helpless children clinging to her neck and enfeebling the strong arms of the parent fighting for the sacredness of the hearth; that their protection would imperil the full exercise of imperial strength. Such alarms and apprehensions can no longer exist. The colonies are the camps and barracks of Imperial forces ready to die for the Empire wherever the foe may be found. This is the lesson we have, by a singular privilege vouchsafed to us, been enabled to teach the world. (Hear, hear.)

He claimed, in the passage that irked Parkes, that 'among living public men of influence of all kinds of opinions' there had not been a dissentient voice.

But the trumpet of war has awakened the dead – has blown its shrill blast through the cemeteries… And the voice of one who speaks to us from a sepulchre, which he selected for himself, and which he ought, I think, to peacefully occupy, and not be perpetually leaving to frighten us, has come to us from below. (Applause and laughter.) He regards our patriotism as illegal, and our enthusiasm as unconstitutional…[12]

Dalley had another important speech to write before the troops departed five days later. In a note to the Governor on 23 February he said he had received a 'strange telegram' from Stuart in New Zealand suggesting that the Chief Justice or the Anglican bishop should say a few words to the troops before they embarked. He had replied disapproving of the idea. 'As to the Bishop the thing was absurd as the force was a national one, not an Anglican one, and every religious body represented in the Corps outside the Church of England would feel perfectly disgusted at His Lordship's valedictory oratory,' he told Loftus. 'You and you alone, My dear Lord, are the man for the duty if it is to be discharged at all.'[13]

Loftus agreed to deliver an address, which Dalley prepared and sent him the day before the embarkation. 'I hope Your Excellency will like it,' he wrote in the accompanying note. 'I am sure you will speak it well. I am very glad you have resolved to head the procession with me. I am sure it is the right thing and will give universal satisfaction. The Quay is the right place for your speech.'[14]

On the Friday evening before the Tuesday departure, one of the stars of a just completed performance of *HMS Pinafore*, Charles Harding, stepped forward and 'sang with stirring effect' a new patriotic song, *To the front: raise high Australia's banner*. Its composer was Charles Huenerbein, the pianist who struck up *Rule Britannia* when Dalley received news of the go-ahead for the contingent at 'Tarengo' less than three weeks earlier; Huenerbein dedicated the song to Dalley. The melody was very pleasing, noted the *Mail*, and the piece was 'likely to find a permanent place among national compositions'.[15]

On Sunday, churches held special services to mark the troops' departure. About a quarter of the 770 men sent to Sudan were Catholics

The troops embark: the scene at Circular Quay.

– close to the proportion in the general community.[16] Around 50 of them heard Archbishop Patrick Moran, who had arrived from Ireland in September 1884 as successor to Archbishop Vaughan (chapter 18), declare that their mission, under 'the Australian flag', was a glorious one. He did not mention Britain or the empire, instead hoping the conflict would prove 'the harbinger of a new era of Christian civilization' in Africa, 'so long enslaved amid the humiliation and sorrows and darkness and vices of barbarism'.[17] This was a very different message from Dalley's.

At St Andrew's Cathedral, the Anglican bishop, Alfred Barry, urged the troops to fight 'in the spirit of generosity, righteousness, mercy, which is the truest chivalry of the soldier'. Their cause was as just as that of Moses, declared Rev. Paul Clipsham at the Wesleyan service.[18] A prominent dissenter among the clergy, the Congregationalist Rev. James Jefferis, kept his views to himself until well after the contingent departed. The colony's motto should have been peace, he declared in a sermon in April. Instead, 'we have entered upon England's heritage of hatred, engendered by a thousand years of war and of conquest, and we must be prepared to stand the consequences'. These might include going to war 'in the burning deserts of Africa or amongst the snows of Afghanistan, or, may God forfend, upon the fields of France, or of Germany…' This

How the Bulletin depicted the troops' departure; it captioned this drawing, 'Embarkation of the Patriotic Troops to Defend Their Native Land (By our special artist at Khartoum)'. 'Dalli Pasha' bears the ensign and 'Splendid Offer of Troops', 'Barri' (Bishop Barry) conducts, 'Justisma Rtin'(the Chief Justice) is armed for battle, and 'Sirj Onrob Ertson' (the Opposition leader) looks on approvingly.

sorry outcome was the result of 'the impetuous decision of one man'.[19]

An exhausted Dalley left the office early on Monday 2 March, feeling unwell. The events of the following day, however, could not be missed. The weather on the public holiday declared for the troops' departure was propitious – dry, a little cloudy and not too hot. Estimates put the number of people who crammed the city to witness the procession from the Victoria Barracks and embarkation at Circular Quay at around 200,000, two-thirds of Sydney's population.

'To say that the people cheered is but feebly to convey an idea of the enthusiasm as the troops passed along,' reported the *Mail*. 'There was one continuous roar of cheering, like the sound of the breaking sea, and there was literally a sea of waving handkerchiefs and hats'. Reporters noted that Dalley was cheered loudly in the procession and at the quay. There, people filled every vantage point, including the rigging of ships, and flags and bunting flew in profusion.

The troops formed into three sides of a square in front of the Governor to hear him deliver his farewell address. 'Soldiers of New South Wales,' he began,

> For the first time in the great history of the British Empire a distant colony is sending, at her own cost, a completely equipped contingent of troops, who have volunteered with an enthusiasm of which only we who have witnessed it can judge, to assist the Imperial forces in a bitter struggle for the suppression of unspeakable cruelty, and for the establishment of order and justice in a misgoverned country. (Hear, hear.) Countless as have been the occasions when the blood and treasure of England have been poured out freely to protect the feeble, to shield the defenceless, and to maintain the right, there has never been one in which humanity is more deeply interested in the triumph of the arms of England than the cause which you have heroically resolved to uphold by your valour. You will be greeted in Egypt by the hearty welcome of thousands of chivalrous soldiers who have never yet looked upon such an action as yours – (cheers) – the eyes of your gracious Queen will be bent upon your exertions – and in every part of the world where our flag floats men and women and children will eagerly read of your exploits and pray for your success. Soldiers, you carry in your keeping the honour of this great colony, which has made such splendid sacrifices to send you to the front with an equipment of which nations most practised in war might have been proud; and you will have the glorious privilege of helping to maintain the honour of the Empire. (Applause.) In your ranks are numbers who are voluntarily leaving the paths of fortune, worldly advantage, the comforts of home, and the sweetness of domestic life, for heroic service in a bloody war, in which already many brave men have been stricken down. You are doing this to show the world the unity of the mighty and invincible Empire of which you are members. Your country charges itself with the care of those dear ones whom you leave behind. All that generosity, tenderness, and gratitude can do to care for them, to succour and console them, will be looked upon as a labour of love by the nation. (Cheers.) Soldiers, you leave us amidst the acclamations of your fellow-citizens, whose hearts will be with you in your camps and your conflicts – amidst an enthusiasm of admiration and sacrifice unexampled – with the sympathies of every true citizen of the Empire – with our earnest hope that it may be your glorious privilege to share in the triumph as in the service, and to come back to us crowned with England's gratitude, as you are now encompassed with her sympathies. Soldiers – On the part of your fellow-citizens, I now say to you – Farewell! And may God ever have you in His holy keeping. (Loud and prolonged cheering.)

The historian K.S. Inglis has likened Loftus's delivery of Dalley's composition to an ancient Roman sending off the legions.[20] Presumably unaware of its authorship, a senior Colonial Office official, after reading the text, made a note that the Governor should be complimented; it was 'the best of his official utterances'. 'Yes, it is a very good one,' Lord Derby concurred.[21]

Colonel Richardson, commandant of the contingent, responded briefly to Loftus's address. Then repeated cries of 'Mr Dalley' arose from the gathering, but he declined the invitation to speak. As the contingent boarded the two troopships, he and, among many others, Chief Justice Martin and opposition leader Robertson (who supported the Sudan mission) made their way on to the coastal steamer *Namoi*. One of more than a hundred steamships on the harbour for the farewell, it proceeded to a spot near the Heads. All on board cheered heartily as the troopships then steamed past.[22]

Back at work, Dalley turned his attention to securing the colony against attack following reports that a new dispute was brewing between Britain and Russia in Afghanistan. He prepared a lengthy minute 'on the necessity of making additional and permanent provision for our defences', which Cabinet discussed on 10 March. Its main proposal, formulated after discussions with Admiral Tryon, was for the colony to fund two warships, to be stationed at Sydney and under a degree of colonial control but still part of the Royal Navy. After further discussions – including with Martin, who as Premier in 1871 ordered a strengthening of Sydney's harbour fortifications after an earlier Russian scare – the government initiated measures to bolster the defences of Sydney, Newcastle and Botany and placed a large order for armaments.[23]

Another country banquet, this time at Dubbo, provided the venue for a particularly vigorous speech on 12 March; the company reportedly 'rose en masse and cheered' when Dalley concluded. He began with jokes about the threatened 'impeachment' of himself and his colleagues when parliament met five days later (on St Patrick's Day). He said that, perhaps 'owing to unconquerable levity of nature', he was not apprehensive about the fate of the bill the government would introduce to provide legislative backing for the Sudan mission, including 'the validation of all acts done and payments made...in anticipation of the sanction of Parliament'.

He claimed that the 'ablest, the most patriotic, the most cultivated' men in the colony were with the government, as were the 'great body of the working men'.

> This I say advisedly, and with a thorough knowledge. Nobody in the country knows them better than I do, is prouder of their support and confidence, has deeper sympathies with them; and I shall dare to say no man in this country has more of their genuine attachment than it is my great distinction to possess, and which, I may remark, is the highest distinction which I prize.

Against the government were

> those, in the first place, who would have disposed of their souls (if purchasers for such extremely damaged articles could have been obtained in an overstocked market of such commodities) for the conception of our idea, and the means of giving it effect; those who hate a generous action, and those who see and feel in a nobler and purer public spirit the death-blow given to fashions and intrigues; these are our enemies; but they are those also of the Empire.[24]

Back in Sydney, Dalley proposed the health of a visiting English journalist, George Sala, at a dinner in his honour at the Athenaeum Club on 15 March. Sala was the man who, admiring Victoria's booming capital, coined the phrase 'Marvellous Melbourne'. Dalley regretted that he had not been in Sydney two weeks earlier. 'If he had witnessed the other day our national enthusiasm, if he had seen our city in its festival of patriotism and chivalry – (cheers) – he would have told our story to the world in language which all would have read and nobody could have misunderstood.'[25]

As parliament was sitting, Dalley could not attend the St Patrick's Day dinner at the Town Hall two evenings later. He would have received a warm welcome, judging by the cheering that greeted mentions of his name. One speaker suggested to applause that his Sudan initiative would help 'the cause of old Ireland' by giving proof of the desire of Irishmen to share in the responsibilities of the empire. Another who opposed the expedition was also applauded.[26]

In the Legislative Council, members were nearly unanimous in backing a resolution expressing 'hearty approval of the conduct of the ministers in despatching the Australian Contingent'; only four offered any criticism.[27] Opening the debate, Dalley outlined 'the considerations which came into my mind on the morning of the 12th February', the day Strickland's letter appeared in the *Herald*. He felt a great opportunity had arisen to show England and the world that the colonies were not an encumbrance to the mother country but 'could give substantial and immediate and valuable assistance in moments of disaster and difficulty'.

> I was not foolish enough to suppose that our aid was essential; but I believed it would be at least acceptable. I did not think that England required our help; but I indulged in the ambition that she would be pleased at our tendering it.

On the question of the offer's legality, he said that, because haste was essential, 'had we pursued the strictly regular and constitutional course of procedure, the work could never have been done at all'. The government had assumed the responsibility, 'and its weight must be borne by them. We have undoubtedly strained the law, and of course we knew it.'

The Council's most distinguished lawyers, Sir Alfred Stephen and the man who was to succeed Martin as Chief Justice, Frederick Darley, gave Dalley strong support, as Martin had done earlier. Stephen volunteered a legal opinion, saying he had consulted 'the authorities on the subject' and concluded that

> a ministry will be justified in incurring expenditure without previous parliamentary sanction in any case where there is a high probability, though not a certainty – which can never be predicated as to any political measure – that it will be sanctioned, and where there are strong grounds of expediency, though not amounting to a case of emergency, calling for or excusing the expenditure; and that which is true of expenditure will obviously be equally true of any public measure which leads necessarily to expenditure.

He spoke emotionally about Dalley – 'most proud I am to call him my friend' – and the Sudan mission, 'the grandest event which could mark the annals of any colony or country under heaven'. He said it would render the government famous and raise the colony 'from the status of a mere dependency to rank as an integral portion of the greatest empire in the world – greater than were those of Greece and Rome'. A colleague, William Suttor, waxed even more lyrical about the expedition's impact on the standing of New South Wales: the convict stain, the 'stigma of Botany Bay', would be 'washed out in the waters of the Nile'.[28]

The debate in the Legislative Assembly extended over five days, ending with rejection, by 64 votes to 23, of the proposition that 'the occasion did not warrant the despatch of troops from the colony without the authority of Parliament'. Only two members voted against the bill authorising the expedition. Aside from the parliamentary sanction issue, arguments put by the government's critics included that the contingent was an unwarranted extravagance, the war was unjust and immoral, and the episode would foster a spirit of militarism and create an unfortunate precedent.[29]

Daniel O'Connor, Dalley's strident, and then contrite, critic in May 1884 (chapter 21), was among the fiercest opponents. England had no need for the colony's troops in Sudan, so by sending them the government had, as well as 'ruthlessly' violating the constitution, committed 'one of the greatest frauds that was ever perpetrated in any part of the habitable globe', he said. But what really made his 'Irish blood boil', he went on, was Dalley's cowardice in bowing and scraping before Germany over New Guinea. He had committed 'treason not only to New South Wales, but also to Australia'.

The 68-year-old opposition leader Sir John Robertson, a colonist since 1822, saw things differently. Great progress had occurred in his time, but 'never in my life did my blood so thrill with emotion as when I saw the soldiers and horses go away, cheered by 300,000 prosperous people, to the Soudan to help our English brothers', he said. He did not mind that the government had acted without parliamentary authority: 'parliamentary government could not be carried on...if ministers did not take responsibility occasionally.' And he was 'proud and glad' that his 'old friend and past colleague' Dalley had taken the leading role. He had ' conducted this business...more ably than any other man would have conducted it'.[30]

24
Back to earth

Robertson's generous feelings extended to Sir Henry Parkes. He told the Assembly, amid exclamations of 'never', that he would be delighted to see the 69-year-old return; parliament 'was not a parliament' without him.[1] He did not have to wait long for the reappearance of his old adversary turned colleague.

When one of the two members for Argyle resigned in mid-March, George Ranken, co-author of the lands report commissioned by the government in 1883 and a supporter of the Sudan commitment, put his name forward. Ranken withdrew a few days later, after Parkes announced that he had decided to stand in protest at the Sudan decision. 'Whatever else the Soudan expedition has done, it has brought me here,' Parkes told an election meeting at Goulburn.[2]

Explaining his withdrawal, the Protestant Ranken claimed he had no chance of success because his opponent would monopolise the Orange vote. He expected to receive the votes of about 700 Catholics, but there were nine hundred Orange electors.[3]

Sectarianism was alive and well in southern New South Wales – to the extent that Orangemen apparently were prepared to put their distaste for the Catholic Dalley ahead of support for an imperial cause. 'Dear boy, this is a great business,' Dalley remarked to a journalist during preparations for the contingent's departure. 'It is gall and wormwood to the bigots, holy water to the Orangemen. Fancy, after all the years they have been calling us plotting Papists and Fenian rebels, the first men from Australia to serve the Queen on the field of battle are being sent by a Paddy and a Holy Roman.'[4]

It seems, though, that Ranken had been unnecessarily 'chicken-

This Bulletin cartoon suggests Dalley put John Osborne up to standing against the re-emergent Parkes. The caption reads: 'Terrible Apparition. Dalley: "Go ahead Osborne. Who–who–hoo– hoo's afraid." Osborne: "All very fine, Dalley; but you weren't game to go in front yourself."'

hearted' (as a *Freeman's* columnist described him[5]) in withdrawing. A Wesleyan minister turned journalist with little public profile, John Osborne, joined the fray and came within 41 votes of defeating Parkes. While Osborne campaigned principally on support for the Sudan expedition, Parkes, with an eye to the mood of the electorate, switched his focus to other issues, especially the government's 'mischievous' land legislation.[6] He denigrated Dalley, 'a gentleman…before the public at the present time as an object of admiration', for his retreats from and returns to public life, and described himself as one who had 'raised the name of the country' more than any other and whose 'life was written in its history.'⁷

Probably a telegram from the popular Robertson, read out at one of Parkes's election meetings and published in the papers, clinched the contest for the veteran. He sincerely hoped Parkes would be elected; 'our parliament is not representative of New South Wales without him'. Parkes was 'sound on the land question, while his opponent supports the destructive law of the present government,' he went on. His last sentence was especially important, seeking to assure supporters of the Sudan mission that it was all right to vote for Parkes. 'The Soudan contingent matter is now legalised,' he wrote, 'and therefore need not be in the way of the choice of the best man.'⁸

Parkes's unconvincing victory came within days of the contingent's arrival at Suakin. The troops landed on 29 and 30 March, and were 'enthusiastically cheered by British Regiment as they marched into camp,' Samuel reported to Dalley immediately he received the news. General Graham had ridden out with his staff to meet them, congratulated them on their appearance, and expressed admiration 'at the spirit which induced them to come and assist the mother country' and pride at having 'such a force' under his command. Shortly before the men went ashore, Dalley cabled Colonel Richardson, the contingent's commander, offering 'best wishes for a successful campaign'.⁹

The previous week 150 British and Indian troops and many more of Osman Digna's fighters had died in a battle at Tofrik, eight kilometres from Suakin. So when the colonial infantry set out as part of a force of ten thousand soon after midnight on 2 April for Tamai, a village 30 kilometres inland where Osman's men were thought to have massed, they expected fierce fighting. They reached Tofrik, where the horrors of the recent battle were plain to see, at sunrise. Then a hard day's march through scorching desert brought them to Tamai, which they found deserted. The next day, as they pressed on through hilly ground, they encountered sporadic fire that left three New South Wales soldiers with flesh wounds. After setting fire to Tamai, the troops returned without incident to Suakin.[10]

The encounter may have been a 'fizzle', as a *Sydney Mail* columnist described it, but it and Graham's comments on the performance of the contingent were big news in Sydney. The colonials 'bore themselves admirably on the march and under fire,' wrote the general: 'by the report of the General Officer Commanding…and from my own observations, I can testify to the soldier-like spirit and endurance shown by Her Majesty's colonial forces'.[11]

The news spurred Dalley to even greater oratorical heights. In a banquet speech at Grafton on 13 April he said he had previously described the day the contingent left Sydney as 'a most eventful one in our history. Let me now say it is the most memorable in the history of Imperial colonisation. (Cheers.)'

> From it will date advantages unforeseen to our own nation, and to others blessings immediate and remote, unspeakable glory not to us only, but the Empire. No British colony will ever be behind us. (Cheers.) All would have desired to be with us. It is the beginning in these days of utilitarianism of a glorious federation of powers and sympathies and aspirations on a basis of chivalry.

Parkes was in Dalley's sights again, particularly his claim in Goulburn that he had 'raised the name of the country' more than any other. The 'brave men' of the contingent, 'by the very fact of their going', had done 'more for the honour and greatness and prosperity of the colony than a thousand men such as he could accomplish in a lifetime,' said Dalley. 'Gentlemen, they have been thanked by their Queen – (cheers) – and, the greatest of all honour to men of courage, they were waited for in Egypt and received with glory into the ranks of the rarest examples of chivalry in Europe, the Imperial Guards. (Cheers.) What a day was that for an infant nation, for you, for me, for all of us…'[12]

Meanwhile, battlefield glory continued to elude the contingent. After their return to Suakin the infantry were put to work guarding the navvies building a railway line intended to carry an army across the desert to the Nile. The artillery had nothing military to do but drill.

Admiral Tryon.

At home, the focus had shifted to the Russian threat. In his 1 April despatch to Derby, Loftus reported that the latest news of strained relations between England and Russia was causing great alarm throughout the Australian colonies. Russian troop movements in Afghanistan were not the only worry; a reported build-up of the Russian naval squadron in Chinese waters, with more ships expected to arrive via the Cape of Good Hope and Java, brought immediate risks. Loftus expressed confidence in the government's efforts to strengthen the defences of Sydney, Newcastle and Botany, 'ably aided' by advice from Admiral Tryon. But he feared 'the presence of a large hostile fleet along the coast of Australia' would expose 'the commercial navy' to 'great danger and possible loss'.[13]

Dalley was keen to assist Britain in its confrontation with Russia as well as in Sudan, asking Samuel to inquire whether the colony could be of any service in providing preserved meats, cattle or horses for the army in India. 'We are ready to act on behalf of Imperial Government and do anything required and forward with despatch,' he cabled on 30 March. The War Office conveyed its thanks and referred the offer to the Indian Viceroy.[14]

Dalley held frequent meetings with Tryon and other military advisers after reports in mid-April suggested the situation in Afghanistan was deteriorating. Decisions taken included strengthening torpedo defences in Sydney harbour and chartering the P&O mail ship *Massilia* and Orient steamer *Lusitania* for use as armed cruisers.[15] Loftus was now concerned that the harbour defences might not ensure Sydney's safety, reporting to Derby that the city was 'within the reach of the guns of an hostile fleet from outside the Heads'.[16] Dalley's request to Samuel on 17

April to immediately secure the services of three Royal Artillery officers – a major and two lieutenants – was a further sign of the prevailing sense of urgency (the War Office quickly obliged).[17]

But he also had another matter on his mind, writing to Loftus the same day 'to ask a great favour'. Despite having said publicly he had no desire for imperial honours (chapter 20), many critics of the Sudan affair claimed his prime motivation in offering the contingent was to secure a knighthood or peerage. In his letter he asked Loftus to forestall any offer of an honour to save him 'from the necessity of declining'. He had never wanted such distinctions, 'and from the time of the death of my poor wife I have quite resolved never to accept them', he wrote. He wondered, on the other hand, whether 'something could be done for Martin C.J., whose Imperial services have never been sufficiently recognised'.

Replying the next day, Loftus promised to do what he could to meet his wishes, while noting that 'the recognition of your valuable services by your Sovereign is not only a mark of personal distinction but it is a mark of gratitude to the colony, and I think that the refusal of it should not be lightly made'. Nevertheless he concurred with Dalley's view of honours and distinctions, adding, 'Genius requires no ribbons to make it shine in the light of day… You have made an imperishable name for yourself not only in Australia but in Europe and your administration will be looked back upon in future years as the commencement of the Augustan Age for Australasia.'

Loftus cabled Lord Derby on the subject in cipher, but news soon leaked out. London's *Daily Telegraph* noted in mid-May that Dalley's refusal to accept any distinction set 'the purity of his motives' for the Sudan offer 'above suspicion or reproach'. It added, 'England would not be more disappointed if Gladstone were to exchange his 'Mr' for 'Sir' or 'Lord' than Australia would be if the most gifted of her living sons should accept a knighthood or a baronetcy.'[18]

Loftus waited until 11 June – after the announcement of a knighthood for Premier Stuart in the Queen's Birthday (26 May) honours – to send Derby a copy of Dalley's letter. In his covering note he described Dalley as 'the ablest man in the Colony', but added 'I fear that he will not remain in office on account of his failing health – and his retirement will be a serious loss to the Ministry and to the Colony'. On the suggested new honour for Martin, he wrote, 'I am aware of the differences which unfortunately took place between him and my predecessor but I think that sufficient time has now elapsed to obliterate that, and I think that the distinction of K.C.M.G. would be honourably bestowed on him and would be duly appreciated by the Bar and the public opinion of the Colony.' It seems memories of Martin's clashes with Sir Hercules Robinson (chapter 15) were too fresh in London; unlike his predecessor (Stephen) and successor (Darley) as Chief Justice and, among others, Parkes, Robertson and Stuart, he was not granted this distinction.[19]

In the second half of April, with little happening in Sudan and the Russian threat agitating colonists, Dalley's thoughts turned again to aiding the British in India. He cabled Samuel on 1 May renewing the offer made a month earlier to send supplies. A week earlier he had asked for urgent advice from the War Office on the 'destination and employment' of the colony's contingent 'if Imperial troops are withdrawn from Egypt'.[20] He also asked Colonel Richardson in a confidential cablegram, 'What about Contingent serving in India, if deemed necessary by Imperial authorities?'

Richardson replied that he had consulted his officers; most thought their men should be despatched elsewhere only after volunteering again, but believed almost all would do so.[21] Samuel advised, after speaking with Lords Derby and Hartington, that operations were unlikely to resume in Sudan. Some British troops would remain at Suakin but the destination of the others was uncertain – either India, Egypt or the Mediterranean. He added that, as the New South Wales contingent was unlikely to be called on for 'immediate active service in Africa' and 'may be required for the defence of their own colony, Her Majesty's Government will under the altered circumstances be guided by the wishes of your Government'.

Despite the fear of a Russian naval attack, Dalley did not think the troops were needed for home defence. He wrote in a minute agreed to by cabinet on 27 April that since the contingent's departure

> we have...not only brought up our defence to the state in which it was when they left our shores, but we have at the present moment a very much larger force than we ever before possessed, while the Imperial Government has within the last fortnight made extraordinary provision at enormous cost for our protection. In the matter of the external defence of our coast and commerce an immense outlay has been undertaken by the Naval Commander-in-Chief of this station.

The minute proposed that the government approve, 'if the Contingent volunteered for service, of its employment if necessary in India and of its maintenance there by the colony on the same terms as in Egypt; and the same might be said of its occupation for military service of any place in the Mediterranean.' Only in this way could the colony 'render effective the assistance which we endeavoured to furnish to the Imperial Government... Our purpose was to assist the arms of England wherever our help was needed.'

The new offer was cabled immediately to Samuel, and to Richardson who was told, 'All depends upon voluntary act of Contingent. Communicate with General on this subject. Of course, members of Contingent who desire to return will be brought back at the expense of the colony.'[22] News of Britain's acceptance of this 'patriotic offer' arrived the next day. In Suakin, enthusiasm was muted. Richardson reported that four out of five of the artillerymen volunteered but, initially, only a third of the infantry. A second count the next day increased that proportion to three-fifths.[23]

This time, press comment was generally adverse, editors arguing that the troops should come home to defend the colony. *Freeman's* was a surprising exception, contending that 'if England needed our assistance in the Soudan she needs it now twenty-fold... Now is the time for us to show to the world how much our sympathy and assistance are worth.'[24]

The argument quickly became academic. Samuel advised Dalley on 2 May that a peaceful settlement of the Afghanistan dispute seemed probable, and three days later that 'peace appears to be assured.' Lord Wolseley, visiting Suakin from his headquarters on the Nile, inspected the colonial troops on 8 May and commended them 'in highest terms'. Five days later Dalley cabled Samuel,

> If no further operations contemplated in the Soudan and peace arrived with Russia there seems no reason to keep our troops at Suakin. Ascertain this at once. We shall if so make arrangements for their immediate return to the colony, defray the cost.

This message crossed with one from Samuel reporting that the War Office had suggested that, as active operations had ceased in Sudan, it was time for the contingent to go home. Dalley replied saying the colony would charter a troopship for the return journey or, if that proved impossible, bring them home on an Orient steamer due to call at Suakin on 5 June. No need, Samuel responded almost immediately; the Admiralty would provide free transport home for the troops. Two men had died of disease at Suakin and 11 were now judged too sick to travel. The remainder departed for Sydney on the steamship *Arab* on 18 May.

It was a very friendly parting. A message from the Queen expressed 'her great gratification that her colonial forces have served side by side with British troops in the field' and wished them 'a prosperous voyage home'. The War Office gave the colony a nine-pounder field battery, which was loaded on to the *Arab*. Dalley arranged for the contingent's horses to be handed over as a gift to the British forces. Lord Wolseley suggested that a company of the colonial troops be taken on a short visit to England, saying 'it would be a most popular thing'. But Dalley declined with thanks, believing 'the colony would prefer the return of the whole force at the same time and by the same vessel'.[25]

On the home front, although the Russian threat had receded, Admiral Tryon submitted a plan to Dalley on 4 May aimed at keeping a hostile fleet at bay. His idea was to encourage the residents of ports around the coast to resist any enemy demands for coal. All colonies should agree 'that in every case, whether a house, a village, or town suffers from an enemy because his demands are bravely refused, the loss incurred will be made good out of the general revenue of these colonies'. Dalley commended the scheme in a circular to the other colonies. Responses – including a prediction by Queensland's Samuel Griffith that unanimity would be hard to achieve 'until some form of federal action is initiated' – were generally wary.[26]

Dalley remained in charge of defence matters but left the Colonial Secretary's office on the return of Stuart on 11 May. The *Mail* thought the Premier looked well enough to resume duty, but a better informed Loftus advised Derby that it was very doubtful he would be able to long bear the fatigues of office, 'and his physicians have warned him of the danger he will incur by overstraining his mental faculties'.[27] In the meantime, Dalley – who had complained to his friend Alexander Oliver, 'They are simply tearing me to pieces here in all hours with work, until I am sometimes…unequal to the least exertion'[28] – had a little more time for other things, including banquets.

Presiding at a Bar dinner on 22 May for the presentation of a portrait of Sir James Martin to hang in the Supreme Court, he made characteristic speeches in praise of Martin and 82-year-old Sir Alfred Stephen. 'Eulogy is at all times pleasing to its object, but when it springs from the kindly heart and flows over the silver tongue of one so genial and so eloquent as our host, it has a charm beyond my power adequately to acknowledge,' Martin responded. Dalley was 'always distinguished…for saying graceful things in the very best manner, and at the very best time,' said Stephen. He again praised the Sudan commitment, adding, 'There is not a man here, nor in the country, who knows [Dalley], who will think that in anything he has ever done he has been looking forward to self-seeking or self-glorification…'

Dalley thanked Martin and Stephen for their public support on Sudan, and joked that he could take the cheers of the assembled judges and barristers as a pardon for his 'gross and unconstitutional' deed. He said he sometimes reproached himself for seeing so little of the members of the profession that he, as Attorney-General, nominally led.

But as you know, I have fallen under various temptations, coming to me in various forms. Literature and politics and, latest of all, a taste for soldiering – (cheers and laughter) – have made me almost a deserter from your ranks. No one has more keenly felt how unworthy in all respects, save in a religious conviction of the responsibilities of my great office, I have been to lead you. (Cheers.)[29]

His next speech, six evenings later, was at the annual dinner held by Sydney's consuls. Fifteen representatives of countries ranging from Peru to Germany were present; their guests included Premier Stuart, opposition leader Robertson and Chief Justice Martin. The Russian consul chaired proceedings, leading Martin to observe, amid laughter, that relations between 'the mother country and another country (turning to the chairman)' were somewhat strained, a situation he hoped would prove temporary.

Dalley's speech was another emotional call for British Australia to welcome others to the region. 'What jealousy should we have of those who bring us strong arms, simple habits, indomitable energies, and minds trained in the best schools in the world?' he asked.

> If we could buy these treasures for ourselves what would be a nobler object of expenditure? But when they come to us as gifts like air and light and water, helping us in our national life to breathe more freely and see more easily and clearly, what can be more dreadful than to turn away from them and shut ourselves up in a poisonous atmosphere of selfishness and darkness? (Cheers.)[30]

Freeman's described his next speech, at a banquet in Wagga five days later, as the best of the many 'brilliant' addresses he had given on the Sudan commitment: 'They deserve to be ranked, and hereafter they will doubtless be ranked, among the very best specimens of Australian oratory.'[31] Reading the text, punctuated every few sentences (in places every few words) with 'cheers' or 'applause', it is not hard to imagine the excitement on the evening.

The despatch of the New South Wales contingent and the offers made by other colonies were, he said, a force for peace as they showed the world that 'if the integrity of the Empire is ever menaced, the British colonies will all be ready'. Also promoting peace, and having 'a glorious power to enforce it', was the alliance he expected to see cemented soon between the Empire and the United States. He scorned the argument that the Russian scare was a reason for returning the troops to Sydney; 'rather...had we known of the greater peril, we should have acted with greater promptitude in despatching all the support we could render.' And home defences were stronger than ever, not least because of 'Imperial expenditure for our own protection to which our paltry contributions were as nothing'.

> Day after day, and night after night, the great and distinguished officer who commands the squadron which guards these seas might be seen advising, organising, preparing for our defence... Let us not in common decency think too proudly of what little service Heaven and our own enviable fortune have enabled us to do for England; but, on the other hand, let us think with unspeakable gratitude of what England was ready and is prepared to do for us. (Cheers.)

He said the colony's action had exalted it in the world's esteem and 'lifted up the public feeling of the country'. He thanked God that nearly all the troops had survived.

> Of all our blessings, this is the richest. We sent them for service – not for slaughter. (Cheers.) They have done all that they were asked to do bravely – (cheers) – cheerfully, and nobly. (Cheers.) They evaded no duty, complained of no labour, were ready to obey every call... We expected, when they left us, that they would uphold our honour. They have done so. (Cheers.)[32]

Dalley took ill again in the weeks between the Wagga dinner and the return of the contingent. His medical adviser, Dr Charles Mackellar, head of the colony's Board of Health, reportedly cautioned him against any return to the long hours and fatiguing journeys of the past few months.[33]

Many members of the contingent also sickened as they steamed home on the *Arab*. Twelve suffering from typhoid or dysentery were hospitalised at Colombo; three subsequently died. One man succumbed on the ship and was buried at sea. Another died after the contingent disembarked at Sydney's North Head quarantine station, where the *Arab* anchored on the night of 19 June. The contingent's total death toll was nine.[34]

With Dalley unwell, the other ministers who played major roles in organising the contingent, Treasurer Dibbs and Works Minister Francis Wright, took charge of arrangements for the troops' welcome.[35] Dalley wrote to Stuart from Manly the day before the *Arab* anchored to thank him for a 'beautiful present' he had sent, which he would 'cherish as a memento of our unbroken intercourse of labour, confidence and attachment'. He added that he was very ill, and 'just now suffering a good deal from a sharp attack of gout'.[36] However, he recovered sufficiently to visit the contingent at their temporary quarters on nearby North Head.[37]

The colony's long drought broke the weekend the troops were in quarantine. Following Dalley's recommendation at a meeting with the Mayor and acting City Engineer in early May, water supplies from the city's severely depleted main source, the Botany Swamps, had been 'curtailed' and plans expedited to pipe water from the Nepean.[38] Loftus was now able to tell Derby that 'the fears of a water famine for Sydney have been happily relieved by copious rains for four days', and good falls had been recorded throughout the colony. He also reported in his despatch of 25 June on the troops' parade through Sydney two days earlier: 'Although the rain fell in torrents during the whole day, the streets were lined with thousands of spectators who proved their enthusiasm by loud and repeated cheering.'[39]

It was a dank homecoming. Without breakfast, and without the warm flannel

A family's greeting during the wet march through the city.

underwear that Dr Mackellar had sent to the quarantine station but somebody had neglected to issue, the troops reboarded the *Arab* early in the morning for the trip to Circular Quay. The Governor and his guard of honour, and the ministry, including Dalley, were there to greet them when they came ashore about 10 a.m. wearing the light khaki battle dress issued in Sudan. One band after another took up the refrain of 'Home, Sweet Home', reported the *Mail*; 'its pathetic music was never heard to finer effect'. *Freeman's* described what came next.

> The colonial military genius for blundering was revealed in many phases during the long and sloppy hour at the Quay; first the bands being ordered to play six distinct and separate tunes near each other at one and the same time; and secondly, the men being put through an amazing amount of manoeuvring before starting, with the only imaginable object of getting the poor fellows thoroughly wet before commencing their long march.

The parade through the city to Victoria Barracks was a grim affair, despite the cheers of the thousands 'bravely' lining the streets. The men trudged 'ankle deep through mud and water to slow music, while exposed all the while to a pelting rain and a marrow-freezing wind'. Then they had to 'stand shivering and hungry in the bleak barrack yard' for a half hour's 'oratorical dumb show'.

The dismal scene at Victoria Barracks.

Loftus began the speechmaking, which few present could hear, with what reads like another Dalley composition. It was a 'subject for our gratitude to Heaven', he told the troops, 'that you have not been called to exercise in any bloody engagement the courage and devotion which prompted you to volunteer for the defence of the Empire'. After Colonel Richardson replied, representatives of Victoria, New Zealand, Queensland and South Australia delivered lengthy congratulatory addresses. Tasmania's representative and Premier Stuart had the good sense not to follow suit, instead handing their speeches to the press.

Proceedings ended with three cheers for the Governor, 'another three for the Hon. W.B. Dalley, and others for the Premier and Ministry'. At the instigation of the thoughtful Dr Mackellar, the troops were all given a glass of spirits before they departed.[40] Dalley joined Lady Isabella Martin and five of her children at the barracks and accompanied them to his former home, 'Greycliffe', Vaucluse, where they were living apart from Sir James. Fourteen-year-old Emily Martin wrote next day to an absent sister,

> imagine my horror when Mother asked Mr Dalley to come home to lunch and he plopped himself on to the seat which already was occupied by Florence, Constance and myself, so we four big people had to drive all the way home on one seat. When Mr Dalley told the Admiral he was coming in our carriage he said 'Why, there are ten people in it already'. He also told us that it looked like a pigeon pie stuffed full.[41]

25
The aftermath

Dalley was used to praise, but perhaps not to the lavish quantities offered at a banquet held two days after the troops' return. Guests of honour were the representatives of the other colonies who had come to Sydney for the welcome home. Premier Stuart chaired proceedings; others present included the Governor, Chief Justice, opposition leader Robertson, Admiral Tryon and Colonel Richardson.

The intercolonial speakers strongly endorsed Dalley's observation that the despatch of the New South Wales contingent had been greeted with 'gracious sympathy', not jealousy, in the other colonies. Sir George Verdon of Victoria thought future generations would cherish the 'authors and fathers' of the 'great enterprise' as they did 'the heroes of former times'. New Zealand's representative reported that his colony's elder statesman, Sir George Grey, regarded it as 'the greatest event of modern times'. Other visitors called Dalley 'a genius' and 'a noble statesman'. His friend Sir James Martin concurred, saying 'no brighter name would be found in aftertimes than that of the father of the contingent, William Bede Dalley. (Cheers.)'[1]

His chief sparring partner on the Pacific annexations issue, Victorian Premier James Service, offered similar sentiments in a speech in parliament soon afterwards. Dalley's 'lightning flash of inspiration' had 'fused these colonies into one, and welded the empire together in such a way that it will never, I believe, be disintegrated again,' he said to loud cheers. The 'highest honour' was due to him and to those who had assisted him in carrying out 'his brilliant conception'.[2]

Two more welcome home banquets were held, for the officers and for the whole contingent. Chairing the officers' event at the Town Hall on 7 July, Colonel Roberts, commander of the NSW Artillery, praised

Dalley for raising 'the military spirit of the colony'; he had shown that he was 'at heart a soldier, and a plucky soldier'. Dalley responded with a vigorous rejection of the argument that by involving itself in an imperial struggle the colony had invited attack by England's enemies. 'If the Empire is at war with any foreign nation, every part of the Empire is the foreigner's enemy,' he said. Decisions to attack would be based on the expected outcome, not on 'which part of the Empire has or has not been most demonstrative in its loyalty'.

> We have assuredly rendered ourselves stronger in the eyes of foreign nations, proclaimed our security from attack, by showing that we are ready to meet it with a light heart, and can spare help to the Empire abroad in her hour of need. (Applause.) And when the time comes, and it is at hand, when these united Australian colonies can put in the field in six weeks in any part of the world where the Empire is involved in war an army of fifteen or twenty thousand men, and still reserve abundant protection for ourselves, we shall have reached the highest point of safety – (cheers) – for then we shall not hear of any expeditions to plunder these colonies. (Hear, hear.)

He again suggested that a more peaceful era had begun, with 'benevolence and brotherhood' replacing the 'old national jealousies'. He defended his policy of welcoming other imperial powers to the region with a reference to King Solomon's prayer for the foreigner at the consecration of the Temple at Jerusalem. Colonial politicians should 'strive to imitate the beautiful spiritualising toleration of the Rabbis in consecrating here the great national temple which we are slowly building up out of the freewill offerings and votive gifts of the civilised peoples of all the world,' he proposed amid cheers.[3]

Nine hundred men, and 500 women who observed proceedings from the gallery, attended the banquet for the contingent – most in their khaki uniforms – hosted by the 'citizens of Sydney' at the Exhibition Building on 28 July. The many speechmakers struggled to be heard at what the *Telegraph* described as 'probably the most thoroughly jovial entertainment of its kind that has ever been witnessed in the colonies'. In the general din – as flowers were thrown from the gallery 'and in return apples and oranges were shooting upwards towards the enraptured ladies' – most

A toast to the soldiers at the contingent banquet. The women, as was customary, watch from the balcony.

speeches were inaudible to all but those within a few metres of the speakers. But when Dalley rose after the Governor,

> Even the ladies bent over the balcony railings to catch his words; the khakee suits crowded up to the platform, whilst a violent effort to maintain silence was made throughout the building. Applause succeeded applause, and when the honourable gentleman gave way at length to Sir John Robertson the cheers that had greeted the father of the expedition were re-inspired by the genial presence of Sir John.

Robertson called for three cheers for his 'dear friend' Dalley, who in his speech had praised the opposition leader's 'chivalrous sense of fair play, of perfect courage, of admirable temper, and of old-world fidelity to old friendships'. Dalley told the troops their actions would 'live in history'. If the government were remembered at all it would be for 'the accident of its being enabled to give your heroic service to the Empire, your patriotic example to the world'. With *The Bulletin* clearly in mind, he criticised those who had ridiculed the contingent.

> The smallness of your numbers, the childishness of our presumption in sending you, even your misfortune in failing to have an opportunity of signalising your devotion on the battlefield – all these have been made the elements of that oppressive, heart-breaking facetiousness, the exercise

The Bulletin's response to Dalley's suggestion at the contingent banquet that 'the oppressive, heart-breaking facetiousness' of 'small humorists' critical of the Sudan venture 'tempts a really humorous man...to ideas of violence'.

of which so dangerously tempts a really humorous man – no matter how intense may be his love of peace – to ideas of violence. (Laughter.) One feels what new and unbearable sadness is given to the world by some of its small humorists. (Renewed laughter.)[4]

Dalley had other speechmaking engagements in July. Proposing the toast to the President at a banquet celebrating United States Independence Day, he noted that 'representatives of all nations and peoples' had found a generous welcome in the US and 'contributed to its stupendous progress'. He repeated his expectation of a 'glorious alliance' between the US and the Empire – a 'federation of the English-speaking peoples of the world' that would guarantee universal peace, 'not for the glory of empire, but for the elevation and protection of mankind'.[5]

His next speech, in praise of a coastal steamer captain whose ship had sunk after running onto rocks, was controversial; could it be seen as

Reading of the Declaration of Independence at the 4 July banquet, 1885. The unofficial colonial flag with Southern Cross and Union Jack adjoins the Stars and Stripes.

interference by the Attorney-General in the Marine Board's examination of the case? He responded to the suggestion by saying it had not occurred to him, 'but the instant that I discovered that the occupation of office interfered with the most public and unreserved expression of sympathy with misfortune in any form, I should get rid of the difficulty by resigning my office.' As it turned out, the board pronounced the day before Dalley spoke, suspending the certificate of the captain, David Walker, for six months. But his intention to chair the testimonial meeting, which raised £250 for Walker, had been announced before the decision.

Dalley said he had sailed often with Walker on the Sydney–Melbourne run, and admired his manliness, gentleness, truthfulness and high courage.

When I read in the papers from day to day of his standing by his wrecked ship, of his seeing everybody safely out of her, of his misery, of the activity of those who were prosecuting him, and heard no single voice in any quarter raised in his favour, I had a picture of the man before me as I saw him 20 years ago on a voyage to Melbourne – through a tempestuous night, tending in the pauses of the storm an almost dying woman and two sick and helpless children, whom he had placed in his own deck cabin. How many hundred times in his numberless voyages for the last 33 years…in all seasons and weathers…has my experience of that night been that of thousands of his passengers?[6]

In mid-August, with parliament due to meet again in three weeks, Dalley made his last ministerial country visit, to Albury. Works Minister Wright and Henry Cohen, the Minister for Justice, accompanied him on the overnight train south. As they approached Albury in the early morning, snow glistened on the mountains – a sight, according to the *Herald*'s reporter, novel to all on board. A large crowd greeted them at the station, including some of the district's Germans whose representative presented an address thanking Dalley for his Maitland speech welcoming the German presence in the Pacific (chapter 22).

He began his speech at the evening's banquet by apologising for the long time that had elapsed since the ministers received the town's invitation to visit. As victims of 'either our excessive labours or it may be of the too abundant hospitality of the people – (laughter) – I do not precisely know which, for I am not clear whether we were disabled by our services or their rewards – we were unable to visit you,' he said. 'But with returning health came back the old sweet temptations…'

Dalley again ridiculed the notion of trying to shut other imperial nations out of the South Pacific, and contended that friendship and cooperation offered 'the only means of universal enlightenment and diffusion of all the blessings of civilisation'. He gave details of the build-up of the colony's defences since the Sudan commitment, including a more than doubling of the number of men in uniform to nearly 8,000. The bulk of the speech was an exhaustive account of progress in implementing the new land law.

He said the government planned to introduce legislation on local govern-ment and public health in the 'brief, and I trust brilliant' session that would bring the parliament's three-year term to an end. Both bills were 'works of enormous difficulty, and consequently of peril to those by whom they are undertaken'.

> If we succeed in passing them into law, our title to public confidence will be strengthened. (Hear, hear.) If we fail, as we may do, we shall have the patriotic consolation of making the work easier and safer for those who will replace us.[7]

If Dalley was doubtful about the government's prospects, Governor Loftus was even more so. In his last despatch to Lord Derby before the resumption he advised that Stuart's health was failing and 'if he attempts to face Parliament, he will do so at the risk of his life'. The Premier was clinging tenaciously to office, turning 'a deaf ear to the advice of his friends and medical advisers', Loftus added. As a result the cabinet was weak, 'and may possibly undergo a defeat on the meeting of Parliament'.[8]

Two months earlier the Governor noted that it had been suggested Stuart move to the upper house as Premier and Dalley transfer to the Assembly. He told Derby he could not assent to this; Stuart would have to accept a less arduous post in a government headed by Dalley, 'the only member of the existing Cabinet who could form a new Ministry'. He reported in the same despatch, though, that Dalley's health also was declining, 'and he is anxious to retire from public life and to have repose'.[9]

Under concerted attack from an opposition bolstered by the return of Parkes, it soon became clear that the government's chances of passing significant legislation were negligible. Dalley introduced the public health bill on the first sitting day, acknowledging that as it had financial implications it would normally be considered first by the Legislative Assembly rather than the Council. Members accepted his proposal that they discuss a version stripped of its financial clauses while the Assembly dealt with the local government bill. This would save time, he hoped, while avoiding a constitutional conflict with the lower house.

Dalley seems to have played a substantial role in preparing the bill, in collaboration with its chief author Dr Mackellar, now a member of the

Legislative Council. His speech commending it was long and passionate. Failure to do everything possible to pass comprehensive public health legislation would be criminally irresponsible, he declared. Sydney's death rate was similar to that in 'cold, wet and foggy' London where large numbers were 'imperfectly fed, insufficiently clad' and unable to buy the fuel needed to stay warm. This was shocking

> when we consider that we have in this city perhaps the finest climate in the world, that we have an abundantly-fed and prosperous people, that up to a very recent period we have enjoyed almost absolute immunity from several of the severer forms of epidemic disease which are born of poverty and suffering, and insufficient nourishment…

The bill was wide-ranging, dealing with, among other things, quarantine, food adulteration, disease prevention in lodging-houses and in public baths and washhouses, and the regulation and inspection of dairies. Perhaps with the personal tragedy of the loss of his wife to typhoid in mind, Dalley spoke at length on the risks posed by unclean dairies and careless storage of milk, a food 'prone to absorb germ life' and spread typhoid, scarlet fever, diphtheria and other diseases.[10]

Speaking on the bill a week later, Dr Mackellar described some current practices that had to be stamped out, including dumping of nightsoil in Sydney's water supply catchment.[11] Unfortunately, proceedings in the Assembly on the day he spoke, 1 October, ensured that there was no chance of the legislation advancing. The government weathered a censure motion against Works Minister Wright, one of a series launched against ministers, and then arranged for parliament to be prorogued until the end of October. It resigned five days later, Stuart finally conceding that he was too ill to continue as Premier.

On Stuart's advice, Loftus asked Dalley to form a ministry. After he declined, giving as the reason 'greatly impaired' health due to overwork, Dibbs was sent for.[12] The Governor accepted the new Premier's advice to dissolve parliament and call immediate elections. Dalley's former junior in the criminal court, John Want, succeeded him as Attorney-General; most of Stuart's other ministerial colleagues continued in the new government.

The evening before the Stuart government resigned, the Premier and most of his ministers, including Dibbs, visited Manly for a lecture by Dalley in aid of the village's park improvement fund and Catholic orphanage. Others who caught the special steamer from Circular Quay arranged for the event included the colony's military leaders Major-General Richardson (promoted from Colonel after the Sudan expedition) and Colonel Roberts. Dalley's subject was 'the Australian Soldier', also the title of a recent talk by Parkes that had attracted an audience, he observed with relish, of 'but 98 persons'.

He rejected Parkes's contention that the great armies of Europe had a disastrous effect on national life; rather, men emerged from their compulsory military service improved mentally, morally and physically. The colony could not emulate European practice by withdrawing 'large numbers of the most energetic members of the community' from their ordinary occupations. But young men whose leisure time might otherwise be 'much more unprofitably employed' were eagerly joining the volunteer forces and receiving training 'beneficial to them and to the nation'.

> We are cultivating a military spirit throughout the country, first of all, because a readiness to die if need be in defence of country is the most absolutely perfect form of citizenship... We are increasing the securities of life and property by organising in all distant parts of the country bodies of men amongst whom will be cultivated habits of respect, obedience, and skill in the use of arms. We are [forming] one great body of patriotic citizen soldiers who will protect us by the very fact of their organization from the possible peril of invasion...

On the Sudan commitment, he said it had attracted warm praise from 'the sovereign, the army, the Parliament, the press, the people of England'; all except 'a few disappointed politicians in this country' had applauded it. He again dismissed the argument that it had increased the risk of an attack on the colony, but said this was growing for other reasons – developments in shipping that meant an enemy could now land 'an enormous force' and the temptations offered by 'our immense increase in national wealth'. Britain had responded generously to the threat:

At the present time her fleets, to the maintenance of which we do not contribute a single farthing, protect our coasts; and as you know, long before danger had assumed any definite form, England had incurred an expenditure for our defence, during a few months, which would have paid our whole military expenditure for 10 years. These are the considerations which justify, nay, compel us into cooperation with her, and…which in moments of real peril, near or distant, will compel every British colony… to stand by the Empire.

Dalley concluded with a reference to the coming elections. The 'noise of men arming for the conflict' was heard throughout the colony; 'battles with which the Australian soldier will have nothing to do will be fought and won within the next three or four weeks, in which we all hope and pray the best men, the bravest, the gentlest, the most chivalrous, may win. (Cheers.)'[13]

The outcome in Dibbs's seat, St Leonards, did not match this hope. Parkes abandoned the Argyle constituency to take on the new Premier and, after thundering about 'the diseased and corrupt state' of parliament under Stuart and making vague promises of a bridge over the harbour, had a convincing win.[14] Dalley admitted in a letter to his friend Alexander Oliver to feeling melancholy: 'My heart bleeds for poor old Mr Dibbs, and all his courage, his truth and his disappointment…'[15]

Dibbs quickly received invitations to stand in ten country electorates, and had an easy win in the one he chose, Murrumbidgee. A few days earlier he was guest of honour at a banquet at St Leonards chaired by Dalley. Amid laughter and cheers, Dalley described Parkes's propensity to materialise 'at critical epochs of our history, as he has always described them'. Whether the crisis was 'a widespread conspiracy to assassinate royal princes' or 'failing to build a bridge from the commanding heights of Fort Phillip to this lovely suburb', he could be relied on to appear when his 'heroic and supremely unselfish exertions' were needed.

Then came a passionate denunciation of the recent political mudslinging. With Parkes clearly in mind, he said,

> Language that would have disgraced any society has been adopted as the fitting utterances of persons who impudently, almost grotesquely, pose as statesmen and high constitutional authorities. (Prolonged cheering.) Abuse, unredeemed by a single gleam of originality or humour, has

been showered upon opponents. (Hear, hear.) Imputations, sometimes ludicrous, sometimes infamous, but always false, have been made upon men concerning whom it would be a cruel wrong to speak in the same breath with their libellers. (Applause.) A great appeal to the judgment of the people has been made to turn upon wholesale and indiscriminate libel.

He urged the voters of Murrumbidgee to help 'save the honour of the country' by returning Dibbs, 'an inspired, gallant, undaunted, and honest man'. Dibbs returned the compliment. Who could doubt, he said, that the new government would have Dalley's advice and assistance, 'for it is impossible for him to change'.

> We know what he did for the late Government, and the incessant labour and toil to which he subjected himself to make the Stuart Government a success – (cheers) – and I believe what he has done and what the Stuart Government succeeded in doing as a Government will be remembered when those who have done their utmost to destroy our fame and reputation are forgotten in the dust. (Cheers.)[16]

A note Dalley sent Stuart in early November shows his eagerness to help Dibbs. Declining Stuart's invitation to go on a three-day trip with him, he wrote that he thought 'duty to Dibbs requires that at this critical time I should be with him'. The difficulties 'confounding' the new Premier could be surmounted if he was well advised: 'Everything depends on prompt and wise diplomacy and a good programme.' Dalley added that he was suffering from 'a very bad head and a feeble heart – the result, I fear, of a little too much excitement and exposure'.[17]

Two more ministers lost their seats at the elections. One was Wright, under attack for an alleged conflict of interest between his ownership of a large carrying business and his position as Works Minister. Dalley observed at a dinner in his honour in November that he had 'administered for two years and a half a great department, without anyone raising the question of the inexpediency or danger of his position'. Then he had been 'suddenly and bitterly attacked night after night, and was finally, in a storm of misrepresentation, swept out of the ranks of your public servants'.[18]

The elections produced a large turnover of members of the Assembly and renewed political instability. When the Legislative Council met again in mid-November, George Thornton, a former Mayor of Sydney who had an unpleasant run-in with Dalley in 1858 (chapter 4) and was now Dibbs's Mines Minister, assumed the post of government representative in the upper house. He promised to do his best, though 'I cannot hope to succeed as [Dalley] succeeded; it is not possible.' William Piddington observed of Dalley, his sparring partner on financial matters over the previous three years, that 'he appears to have formed so high an ideal of the character of a minister and member of Parliament that I think the House and the country will feel a great loss by his retirement'. Thanking members for their 'forbearance, consideration and support', Dalley said the three years, 'while they have been the most laborious they have at the same time, so far as public life is concerned, been the pleasantest years of my life'.[19]

Pleasantries were much fewer in the Assembly. The government just survived a no-confidence vote after a heated debate that lasted nine days. It resigned two weeks later, on 16 December, when defeat loomed over proposals to deal with the colony's million-pound budget deficit, partly caused by military spending but mainly a legacy of the drought.[20] The new Governor, Lord Charles Carrington, who had arrived five days earlier – Loftus departed on 9 November after a series of farewells at which Dalley was prominent – called on Robertson to form a new government. The 69-year-old, who was far from well, took office reluctantly and had difficulty forming a ministry after Parkes refused his offer of the Colonial Secretaryship.[21]

Robertson's government was defeated two months later, with Parkes supporting a censure motion over its financial proposals. Robertson accused his fellow political veteran of playing 'treacherous games'; Parkes had helped him 'put the former Government out, and then left me high and dry'. Parkes regarded himself as 'a God Almighty', Robertson added, and he would be reluctant to trust him again: 'It is all I – I – I with him.'[22] Sir Patrick Jennings, Colonial Secretary in Dibbs's government, formed the next administration, which lasted 11 months.

Popular with politicians of all stripes, Robertson was feted at a birthday dinner at the end of November at which Dalley, Martin and Admiral Tryon spoke. Others present included Stuart, Dibbs, Jennings and the Catholic Archbishop Patrick Moran, recently returned from Rome after being made a Cardinal.[23]

Dalley called at the Australian Club to change on his way to the dinner, and found a 'heartbreaking' letter from Martin there. The subject was his continuing separation from his wife; it appears that he hoped Dalley, who was on good terms with her, could help bring about a reconciliation. Dalley replied briefly, saying that 'for poor Eleanor Emiline in Heaven' [the daughter whose death in 1880 precipitated the breakdown of the marriage (chapter 17)] he would consider the rest of his life well spent if he could be the instrument of bringing together again 'two beings so dear to me by all ties'.[24]

Dalley wrote occasional chatty letters to Lady Martin, including one a few weeks earlier replying to a telegram suggesting he join her at a performance of Gilbert and Sullivan's *Patience*. Her message had arrived only a few moments before the fiddlers began tuning up, he began.

> Our telegraph people here put a check upon the dangerous excitement of this means of communication by keeping the messages an hour or two for deliberate perusal and careful study; and then deliver them by a romantic boy who prefers flowers, birds' nests, fish and long rambles to a swift discharge of duty.

But he could not have gone anyway because he was entertaining the widow of a noted flautist whose only child had died recently at the age of 13. He had encountered her 'a day or two ago on the pier looking so sad and lonely that I begged her to come up and see us'.

> She came to dinner last night and Bess [presumably the cook] surpassed herself – and a German gentleman sang for us and we suffered her troubles for an hour or two. I feel as complacent as possible and am quite satisfied that I shall meet her in Heaven for I prepared for this feast and presided over it with a headache that has lasted for 30 hours and preferred dining with the poor afflicted lady to accepting the Admiral's invitation to 'dine' last night on board the 'Nelson' [the navy flagship] at a farewell dinner to Lord Augustus [Loftus].[25]

The day after the Robertson dinner Dalley wrote again to Martin, this time at length. 'Nothing has given me greater distress than the deplorable estrangement which, however originating, has for so long destroyed the peace and happiness of the family,' he began. He had told Lady Martin he thought the family should be together, especially now that their daughters were 'going into womanhood' and the colony's social life was about to be 'entirely altered' with the arrival of 42-year-old Governor Carrington with his wife and children. But he had not presumed to speak 'to you, my dear Chief', on the subject. He felt sure that Martin's failure to mention his troubles previously had been 'out of your sympathy with my own troubles'.

So far as he could gather, he went on, Lady Martin's only objection to returning home to Potts Point was that the house and grounds were too small.

> Although 'Clarens' is one of the loveliest of residences, and your genius has made it a beacon of beauty, I am entirely of her opinion that it is neither large enough for the family – nor for your station with its necessary special liabilities. A great house – with extensive grounds – is, I think, essential to both.

He offered, if his health allowed, to help Lady Martin find a suitable place and then fit it out for the family. The remainder of his life would be 'well and happily employed', he reiterated, if he could help bring about 'the re-establishment of your happiness and the maintenance of the dignity of a domestic life as dear to me as my own'.[26]

26
Church and state

Dalley's prominent role in the lay affairs of the Catholic Church resumed with the arrival of Archbishop Moran in September 1884. 'Immense throngs' turned out on a sunny Monday to greet the archbishop at Circular Quay. The next day Dalley called to pay his respects, and apparently impressed on Moran the virtues of 60 acres owned by the church at Manly as a site for Sydney's archiepiscopal residence.

Two days later, on 11 September, Moran visited Manly with the bishops of Adelaide, Ballarat, Maitland, Goulburn, Rockhampton and Armidale, who had come to Sydney for his welcome. Dalley served as guide as they inspected the church land. Moran was so taken with what he saw that he announced immediately that an ecclesiastical college as well as his residence would be built there.

Archbishop Polding had chosen the Manly site 25 years earlier, after the government offered the church 60 acres to match a land grant made to the Anglicans at Randwick. Kevin Walsh, in his history of the Manly seminary, St Patrick's, speculated that Polding's 'personal and sympathetic interest in ministrations' at the adjacent North Head quarantine station attracted him to the location. But he erected only a wooden cross there and left the land to the fishermen who squatted on it, as did his successor, Archbishop Vaughan.

Walsh reported that, according to 'Catholic lore (fed in this instance by the stories of William Bede Dalley)', John Robertson, Lands Minister at the time, persuaded a largely unsympathetic cabinet to approve the grant 'by pointing out it would set a protective barrier of Romanists between sundry foreign diseases and the rest of the population'. Robertson added, so the story goes, that Catholics were 'so think-

Cardinal Moran.

skinned they would not take smallpox'. Presumably Dalley made that up.¹

Moran was summoned to Rome in May 1885 and left a few weeks later amid speculation that he was to be appointed Archbishop of Dublin. With work already under way on the site, Dalley was called on shortly afterwards to help fend off an attempt, which failed, to have some of the land resumed.²

News that Moran was to return as a Cardinal reached Sydney in September. His elevation was a compliment to the marvellous progress of the Australian colonies as well as to the man, Dalley told a meeting at St Mary's Cathedral that resolved to present him with a carriage and pair on his return. Who could have imagined that 'within little more than the allotted period of human life this distant country would become one of the hinges upon which the administration of the universal Church would turn?'

Just as pleasing, he went on, was the community's response to the news. 'With the improved intelligence and (thank God for the unspeakable blessing!) with the nobler toleration of the times', an event that not long ago would have provoked 'unmeaning jealousies and unkindly feelings' was now regarded with 'generous satisfaction'. He urged Catholics to 'be on their guard to carefully cultivate, and on all occasions display, a noble spirit of liberality'; this would be 'the most effectual way of honouring themselves and their Cardinal Archbishop'.³

Dalley delivered a similar message in his speech at the laying of the foundation stone of St Patrick's Seminary on 19 November 1885, two weeks after Moran's return. About 200 clerical and lay guests watched the Cardinal perform the ceremony with an ivory mallet and silver trowel donated by the building's architects. Then all gathered for lunch in a marquee erected behind a beach 'on the most romantic portion of the

Seminary estate'. Proposing Moran's health, Dalley assured him he would experience 'on all sides' at Manly 'that noble liberality of sentiment which, except religion itself, is the most beautiful work of higher civilization'.[4]

Liberality was again his theme when he spoke at the opening of a bazaar to raise funds for Sydney's St Vincent's Hospital, run by the Catholic Sisters of Charity, at the end of November. The organisers had decked the Exhibition Building out as a 'Soudan Encampment' for the event. 'It makes a wonderfully pretty picture,' reported *Freeman's* – 'that antique Egyptian market square, with its rows of odd-looking shops...; its dainty bits of Nile scenery gleaming amidst the battered yet noble fragments of mysteriously ancient architecture; its profuse display of Oriental flags and symbols...' Participants wore all sorts of costumes – 'here a Swiss peasant and a classic Athenian maiden grouped with a lady radiant in the gorgeous apparel of the Elizabethan Court; there a lassie in highland plaid and Young Australia, all flowers and ribbons, mingling with a bevy of Egyptian princesses, and strangest of all, an ambulance nurse chatting familiarly with a queenly descendant of Cleopatra – suggest the realization of utopian dreams in the peaceful and happy blending of all the races of the world'.

Dalley extolled the care the hospital and its nuns gave 'those of all religions or of none'. The Catholic Church had 'the merit of its foundation, and, so far as the nurses were concerned, the glory of its service', he said. But the entire community supported the hospital, and he believed its most generous benefactors were 'not of our communion'.

> It is thus a standing memorial of that liberality which we should all cultivate in all relations of life. There are some miserable creatures who would make even the administration of our public charities the arena for the display of religious intolerance. The very existence of such a charity as this is a reproach to such degrading intolerance, and upholds our character as a civilized community. (Loud and long-continued applause.)[5]

Dalley was part of the official welcoming party for Governor Carrington in early December and took a prominent place at a banquet in his honour at the Town Hall two weeks later. In mid-January 1886 the

Lord Carrington.

Governor and his entourage made an evening visit to Manly to attend a concert of piano pieces and song in aid of the village's Catholic orphanage. Dalley, who probably arranged the viceregal presence, greeted them on a pier 'gaily decorated with flags' and introduced them to their host, the mayor.⁶

A week later the new Governor attended a banquet, chaired by Dalley, in honour of Sir Alexander Stuart. The former Premier was to leave shortly for Britain to represent the colony at the Colonial and Indian Exhibition being staged to demonstrate the 'wealth and industrial development' of the empire. Responding to Dalley's speech in his praise, he described his Attorney-General as 'my dearest friend in public and in private life'.⁷

Stuart showed Queen Victoria around the New South Wales stand at the London exhibition in late May, and shortly afterwards related the following incident to the historian James Froude. Pointing out a picture of Dalley attached to the frame of a photograph of the Sudan contingent, Stuart said, 'Although, your Majesty, I was Premier of the colony when the contingent was sent to the Soudan, this is the statesman, Mr Dalley, who actually sent it. I was ill at the time and out of the colony.' The Queen replied, 'I presume he is an Englishman, who may even have achieved some distinction before emigrating to Australia.' 'No, your Majesty,' said Stuart. 'Mr Dalley was born in the colony, and did not come to England till he had achieved some distinction. He is the son of Irish parents, and a Roman Catholic, and your Majesty has no more loyal subject in the Empire.'⁸ Presumably he did not add that Dalley's parents came to the colony as convicts.

On the evening of 12 February, the anniversary of the offer of the Sudan contingent, Dalley joined Carrington at a dinner to commemorate the Governor's appointment as honorary colonel of the colony's reserve cavalry.⁹ The next day the Governor, once a captain of the Royal Horse Guards, mounted a fine horse to inspect more than five hundred members of the contingent who had mustered at Moore Park to receive their campaign medals. Recently arrived from England, these displayed the Queen's head on the face and a sphinx on the reverse. Dalley was among the official party who heard Carrington give his view of the impact of the Sudan commitment. It had been

> watched in England with an interest which can alone be understood by those who witnessed it. On the Continent of Europe it was felt that the Empire, however distant its portions, was a mighty Union, animated with the same noble purposes, and thrilling with the same national emotions; and while this was felt throughout Continental Europe, the news of your action was received with admiration and sympathy by that great American people who have so wondrously increased the renown of our race.[10]

Dalley's speaking engagements continued unabated. He advised the eight hundred people who gathered for the first annual picnic of the colony's Licensed Victuallers' Association in late February that temperance campaigns could best be countered by ensuring that licensed premises were conducted respectably. Chairing the St Patrick's Day banquet at the Town Hall, he urged Irish Catholics to remember their obligation to those 'neither of your race or faith' who had promoted the colony's civil and religious liberty, and to identify fully 'with all that delights, interests, and benefits your fellow citizens'. To 'prolonged applause' he read from a recent London *Spectator* a verse whose 'pathos' and 'beauty' had moved him.

> Let the orange lily be thy badge,
> My patriot brother!
> The everlasting green for me,
> And we for one another![11]

His next two banquet speeches were in praise of sportsmen. First was John Tait, a 72-year-old racehorse owner and trainer, winner of four Melbourne Cups. Tait had 'to as large extent as any man in the country contributed to the holiday happiness of the community', said Dalley.

He added that 'in former years' he had 'often and gladly' witnessed Tait's triumphs.[12] Second was 35-year-old Bill Beach, who was about to leave for London to defend – successfully – his title of champion sculler of the world. The rejoicing would be even greater in England than in the colony if he succeeded, Dalley predicted. 'They who are our masters in all that is great, and strong, and worthy, will rejoice that we are growing up such scholars in manliness, and are educating ourselves for our share in the labours of the empire.'[13]

Dalley spoke at length again on imperialism in the Pacific in April after Premier Jennings came under fire for suggesting that France should be allowed to annex the New Hebrides under certain conditions, the main one being that it stop transporting convicts to the Pacific. In the first of two stirring speeches in the Legislative Council, he described those demanding an exclusively British South Pacific as 'people who mistake sensational vapouring for statesmanship and patriotism'.[14] Daniel O'Connor, in the Assembly, took the bait, calling Dalley the apostle of a 'cringing and servile policy'. In England, he suggested, a man who so humiliated and insulted the empire 'would at least have been sent to the Tower'.[15]

The colony could only benefit from French annexation of the New Hebrides, Dalley declared in his second speech on 21 April.

> I thank God that mine is not the patriotism which would aspire to shut out from these seas the enterprise, the commerce and the civilisation of the great nations of Europe, and deprive these Australasian colonies of all the riches of the neighbourhood, and intercourse, and honourable rivalry in commerce of men and women at least as well educated, as virtuous, and as industrious as ourselves.[16]

The next day Dalley joined the Governor, the Premier, Admiral Tryon and opposition leader Robertson on a harbour cruise and picnic for General Sir Arthur Fremantle, commander of the guards brigade to which the Sudan contingent had been attached. Officers of the contingent and of the local forces hosted the outing. Two days later, he entertained Tryon and, among others, the Premier and his new Victorian counterpart, Duncan Gillies, at the Australian Club. Tryon returned the hospitality, on HMS *Nelson*, after another two days, this time with the Queensland Premier, Samuel Griffith, also present.[17] Noting Dalley's absence due to illness from a dinner hosted by the American consul, Gilderoy Griffin, later in the week, a columnist in the *Mail* wrote,

> 'And what else can he expect,' said a sympathetic friend, 'sitting by the sea there till he gets an appetite, and then feeding on turtle and champagne till the gout lays him by the heels?' Strange what erroneous notions people form of prominent men. Now, there will doubtless be many people in the colony as much surprised as was that good man to be told that at least five days out of the week Mr Dalley goes to his bed before 9; that he invariably rises at 6, in summer by 4; and in eating and drinking is far more familiar with toast and tea than with turtle and champagne.[18]

Perhaps that was the usual routine since he left government, but not recently. Bursts of impassioned speechmaking in the Council had left him unwell before, as, of course, had excessive banqueting. Probably the combination contributed to his renewed illness.

He was well enough at the end of May to open an 'all nations fair' in aid of a new charitable home run by the Sisters of St Joseph, and again praised the contributions of 'generous and unostentatious' members of other faiths to Catholic charities. They were further proof that New South Wales enjoyed a civilisation that made 'the efforts of the intolerant and the fanatical mere exhibitions of impotent malignity', he said.[19] On 21 June he spoke at a banquet at the Town Hall to mark the start of Queen Victoria's 50th year on the throne. The colonists were the devoted subjects of a 'gentle, tender, afflicted Sovereign' who had 'tasted the highest happiness' and 'borne bitter sorrow', he declared. By 'her graces and her virtues', she 'adorned and crowned an Empire founded, built up, and sustained by the valour of great souls, and by a loyalty unparalleled in the history of princes. (Cheers.)'[20]

Other speakers at the jubilee banquet included the Governor, Chief Justice Martin and Sir John Robertson, who had retired from Parliament three days earlier. A leg injury sustained the previous September in the National Park south of Sydney – when he fell as he jumped between

Right Honourable: Dalley on the cover of Illustrated Sydney News after his appointment to the Privy Council in 1886. His physical decline is evident from comparison of this portrait with the one published in the News three years earlier (page 275).

rocks, 'as agile as a rock wallaby' as he put it[21] – laid Robertson low. The pain had worsened after a temporary improvement.[22]

His retirement coincided with news of the death in London, from typhoid, of Sir Alexander Stuart. A leading article in *Freeman's* that coupled the two events looks like Dalley's work. Never was there 'an honester, more unselfish public man' than Stuart, it observed. And Robertson, 'the brave old hero of a hundred fights', left the political fray without a 'single genuine enemy'. He was a man whose 'peculiar personal qualities' were 'in themselves a public service in their effect on the general tone of public life'.[23]

On 30 June the papers carried the news that Dalley had been awarded an honour he could not refuse, membership of Her Majesty's Privy Council. He remained, as he wished, 'plain Bill Dalley', but this honour was a much more exclusive one than the knighthood he had rejected. He was the first Australian colonist to receive it and the style that went with it, 'Right Honourable'.

On the same day the Legislative Council formally accepted a marble bust of Dalley commissioned by members a year earlier; it is one of seven such busts that now adorn the chamber. Taking the opportunity to congratulate him on his imperial honour, William Piddington said he considered Dalley 'as pure a specimen of real and genuine patriotism as can be found from one end to the other of the British empire'.[24] No doubt many people wrote with kind words; a few of his replies have survived.

He told Alexander Oliver he derived pleasure from the award 'mainly because it is requited with such favour and gratification by dear friends'.[25] To William Archer, his collaborator in the John Henry Newman commemoration (chapters 16, 17), he wrote of his pleasure at receiving the congratulations 'of one for whose character and culture I always felt the deepest affection and respect'.[26] In a letter to 'My Dear Colonel', probably Colonel Roberts of the colonial artillery, he wrote, 'At no time had I any passion for personal distinctions and as you know for years my eyes have been fixed rather upon the past and all that lies in it of love and happiness than upon the future with its honours and rewards.'[27]

Dalley wrote to Lord Loftus, back home in England, towards the end of July to 'express...the extent of my personal obligations to you...for a large share of this royal recognition of my humble service performed under your own eyes and so greatly assisted...by your most generous support'. It is not a cheery letter; the Sydney news he passed on was bleak. Nothing could be more disheartening 'than the positively disgraceful scenes in our legislature', Dalley wrote. Jennings was holding on as Premier, but only because of 'apprehension, approaching horror' at the return to power of Parkes, who had replaced Robertson as opposition leader. He feared that Robertson, 'poor dear old Jack', was 'about to leave us forever' having become 'sadly broken' and now reeling from the death of a daughter in childbirth. His own health was so bad he had been confined to bed for the past three weeks.[28]

Dalley was well enough to attend the American Independence Day banquet at the beginning of the month. This was notable as the first of these annual celebrations, hosted by the US consul, to be attended by the Governor. Carrington proclaimed his sympathy 'with that movement which in the interests of the world would bind England and America together in the strongest ties of union'. Dalley and the other main speaker, Sir James Martin, offered similar sentiments. Amid cheers, Dalley called the Declaration of Independence one of the 'greatest charters of the liberties of mankind'. Reading it provided a 'pathetic' reminder of 'the melancholy mistakes of those English statesmen who compelled their offspring into a revolt in defence of liberty', he said. England had since given 'to her adventurous children in all parts of the world the liberty which she refused you... By her splendid atonement for the injury done to you, she was to memorialise your victory...'[29]

The next day Dalley chaired a meeting to organise a public banquet, on 19 July, in honour of Robertson. The event was postponed indefinitely a few days later, at Robertson's request, because of Dalley's illness.[30] In the meantime the Legislative Assembly had given overwhelming support to a government proposal to grant Robertson, who was in financial difficulties, £10,000 in recognition of his long and valued public service. Parkes, arguing that the grant would set a dangerous precedent, was one of the few dissenters. Possibly another heated comment about him by Robertson in May – that he had done more to injure the colony's public life than any other man – influenced Parkes's position (18 months later the generous Robertson said that, despite their differences, he considered Parkes the colony's greatest statesman).[31]

Speaking in the Legislative Council on 28 July, two days after writing his gloomy letter to Loftus, Dalley strongly supported the grant. He maintained that if a precedent were set it would be a good one. In a career of nearly 40 years, Robertson had been the colony's 'most busy, active, unselfish public servant'.

> Whenever, in the life of an individual or in the history of a nation, something unusual occurs which must be met and must be recognised – which must be done if justice is to be done... – there a precedent is created, and necessarily so... [Our] sole responsibility...is to satisfy ourselves that the circumstances justify our action; and if this be so...not to permit ourselves to be disturbed...as to the creation of a precedent, unless, indeed, it be by the gratification [of creating it].[32]

The Robertson banquet went ahead eventually on 11 September, chaired by Dalley. It was a 'farewell festival', he said, a 'national goodbye

An elderly Sir John Robertson.

to a strong, brave, tender heart'. Among the 140 present were many politicians from both sides of parliament; Parkes, who sent his apologies, was the most notable exception. Proposing Robertson's health, Dalley described him as a man of 'sweetly-endowed nature' who had 'never shaken in the least degree the love and trust' of his fellow creatures.

For the generosity with which he brightened and elevated public life the world has repaid him with abundant interest, and he passes out of the arena which most men are compelled to leave with bitter regrets and many things done which have wounded gentleness, bruised hearts, sundered kindly relations – he leaves, I say, only stricken down by his own infirmities, and ready and willing to look all in the face as friends and hold all hands in his own. (Loud cheers.)

'People have been too good to me,' Robertson responded to cries of 'No, no'. 'Well, I know myself better than you do. I know how to criticise my own career.' He offered good-humoured tributes to eight 'great men' with whom he had been associated. First was Charles Cowper; others included Martin, but he did not mention Parkes. Of Daniel Deniehy, he said, 'No more distinguished man ever appeared here'. He recalled that he 'used to call Dalley and Deniehy "my boys," and used to lecture them pretty freely, and now here is Mr Dalley the boss of the whole crowd. (Loud laughter.)'[33]

The Robertson dinner came towards the end of two months of socialising and speechmaking that culminated in Dalley becoming so ill that he was granted leave of absence from the Legislative Council for the remainder of the session.[34]

He spoke at the laying of the foundation stone of a new wing of St Vincent's Hospital by Cardinal Moran in early August, describing the hospital as a monument to the colonists' 'wide-stretching benevolence' and abhorrence of sectarianism. Lord and Lady Carrington attended this event, prompting *Freeman's* to observe that it was only the third Catholic gathering in the colony's history at which the Queen's representative had taken a prominent part; the others were the laying of the foundation stone of the first St Mary's Cathedral by Governor Macquarie in 1821 and Sir John Young's appearance at a memorable public meeting after the cathedral burnt down in 1865 (chapter 8).[35]

In the Legislative Council, Dalley spoke at length in mid-August in support of his view, challenged in the Assembly, that the Council had the power to amend any legislation.[36] He defended the competence of the colony's artillery forces in a long speech at the beginning of September. Later in the month he spoke in favour of a customs duty bill, fiercely attacked by Parkes and his supporters, intended to help remedy the colony's budget deficit.[37] In his last contribution before taking leave he argued against allowing a barrister to address the Council on a land law issue, rejecting suggestions that his own appearance in 1881 on behalf of Chinese merchants opposed to Parkes's immigration restriction bill provided the precedent.[38]

Dalley accompanied the Governor and his wife, Cardinal Moran and others on a visit in late August to the offices where Andrew Garran, recently retired as editor of the *Herald*, was overseeing production of a lavish publication, *The Picturesque Atlas of Australasia*. After admiring many of the illustrations prepared for it, the party retired to a nearby hotel for a banquet. Dalley, the main speaker, predicted the *Atlas* would stimulate many to visit Australia to see 'our scenes of beauty and of majesty'.[39]

He took his children to a 'comedietta' and farce performed in aid of the Manly cricket club at the end of August, and a week later attended a banquet at Sydney's German Club.[40] In mid-September he presided at the inaugural banquet of the Manly Club, and in a merry speech suggested members should insist on the club having 'few banquets and no speeches'. If politicians could be induced to spend a day or two of their week 'amidst such scenes of calm and beauty', he said, they might 'abandon the error of supposing violence of speech to be synonymous with principle, and of mistaking personal malignity for high-toned difference of opinion'.[41]

His renewed illness in October was apparently not the product of overwork or overindulgence. In a letter to 20-year-old Mary Martin, who managed the household at 'Clarens' for her father, Sir James, he explained why he probably could not come to dinner two days later, on 14 October. For eight days a head cold, which had 'taken a somewhat severe bronchial form', had left him sleepless and with little voice. Then, feeling better, he had set out for his 'paradise by the sea' at Bilgola. But at Narrabeen Lagoon his horse shied at a fishing boat and the buggy capsized into the water, 'precipitating me 14 feet away'. He was now suffering 'very much' from the shock and exposure.[42]

Relations between Sir James and Lady Martin had improved in recent months, to the extent that she now came to 'Clarens' to act as hostess at his dinner parties.[43] Admiral Tryon was to attend the 14 October event, and Dalley, who signed his letter 'Always your loving uncle', asked Mary to give his love 'to the great father and dear mother…and if you sit next to him give my love to the Admiral'. Dalley wrote to Lady Martin the day after the dinner to express regret at missing it and suggest that she and Sir James join him for lunch, with Sir Alfred Stephen, at Manly the following Monday. After the meal he would take them on a 'delightful' trip to Dee Why, which should 'do the dear Chief all the good in the world'. He proposed returning with them to dinner at 'Clarens', bringing two of his children, 11-year-old Eleanor and 10-year old John Bede, 'who would amuse the dear Chief immensely'.[44]

A week later, illness prevented Dalley speaking at the laying of the foundation stone of a Little Company of Mary charitable institution.[45] An undated letter to Mary Martin declining another dinner invitation is probably from this time. He wrote that he could neither eat nor talk, and had been suffering 'a sharp attack of gout in my left wrist which starts occasionally up my arm as if like some aspiring girl it were seeking a way to my heart'. He promised to call at 'Clarens' the first day he was able to 'come to town'.[46]

Dalley visited during the week beginning 1 November, having received news that Sir James's long-standing heart problem had taken a severe turn for the worse. His condition fluctuated, but after a setback on 3 November Charlotte Martin, wife of one of his brothers, felt the need to send an anxious note to Cardinal Moran. Sir James was dangerously ill and might die, she wrote. 'His wife and children are Protestants but he is a Catholic, and so far as I know has always believed in the Doctrines of the True Faith. He may die without a priest, for I do not know that one will be sent for, therefore you will forgive my writing to you and asking you to visit him?'[47]

A talk Martin gave to the Christian Evidence Society in August 1885 convinced *Freeman's* that, although not a churchgoer, he was certainly a Catholic at heart.[48] One of the paper's writers claimed later that Sir James had expressed to Dalley a strong desire to be reconciled to the church, but had replied 'not yet' when his friend offered to fetch a priest.[49] Dalley reportedly was with Martin until nearly 11 p.m. on 4 November, when there seemed to be no immediate cause for alarm.[50] The 66-year-old Chief Justice died less than an hour later, without the last rites.

The Anglican Bishop of Sydney, Alfred Barry, officiated at his burial two days later in the Long family vault at St Jude's, Randwick, where he joined three children who had predeceased him, Lady Martin's father and her sister Eleanor Dalley. Lady Martin had declined the offer of a public funeral in a letter written on her behalf by Dalley. While she wished the interment to be 'of a strictly private nature', the family was grateful for the government's offer marking its sense of 'the great public service rendered to the country by Sir James', he wrote.[51]

27
Looking back

Dalley delivered one of his grand eulogies two weeks after Martin's burial, at the unveiling by Lord Carrington of an impressive monument to Henry Kendall at Waverley Cemetery. He was among those who, as the epitaph on the marble column puts it, had 'loved and admired' the poet and contributed to the monument's erection 'in grateful and lasting remembrance of his genius'. He arranged the Governor's attendance, and proposed suitable words for Charlotte Kendall to inscribe in a volume of her husband's work to be presented to Carrington. Also in touch with her about the wording of the epitaph, he rejected use of the phrase 'poet laureate' because of its 'special meaning'.[1] He selected two appropriate lines from Shelley's 'Adonais: An Elegy on the Death of John Keats':

> Awake him not! Surely he takes his fill
> Of deep and liquid rest, forgetful of all ill.

Mrs Kendall was introduced to the Governor before the unveiling, and two small daughters presented wreaths to the vice-regal couple. Three Kendall sons were also among the large group of guests who gathered in the afternoon sun. Political figures there included Sir John Robertson and the excitable Daniel O'Connor, a member of the monument committee.

Dalley's lengthy speech was greeted with 'great applause'. The honour done to Kendall was testimony to the colony's spiritual growth, he said. A young and vigorous nation's accolades usually went to the conspicuous – those 'who use the hour, live for it'. But here they were recognising one who had made the 'music which softly steals into the soul – which compassionates and consoles – which sings of love and pity and suffering – which tells of the anguish of disappointments – of noble aims unattained – of baulked ambitions; or which invests the common and familiar things of life with a freshness and beauty to which our eyes had not before been opened...' He regarded Kendall's poetic descriptions of nature as his best work.

> You read some of these touching pieces with a peculiar tenderness for the gifted but solitary child whose heart is so full of beauty, and of the passionate desire to speak of it. And you feel as if you could wish the young eager singer a future of peace and love and simple pleasure...

Dalley concluded with a reference to the death of Martin, who, he was sure, would also be remembered tenderly. In his case, 'you think gratefully of the life of ceaseless labour in the highest walks of intellectual excellence, of the clear eyes perforce turned away from the spiritual forms and lovely images of the imagination'. In Kendall's, 'you cherish the gentle memory of the childlike genius who loved the beautiful and lived to try and tell you of his pleasures and consolations in its worship'.[2]

Dalley, who straddled the two worlds, twice declined the opportunity to succeed Martin as Chief Justice. Premier Jennings sounded him out shortly after Martin's death. 'Without an instant's hesitation I declared that under no circumstances could I presume to undertake so vast a responsibility,' Dalley wrote to Frederick Darley.

> I pointed out that the state of my health forbade the idea that I was or would become physically equal to discharge of the onerous duties of so great an office; and that in other important respects I was not possessed of the qualifications which would justify me in presuming to occupy a place difficult to fill under any circumstances, and which, owing to the distinguished ability and attainments of its late lamented occupant, was an office even the most highly qualified would be slow to accept.[3]

While clearly not up to the task physically, Dalley perhaps was being too modest about his legal attainments. Although most of his appearances as a barrister had been in the criminal courts, the opinions he prepared as Attorney-General demonstrated his capacity in other areas of the law. Alexander Oliver noted after his death that 'in almost every case in which he advised the Government to take a judgment of the Supreme Court to the Privy Council, no matter whether their Honors had been unanimous or not', he succeeded in the appeal. 'Some of these cases were of extraordinary complication, and others involved the subtlest questions of constitutional law.'[4] Darley commented that Dalley's acceptance of the position 'would have afforded unqualified gratification to his profession'.[5]

Sir Frederick Darley.

Darley was Jennings's eminently qualified second choice for the vacancy, but declined the post because the salary, £3,500, was much less than he was earning at the Bar. The Premier then turned to Julian Salomons, also a very capable and successful barrister, who accepted but quickly resigned, upset at the cool reception he received from some of his fellow judges. He reported that one, Justice Windeyer, had received him with 'marked brusqueness and discourtesy' and declared his appointment 'outrageous'.[6]

Sir Patrick Jennings.

Jennings next formally offered the position to Dalley who, before responding, sought to change Darley's mind. He wrote persuasively to his friend, and then spoke to him at length both at his chambers and at home. His object, as he put it in the letter, was

> to urge upon you the immediate discharge of a great public duty – the greatest patriotic service, indeed, which you can render to a country to which your own obligations are not inconsiderable – and that is the acceptance of this great office, the delay in filling which is a public misfortune which can only be exceeded by the calamity of its being filled unworthily. It is in your power to avert by a single act of sacrifice both disasters.

He implied that, if Darley stuck to his guns, he would feel compelled to accept the job – and in effect begged him to prevent this. 'No one knows better than you do,' Dalley wrote, 'that for my own sake and that of a young family of which I am the sole guardian and protector – and above all for the sake of the public – it would be wrong on my part to do what I am asked to do.' Jennings renewed the offer to Darley, and he accepted immediately.[7] A distinguished Chief Justice, he presided over the Supreme Court for 21 years.

Dalley attended congratulatory functions for Darley hosted by Premier Jennings and the President of the Legislative Council, Sir John Hay, during December.[8] Earlier in the month he took a prominent part in the triumphant welcome home from England of the sculler Bill Beach. 'Not since the departure of the troops for the Soudan has there been such excitement,' the *Mail* observed. Around a hundred thousand people turned out to see him land at Circular Quay and cheer the procession to the Town Hall. There, after Beach was presented with an illuminated address, Dalley made a brief speech of welcome in the name of the colony. He congratulated the champion on bearing himself with 'much modesty and gallantry' and achieving 'an honourable triumph not only for yourself but for your country'.[9]

In mid-December he presided at the break-up ceremony at St Aloysius' College, the Jesuit school in the city attended by his 13- and 10-year-old sons William Bede and John Bede. Both boys were among the student performers, William playing the piano and taking part in French and German dialogues and John reciting from Macauley's 'Horatius'. Dalley began his speech by joking that 'since the abolition of all other forms of human torture public speaking alone remains', and promising to be brief. He praised the Jesuit teachers for fostering thought and understanding rather than 'a triumph of memory'. He also praised the *Herald* as a paper 'most creditable to our intelligence and civilisation', and told of an article he had read in it recently about the work of Jesuit missionaries among Aborigines in the Northern Territory.

> It is a most beautiful experiment of colonization, one of the most interesting attempts to save by love and sacrifice the few happy ones who remain out of the tens of thousands who have perished as directly and cruelly from our so-called civilization as if we had marched against them disciplined troops, and persistently shot them down with repeating rifles.[10]

Two days before Christmas he opened a new aquarium near the Manly pier. It was, he said, a place of amusement, pleasure and instruction 'which we may hope will give as much profit to [its proprietors] as it will assuredly give happiness not only to the strong, the healthy, and the wise, but to those who are dearer to us all – the gentle, the feeble, and the children, who will find solace and delight in this place.'[11]

Earlier in the week he had accompanied the Governor and, among others, two visiting lords on a Hawkesbury River excursion. Again with Carrington, he visited a 'horsebreeding establishment' at Richmond on the upper Hawkesbury two days later; his brother-in-law William Long, a prominent racehorse owner, was one of this party. On Boxing Day he joined the Governor, Lady Carrington, Admiral Tryon and Premier Jennings at the Randwick races.[12] Less than two weeks later he was a member of an unlikely deputation – the others were Parkes, Cardinal Moran and his secretary Rev. Dr Denis O'Haran, and the Anglican Bishop Barry – pleading with Carrington to spare the lives of six convicted rapists.

They were among 11 young men – ages between 17 and 22 – charged following the 'Mount Rennie outrage', the gang rape in September 1886 of a 16-year-old servant girl in bushland near Waterloo. At the trial, conducted by Justice Windeyer in November, the jury found nine of them guilty but recommended mercy on account of their youth. The judge took a different view, declaring his belief, before sentencing all to death, that leniency exercised after similar crimes in the past had led to 'this culminating horror'. 'The time has come when a terrible example must be made of those who seem to be restrained by no pity for their victims, no sense of shame, no dread of the loathing of their fellows,' he said. 'Crimes such as yours it is too clear can only be restrained by the fear of death, the fate which awaits you.'[13]

The issue of the death penalty for rape had long aroused emotions in the colony. After Dalley, following English precedent, introduced an abolition bill in 1857, most of his fellow members of the Legislative Assembly avoided committing themselves by absenting themselves when it came up for discussion and vote (chapter 3). He subsequently changed his mind on the question at least twice (chapters 15, 16), and execution for rape remained on the books when he secured passage of the Criminal Law Amendment Act in 1883 (chapter 19). Of the other Australian colonies, only Tasmania still retained it in 1886.

One argument for abolition was that juries would be less likely to convict if they knew a guilty verdict would lead to hanging. A member of the jury at the Mount Rennie trial wrote to the *Herald* at the end of December claiming that if he and his fellow jurors had thought their 'recommendation to mercy would be thrown overboard' they probably could not have reached agreement on a verdict.[14] Precedent over many years would have given them confidence that any death sentence pronounced would be commuted.

This time, after a long meeting on 16 December attended by Justice Windeyer, the Executive Council (the Governor and ministers) concluded that six of the nine should hang; the sentences of the others were commuted to life imprisonment. Public agitation both for and against clemency, already under way, now became clamorous with meetings called and petitions circulated in country centres as well as the city. Cabinet considered the matter again on 30 December, after a meeting opposing the executions attracted an overflow crowd to Sydney Town Hall. Witnesses were quizzed and written statements considered as ministers, in effect, took on the role of appeal judges. They decided to uphold the Executive Council's earlier decision, an outcome confirmed when the Council met again on 4 January 1887.[15]

The next day Dalley, Parkes and the church leaders made their appeal to the Governor to save the six men due to hang two days later. The deputation sprang from a visit by the journalist Frank Myers, a prominent advocate for clemency, to Dalley at Manly the previous day. Dalley reportedly told Myers that he had been 'unremitting in urging a merciful view of the case upon those whom he could properly approach'. When Myers suggested he join his old adversary, Parkes, in an approach to the Governor, he agreed without hesitation.

The idea of including the church leaders in the deputation was Dalley's. After a long discussion with Parkes he called on Barry and Moran, who 'at once consented'. Parkes spoke first when Carrington received them at Government House, arguing principally that the executions would damage the colony's reputation. Dalley began by sympathising with the Governor over the pain and suffering his role in the case was causing him. He criticised the conduct of the trial; unprecedentedly long sittings into the night had exhausted both counsel and jurors. And he considered the re-examination of witnesses by ministers 'grossly unconstitutional', with weight being given to statements made 'not on oath…and given not in the presence of the prisoners or their legal representatives'. Moran pleaded for consideration of the 'youth and ignorance of the culprits' and decried 'the popular frenzy for blood'. Barry was concerned that if the executions went ahead juries would refuse to convict in future rape cases.

Responding, Carrington indicated that he was unlikely to change his mind. 'If I accede to your application', he said,

> it seems to me that I must necessarily do so in all future cases, for a worse case than the present can scarcely be imagined. In so doing, shall I not, in effect, be repealing the present law, and setting my own arbitrary action against the deliberate decision of the people of the country as expressed by their own elected representatives in the Legislative Assembly assembled, and by the Legislative Council as well?[16]

He decided to commute the sentences of two to life imprisonment, leaving four to hang. One of the reprieved pair had been declared innocent by another of the condemned youths, and Justice Windeyer had recommended clemency for the other. The executions were performed simultaneously the next morning, before more than a hundred and twenty spectators, on newly erected gallows in the grounds of Darlinghurst Gaol. The procedure was bungled, resulting in three of the youths dying slowly by strangulation.[17]

Frank Myers recalled Dalley remarking after the meeting with Carrington, 'No use, no use, the man is adamant.' And then, 'I must get home; this has shaken me.' It seems Premier Jennings was also severely shaken by the Mount Rennie affair. Later press reports claimed he was one of four ministers at the final Executive Council meeting who favoured reprieve for all the condemned youths. The other four, including Dibbs, took the opposite view and prevailed.[18]

Jennings had been in dispute with Dibbs for months over financial issues, and a new conflict blew up between them in early January. Despite still commanding a majority in the Assembly, he resigned four days after the executions and advised Carrington to call on Parkes. The 71-year-old accepted office on condition that new elections were called immediately, and was rewarded with a sweeping victory.

Away from the political turmoil, Dalley made the main speech at a banquet celebrating the appointment of a new Mayor of Sydney, Alban Riley, in mid-January.[19] He also wrote a review for the *Herald* of a book of poems by John Farrell, a 35-year-old bushman and brewer who had turned to journalism and poetry and become a frequent contributor of verse to *The Bulletin*. Dalley compared Farrell's collection, *How He Died and Other Poems*, to the work of the American Bret Harte: 'In each case the pioneer and adventurer are more fascinating types for the poet than the comfortable, law-abiding prosperous citizen.' Some of Farrell's poetry might 'shock the reverential,' he went on. It was 'peculiarly Australian', and 'full both of a rugged manliness and a womanly pathos'.[20]

Farrell was one the aspiring writers Dalley had helped in various ways. In a letter to another of them, Frederick Broomfield of *The Bulletin*,[21] he recalled Farrell sending him some verses in the early 1880s and requesting his comments. 'They were marked with occasional strokes of power,' he wrote,

> but were rude and unlettered, and showed such defective culture that I thought the kindest thing I could do was to tell him frankly that though I was convinced he had 'the vision and the faculty divine,' he would require the 'inspiring aid of books,' study, patience, and a severe discipline of refinement before he could produce anything worthy of his genius. He thanked me in very touching words, told me he would do what I advised, and when one day I read his poem of 'How He Died' I wrote to him on the spot, declaring that I recognised his hand at once.[22]

In his *Herald* review, Dalley quoted from a poem in which Farrell lamented the death of General Gordon, who had lived 'The noblest life, since Christ's, that men have known.' But the poet was not a supporter of the colony's Sudan commitment, as his 'dedicatory sonnet' to Dalley at the front of his book makes clear.

> I, holding to this truth that sudden swords,
> Uplifted at a nod to harvest lives
> Of unknown brethren, are as murderers' knives
> In sight of God, and all the brave rewards,
> With blood stuck on the breasts of war's loud lords,
> For fettering hands that wronged them not, with gyves,
> When later day with lordlier light arrives –
> Shall show to men as foul as Judas-hoards.
> But knowing him, who, past the blue sweet bay
> Hides in a home with love and laurel crowned,
> Most honoured by high nations far away;
> Most loved by those, who, standing closeliest round,
> See all his life, 'mid kinglier tributes lay
> This book of mine before him on the ground.

Dalley became severely unwell in February. Two doctors reportedly were 'in almost constant attendance' on him at Manly after a fainting fit on the 11th, and visitors were banned.[23] Ten days later, 'still rather feeble, though able to walk', he travelled to 'Numantia' for some mountain air, perhaps under the care of Lady Martin. His Manly doctor was summoned a few days later after a relapse, but arrived to find the patient again improving.[24]

Back home, but 'still under medical treatment' and 'forbidden to hope to resume, for a considerable time, his place in Parliament', Dalley spoke to a *Herald* reporter in late March about allegations that he had acted without Cabinet approval in ordering armaments worth £250,000 for the colony in May 1885. The storm erupted soon after parliament resumed early in the month, and died two weeks later when Premier Parkes and his Treasurer produced a document demonstrating that Cabinet had been consulted. Dalley thanked them for 'the spirit of fairness and justice' they had displayed while pointing out that the sum involved was much smaller than stated, about £120,000; £250,000 was the cost of all war materials ordered during 1885.[25]

He reappeared in the Legislative Council on 4 May to support an address to the Queen from the two houses of parliament congratulating her on the completion of her jubilee year. 'In no portion of your vast dominions are the sentiments of loyalty and love for your throne and person more warmly cherished than by the inhabitants of New South Wales,' the address, which was carried by acclamation, concluded. Dalley returned to two oft-traversed themes in his speech. One of the most glorious characteristics of Victoria's reign was the establishment of 'universal religious tolerance', he said. And she had witnessed in the Australian colonies the growth of 'powerful peoples' who 'now proudly and gratefully undertake' to participate in the empire's defence.[26]

On 23 May he joined 11 other members of the colony's first Legislative Assembly at a dinner, convened by Parkes, to commemorate the 31st anniversary of its first sitting. 'I think the idea of your banquet… is not only a happy but an extremely affecting one,' Dalley told the Premier in a letter accepting his invitation to attend and speak in memory of the 43 foundation MPs who had died (another eight had left the colony or were too ill to attend the dinner). 'I am sure I need hardly tell you with what real sympathy with your efforts to make your celebrations a complete success I shall gladly undertake the duty which you have honoured me in asking me to discharge.'[27]

Relations between Dalley and Parkes had clearly improved in recent times (a cynic might speculate that the Premier was relieved his ailing rival no longer posed any political threat to him). Chairing proceedings at the dinner, Parkes introduced Dalley generously, predicting that the 'gifted gentleman' would deal with his topic 'in a way beyond any power of mine'.

Praising their deceased contemporaries, Dalley named Cowper, Plunkett, Forster, Deniehy and Martin among those he thought would have been 'not undistinguished in the first of Legislative Chambers'. The 'genius of Deniehy would have kindled with enthusiasm and delight the most severely critical and refined, and the massive grandeur of Martin would have inspired the admiration of the most thoughtful of hearers'.

He also spoke of the survivors, including Parkes who 'in age, and service, and in station' was 'entitled to respect, and honour, and gratitude', and 'our dear and venerable friend' Robertson who had been 'supported through great labours by the loyal attachment which the sweetness of his nature, as much as his intellect, has created and sustained'.

He thought reflecting on 'vanished greatness and departed worth' was a valuable activity, prompting 'kindlier thoughts and tenderer words and nobler views of life'. *Freeman's* commented that, 'often as his happy eloquence has charmed us, we do not think it was ever much happier'. The paper detected a 'marked difference' in his references to Parkes and Robertson: 'In the one case it was a matter of mere courtesy, and rather strained at that; in the other the cheerful outpouring of a personal as well as a public affection…'[28]

Possibly so, but there was no lack of warmth in Dalley's letter to Parkes a few days later thanking him for sending a printer's proof of the speech and 'for the opportunity which your hospitality afforded me of saying a few words on the deeply interesting subject which you entrusted to me.' He added, 'Had I known of your seventy-second birthday [on 27 May] I should certainly have presumed to add mine to the numberless congratulations which you must have received.'[29]

At the end of May Dalley joined Cardinal Moran at a meeting to raise funds for further work on St Mary's Cathedral, a project to mark the colony's centenary. He noted that the time was one of 'glorious celebrations' – the Pope's 50th year as a priest, the Queen's jubilee and, next year, the 100th anniversary of the arrival of the First Fleet. He recalled the 'poor trembling bands of Irish exiles' who had laboured 'in suffering and bitter poverty and discouragement' to build the first St Mary's.

> Our work in these days of sunshine, of glorious freedom, of sympathy on all sides, of abundant means and of a blessed liberality of sentiment, which leads those to help us in adorning this temple who will not use it as a house of prayer – I say our work is an easier one. (Loud applause.) It is still a great one…[30]

Two weeks later he spoke at the laying by the Cardinal of the foundation stone of a new church at Manly, and made by far the largest donation, £150, to the project. The builders faced quite a challenge in creating a humble parish church worthy of the natural beauty of the location and overlooked by the 'magnificent' St Patrick's seminary, which had risen 'as if by some spiritual magic on the hills above', he said. Referring to riots two days earlier at a meeting at the Town Hall called to plan celebrations for the royal jubilee, he commended Moran for stating forcefully that Catholics had no sympathy with such outrages.[31]

This was the second such meeting disrupted by noisy dissidents. The platform was rushed, fights broke out and calls for cheers for the Queen were greeted with groans and yells. Making amends, some thirty thousand turned out for a loyal demonstration at the Exhibition Hall five days later. The next day both houses of parliament adopted a resolution 'to place upon record the fervent expression of the loyalty of the people of New South Wales' to the throne and Queen.

In the Legislative Council, Dalley contended that none of England's colonies was more devoted to the throne. Nowhere had 'the purity and unselfishness and strength of this feeling' been more 'nobly manifested' – through despatch of the Sudan contingent. By this action, 'into which was concentrated sympathy, sacrifice, generosity, and valour', the 'relation of the colonies to the world' had been changed; 'to be an Australian colonist became a European distinction.' He linked opposition to the contingent to the riots. A 'certain section, insignificant but for its malignity', had tried to 'mar the lustre of the action of this peculiarly favoured colony'.[32]

Dalley's next speaking engagement was at the American Independence Day banquet. Also on the speakers' list was Sir Alfred Stephen, now 84 years old, who sought Dalley's opinion of the speech he had drafted proposing the health of the President. It was 'everything that such an address from such a speaker on a national subject should be,' Dalley assured him in a letter written three days before the event. 'Brief and statesmanlike in tone – very graceful – chivalrously courteous – it is a little gem.'

Dalley told Stephen he regretted the Governor would not be attending, as he had the previous year. 'In my view this drawing together more affectionately the bonds that unite us with America is one of the noblest works of modern public life, and its performance is one of the special services which can be most gracefully and acceptably rendered by high Imperial officers.'[33]

At the banquet, he proposed the toast to 'the day we celebrate' in an emotional speech. 'The millions of the British Empire' had observed the American Civil War two decades earlier 'with broken and yet with proud hearts,' he said. 'We lamented the slaughter, and yet were proud of the combatants. And we celebrated the close of that dreadful war with gratitude to Almighty God for its end and for its result.' Now the Empire and the Republic were 'growing dearer and dearer to each other, and religiously preparing for the advent of that time when, in the glorious words of George Eliot,

> All our race shall come
> From north, west, east – a kindred multitude –
> And wake large fellowship, and raise inspired
> The shout divine, the unison of resolve.'[34]

28
Centenary

In his next big speech, in the Legislative Council three days after the Fourth of July celebration, Dalley gave strong support to Parkes's plans to mark the colony's centenary. The government that put them forward was one 'with which I have, as all the world knows, no connection whatever, except one of honest desire to give them my support when I think their action tends to the advantage of the country,' he said. He believed its intentions in advancing the proposals were honest and unselfish.

Creating a great public park – Centennial Park – out of the Lachlan Swamp, once Sydney's main water supply, was the centrepiece. Much more controversial was a 'State House' to be built in the park. This would include a grand hall or amphitheatre, a museum, a portrait and statue gallery, and a 'public mausoleum for the interment of those who have been honoured by a public funeral pursuant to a resolution of both houses of parliament'. To pre-empt cynics who would naturally assume he intended to occupy a prominent spot in the mausoleum, Parkes declared he had 'taken care that I shall be buried far away in the mountains'.[1]

Supporting the mausoleum idea, Dalley said most civilised nations, ancient and modern, had 'some magnificent receptacle for the ashes of their illustrious dead'. Standing 'near the ashes of those who had given all the vital forces of their lives to the service of the country' was an uplifting experience, and he imagined school groups, 'disporting themselves in the garden', being summoned by their teachers:

> 'My children, come here to this building where all is deposited of the remains of those who were the great public servants of their time and have been brought here that you may study over their tombs the history of the country!'

Likewise, 'persons taking their pleasure in the gardens' could visit the museum to 'inspect…those solemn instruments by which from time to time increased freedom and power have been given to the people – the manuscripts of illustrious men connected with the government of the country, documents which have become the law of the land, and the despatches of Governors'.[2]

He wrote to Parkes from Manly a week later offering to help in any way, 'so far as my broken health will permit me', with the centennial proposals. Writing again on 7 August from 'Ringarooma', Mittagong, where he had gone to seek 'perfect peace and a purer air', he regretted not having called on the Premier, but had been very weak, 'suffering severely from sleeplessness', and unable to attend to any business. He suggested Parkes consult William Wardell, the architect of St Mary's Cathedral and 'I think unsurpassably the most thoroughly cultivated member of his profession', on the style and cost of the State House. No criticisms he had read weakened 'in any way the force of your proposals', and he would be 'proud and glad' to render any 'poor assistance' that would be 'acceptable to you'.[3]

Dalley's retreat to the southern highlands followed a Hawkesbury River excursion and luncheon speech, in honour of Lord Thomas Brassey, a future Governor of Victoria, on 9 July, and another long and impassioned speech in the Legislative Council three days later. The topic was payment for members of the Legislative Assembly, which he strongly supported. Nobody could simultaneously earn a living and satisfactorily represent the people in parliament, he said. As a member of the Assembly he had 'had the honour and happiness of intimately associating…with the men occupying the first place in it', and

> I knew none of those who were greater, more laborious, and more unselfish than some who discharged their duties almost under privations; and I never received a greater blow to my own ease and contentment than from one of these, known to many distinguished members of this House, who informed me one night that he had never been in a position during all the weary and wasting nights of debate to justify his procuring food itself in the refreshment-room.[4]

Dalley and Sir Alfred Stephen were among only nine Council

members who voted for remuneration of their Assembly brethren; 30 voted against. The proponents prevailed two years later.

The Mittagong sojourn did not improve Dalley's health, and newspapers reported in mid-September that he had retired from public life 'for, it is feared, a long time, if not permanently'. His doctors prescribed 'perfect quiet and freedom from every kind of excitement'.[5] No improvement was reported until mid-December, when *Freeman's* noted that 'he seems to have taken a fresh lease of life, and may soon be seen once more amongst us'.

> With us, all creeds and classes, rich and poor, high and low, have taken the deepest interest in Mr Dalley's recent struggle with the grim old wrestler who sooner or later puts the 'half-Nelson' on and throws us all. The tidings that the brilliant favourite is rallying will therefore be glad news for all to-day…[6]

Some undated letters to Lady Martin are probably from the period after his return to Manly. In two of them Dalley writes of plans for a day trip with her and her sister Selina Cheeke to his house at Bilgola: 'I am sure you will immensely enjoy this little trip… I shall have a comfortable carriage, quiet horses and a careful driver.' He had to cancel at the last minute 'as I can hardly move or think without effort and have been very feeble'. In another letter, written after a visit by Lady Martin, he said he had given 'entire control of the children' to a governess, Miss Trotter, and felt he was nearing 'the clearing up of all mysteries'.[7] He signed his last will on 18 November, days after reportedly experiencing 'urgent symptoms' that soon passed but left him 'exceedingly weak'.[8]

He reappeared on the public stage at the opening of the new wing of St Vincent's Hospital by Lady Carrington on 21 January 1888. Official guests included five archbishops and bishops from the country and neighbouring colonies, in Sydney for the centennial celebrations, as well as Cardinal Moran. Also there was Sir John Robertson, who rose 'in response to repeated calls' and was greeted with great cheering when he expressed his delight at seeing his 'old friend' in public again.

Dalley, according to the *Freeman's* report, was loudly cheered throughout his short speech. The hospital was 'a perpetual manifestation of heavenly pity for affliction, and a living protest against an intolerant and cruel fanaticism', he said. It had been established with the heartiest encouragement of the tender-hearted Archbishop Polding, who, 'if he hated anything in the world, held in deepest abhorrence those who carried sectarianism into charities and poisoned the fountains of pity.' The reporter thought his voice was perhaps a little weaker than a year ago, but still carried 'all its old charm and all its old magic'.[9]

Probably a day or two earlier, Dalley received a *Daily Telegraph* reporter at home at Manly. The paper had asked for a lengthy article on his 'imperial views'. He replied that, while not up to the physical task of writing it, he was happy to be interviewed. The result filled more than four broadsheet columns of the paper.

Dalley regretted that the idea of the State House (with mausoleum) appeared to have been abandoned in the face of ridicule and unfair criticism. He also regretted that 'representative men, not only from the mother country but from America and the great countries of Europe' had not been invited to the centennial celebrations to witness 'our marvellous development'.

He reiterated his view that other European powers should be welcomed in the region, not feared. And he had no regrets about the Sudan enterprise. It had been applauded in all parts of the world, 'save here…where some few of those persons, who seem to be inspired with an ambition to obscure the glory of an event which they could never have originated, endeavoured to darken the splendour of this greatest historical action of the colonies of England up to the present time.'

The disappointment and hint of bitterness apparent in that passage were also evident later in the interview. Some 'persons in high stations' who had 'enthusiastically sanctioned' the contingent had recently made 'some extremely guarded utterances' on the subject; he would have expected 'more wisdom and more chivalry' from them. And the 'audacious misrepresentations' made about his alleged unsanctioned purchases of military equipment when he was acting Premier had shocked him.

What has given me at times acuter pain than the extent of the calumnies on my public character has been the silence with which they have been received by persons who had peculiar advantages of knowing their cruel falsehood, and who yet preserved absolute silence while they were being circulated.[10]

A happier Dalley appeared at a gathering of around 5,000 people at St Mary's Cathedral on the evening of 24 January to 'formally initiate as a centennial memorial the movement for the completion of our cathedral'. The Governors of all the Australian colonies and Fiji were there, together with four archbishops and seven bishops. Dalley received a 'tremendous ovation' when the Cardinal called on him to welcome the Governors on behalf of the Catholic community.

Their presence was a compliment to 'the great Catholic body of colonists' and a 'homage to liberality of opinion', he said. They were following in the footsteps of other great Governors – Macquarie, who laid the foundation stone of the first St Mary's; Denison, present at the laying of the foundation stone of St John's College; and Young, who 'eloquently stimulated the generosity of the public' after the cathedral fire of 1865. This 'inheritance of liberality and sympathy…cannot have been without the most beneficial influence upon the community.'

Dalley was in top form the next day when the 'laity of Sydney' treated the visiting prelates to a harbour excursion and luncheon at Cabarita on the Parramatta River. Presiding at the feast, he proposed the health of Governor Carrington in words that at least one eulogist observed could be applied to himself. 'There are some men', he said,

> who seem to have been sent into the world with the beautiful mission of simply making themselves agreeable and delightful. They are endowed with those rare qualities which find their own happiness in widely diffusing it, they discover the fascination of unselfishness, and the perfect felicity of devoting life to the work of making it more attractive to those who enjoy it, and more tolerable to those who suffer. They are the missionaries of true courtesy – preaching in every action of their lives the beauty of goodness, of kindness, of consoling words, and generous actions. The world, which in spite of all (Heaven forgive me for the heresy of making so unorthodox a statement in this holy company) is not a bad world to those who love it, receives these missionaries with welcome, and rewards them with love. Now, in the person of our Governor, we have a beautiful example of one of them…

Toasting the bishops and archbishops, he spoke of the extraordinary progress of the Catholic Church in the colony since the arrival of the first 'manacled missionaries', transported 'for an alleged share in what was called the Irish Rebellion'. He praised the success of its leaders in fostering good relations with non-Catholics, demonstrating that their churches were 'schools of pure charity and tender forbearance, of justice and mercy and peace…'[11]

Speechmakers during the long afternoon's celebration included six prelates, politicians and a judge. Winding up proceedings with the toast to Dalley, Thomas O'Mara, an MP who opposed the Sudan expedition but greatly admired its author, described him as 'beyond all question… the most cultured and the most popular man in all Australia'. He was also the 'most eloquent man in the southern hemisphere' and 'the first citizen in the land' in talent, culture, patriotism, public service, and 'highest of all his titles', in the 'universal esteem of all classes and all creeds in the community. (Loud cheers.)'

Dalley responded with a moving and much cheered off-the-cuff speech mostly in praise of Protestants who had sprung to the support of Catholics labouring 'under a cloud of calumny, cowardly persecution [and] infamous misrepresentation' during the Fenian scare of 1868. There was the 'gifted, unselfish, chivalrous' William Forster and 'my dear friend' William Macleay. 'Nor can we forget the gallantry and tenderness and sympathy of dear old Sir John Robertson.'

> When I think of these men I am overwhelmed with a sense of our obligations to the justice and courage of some of the best of our Protestant fellow-citizens. (Great applause.) Will you permit me to say that in all our public actions we should be careful so to conduct ourselves as to preserve this precious relationship? Nothing would be so calamitous as to weaken its power, while to destroy it would be to cripple our influence for good upon that civilization which in this country, thank God, we have upheld with all our strength. (Cheers.)[12]

That Dalley was still far from well is clear from his reply, written on 27 January, to a 'most elegant and loving' letter from Sir Alfred Stephen congratulating him on his *Telegraph* interview vindicating 'the course which I have pursued in public affairs'. He was still 'too feeble and prostrated' to do all that was 'absolutely essential for our credit's sake in the eyes of both our own people and foreigners', he wrote, but hoped to take the matter up again in the Legislative Council 'where you will be beside me and with me'.

> But I have been so ill that I hardly dare to cherish the hope that I shall do much again. I have been compelled to abstain from all share in the festive celebrations save those immediately connected with our Church, in which I perilously participated for the sole purpose of keeping our people – unhappily so prone to make mistakes in public and particularly in Imperial questions – to the right path. Thank God, they behaved most nobly.[13]

Soon afterwards Dalley was feeling well enough to contemplate a visit to England. In a note dated 6 February thanking the book and art dealer Jacob Clarke for offering a letter of introduction to his brother, he said his 'arrangements for leaving the colony' were incomplete.[14] It was a passing prospect. Three months later he told Dibbs, who had sent on a letter from Lord Loftus, that he no longer entertained any hope of undertaking the trip and seeing the former Governor, whose 'great kindness to his advisers' he remembered with 'tenderness and gratitude'.[15]

Dalley made another much-cheered speech, at a banquet for the newly arrived Irish rector of St John's College, Dr James O'Brien, on 23 February. Welcoming O'Brien, he paid tribute to three earlier 'apostles of culture' who had courageously left 'the sanctity of long association for the busy, struggling, awakening life of young communities.' Professor Badham had brought 'the rarest scholarship and the gayest youthfulness of feeling…' Bishop Charles Davis – who came to Sydney in 1848, played an important role in the university's foundation, and died in 1854 – was 'as liberal as he was saintly… I went the other day to the grave in which he sleeps… and wondered that such a man had been lent to us in our earliest days.' Then there was the founding St John's rector Dr John Forrest, 'who was sent…to show you what a good sound scholar, what a dear friend, what a delicate humorist and a perfectly tolerant gentleman, may be found in the person of an Irish Catholic priest. (Great applause.)'[16]

One of the stories told later of Dalley was of his rush to catch the last ferry to Manly after that banquet. He had arranged for his favourite cabman, Patrick Moloney, jocularly referred to as 'my Fenian cabman', to pick him up at St John's. Hastening to the door at 20 to 11, he told the journalist to whom he had offered a lift to town that his 'heavenly cabman' was to be there at ten. But when they emerged no cab was waiting. Dalley, the journalist recalled,

> as if summoning some spirit from the mystic darkness, lifted up his voice and shouted, 'Malony, you Fenian, where are you?' ... In a twinkling of an eye the bold Malony was at the door with his cab and his emphatic 'Right, sir!' We jumped in. 'Where to?' asked Malony. 'Drive for your life to the Manly wharf, but stop for a second at the *Herald*. I've got the editor on board, and he's late with a scorching article on the Pope.' Malony broke his record for furious driving; Dalley caught his boat; and I live to tell the tale.[17]

Dalley left his Manly 'castle' soon afterwards. Letters from late March to early May give his address as 'Fernside', Bowral;[18] again he was seeking refreshment from the southern highlands air. He had intended to speak at the St Patrick's Day banquet at the Sydney Town Hall and prepared a speech on current Irish matters, but sent his apologies.[19] By 25 May he and the family had moved into a rented house not far from the city, 'Annery', Darling Point.[20] The Manly and Bilgola properties were sold on 1 May.[21]

He declined with regret the Cardinal's invitation to a dinner at Manly on 3 May. Three days later he spoke in the cathedral, packed for a farewell presentation to Moran before another Rome visit. As spokesman for the laity, Dalley presented an address and £500 cheque to the departing prelate. Eloquent as ever, he praised Moran for the archdiocese's remarkable progress during his four years in charge. Thirty-three new churches and 36 schools had been built, and priest numbers had more than doubled. He had fostered 'all that tends to exalt and perfect human society', and raised from their foundations institutions

> that help us to conceive of God and of his love with a deeper awe and reverence, and of our fellow-creatures of all classes, and colours, and tongues, and creeds, with a profounder sympathy and a sweeter compassion. (Cheers.)

Moran's response would have pleased Dalley. Catholics should always aim 'to heal dissensions and to promote union in all sections of the community', he said. They should cherish their Protestant fellow citizens, many of whom had been 'fearless and brilliant champions of religious equality and civil liberty'. Dalley was part of the large party that escorted the Cardinal to his ship at Circular Quay two days later, and saw him, 'fairly wreathed in smiles' as he 'responded to the enthusiastic ovation', to the Heads on one of seven accompanying steamers.[22]

Moran left at a time of renewed anti-Chinese clamour in the colony. 'Wholesale immigration' through Darwin, where the poll tax imposed at other ports was not collected, was the main worry early in the year.[23] Agitation grew in April with the arrival at Melbourne of a steamer bearing 'a number of Chinamen for distribution amongst the different ports'; the *Mail* advised politicians to respond calmly to the 'wild talk at public meetings'.[24] The arrival in Sydney harbour of hundreds of Chinese on this ship and another at the beginning of May prompted an overflow meeting at the Town Hall that called for a total ban on their entry. Afterwards, an 'excited crowd' estimated at more than 5,000 marched to Parliament House, demanding that Premier Parkes receive a deputation.

Parkes delivered a mixed message when he did so the next morning. While noting that the proportion of Chinese in the colony's population was less than half that in 1861, he said he entirely supported the deputation's position.[25] He ordered tough action, declaring 'the Government has decided at all hazards to prevent Chinese landing in this colony', except those with naturalisation certificates. He was flouting the law, which allowed in those who paid the poll tax or had certificates exempting them from it, given to residents who left the colony to visit China.

On 16 May the Legislative Assembly rushed through legislation greatly increasing the poll tax and reducing the number of Chinese a ship could bring in, imposing an annual licence fee on them, restricting their movements and where they could live, and most controversially, indemnifying the government for its actions since 1 May and preventing legal redress. 'I cast to the winds your permits of exemption,' Parkes declared. 'I care nothing about your cobweb of technical law.'

The next day the Supreme Court ruled that those with exemption certificates must be allowed to land. A second case produced a similar decision for those able to pay the poll tax. In early June Chief Justice Darley delivered a withering judgment in the case of a man refused permission to land despite being ready to pay the tax. Never before had the law, once pronounced, been similarly 'set at defiance', he declared, and an illegally held Chinese who took a life 'in order to obtain his liberty' would be committing justifiable homicide, not murder.[26]

The Legislative Council refused to follow the Assembly in curtailing discussion of Parkes's bill. Dalley spoke for more than an hour in the second reading debate on 30 May, and showed he had 'lost none of that wondrous power of fact-marshalling, and penetrating into the very sap of subjects which was the marvel of all who had the good fortune to hear him more frequently in his young and golden days,' commented 'The Flaneur' in *Freeman's*.[27]

As he did when Parkes introduced legislation to restrict Chinese immigration in 1879 (chapter 16), Dalley announced his intention to vote for the second reading in deference to the 'general public feeling', but support amendments to remove the bill's most objectionable features. The feeling against an increase in numbers of Chinese in the colony had been 'wildly, and cruelly, and unjustly inflamed', but there was no reasonable probability of it diminishing, he said.

> Under these circumstances it is neither desirable for the Chinese themselves nor for the country that a state of things should exist which will expose them to hatred, surveillance, capricious cruelty, and us to the dishonour of being without sympathy with, or compassion for, those who are helping to build up the fabric of our prosperity by their industry.

The colony might lose its 'title to civilisation' by failing to protect their lives and property, he feared. Then the 'alleged degradation which flows from their presence' would be of 'our creating, not theirs'. It would proceed 'not from their disobedience of our laws, but from our own inability to enforce them for their protection, and from our want of sympathy with the first principles of justice, and pity, and mercy'. Referring to the anti-Chinese agitation and the government's attempts to defy the law, he added,

> I confess, with shame, that my heart was filled with indignation at the silence of Christian ministers in this city, in the midst of recent events which appealed so strongly to them to speak a word in behalf of eternal justice, of human pity…[28]

A week later Dalley moved an amendment, which was accepted by the Council, to limit the bill's indemnity provision by upholding the right of those affected by illegal acts of the government to go to court.[29] He was too ill to take any further part in the debate, which saw the Council remove the provisions making life harder for the Chinese already in the colony. Both houses passed the amended bill in early July.

Dalley managed to again attend the American Independence Day luncheon. Never had there been such 'a triumph of human industry' as that presented by the US, he declared: 'it follows that no anniversary of any human event should be so religiously, so enthusiastically, and so universally celebrated as this.'[30] He wrote to Sir Alfred Stephen two weeks earlier hoping he, too, would attend, and offering to drive the old man to the Botany picnic grounds, 'take charge of you, and restore you within two hours to [your home in] College Street'. He added, 'I am really too infirm to subject myself to these excitements but I shall be imprudent if you will be courageous.'

Accepting the invitation, Stephen recalled, perhaps insensitively, the 'epitaph' to Dalley he had written in court in Bathurst in 1859 predicting the young barrister's early demise from excessive cigar smoking (chapter 5). 'I remember the epitaph as if it was sculptured yesterday and the unintended compliment elicited by your versatility,' Dalley replied. In a postscript to his letter, signed 'Yours most reverentially and affectionately', he told Stephen he was living so close to St Mark's Anglican church, Darling Point, 'that I speak in whispers lest my ecclesiastical conversations may be overheard and supposed to be the vicar's sermons (who is said to he 'high').' He added,

I have a decent cook – a few bottles of dear old Martin's best wine – and I could send any day at 1 or 1.30 a pair of charming gentle horses well driven to bring you out to lunch and send you home as early as you like. When will you come?[31]

Dalley wrote a collection of brief literary thoughts – 'Pensées' – for the first issue of Sydney's *Centennial Magazine* around this time. The *Mail* found it 'emphatically the best and brightest' piece in the magazine; it reminded *Freeman's* of Dalley's 'table talk'.[32] He speculated that, but for a chance event in his life, Gibbon might have written 'delightful classical romances' in French rather than *The Decline and Fall of the Roman Empire*. He was inclined to think Keats's 'Ode on a Grecian Urn' was a work of pure imagination rather than inspired by a real vase, and thought it most unlikely that the Duke of Wellington had really said 'the battle of Waterloo was won on the playing fields of Eton'.

Writing of John Henry Newman, a 'master spirit' of the age who had largely and permanently affected 'the most ingenuous and the most refined youth of three generations', he noted that the old man must soon be 'called away'. When that happened, 'the best men of all forms of opinion' would 'vie with each other in attempting to estimate the value of the life lost'. The longest section of the article mourned the recent death of the poet Matthew Arnold, who had written of death – particularly that 'of youth, of genius, of sacrifice, of love and pity' – in a way that made it often seem 'more sweet and beautiful and less sad' than the preceding life.[33]

Thanking Alexander Oliver in late July for the 'generous tenderness, affectionate curiosity and cultured gossip' of a recent letter, Dalley wrote that he had felt Arnold's death 'very much'. And the 'hideous' anti-Chinese business had done him 'indescribable injury'. Opponents of the outcry had seemed 'powerless against infamous wrong, and I felt my personal feebleness as a calamity. I hardly dared to look a Chinaman in the face while our brutalities were triumphantly going on.'

He added that his health had deteriorated to the point where 'the mere physical exercise of writing disables me'. Insomnia had 'returned with intense force and literally almost the cry has come to me 'Sleep no more!' I never go anywhere – and scarcely ever see any one, except occasionally for Martin's wife.' He invited Oliver to visit; there was nearly always 'some choice fish – sole or flounder or black rock-cod' – in the larder.[34]

Dalley apparently hoped to deliver another eulogy to Daniel Deniehy, whose remains were reburied at Waverley cemetery on 15 September. Daniel O'Connor instigated the reinterment, and announced that Dalley would give the oration when the monument planned for the site was unveiled.[35]

The reburial was accompanied by controversy over whether the right bones had been retrieved from Bathurst,[36] and by an anonymous letter to the *Herald* making the extraordinary claim that Deniehy had been denied Catholic rites at his original burial because he had offended Dalley in his satire 'How I Became Attorney-General of New Barataria' (chapter 5). O'Connor sprang to the defence of his old sparring partner in the next day's paper, writing that his heart was 'as tender and free from every ungenerous throb as his nature is high and his intellect above measure.'[37] Dalley wrote to O'Connor,

> I am exceedingly obliged to you for your very chivalrous reference to the ruffianly correspondent of the *Herald* who dared to attribute the desecration of our poor Deniehy's remains to a desire on the part of our Church to gain my favour. I scarcely even allowed for a moment poor Deniehy's references to me in the article referred to, to ruffle my equanimity – certainly never to disturb the deep laid foundations of our friendship. He was as dear to me during the latter dark and disastrous days of his sad life as he was at the most brilliant and hopeful period of his existence, and no-one felt a keener suffering at the dishonour of his poor remains than I did.

He added that he sympathised with O'Connor over the 'storm of abuse and misrepresentation' he had been subjected to for his 'touching and unselfish action'. 'Should God give me strength' he went on, 'I shall take care some day that what you have done will be fairly known by the public.'[38] Unfortunately, that strength was not granted to him.

On 27 August Alexander Oliver's wife Celia gave birth to a boy, whom they christened Dalley George Tryon. A month later, four of the Dalley children visited the Olivers at 'Shelcote', Neutral Bay, to admire the baby named in honour of their father. 'I have been very queer unhappily for the last few days and I was ill on the blissful day when our poor little 'Magi' went to their innocent adorations at the crib at 'Shelcote", Dalley wrote in a note of thanks. 'They came back full of happiness and gratified for all the kindness...'[39]

His last known letter, written three days later, on 3 October, is a sad one. Replying to a request by Robert Burdett Smith, representing New South Wales at the Melbourne International Exhibition, for a portrait of himself to go with the Sudan contingent display, he declined with thanks. In sending the contingent, 'which has done more to elevate these Australian Colonies in the eyes of the universal world than anything which has taken place since their foundation, I have only tasted suffering, the grossest misrepresentations, and have been charged with every kind of offence in the gratification of a selfish and inordinate ambition,' he wrote.

> I now scarcely ever open my mouth about a subject in which I thought I should have shared in the glory of our country in its achievement. You will understand how reluctant I am to take any step to give the least justification for suggestions that I had any personal purposes to serve in an action which you, at all events, do not require to be informed, was undertaken in the purest spirit of devoted unselfishness, and the labour attending which, added to that which I undertook for my poor dear friend Stuart, has ruined my constitution and wrecked my life.[40]

Dalley died aged 57 – according to the death certificate of cardiac disease, renal disease and uraemia – on the evening of Sunday 28 October. He had received the last rites, and his children and sister were at the bedside.

29
'Tongue of silver, heart of gold'

Lord Carrington coined that phrase in a tribute to Dalley, and the poet and journalist Frank Hutchinson made it the theme of a memorial cantata.[1] Chief Justice Darley called Dalley 'the most highly gifted, eloquent Australian who ever graced the Senate or adorned the forum of his country'.[2] The Attorney-General, George Simpson, thought him 'the kindest man I ever met'.[3] As Dalley had predicted would happen when John Henry Newman died, men vied with each other 'in attempting to estimate the value of the life lost'. So did the newspapers, which devoted many columns – in the case of *Freeman's* many pages – to glowing leaders, obituaries and anecdotes. Dalley had become 'the Australian representative man' in the eyes of the world, said Melbourne's *Argus*.[4] To *Freeman's*, he was 'Australia's peerless son…whom to know was to love'.[5]

In the Cardinal's absence, the colony's senior bishop, James Murray of Maitland, presided at the dirge and requiem high mass at the cathedral on 30 October. Some 6,000 people, as many as the building could hold, heard the Jesuit Rev. William Kelly of St Aloysius' College deliver a moving panegyric to a man whose eloquence was always directed to the 'nobler sentiments of the human heart'. Another 10,000 waited outside, in threatening weather, for the funeral procession to leave. Flags flew at half-mast, shops were draped in black and thousands lined the streets as more than 400 carriages and hundreds on foot made their way to Waverley Cemetery. There, two to three thousand followed the hearse down the hill to the grave, where Bishop Murray performed the rites. 'Conspicuous amid the throng were many white-haired veterans of political life,' *Freeman's* reported; notable among these were Sir John Robertson and the Legislative Council President, Sir John Hay.[6]

Talk of erecting a statue of Dalley began within days of his death. Alexander Oliver endorsed the idea in the *Herald*, saying it would express 'the large, and among many of us the passionate, admiration in which Mr Dalley was held in the colony of his birth'.[7] Robertson took the lead, calling a well-attended preliminary meeting on 10 December that set the wheels in motion. Somewhat dampening the enthusiasm, Joseph Abbott, a colleague of Dalley in the Stuart government, pointed out that the statue of Rev. John Dunmore Lang, initiated in 1882 (chapter 17), was still to appear in Wynyard Square (it was eventually unveiled in 1891). And George Dibbs noted that people had been slow to subscribe to monuments to great men; he particularly regretted the lack of recognition of Wentworth and Bland. Robertson agreed, and named Cowper as another neglected figure, but urged those present to concentrate on the task at hand, honouring Dalley.[8]

Absent from the meeting was William Long, who wrote to Robertson declaring his 'firm friendship' with his brother-in-law Dalley but naming five others who he thought had prior claims to a statue.[9] Whatever Long's motivation, the next meeting, a week later, may have prompted second thoughts. The hall was packed and an array of eminent political, legal and religious – Protestant as well as Catholic – figures joined Robertson on the platform. Notable absentees who sent warm messages of support included Carrington and Darley.

Sir Alfred Stephen spoke first, saying he supported the movement 'on every ground, personal and public'. Dalley had always spoken, felt and acted 'under the impulses of duty' and was therefore 'in the best sense' a patriot, he said. 'In a world-embracing spirit, he lifted up his voice on behalf of the Chinese among us. He reminded us, also, that the broad Pacific held other nations than our own, and that it was wise to regard them as friends.' His 'crowning act' was sending the Sudan contingent, which had 'taught geographers and politicians who and what we are, and where to be found; and that we claimed to be a portion, not a dependency merely' of the 'mighty' empire.

Cardinal Moran, received with 'deafening applause', hoped future generations would seek to emulate Dalley's honourable career: 'Who more fervent and fearless than he in every path of enlightenment and progress?' The Presbyterian Moderator Very Rev. John Auld said Dalley 'belonged to us all', and regarded his loss as 'a public calamity'. An emotional Sir Patrick Jennings thought Dalley 'the most loveable man' he had met; 'he was so simple, so genial, so natural, so unaffected that one forgot in his presence he was so great a man'. The US consul, Gilderoy Griffin, spoke of the 'peerless grace and lofty beauty of his soul'.

The speaker who most impressed *Freeman's* was the Anglican Bishop Barry who, according to the paper, put into words 'the unexpressed thought that was in all men's minds' – that Dalley had so worthily represented the 'noble side' of Australia's young national life, 'its imaginative side, its sentiment, and its romance'. In honouring Dalley the community honoured itself 'because it showed it could produce greatness and appreciate it when produced', said the bishop. Dalley had had 'an instinct for great things', which he knew how to distinguish from the 'very small things' that made up so much of political life in the colony. The 'element of poetry, of imagination, and appreciation of [the] noble and beautiful' he contributed had ameliorated the often 'somewhat prosaic ugliness' of modern life. Like Moran's, Barry's remarks were greeted with 'deafening applause'.

Robertson had the last word, saying he had acted to honour the memory of his 'dear old friend' out of a sense of duty as well as affection; nobody had served the country more faithfully, or better deserved the tribute it was proposed to pay him. About £300 was subscribed at the meeting, leaving a large sum still to collect after the initial enthusiasm passed.[10]

In London in the meantime, with memories of the Sudan adventure still fresh, Dalley's death was reported widely, and he was much praised, in the press.[11] Lord Rosebery, now president of the Imperial Federation League, quickly initiated plans for a memorial. He had been impressed by the colonial orator during his visit to Sydney in 1883 and cabled 'Well done, New South Wales' when the Sudan offer was accepted.[12] In May 1889 the Dean and chapter of St Paul's Cathedral, site of the tombs of imperial heroes including Nelson and Wellington, accepted his proposal to fix a tablet in honour of Dalley to the crypt wall. That the first colonial so honoured was a Catholic apparently caused no concern.[13]

In Sydney, Major-General Richardson and about 20 other members of the Sudan contingent met within days of Dalley's death to consider how his memory could best be perpetuated, and proposed that the veterans fund a memorial tablet in St Mary's Cathedral.[14] This proposal lapsed, but Dalley is honoured in the cathedral with a stained-glass window installed in the western transept in 1892. Those who helped pay for it included the Protestants Lord Carrington, Robertson and Darley.[15] The plaque notes Dalley's services 'to his Church, his Country and the Empire'.

Smaller gestures of respect included a motion of condolence carried by the Manly Borough Council. The mayor spoke of Dalley's 'unostentatious, ungrudging and constant charity', including giving the overseer of the borough 'permission to put his name down for any amount he thought fit in every case of real distress that came under his notice'.[16] Many stories were told of his generosity; one eulogist, possibly exaggerating, wrote that every morning 'brought a sheaf of begging letters and every day applicants for bounty at the door, and rarely it was that an appeal was made in vain to the tender-hearted master of the house'.[17]

Perhaps this partly explains why, despite his large inheritance, success at the Bar and the sale of the last of his real estate in early 1888, Dalley did not die particularly wealthy. The net value of the estate declared by William Long and the other executors was £5,557. Confirming that he was a generous donor to the Catholic Church, the debts listed at his death included £140 promised to the Manly Beach mission and £183 15s to the cathedral fund.

Other debts included small sums owed to two governesses, another female servant, and the coachman, butler, housemaid and cook – an interesting insight into a vanished life style. Probably the butler was Michael Collins, who the will provided should be retained, if he wished, as servant to the Dalley boys until they came of age. Dalley asked in the will – which provided equally for the five children – that if possible the boys remain at St Aloysius' as boarders and then go to St John's College at the university. The executors decided, instead, to send them to Catholic colleges in England – at least fulfilling his desire that they be brought up 'in my own religion'. They departed, under the care of one of the governesses, Miss Hogarth, in February 1889.[18]

The girls, as Dalley had wished, went to live with his sister, Christina Greig, in Melbourne. The will provided for her to receive £20 a month for the rest of her life, and for the other governess, Miss Trotter, to join the Greig household as 'a companion and attendant' to his daughters. Miss Trotter, who was to receive a pound a week for life as well as her servant's pay, seems to have been a favourite. Dalley told Lady Martin an amusing tale in October 1886 of the family presenting her with an illuminated address on her safe return to Manly after a trip to the city.[19] And he proudly recounted to 20-year-old Mary Martin one of his six-year-old Mary's 'dialogues' with Miss Trotter.

> Mary: Trots, tell me a conundrum!
> Trotter: Why my darling are old maids receiving an offer of marriage like convicts?
> Mary: I give it up Trots.
> Trotter: Because they go off in transports.
> Mary: What do you mean by transports?
> Trotter: Vessels in which people who have committed crimes are sent out to the colony.
> Mary: Trots, what crime did you commit? Why did they send you out?[20]

Many eulogists mentioned Dalley's devotion to his children, and tellers of stories about him added scraps of detail. He was to be seen 'marching about Manly accompanied by five children, five nurses and five dogs', wrote one, who also told a tale of the family in church.

> One Sunday morning Dalley and his children were attending Mass at the Manly Catholic Church when Dalley felt a nudge from [youngest son] Charlie, who was sitting next to him. Dalley tried to suppress the boy, but without success. He had his eye rivetted on a window, which represented St John and the Lamb, and kept asking, 'what is the gentleman doing with the sheep, Daddy?' The father's sense of humour alone saved the boy from severe castigation that day.[21]

The writer of the *Argus* obituary, clearly someone who knew Dalley well, wrote that 'utmost simplicity' reigned at home in Manly, with 'governesses and housekeeper' joining 'the privy councillor and all the children' at the breakfast table and 'the whole establishment...migrating' to Bilgola soon after daybreak on hot summer days. The same article gives probably the best description of him – allowing for the exaggerations of eulogy – as dinner host. Dalley 'delighted in entertaining', and had an inexhaustible memory and 'ever-flowing spring of humour' that made 'light and laughter spontaneous and continuous'.

> He seemed to have all the stories that had ever been told arranged and assorted, the most appropriate ever on the tip of his tongue. He could surround, elucidate, and amplify any matter with innumerable quotations. Relating old matters of church history, writings of the fathers, records of the saints, he would diffuse about him a sentiment as of an ancient cathedral; lights of learning, research, and living sympathy seemed to radiate as through richly stained windows; the mellow music of the organ would at times have been fitting accompaniment to the solemn and measured cadences of his voice. Breaking away in wild flights of Rabelaisian humour, his laughter would lead the general chorus. He knew all literature; his sympathy with the ancients never died, and with all modern and mediaeval authors he was in constant intercourse...[22]

'The Flaneur' in *Freeman's* made the bold prediction that, 'while Australia lasts, her children will ever treasure the memory and speak with flashing eyes and proudly parted lips of the first and greatest of her young day's sons – William Bede Dalley!'[23] Frank Myers was more realistic; Dalley would dwell 'in the innermost sanctuaries' of the memories of those who knew him 'while memory endures', he wrote in 1907.[24] But memory has a limited life.

Unlike some prominent figures, including Parkes who kept vast quantities of correspondence and wrote his own draft of history,[25] Dalley did not actively seek future fame. He is not remembered for any great legislative measures, and his writings, though prolific and a pleasure to read, were ephemeral; plans reported within days of his death to collect and publish them came to nothing.[26] The Boer War and the horrors of World War I soon pushed the Sudan expedition – whether grand turning point in imperial history, farce or something in between – into the shade. So it is hardly surprising that Dalley's is not a household name today.

But his legislative achievements – particularly in securing the Stuart government's criminal law and land reforms – were considerable. So was his contribution to, in the *Herald*'s words, raising 'the tone of this young community', not least through his appeals for religious harmony and respect for the Chinese. He was a man 'so unique in his personality, … so unlike all his contemporaries', that he 'completely made for himself the niche which he filled,' another *Herald* leader observed.[27] One rare trait was the reluctance of his forays into government. Once committed, though, the work level was intense. As *Freeman's* put it, among Dalley's 'remarkable and charming' characteristics was

> the whole heart which he threw into every action of his life, whether it was a great speech or a good story, a military expedition or a fishing party, a 'round' with a political opponent or a romp with the boys. It was much more than mere energy; it was the perennial spring of a bold, bright, happy, inexhaustible nature…[28]

Charles Dalley, two days short of his 12th birthday, was the only family member who could attend the unveiling by Lord Rosebery of the memorial tablet in the St Paul's Cathedral crypt on 17 July 1890; his brothers were ill. Others there included Lord Knutsford, Secretary of State for the Colonies; Lieutenant-General Sir Gerald Graham, commander of the forces in Sudan; and Admiral Tryon. In his brief speech, Rosebery described Dalley as 'not merely a colonial minister, but an imperial statesman'.

The memorial comprises a head and shoulders profile of Dalley sculpted in white Carrara marble set in an octagonal slab of grey marble, with an inscribed marble tablet below. The inscription reads, 'In memory of William Bede Dalley, the Australian statesman and patriot. This tablet has been erected by contributions from all parts of that world-wide empire which he cherished, served, and strove to maintain. He was born in 1831. He died in 1888.'[29]

Seven more years passed before the statue – the first of a native-born

Australian to grace Sydney's streets and parks – was unveiled. Only two colonists had been honoured similarly before – Thomas Sutcliffe Mort (Dalley spoke at the unveiling of his statue in 1883 – chapter 19) and Lang. The other statues already standing were of Captain Cook, Governor Bourke, the Queen and Prince Albert.

Funds flowed in slowly, not helped by competing demands, such as for the St Mary's Cathedral extensions, and the economic depression of the early 1890s. Only £825 was to hand when the first subscription list was published in July 1892, well short of the required sum.[30] By then Sir John Robertson had been dead a year, and prospects for completing the project looked bleak.

Perhaps a brief visit to the colony in 1895 by Dalley's second son, John Bede, then a student at Cambridge, helped revive interest. 'He is very like his father, with the same quick eye, the same happy manner, and the same charm of bright and witty conversation,' commented *Freeman's*.[31] Whatever the spur to renewed action, the committee was ready to select a sculptor in early 1896. English-born James White, who won the commission and later produced the statue of Robertson that stands in the Domain, displayed a full-size clay model in his Strand Arcade shop from May 1896. Darley and Dibbs were among those who dropped in to admire it. In September the trustees of Hyde Park approved the site near St Mary's Cathedral proposed, reportedly by Cardinal Moran, for the statue.[32] White cast the bronze likeness of Dalley at his foundry at Petersham in early 1897.

At the unveiling by the Governor, Lord Hampden, on 20 April – in the presence of the Cardinal and two former Premiers (Jennings and Dibbs) and a crowd of 10,000 – Charles Dalley, now 18, again represented the family. Delivering a brief speech of thanks to the Governor, he was 'very nervous, and spoke with difficulty'; at one point an encouraging voice from the crowd urged 'take your time'.[33] In this respect, he clearly did not take after his father.

Charles, who had embarked on a military career, died in a hunting accident in England two years later. His remains were returned to Sydney and, after a requiem mass and last blessing pronounced by Moran at the cathedral, interred in Dalley's vault at Waverley cemetery. Topped by a stone monument in the shape of a miniature cathedral with a large ornamented Celtic cross at the eastern end – the design of William Wardell – this was completed about a year after Dalley's death. On its reopening to receive his son, a miniature marble altar was unexpectedly found inside – a gift of the monumental mason and another sign of the regard in which Dalley had been held.[34]

Notes

Introduction

1. *SMH* 21 April 1897; *FJ* 24 April 1897
2. *Sunday Sun* 5 Jan 1930
3. *FJ* 24 April 1897
4. *Empire* 15 April 1865
5. *FJ* 24 April 1897
6. *Bulletin* 3 Nov 1888
7. *SMH* 31 Oct 1888

1. Looking up

1. *ADB*, Vol. 1, pp. 128–33; Immigrant and convict statistics in Vamplew, pp. 4–5
2. *Australian* 15 May 1838, 14 March 1840, 3 March 1842
3. *ADB*, Vol. 2, pp. 290–91
4. Sir Philip (1925–34), Sir Kenneth (1950–60) & Sir Laurence (1974–88) Street
5. Barker, p. 55
6. *Macquarie Dictionary*, Sydney, 1981
7. The Cork City Assizes record gives her age as 30 when convicted in April 1824. This conflicts with the age of 65 stated on the certificate recording her death on 8 March 1869.
8. O'Farrell, p. 23, records that there were 16,088 Catholics in 1833.
9. Genealogical detective work by the late Mr D.K. Muir, reported in a typescript placed in the Mitchell Library and elsewhere, is gratefully acknowledged as a key source on the early lives of John and Catherine Dalley.
10. His age was recorded as 15 years and 7 months when he died on 31 January 1845.
11. 5 July is the generally accepted birth date, but one record held by the NSW Births, Deaths and Marriages office gives it as 15 August (another says 5 July and a third gives no date). The inscription under the statue in Hyde Park nominates 5 August 1831.
12. Dowd, 'William Bede Dalley', pp. 204–05, discusses alternative suggestions on where he was born.
13. After two marriages – to Owen Davies in 1839 and George Bainbridge in 1842 – she died on 7 May 1867 and was buried in the Dalley family plot at the Devonshire St cemetery. When this cemetery was resumed for Central Railway Station she was reinterred with John and Catherine Dalley and four of their children at Botany (Bunnerong) cemetery.
14. The Dalley monument in the Botany Cemetery Pioneer Memorial Park carries the inscription: 'John Dalley died 14th November 1871 aged 70 years, also James Dalley infant son of Mr John Dalley of lower George Street Sydney, died 9th May 1836 aged 14 months & 12 days, also Catherine Bainbridge died 7th May 1867 aged 42 years,

also James Dalley died 7th May 1838 aged 6 hours, also Hannah Dalley died 17th February 1839 aged 2 years & 4 months, also John Dalley junior died 31st January 1845 aged 15 years & 7 months, also Catherine Dalley died 8th March 1869 aged 65 years.' (Transcription in Johnson, K.A. and Sainty, M.R., *Sydney burial ground 1819–1901: Elizabeth and Devonshire streets and history of Sydney's early cemeteries from 1788*, Sydney 2001.) The ages of the children seem to have been recorded precisely, but not those of the three adults.
15. *Australian* 3 July 1838
16. *Australian* 27 Sept 1836 & 30 Jan 1841
17. eg. *SMH* 28 Aug 1841, 4 Nov 1843, 11 July 1844
18. *SMH* 25 Nov 1844
19. *FJ* 24 April 1897
20. *SMH* 3 Nov 1888, As You Like It column
21. Bertie, pp. 9–10
22. McGuanne, p. 10
23. *FJ* 10 Nov 1888
24. *SMH* 6 June 1871
25. Boldrewood, pp. 5-6
26. Quoted in Prendergast, p. 67
27. Polding to Abbot Gregory, 17 May 1839, Polding letters Vol. 1, p. 136
28. The *SMH* death notice (1 Feb 1845) notes that he had died after a long illness.
29. *Chronicle* 11 Dec 1841, 12 Dec 1842, 23 Dec 1843, 21 Dec 1844 & 20 Dec 1845
30. *Australian Encyclopaedia*, Vol. 2, p. 187
31. *Empire* 31 Dec 1856
32. Polding to T.P. Heptonstall OSB, Polding letters Vol. 1, p. 12
33. Dalley to Therry 30 July 1846 & 14 Sept 1847, www.unisanet.unisa.edu.au/research/condon/CatholicLetters
34. *FJ* 21 Aug 1851
35. *Australian* 16 Aug 1836, 10 Oct 1842, 2 Nov 1842, 28 Dec 1842; *SMH* 29 Aug 1844, 2 Nov 1844
36. Sources on Deniehy's life include Bladen 1884, Dowd 1947, Pearl 1972, and Walsh 1988. For Stenhouse, see Jordens 1979
37. Blair, Deniehy, p. 385
38. Blair, Parkes, p. 616
39. Deniehy, 1859
40. *FJ* 25 March 1882
41. Palmer, p. 140
42. H.F.M., *New Triad* 1 June 1928, p. 17
43. *SMH* 1 July 1852
44. *SMH* 16 Aug 1853
45. *SMH* 6 Sept 1853
46. Examples are in David Headon and Elizabeth Perkins (eds), *Our first republicans: John Dunmore Lang, Charles Harpur, Daniel Henry Deniehy: selected writings, 1840–1860*, Sydney 1998
47. *SMH* & *Empire* 12 March 1856
48. *Empire* 31 Dec 1856

2. Into the fray

1. Ownership of freehold land worth at least £100, occupying property with an annual value of at least £10 or paying that much to occupy a lodging or room, or having an income of at least £100 per year.
2. *SMH* 12 March 1856
3. To Labouchere, 4 March 1856, Denison p. 341
4. Denison, p. 322

5. Discussed in Loveday and Martin, eg. pp. 9 & 23
6. Denison, p. 365
7. Denison, p. 370
8. *FJ* 10 May 1856
9. Shine, p. 15
10. *Empire* 5, 21 & 23 Aug 1856
11. *Argus* 29 Oct 1888
12. H.F.M., *New Triad* 1 June 1928, p. 17
13. *Empire* & *SMH* 30 Aug 1856
14. Bennett, *History of the NSW Bar*, p. 77
15. *SMH* 30 Aug 1856
16. *SMH* 12 Sept 1856
17. Bennett, *Sir James Martin*, pp. 97–98. His chapter 5 gives a detailed account of this episode.
18. 1856 Census, Vamplew, p. 29
19. *Empire* 30 Sept 1856
20. *Empire* 1 Oct 1856
21. *Empire* 8 Oct 1856
22. *Empire* 11 Oct 1856
23. *Empire* 27 Dec 1856
24. *Empire* 27 Dec 1856
25. *Empire* 29 Dec 1856
26. Walker, p. 65
27. Principally *Empire*, also *SMH* 30 Dec 1856
28. *Empire* 31 Dec 1856

3. Assembly and Circuit

1. *Empire* 31 Dec 1856
2. *Empire* 3 Jan 1857
3. NSW LA V&P, 2 Jan to 19 Feb 1857
4. *Empire* 17 Feb 1857
5. *Empire* 24 Feb 1857
6. He mentioned 'the state of his health' at the Parkes testimonial meeting (*Empire* 3 Feb), and Forster noted at the electoral reform meeting that Dalley had missed the 27 January vote on his reform bill being 'confined to his bed through illness' (*Empire* 24 Feb).
7. *Empire* 4, 5 & 11 Feb & 29 May 1857
8. *Empire* 5, 6 & 11 Feb 1857
9. Blacket, pp. 2–3
10. *Empire* 29 March 1858
11. *Empire* 3 April 1857
12. *Bathurst Free Press* 21 March 1857
13. *Empire* 26 Aug 1857
14. *SMH* 7 Nov 1857
15. *Empire* 14 Nov 1857
16. *Empire* 17 April 1857
17. *Empire* 1 May 1857
18. Lehane, pp. 21–22
19. *Empire* 4 Aug 1867
20. McMinn, pp. 188-89
21. *Empire* 2 Sept 1857
22. *Empire* 22 Sept 1857
23. *Empire* 18 Oct 1857
24. *Empire* 2 Nov 1857
25. *Empire* 2 Dec 1857 & 22 May 1858
26. *Empire* 5 & 27 Nov & 5 Dec 1857 & 16 June & 28 Aug 1858
27. *Empire* 14 Nov 1857
28. *Empire* 17 & 24 Nov & 8 Dec 1857
29. *FJ* 28 Nov 1857
30. *SMH* 25 Nov 1857
31. *SMH* 3 Dec 1857
32. *Empire* 21 Jan 1858
33. *Empire* 23 Dec 1857
34. *Empire* 21 Jan 1858
35. *Empire* 8 Jan 1858
36. *Empire* 1 Jan 1858
37. *Empire* 4 Jan 1858
38. Fowler, p. 72

39. Walker pp. 66–67
40. *Empire* 15 Jan 1858
41. *Empire* 19 Jan 1858
42. *FJ* 27 Jan 1883

4. In and out of office

1. *Empire* 16 Jan 1858
2. *Empire* 23 & 27 Jan & 6 Feb 1858
3. *Empire* 21 Jan 1858
4. Molony, pp. 251–60; Powell, pp. 103–04
5. *Empire* 10 Feb 1858
6. *FJ* 27 Feb 1858
7. *FJ* 1 May 1858
8. *FJ* 5 May 1858
9. *FJ* 12 May 1858
10. *Empire* 30 April 1858
11. *Empire* 7 May 1858
12. Polding documents and resource material, Vol. 2, p. 178
13. *FJ* 8 May 1858
14. *FJ* 9 June 1858; *Empire* 26 June & 1 July 1858
15. *Empire* 13 March 1858
16. *Empire* 23 & 24 March 1858; *Bathurst Free Press* 7 & 14 April 1858
17. *Empire* 9 April 1858
18. *Empire* 23 April 1858
19. *SMH* 2 June 1858
20. *Empire* 5 June 1858
21. *Empire* & *SMH* 12 June 1858
22. *Empire* & *SMH* 14 April 1858
23. By Richard Sadlier, *SMH* 26 Oct 1870, and Parkes, *SMH* 26 March 1872
24. *Empire* 23 April 1858
25. *Empire* 27 April 1858
26. *Empire* 8 May 1858
27. *Empire* 2 June 1858
28. *Empire* 31 July 1858
29. *Empire* 5 Aug 1858
30. *SMH* 17 Nov 1858
31. *Empire* 14 Nov 1857 & 4 Aug 1858
32. *SMH* 25 Nov 1858
33. *SMH* 26 Nov 1858
34. *FJ* 13 Oct 1858 contains the correspondence
35. *SMH* 30 Oct 1858
36. *FJ* 27 Nov 1858
37. *SMH* 18 Dec 1858
38. *SMH* 21 & 30 Dec 1858; *FJ* 25 Dec 1858
39. *FJ* 8 Jan 1859
40. *SMH* 13 Jan 1859
41. *SMH* 19 Jan 1859
42. *SMH* 27 Jan 1859
43. Dalley to Parkes 3 Feb 1859, ML A921, 153
44. *SMH* 4 Feb 1859
45. *SMH* 5 Feb 1959
46. *SMH* 11 Feb 1859

5. Twank and Tiptop

1. *SMH* 7 & 8 Dec 1858
2. *SMH* 7 Jan 1859
3. *SMH* 22 Jan 1859
4. *SMH* 9 Feb 1859
5. *FJ* 23 Feb 1859
6. *FJ* 2 March 1859
7. Polding letters Vol. 2, pp. 279
8. Powell, p. 130
9. *SMH* 4 March 1859
10. *SMH* 5 April 1859
11. *SMH* 23 & 26 March 1859
12. *SMH* 20 April 1859
13. *SMH* 7 April 1859
14. *SMH* 28 April 1859
15. Walker, p. 72
16. *SMH* 11 May 1859
17. *SMH* 18 May 1859

18. *SMH* 24 May 1859
19. *SMH* & *Empire* 21 June 1859
20. *FJ* 25 June 1859
21. *Empire* 31 May 1859
22. *Empire* 16 June 1859
23. *Empire* 27 & 29 June, 1 & 2 July 1859; *FJ* 12 Oct 1859 & 16 May 1860
24. *SMH* 18 Aug 1859
25. *Empire* 2 & 4 July 1859
26. *Empire* 3 Sept 1859
27. *SMH* 10 Sept 1859
28. *SMH* 15 Oct 1859
29. Powell, pp. 105-07
30. *Empire* 30 Nov 1859
31. *Empire* 17 Dec 1859
32. *Empire* 16 Dec 1859
33. *Southern Cross* 22 Oct 1859
34. *Southern Cross* 3 Dec 1859

6. The other side

1. As Catherine Dalley, she married a Captain Owen Davies in 1839. Their one child was born in 1840. Following the death of Davies, she married George Bainbridge in 1842.
2. Canon Robert Allwood officiated.
3. *FJ* 16 Feb 1859
4. Donovan, p. 446; *Bulletin* 26 Feb 1881; *FJ* 8 Oct 1898
5. N.S.W. Parliamentary Debates 1888, p. 193
6. *Southern Cross* 27 Feb 1860
7. *Empire* & *SMH* 24 Feb 1860
8. *SMH* & *Empire* 27 Feb 1860
9. *Empire* 23 Feb 1860
10. *Argus* 1 & 7 March 1860; www.ssgreatbritain.org/history/ss/
11. *SMH* 30 March 1872
12. *Empire* 14 Sept 1860

13. *Empire* 8 Nov 1860
14. *Empire* 14 Nov 1860
15. *Empire* 16 Nov 1860
16. *Empire* 3 Dec 1860
17. *Empire* 6, 8, 12 & 13 Dec 1860
18. *Empire* 22 Dec 1860; *FJ* 26 Dec 1860
19. *Empire* 22 Jan 1861
20. *Empire* 2 & 13 March 1861
21. *Empire* 22 Nov 1861
22. *Empire* 18 Oct & 6 Dec 1861, & 17 Jan 1862
23. *SMH* & *Empire* 21 May 1861
24. *FJ* 29 June 1901
25. Martin, *Letters from Menie*, pp. 20–23
26. 'Menie' to Parkes 14 Oct 1861, ML A933, 149
27. Dalley to Alexander Oliver 2 Oct 1885, Oliver Papers Box 14, University of Sydney Archives
28. *FJ* 8 April 1899
29. *FJ* 31 March 1866
30. Dalley to Clarinda Parkes 19 Aug 1861, ML A1045, 199
31. Martin, *Letters from Menie*, pp. 25–26
32. 'Menie' to Parkes 14 Oct 1861, ML A933, 149
33. Martin, *Letters from Menie*, p. 40
34. *Empire* 18 Oct 1861
35. *Empire* 15 May 1862
36. *Empire* 12 Oct 1861
37. *Empire* 6 Dec 1861
38. Dalley to Parkes 9 Oct 1861, ML A921, 165
39. *Empire* 24 & 30 Dec 1861
40. Parkes to Dalley 18, 23 & 26 Nov 1861, ML A931; Dalley to Parkes 19 & 25 Nov & 13 Dec 1861, ML A921
41. Dalley to Parkes undated, ML

A921, 231; Dalley to Parkes 1 Jan 1862, ML A921, 185
42. Dalley to Parkes 27 Jan 1862, ML A921, 188
43. *Limerick and Clare Advocate*, quoted in *Empire* 24 March 1862

7. Among bushrangers

1. Dalley to Parkes 27 Jan 1862, ML A921, 188
2. *FJ* 25 May 1895 & 11 April 1907
3. Dalley to Parkes 3 & 15 April & 22 May 1862, ML A921 191, 197 & 201
4. Parkes to Mrs Parkes 24 May 1862, ML A1044
5. Dalley to Parkes undated, ML A881, 85
6. Martin, *Henry Parkes*, p. 190
7. Parkes to Mrs Parkes 16 June 1862, ML A1044
8. *Empire* 5 June 1862
9. *SMH* 9 June 1862
10. *Empire* 8 & 11 Oct 1862
11. *Empire* 7 Nov 1862 & 19 Oct 1864
12. *Empire* 5 Sept 1862
13. *Empire* 5 Feb 1863
14. *Empire* 3, 6, 7 & 10 Feb 1863
15. Bennett, *Sir James Martin*, pp. 184-85
16. *Empire* 28 Feb & 3 March 1863
17. *Empire* 16, 19 & 21 March 1863
18. *SMH* 24 March 1863; *Empire* 27 Feb & 24, 25, 26 & 27 March 1863
19. *Empire* 24 April 1863
20. *Empire* 21 Feb & 30 May 1863
21. Bennett, *Sir James Martin*, p. 118
22. *Empire* 3 June 1863
23. *Empire* 6 Feb & 18 Nov 1863
24. *Empire* 24 Nov 1863
25. *Empire* 2 Dec 1863; Bennett, *Sir James Martin*, pp. 233–36
26. *Empire* 11 Feb 1864
27. *Empire* 8 Oct 1863
28. *Empire* 28 Aug 1863
29. *Empire* 5 & 8 Oct 1863
30. *Empire* 24 June 1863
31. *Empire* 23 July 1863
32. *Empire* 21 Sept & 15 Oct 1863
33. *Empire* 3 July 1863
34. *Empire* 8 July 1863
35. *Empire* 22 Oct 1863
36. *Empire* 13 Nov 1863; Bennett, *Sir James Martin*, pp. 133–34
37. *Empire* 25 Jan & 27 Sept 1864
38. *Empire* 12 Jan 1864
39. *FJ* 19 March 1864
40. *Empire* 30 Sept 1863
41. *Empire* 21 Dec 1863
42. *Empire* 4 April 1864
43. *SMH* 15 & 20 April 1864
44. *Empire* 21 May 1864
45. *Empire* 23 May 1864
46. *Empire* 9 July 1864

8. The journalist

1. Quoted in Jordens, p. 70
2. Correspondence of Nicol Drysdale Stenhouse, NL mfm G 15845
3. Barton, *Literature*, p. 66
4. Quoted in Barton, *Poets and Prose Writers*, pp. 166 & 178
5. *FJ* 3 Nov 1888
6. Barton, *Literature*, p. 65
7. *FJ* 5 March 1898
8. *Sydney Times* 23 April 1864
9. *FJ* 28 June 1890
10. *FJ* 15 Oct 1864 & 14 Jan 1865
11. *FJ* 15 Oct 1864
12. *FJ* 3 Sept 1864

13. *FJ* 7 Sept 1864
14. *FJ* 30 Dec 1865
15. *FJ* 24 Sept 1864
16. *FJ* 17 Aug & 15 Nov 1864, & 14 Jan 1865
17. *FJ* 7 Sept 1864
18. *FJ* 2 June 1858
19. *FJ* 18 March 1865
20. *FJ* 25 March 1865
21. *FJ* 15 April 1865
22. *Empire* 15 April 1865
23. *SMH* 20 April 1865
24. *FJ* 3 & 6 May 1865
25. *SMH* 11 & 13 May 1865
26. *SMH* 28 Sept 1865
27. *FJ* 28 Oct 1865
28. *FJ* 1 July 1865
29. *FJ* 8 July & 7 Oct 1865
30. Polding to Wardell 10 Oct 1865 (http://www.sydney.catholic.org.au/Cathedral/desc.shtml)
31. Piddington, p. 3
32. *Empire* 10 Nov 1860
33. *FJ* 20 March 1861
34. *Empire* 1 Aug 1861
35. *FJ* 3 Aug 1861
36. Blair, *Deniehy*, p. 386
37. Stenhouse to Rowe, 22 July 1864, Correspondence of Nicol Drysdale Stenhouse, NL mfm G 15845
38. *FJ* 3 Sept 1864
39. *FJ* 12 April 1865
40. Quoted in Walsh, G., p. 85
41. Letter by J.G. O'Connor, *EN* 30 March 1882
42. *EN* 1 April 1882
43. Dalley to Stenhouse 24 Oct 1865, Correspondence of Nicol Drysdale Stenhouse, NL mfm G 15845
44. Barton, *Literature*, p. 60
45. *FJ* 28 Oct 1865

9. Libel and murder

1. *Empire* 31 Oct 1865
2. *Empire* 4 Nov 1865
3. *Sydney Punch* 14, 21 & 28 Oct & 4 Nov 1865
4. *FJ* 21 Oct 1865
5. *FJ* 6 Jan 1866
6. *FJ* 20 Jan 1866
7. *FJ* 3 March 1866
8. *FJ* 24 Feb 1866
9. *SMH* 14 Feb 1866
10. *SMH* 16 Feb 1866
11. *SMH* 24 Feb 1866; Bennett, *Sir James Martin*, pp. 187–91
12. *FJ* 24 & 31 March 1861
13. *Wagga Wagga Express* 28 April 1866; *SMH* 1 May 1866
14. Buchanan, p. 52
15. *Empire* 17 Aug 1866
16. *DT* 29 Oct 1888; *FJ* 24 April 1897
17. *SMH* 21 & 23 Feb 1867
18. *SM* 23 March 1867
19. *SMH* 19 March 1867
20. *SM* 18 May 1867
21. *SM* 28 Sept & 5 Oct 1867; Bennett, *Sir James Martin*, pp. 236–37
22. Kirkpatrick, p. 177
23. O'Sullivan gives a detailed account of the Clarke gang's exploits and trials.
24. *SM* 1 June 1867
25. *SM* 15 June 1867
26. *SM* 1 June 1867
27. *SM* 21 Sept 1867
28. *SM* 24 Aug 1867

10. Parkes and the Irish assassin

1. *SM* 1 Feb 1868
2. *SM* 9 Nov 1867

3. *SMH* & *Empire* 23 Jan 1868
4. *SMH* 24 Jan 1868
5. *SM* 11 Jan & 8 Feb 1868
6. Dalley to Parkes ML A921, 206; A881, 83; A921, 207, 240 & 242
7. Dalley to Parkes 7 June 1867, ML A881, 95
8. Dalley to Parkes 2 Oct 1867, ML A921, 209
9. *SMH* 14 March 1868
10. *SMH* 17 March 1868
11. *SMH* 14 March 1868
12. Contemporary newspapers reported the O'Farrell affair in great detail. Secondary sources include: Amos, K., *The Fenians in Australia 1865–1880*; Travers, R., *The Phantom Fenians of New South Wales*; Lehane, R., *Forever Carnival*.
13. H.F.M., *The New Triad*, 1 June 1928, p. 17
14. Woods, pp. 240–43
15. *FJ* 19 Dec 1868
16. *SM* 18 April 1868
17. Polding to Gregory, 19 May 1868, Polding letters, Vol. 3, p. 298
18. *SM* 25 April 1868
19. *Sydney Punch* 25 April 1868
20. *Yass Courier* 20 & 23 May 1868
21. *SM* 27 June & 11 July 1868
22. *SM* 25 July 1868
23. *Sydney Punch* 22 & 29 Aug 1868
24. *SM* 29 Aug 1868
25. *SM* 5 Sept 1868

11. Settling down

1. Martin, *Henry Parkes*, pp. 244–46
2. Quoted in *FJ* 3 Oct 1868
3. *SM* 24 Oct 1868.
4. *Sydney Punch* 12 Dec 1868
5. *Empire* 21 Dec 1868
6. *Sydney Punch* 24 Dec 1868
7. Martin, *Henry Parkes*, p. 248
8. Quoted in Travers, p. 158
9. *Sydney Punch* 6 Feb 1869
10. *Sydney Punch* 20 Feb 1869
11. *SM* 22 March 1869
12. Polding to Gregory, 26 Feb 1869, Polding letters, Vol. 3, p. 322
13. *SM* 9 Jan 1869
14. *SM* 16 Jan 1869
15. Badham to Stenhouse, date unclear (probably May 1869), Stenhouse Correspondence, NL mfm G 15845
16. *Sydney Punch* 25 March & 15 May 1869
17. *SM* 5 June 1869
18. *SM* 26 June, 3 July & 2 Oct 1869; Woods, pp. 214–19; Mortensen, pp. 1–22
19. *ADB* entries – Cowper, Robertson, Towns
20. Woods, p. 217
21. *SMH* 11 Dec 1871; *SM* 30 March & 13 April 1872
22. Palmer, pp. 139–40; his description of the 'dapper little barrister' is quoted in chapter 1.
23. Report of the Royal Commission, 1869
24. *SMH* 17 Feb 1873
25. *SM* 28 Aug, 4, 11, 18 & 25 Sept, 27 Nov & 11 Dec 1869
26. Hyndman, p. 119
27. *SM* 28 Aug 1869
28. *SMH* 2 Dec 1869
29. *FJ* 11 Dec 1869
30. *EN* 6 Dec 1869
31. *FJ* 11 Dec 1869
32. *Yass Courier* 21 Dec 1869 & 4 Jan 1870

12. The dolphin and the anchor

1. SM 27 Jan 1870
2. SM 12 & 19 March 1870 & 28 April 1877
3. SM 13 Aug 1870
4. FJ 22 Oct 1870
5. Documents re Polding episcopacy, Vol. 2, p. 178; FJ 5 Nov 1870
6. Powell, p. 157
7. SM 18 Feb 1871
8. Dalley to Lord Loftus, nd, ML A3057
9. SM 19 Feb 1870
10. *Empire* 26 Nov 1870
11. *Empire* 22 Dec 1870
12. FJ 30 June 1900
13. FJ 5 Aug 1882
14. FJ 24 Aug 1878
15. SM 1 July 1871
16. SMH 6 June 1871
17. Reprinted in SM 14 Oct 1871
18. SM 25 Nov 1871
19. SMH 31 March 1873
20. *Brisbane Courier* 11 & 14 Nov 1871
21. FJ 18 Nov 1871
22. SM 3 Feb 1872
23. SMH 11 March 1872
24. SMH 12 March 1872
25. SMH 13 March 1872
26. SMH 15 March 1872
27. SMH 16 March 1872
28. Martin, *Henry Parkes*, p. 258
29. SMH 19 March 1872
30. SMH 21 March 1872
31. SMH 22 March 1872
32. SMH 26 March 1872
33. SMH 30 March 1872
34. SMH 22 May 1872
35. Dalley 1872

13. A married man

1. *SMH* 3 June 1872
2. *FJ* 22 Jan 1881
3. Froude, p. 176
4. Dalley to Lady Martin, nd, MLMSS 2425/5, 79
5. Myers, p. 3
6. SMH 22 June 1872; FJ 6 July 1872
7. FJ 20 Dec 1873
8. Dowd, *William Bede Dalley*, p. 241
9. FJ 6 Sept 1873
10. Anne Pohlmann to T.W. Campbell, 22 July 1999. Annie O'Brien was her grandmother's sister.
11. FJ 24 April 1897 & *Austral Light* August 1897, p. 441
12. Muir, p. 5; Dalley's last letter found from Greycliffe is dated 21 July 1879 and first from Clairvaux 5 Feb 1880. A letter of 21 October 1879 was written at 'Manly Beach'.
13. FJ 29 June 1901
14. SMH 24 June 1872
15. SM 24 Aug 1872
16. SM 17 Aug 1872 (first published in SMH)
17. FJ 31 Aug 1872
18. SM 26 Oct & 2 Nov 1872
19. SM 16 Nov 1872
20. SM 23 Nov & 7 Dec 1872
21. SMH 10 Feb 1873
22. SMH 24 March 1873
23. SMH 5 March 1873
24. *Yass Courier* 4 April 1873
25. SMH 7 May 1873
26. SM 24 May, SMH 3 June & SM 5 July 1873
27. Reprinted in FJ 19 June 1897
28. SM 24 May 1873
29. Rutledge, pp. 207–22; Lehane, pp. 216–18

30. *SMH* 15 Dec 1874
31. *SMH* 16 Dec 1873
32. *SMH* 19 May 1874; *SM* 14 Nov 1874
33. Parkes's views on this matter are set out in his pamphlet, 'The Case of the Prisoner Gardiner'. Nairn, in 'The Governor, the Bushranger and the Premier', discusses the divergent views of the time on the respective responsibilities of the Governor and Ministers.
34. The petitions and related documents are in NSW LA V&P 1873–74, Vol 2, 205-215
35. *SM* 28 March 1874
36. Parkes, pp. 18–28
37. *SM* 25 July 1874
38. *SM* 28 Nov 1874

14. Robertson's Attorney-General

1. *FJ* 19 Dec 1874 & 2 Jan 1875
2. *SMH* 15 Dec 1874
3. Robinson to Carnarvon, 11 Feb 1875, CO 201/579
4. *FJ* 1 Jan 1976
5. Dalley, Opinions
6. *ADB* Vol. 5, pp. 378-82
7. *SMH* 21 April 1875
8. *SM* 15 Jan & 25 March 1876
9. *ADB* Vol 5, pp. 42-44
10. *SMH* 21 April 1875
11. *SMH* 30 April 1875
12. *SM* 19 June 1875
13. N.S.W. Parliamentary Debates 1883, p. 1118
14. *SM* 22 May 1875
15. *SM* 15 May 1875; *SMH* 6 Aug 1875
16. Robinson to Carnarvon, 4 June 1875, CO 201/579
17. *ADB* Vol 5, pp. 185-87
18. Robinson to Carnarvon, 22 Oct 1875, CO 201/579
19. *SM* 28 Aug 1875
20. *ADB* Vol 4, p. 235
21. *SM* 21 Aug 1875
22. *SMH* 1 Sept 1875
23. *SM* 20 Nov 1875
24. *SM* 11 March 1876
25. *SM* 6 & 20 May 1876
26. Dalley to Manning 10 May 1876, ML CY1823
27. *SMH* 16 Dec 1875
28. *SM* 12 Feb 1876
29. *FJ* 25 March 1876
30. *SMH* 4 March 1876
31. *SMH* 7 March 1876
32. *SM* 24 April 1876
33. *SMH* 16 June 1876
34. *SMH* 26 July 1876
35. *SMH* 11 Aug 1876
36. *SM* 30 Sept 1876

15. Three more governments

1. *SM* 30 Sept 1876
2. *SMH* 18 Nov 1876
3. *SMH* 6 Nov 1876
4. Woods, pp. 245–364, gives a full account of the tortuous process that produced the Criminal Law Amendment Act of 1883.
5. *SMH* 18 Jan 1877
6. Woods, p. 248
7. *SMH* 22 Dec 1876
8. *SMH* 11 Jan 1877
9. *SMH* 31 May 1877
10. *SMH* 28 Feb 1877
11. *SMH* 1 March 1877
12. *SMH* 27 Jan 1877
13. *SMH* 9 Feb 1877
14. *SMH* 15 Feb 1877

15. SMH 15 March 1877
16. Reprinted in FJ 10 March 1877
17. Wynne, pp. 216-17
18. FJ 17 March 1877
19. FJ 24 March 1877
20. Reprinted in FJ 31 March 1877
21. SMH 26 March 1877
22. SMH 27 March 1877
23. SMH 17 May 1877; SM 14 July 1877
24. SM 9 & 16 June 1877
25. SMH 8 June 1877
26. SM 2 June 1877
27. SM 11 Aug 1877
28. SMH 12 Sept 1877
29. SMH 15 Sept 1877
30. SMH 23 March 1878; SM 10 Jan 1880
31. SM 10 Nov 1877
32. SMH 24 Jan 1878
33. SMH 17 Jan 1878
34. Senate Minutes, University of Sydney Archives
35. Bennett, *Sir James Martin*, pp. 286–96, tells the full story.
36. Robinson to Carnarvon 27 July 1875, CO 201/579
37. Quoted in Grainger, p. 129
38. SM 15 Dec 1877
39. FJ 25 May 1878
40. FJ 29 June 1878

16. Political battles and a busy pen

1. SM 22 June 1878
2. Dalley to J.R. Clarke 4 Feb 1879, ML CY2421
3. SMH 7 March 1878
4. SMH 3 May 1878
5. SMH 17 May 1878 & 13 March 1879
6. SM 17 Aug 1878
7. Reprinted in FJ 30 Nov 1878
8. Reprinted in FJ 21 Dec 1878
9. SMH 30 Jan 1879
10. SMH 13 March 1879
11. SMH 25 April 1879
12. SM 3 May 1879
13. SMH 7 & 15 May 1879
14. SMH 27 March & 15 May 1879
15. SM 27 July 1878
16. SM 17 Aug 1878
17. SM 7 Dec 1878
18. SMH 3 April 1879
19. SM 5 April 1879; SMH 23 April 1879
20. SMH 20 June 1879
21. SMH 3 July 1879
22. SM 12 July 1879
23. Dalley 1879 (a)
24. SMH 21 May 1879
25. FJ 29 Sept 1877
26. SM 8 Feb 1879
27. SMH 4 Feb 1879
28. FJ 22 Feb 1879; the poem is in Kendall's 1880 anthology *Songs from the Mountains*.
29. Dalley to Butler 5 March 1879, Kendall correspondence, ML CY1211
30. Jennings to Dalley 11 June 1879, MLDOC 3384
31. SMH 18 Sept 1879
32. SM 8 March 1879
33. SMH 21 April 1879
34. Dalley to Archer 2 June 1879, Archer collection 3/1, University of Melbourne Archives
35. FJ 21 June & 19 July 1879
36. Dalley to Archer 2 June 1879, Archer collection 3/1
37. FJ 23 Aug 1879
38. FJ 13 Sept 1879
39. FJ 10 July 1880

40. *FJ* 1 Nov 1879
41. *FJ* 14 June 1879
42. *SMH* 18 July 1879

17. Dark times

1. Lady Stephen's Diary 6, 8, 11 & 12 Sept 1879, ML MSS 777/3
2. *FJ* 23 Aug 1879
3. *FJ* 2 Aug 1879
4. *FJ* 28 June 1879
5. Fogarty, pp. 250–53, discusses the motives and response.
6. Dalley to Archer 10 Sept 1879, Archer collection 2/43/1, University of Melbourne Archives
7. Dalley to Archer 21 & 30 Sept 1879, Archer collection 2/43/2 & 2/43/3
8. Dalley, 1879 (b)
9. *FJ* 18 Oct 1879
10. *FJ* 15 & 22 Nov 1879
11. *SMH* 14 Nov 1879
12. *SMH* 28 Jan 1880
13. *SM* 13 March 1880
14. N.S.W. Parliamentary Debates 1880, pp. 1432-43
15. *SMH* 4 Dec 1879
16. *SMH* 19 Dec 1879; *SM* 10 Jan & 22 May 1880
17. *SM* 13 March 1880; N.S.W. Parliamentary Debates 1880, pp. 1602–07, 1644–45 & 1734–38
18. Dalley to Stephen 13 April 1880, ML CY4592, 95
19. Dalley to Parkes 10 April 1880, ML A881, 96
20. N.S.W. Parliamentary Debates 1880, p. 1860
21. *SMH* 12 April 1880
22. Reprinted in *FJ* 1 May 1880
23. *FJ* 17 April 1880
24. Grainger, pp. 139–42; Bennett, *Sir James Martin*, pp. 308–11
25. *SMH* 21 June 1880
26. *SMH* 11 Oct 1880
27. *SMH* 12 Oct 1880
28. *SM* 11 Dec 1880
29. Dalley to Kendall 3 Sept & 3 Dec 1880, Kendall correspondence, ML CY1211
30. *SMH* 12 Jan 1881
31. *SMH* 27 Dec 1880
32. *SMH* 18 Jan 1881; *FJ* 22 Jan 1881

18. In praise of troubled genius

1. *Bulletin* 26 Feb 1881
2. *FJ* 29 Jan 1881
3. *SMH* 15 Feb 1881
4. From information compiled by Muir and addresses given in Dalley correspondence
5. *SM* 26 July 1884
6. *SMH* 11 March 1933
7. *SM* 5 March 1881; Birch and Macmillan, pp. 184 & 211–12
8. *SMH* 15 & 22 Feb 1870
9. *SM* 30 April 1881, 14 Jan 1882 & 29 April 1882
10. Paul Sendziuk, review of Alison Bashford, *Imperial Hygiene: A Critical History of Colonialism, Nationalism and Public Health*, Basingstoke, 2004 http://www.arts.monash.edu.au/eras/edition_6/sendziuk.htm
11. *SM* 16 July 1881
12. *SM* 8 May 1880
13. *SM* 23 & 30 April 1881
14. *SM* 28 May 1881
15. *SM* 25 June 1881
16. *SM* 16 July 1881
17. *SMH* 11 Aug 1881

18. N.S.W. Parliamentary Debates 1881, p. 631
19. SM & *FJ* 27 Aug 1881
20. SM 20 Aug 1881
21. SM 24 Sept 1881
22. SM 15 Oct 1881
23. SM 1 Oct 1881
24. *Encyclopaedia Britannica* 2005, entry for Horace Walpole
25. *The Sydney University Review*, No. 1, 1881, pp. 7–17
26. SMH 18 Oct 1881; *FJ* & SM 22 Oct 1881
27. *FJ* 24 Dec 1881
28. Lehane pp. 278–81
29. Letter by 'A Friend of Deniehy', SMH 21 Sept 1888
30. *FJ* 24 Dec 1881
31. Lehane, p. 293
32. *FJ* 30 June 1900
33. *FJ* 1 Oct 1881
34. *FJ* 4 Feb 1882
35. Lehane pp. 260–68
36. Myers, p. 4
37. SMH 25 Feb 1882; SM 4 March 1882; *ADB* Vol. 3, pp. 74-75
38. *FJ* 4 March 1882
39. *FJ* 25 March 1882
40. SMH 8 May 1882
41. Dalley to Ranken 25 April 1882, in 'Letters about Windabyne', Australian Literature Database, University of Sydney
42. Dalley to Clarke 12 May 1882, ML CY2421
43. Two telegrams to Mrs Kendall 29 July 1882, in Charlotte Kendall correspondence, ML CY1523
44. Dalley to Oliver 13 Aug 1882, Oliver Papers Box 14, University of Sydney Archives
45. SM 12 Aug 1882
46. *The Sydney University Review*, No. 4, 1882, pp. 430–33

19. He's back

1. *SMH* 22 Aug 1882
2. SM 5 May 1883; Dalley to Mrs Kendall, nd, ML CY1523
3. Dalley to Mrs Kendall 27 July 1885, ML CY1523
4. SM 31 March 1888; Dalley to Mrs Kendall 19 Sept 1886, ML CY1523
5. Dalley to Mrs Kendall 29 May 1888, ML CY1523; FJ 15 Sept 1888
6. Dalley to Clarke 30 Sept 1882, ML CY2421
7. Dalley to Oliver 13 Aug 1882, Oliver Papers Box 14, University of Sydney Archives
8. *The Sydney University Review*, No. 4, 1882, pp. 329–47
9. *FJ* 14 Oct 1882
10. *FJ* 4 Nov 1882
11. Dalley to Stuart 16 Nov 1882, Robert Towns & Co Records, ML CY3018
12. *FJ* 2 Dec 1882
13. *FJ* 2 Dec 1882
14. SM 2 Dec 1882
15. SM & *FJ* 6 Jan 1883
16. SM 20 Jan 1883
17. SM 27 Jan 1883
18. *DT* 20 March 1883; SM 24 & 31 March 1883
19. N.S.W. Parliamentary Debates 1883 pp. 131–32
20. N.S.W. Parliamentary Debates 1883 pp. 177–84
21. Woods, p. 345
22. Woods, pp. 348–56; N.S.W.

Parliamentary Debates 1883 pp. 1228–30, 1274–78, 1300–05
23. N.S.W. Parliamentary Debates 1883 pp. 1533–38
24. N.S.W. Parliamentary Debates 1883 pp. 197–203, 254–86, 383–447, 552–72, 604–11, 807–13
25. *SMH* 3 Sept 1883
26. *SMH* 8 April 1884
27. N.S.W. Parliamentary Debates 1883 pp. 984–95
28. *Empire* 20 Jan 1864; *FJ* 7 Dec 1864 & 31 May 1865
29. *SM* 11 April & 23 May 1885
30. N.S.W. Parliamentary Debates 1883 pp. 1117–19, 1591–94
31. N.S.W. Parliamentary Debates 1883 pp. 1827–29
32. N.S.W. Parliamentary Debates 1883 pp. 1848–49
33. N.S.W. Parliamentary Debates 1883 pp. 1538–45
34. N.S.W. Parliamentary Debates 1886 pp. 1167–92
35. *SM* 26 May 1883
36. N.S.W. Parliamentary Debates 1883 pp. 2021–42
37. *SM* 19 July 1884
38. *FJ* 17 Feb 1883
39. Reprinted in *FJ* 14 April 1883
40. *SM* 16 June 1883
41. *FJ* 3 March 1883; *SM* 5 May 1883
42. *SMH* 23 April 1883
43. *SMH* 20 June 1883; *SM* 23 June 1883
44. *SMH* 20 July 1883
45. *SM* 18 Aug 1883
46. *SM* 11 Aug & 8 Sept 1883
47. N.S.W. Parliamentary Debates 1883 pp. 68–69
48. *SM* 10 Nov 1883
49. N.S.W. Parliamentary Debates 1883 pp. 295–302

20. The 'Dining-out Administration'

1. *SMH* 23 July 1883
2. *SM* 28 July 1883
3. *SMH* 20 July 1883
4. *SMH* 23 July 1883
5. *SM* 18 Aug 1883
6. *FJ* 27 Sept 1884
7. Piddington, p. 6
8. *SM* 25 Aug 1883
9. *SMH* 1 March 1884
10. Piddington, p. 4
11. *SMH* 29 Aug 1883
12. *SM* 1 Sept 1883
13. *SMH* 3 Sept 1883
14. *FJ* 29 Sept 1883
15. *SMH* 2 Oct 1883
16. *SMH* 8 Oct 1883; *FJ* 13 Oct 1883
17. *SM* 13 Oct 1883
18. N.S.W. Parliamentary Debates 1883 pp. 1145 & 1148
19. N.S.W. Parliamentary Debates 1883 pp. 13–17
20. *FJ* 13 Oct 1883
21. N.S.W. Parliamentary Debates 1883 pp. 401–02, 484–88, 1172–83
22. *SMH* 29 Oct 1883
23. Rosebery, p. 51
24. *SMH* 26 Nov 1883
25. *SMH* 11 Dec 1883
26. Thompson and Stargardt give full accounts of these events.
27. *SM* 1 & 8 Dec 1883
28. Thompson, p. 87
29. Stargardt, pp. 80–81; Thompson, pp. 88–93

30. N.S.W. Parliamentary Debates 1883 pp. 1133–39
31. N.S.W. Parliamentary Debates 1884 pp. 4246–54
32. N.S.W. Parliamentary Debates 1884 pp. 6149–54

21. The land war won

1. *FJ* 12 Jan 1884
2. N.S.W. Parliamentary Debates 1884 pp. 1260–68
3. N.S.W. Parliamentary Debates 1884 pp. 1614–19
4. N.S.W. Parliamentary Debates 1884 p. 1635
5. *SM* 16 Feb 1884
6. *SMH* 28 Feb 1884
7. *SMH* 23 July 1883
8. N.S.W. Parliamentary Debates 1884 pp. 1547–53
9. *SM* 1 March 1884
10. N.S.W. Parliamentary Debates 1884 pp. 1882–97
11. N.S.W. Parliamentary Debates 1884 pp. 2144–48
12. *SM* 15 March 1884
13. *SM* 22 March 1884
14. *Australasian* 22 March & 12 April 1884
15. *SMH* 5 April 1884
16. *SMH* 8 April 1884
17. N.S.W. Parliamentary Debates 1884 pp. 2669–74
18. N.S.W. Parliamentary Debates 1884 pp. 3420–26
19. Moran, p. 475
20. *FJ* 10 May 1884
21. N.S.W. Parliamentary Debates 1884 pp. 2669–74
22. N.S.W. Parliamentary Debates 1884 pp. 3337–42; DT 16 May 1884; FJ 24 May 1884
23. *FJ* 24 May 1884
24. N.S.W. Parliamentary Debates 1884 pp. 3218-20
25. N.S.W. Parliamentary Debates 1884 pp. 3417–20, 3647–53 & 3768–76
26. N.S.W. Parliamentary Debates 1884 p. 3575
27. N.S.W. Parliamentary Debates 1884 p. 3656
28. N.S.W. Parliamentary Debates 1884 pp. 4292–93 & 4300
29. N.S.W. Parliamentary Debates 1884 pp. 4378–80 & 4407–12
30. *SM* 9 Aug 1884
31. N.S.W. Parliamentary Debates 1884 pp. 4826–27
32. *SM* 23 Aug 1884
33. N.S.W. Parliamentary Debates 1884 pp. 4844–53
34. N.S.W. Parliamentary Debates 1884 p. 4918
35. N.S.W. Parliamentary Debates 1884 p. 5091
36. N.S.W. Parliamentary Debates 1884 p. 5057
37. N.S.W. Parliamentary Debates 1884 pp. 5338–39
38. N.S.W. Parliamentary Debates 1884 pp. 5377–83
39. *SM* 11 Oct 1884
40. N.S.W. Parliamentary Debates 1884 pp. 5706–12
41. *SM* 11 Oct 1884
42. *SM* 22 Nov & 13 Dec 1884 & 24 Jan 1885
43. N.S.W. Parliamentary Debates 1884 p. 5967

22. In charge

1. Dalley to Stuart 20 Nov 1884, Robert Towns & Co Records, ML CY3018
2. SM 29 Nov 1884
3. SMH 11 & 12 Dec 1884
4. *FJ* 20 Dec 1884
5. *FJ* 8 Nov 1884
6. Dalley to Parkes 16 Dec 1884, ML FM3/796
7. SM 28 March 1885
8. SM 22 Nov 1884
9. Dalley to Erskine 9 & 27 Dec 1884, NLA MS 2541
10. CO 201/602
11. *SMH* 20 Dec 1887
12. CO 201/602; Bennett, *Sir James Martin*, pp. 266–68; Bolton, pp. 40–41 & 49
13. *DT* 23 Dec 1884
14. *SMH* 24 Dec 1884
15. SM 17 Jan 1885
16. SM 24 Jan 1885
17. Reprinted in *FJ* 7 Feb 1885
18. SM 7 Feb 1885
19. postscript to Loftus to Derby 3 Feb 1885, CO 201/602; Thompson, p. 96
20. Loftus to Derby 31 Dec 1884, CO 201/602
21. Dalley to Loftus 2 March 1885 ML CY2394; FJ 15 April 1899
22. Loftus to Derby 31 Dec 1884 & 2 Jan 1885, CO 201/602
23. Samuel to Derby 7 Jan 1885, CO 201/602
24. Dalley to Samuel 19 Jan 1885, CO 201/602
25. Dalley to Samuel 31 Jan 1885, CO 201/602
26. Loftus to Derby 3 Feb 1885, CO 201/602
27. Fitzgerald, p. 189
28. Tryon to Northbrook 14 May 1885, CO 201/602
29. *SM* 7 Feb 1885
30. *ADB* Vol. 6, pp. 98-99
31. Inglis and Saunders, in books published in 1985 to mark the centenary of the New South Wales contingent, tell the story of the Sudan campaign.
32. *SMH* 12 Feb 1885
33. Garran, p. 27
34. Inglis, p. 23
35. Barrett tells the stories of 'Ned' Ryan, who rose from Irish convict to 'patriarch of the Lachlan', his son John Nagle Ryan and other Galong characters.
36. *FJ* 15 Jan 1887
37. *SMH* 16 Feb 1885
38. Charles Huenerbein subsequently composed a patriotic song, *To the front: raise high Australia's banner*, which he dedicated to Dalley (chapter 23).
39. Barrett, pp. 147–50; *SMH* 16 Feb 1885; *FJ* 11 Dec 1897

23. To Sudan

1. Froude, pp. 163, 169–73
2. *FJ* & *Bulletin* 21 Feb 1885
3. SM 21 Feb 1885
4. Froude, p. 172
5. Froude, pp. 175–79
6. Loftus gave the date in his 19 February London despatch.
7. SM 28 Feb 1885
8. *SMH* 3 March 1885
9. *SMH* 14 Feb 1885; Colonial Office minute 4 March 1885, CO 201/602

10. *SMH* 27 Feb 1885
11. *SMH* 24 March 1885
12. *SMH* 27 Feb 1885
13. Dalley to Loftus 23 Feb 1885, ML CY2394
14. Dalley to Loftus 2 March 1885, ML CY2394
15. SM 7 March 1885; State Library of NSW Music file/HUE
16. Inglis, p. 44
17. *FJ* 7 March 1885
18. Inglis, p. 47
19. *DT* 20 April 1885
20. Inglis, p. 56
21. Colonial Office minute 15 April 1885, CO 201/602
22. SM 7 March 1885
23. *DT* 28 Jan 1888; Bennett, *Sir James Martin*, p. 203
24. Shine, pp. 49–51
25. *SMH* 16 March 1885
26. *FJ* 21 March 1885
27. Saunders, 'Parliament and the New South Wales Contingent', p. 229
28. N.S.W. Parliamentary Debates 1885 pp. 1–16, 61–76
29. Saunders, 'Parliament and the New South Wales Contingent', pp. 249–50
30. N.S.W. Parliamentary Debates 1885 pp. 101–18

24. Back to earth

1. N.S.W. Parliamentary Debates 1885 p. 107
2. *Goulburn Herald* 21 March 1885
3. *SMH* 23 March 1885
4. Donovan, p. 443
5. *FJ* 28 March 1885
6. *Goulburn Herald* 28 March 1885
7. *SMH* 27 March 1885
8. *Goulburn Herald* 28 March 1885
9. Samuel to Dalley 30 March 1885 & Dalley to Richardson 28 March 1885, State Records NSW, Special Bundle The Soudan Contingent 1885, CGS 906, 4/853
10. Inglis, pp. 96–102
11. General Graham's report, 8 April 1885, State Records, Special Bundle The Soudan Contingent
12. Shine, pp. 52–54
13. Loftus to Derby 1 April 1885, CO 201/602
14. State Records, Special Bundle The Soudan Contingent
15. SM 2 May 1885
16. Loftus to Derby, 16 April 1885, CO 201/602
17. State Records, Special Bundle The Soudan Contingent
18. Reprinted in *FJ* 30 May 1885
19. Letters re Dalley honour NLA MS 3353
20. State Records, Special Bundle The Soudan Contingent
21. Inglis, p. 120
22. *SMH* 29 April 1885
23. Inglis p. 122
24. *FJ* 2 May 1885
25. State Records, Special Bundle The Soudan Contingent
26. Attachments to Loftus to Derby 14 May & 10 June 1885, CO 201/602
27. SM 16 May 1885; Loftus to Derby 14 May 1885, CO 201/602
28. Dalley to Oliver nd, Oliver Papers Box 14, University of Sydney Archives
29. *SMH* 23 May 1885
30. *SMH* 29 May 1885

31. *FJ* 6 June 1885
32. *SM* 6 June 1885
33. *FJ* 20 June 1885
34. Inglis, pp. 128–29; Australian War Memorial website
35. *FJ* 20 June 1885
36. Dalley to Stuart 18 June 1885, Robert Towns & Co Records, ML CY3018
37. Inglis, p. 129
38. *SM* 9 May 1885
39. Loftus to Derby 25 June 1885, CO 201/602
40. *SM* & *FJ* 27 June 1885
41. Emily to Mary Martin, 24 June 1885, MLMSS 2425/7, 93C

25. The aftermath

1. *SMH* 26 June 1885
2. *SM* 11 July 1885
3. *SMH* 8 July 1885
4. *DT* & *SMH* 29 July 1885
5. *SM* 11 July 1885
6. *SMH* 23 July 1885
7. *SMH* 20 Aug 1885
8. Loftus to Derby 20 Aug 1885, CO 201/602
9. Loftus to Derby 25 June 1885, CO 201/602
10. N.S.W. Parliamentary Debates 1885 pp. 360–69
11. N.S.W. Parliamentary Debates 1885 pp. 552–60
12. Loftus to Derby, 7 Oct 1885, CO 201/602
13. *SMH* 6 Oct 1885
14. Martin, *Henry Parkes*, p. 354; *FJ* 24 Oct 1885
15. Dalley to Oliver nd, Oliver Papers Box 14, University of Sydney Archives
16. *SMH* 28 Oct 1885
17. Dalley to Stuart nd, Robert Towns & Co Records, ML CY3018
18. *SMH* 24 Nov 1885
19. N.S.W. Parliamentary Debates 1885 pp. 6–7
20. *SM* 5 & 19 Dec 1885
21. *SM* 14 Nov 1885; *FJ* 19 Dec 1885
22. N.S.W. Parliamentary Debates 1885 pp. 6-7
23. *SM* 5 Dec 1885
24. Dalley to Martin 30 Nov 1885, MLMSS 2425/1
25. Dalley to Lady Martin nd, MLMSS 2425/5
26. Dalley to Martin nd but context shows 31 Nov 1885, MLMSS 2425/1

26. Church and state

1. *SM* 20 Sept 1884; *FJ* 24 April 1897; Walsh, K.J., p. 43
2. Walsh, K.J., pp. 74–76
3. *SMH* 29 Sept 1885
4. *FJ* 21 Nov 1885
5. *FJ* 28 Nov 1885
6. *SM* 2 Jan & 23 Jan 1886; *FJ* 26 Dec 1885 & 23 Jan 1886
7. *SMH* 26 Jan 1886
8. *FJ* 17 July 1886, reprinted from *DT*
9. *FJ* 20 Feb 1886
10. *SM* 20 Feb 1886
11. *SMH* 19 March 1886
12. *SMH* 20 March 1886
13. *SMH* 25 March 1886
14. N.S.W. Parliamentary Debates 1886 pp. 1196–99
15. N.S.W. Parliamentary Debates 1886 p. 1278
16. N.S.W. Parliamentary Debates 1886 pp. 1474–77

17. SM 1 May 1886
18. SM 8 May 1886
19. SMH 1 June 1886
20. SMH 22 June 1886
21. SMH 13 Sept 1886
22. SM 26 June 1886
23. FJ 26 June 1886
24. N.S.W. Parliamentary Debates 1886 p. 2993
25. Dalley to Oliver 30 June 1886, Oliver Papers Box 14, University of Sydney Archives
26. Dalley to Archer 2 July 1886, Archer collection 2/43/4, University of Melbourne Archives
27. Dalley to 'My Dear Colonel' nd, Robert Towns & Co Records, ML CY3018
28. Dalley to Loftus 26 July 1886, ML CY2394
29. SMH 6 July 1886
30. SMH 7 July 1886; SM 17 July 1886
31. SM 19 May & 10 July 1886, & 22 Oct 1887
32. N.S.W. Parliamentary Debates 1886 pp. 3639–42
33. SMH 13 Sept 1886; FJ 18 Sept 1886
34. SM 16 Oct 1886
35. FJ 14 Aug 1886
36. N.S.W. Parliamentary Debates 1886 pp. 4082–87
37. N.S.W. Parliamentary Debates 1886 pp. 4519–23 & 5019–25
38. N.S.W. Parliamentary Debates 1886 pp. 5202–03
39. SM & FJ 28 Aug 1886
40. SM 4 & 11 Sept 1886
41. FJ 25 Sept 1886
42. Dalley to Mary Martin 12 Oct 1886, MLMSS 2425/6
43. Grainger, pp. 147–48
44. Dalley to Lady Martin 15 Oct 1886, MLMSS 2425/5
45. FJ 30 Oct 1886
46. Dalley to Mary Martin nd, MLMSS 2425/6
47. Charlotte Martin to Moran 4 Nov 1886, Sydney Archdiocesan Archives Box U2209
48. FJ 15 Aug 1885
49. FJ 31 March 1900
50. SMH 7 Nov 1886
51. SMH 7 & 8 Nov 1886: FJ 13 Nov 1886

27. Looking back

1. Dalley to Mrs Kendall 19 Sept, 11 Oct & nd 1886, Charlotte Kendall correspondence, ML CY1523
2. SMH 22 Nov 1886; FJ 27 Nov 1886
3. Dalley to Darley 27 Nov 1886, in SMH 29 Nov 1886
4. SMH 31 Oct 1888
5. SMH 30 Oct 1888
6. Bennett, 'Sir Julian Salomons', has a full account of this episode.
7. SMH 29 Nov 1886 published Dalley's letter and subsequent correspondence.
8. SM 18 Dec 1886 & 1 Jan 1887
9. SM & FJ 11 Dec 1886
10. FJ 18 Dec 1886
11. SMH 24 Dec 1886
12. SMH 23 Dec 1886; SM 25 Dec 1886 & 1 Jan 1887
13. SM 4 Dec 1886
14. SMH 31 Dec 1886
15. SMH 30 & 31 Dec 1886 & 5 Jan 1887
16. SMH 6 Jan 1887

17. *SMH* 8 Jan 1887
18. Myers, p. 4; Campbell, p. 76
19. *FJ* 22 Jan 1887
20. *SMH* 22 Jan 1887
21. Dalley secured work for Broomfield as editorial assistant on the *Picturesque Atlas of Australasia* – *ADB* Vol. 7, pp. 435–36
22. In memoir by Bertram Stephens in Farrell, 1905 and later editions
23. *SM* & *FJ* 19 Feb 1887
24. *SM* & *FJ* 26 Feb 1887
25. *SMH* 24 & 26 March 1887
26. N.S.W. Parliamentary Debates 1887 pp. 1292–93
27. Dalley to Parkes nd, ML A921, 234
28. *SMH* 24 May 1887; *FJ* 28 May 1887
29. Dalley to Parkes 29 May 1887, ML A921, 143
30. *FJ* 4 June 1887
31. *FJ* 18 June 1887
32. N.S.W. Parliamentary Debates 1887 pp. 2112–14
33. Dalley to Stephen 1 July 1887, ML CY4592, 207
34. *FJ* 9 July 1887

28. Centenary

1. Martin, *Henry Parkes*, p. 370
2. N.S.W. Parliamentary Debates 1887 pp. 2671–73
3. Dalley to Parkes 14 July & 7 Aug 1887, ML A921, 216 & 145
4. N.S.W. Parliamentary Debates 1887 pp. 2845–49
5. *SM* & *FJ* 17 Sept 1887
6. *FJ* 17 Dec 1887
7. Dalley to Lady Martin, MLMSS 2425/5
8. *SM* 19 Nov 1887
9. *FJ* 28 Jan 1888
10. *DT* 23 Jan 1888
11. *SMH* 26 Jan 1888; *FJ* 28 Jan 1888
12. *FJ* 4 Feb 1888
13. Dalley to Stephen 27 Jan 1888, ML CY4592
14. Dalley to Clarke 6 Feb 1888, ML CY2421
15. Dalley to Dibbs 12 May 1888, Loftus correspondence ML CY2394
16. *SMH* 25 Feb 1888; *FJ* 25 Feb 1888
17. *FJ* 24 April 1897
18. Dalley to Charlotte Kendall 25 March 1888, ML CY1523; Dalley to Daniel O'Connor 5 April 1888, ML CY3947; Dalley to Miss Parkes 17 April 1888, ML FM 3/796; Dalley to Dibbs 12 May 1888, ML CY2394
19. *FJ* 24 March 1888
20. This is the date of a letter from Dalley to Parkes regarding the appointment of a railway commissioner – ML A921, 219
21. Muir, p. 7
22. *FJ* 12 May 1888
23. *SM* 25 Feb 1888
24. *SM* 5 May 1888
25. *SM* 12 May 1888
26. *SM* 26 May 1888; *FJ* 9 June 1888; Bennett, 'Frederick Darley', p. 52
27. *FJ* 16 June 1888
28. N.S.W. Parliamentary Debates 1888 pp. 5019-25
29. N.S.W. Parliamentary Debates 1888 pp. 5255-61
30. *FJ* 7 July 1888
31. Dalley to Stephen 20 & 24 June 1888, ML CY4592

32. SM & FJ 18 Aug 1888
33. *Centennial Magazine*, Aug 1888, pp. 23–25
34. Dalley to Oliver 26 July 1888, Oliver Papers Box 14, University of Sydney Archives
35. FJ 22 Sept 1888
36. Pearl, pp. 130–31
37. SMH 20 & 21 Sept 1888
38. Dalley to O'Connor 21 Sept 1888, ML CY3947
39. Dalley to Oliver 30 Sept 1888
40. Dalley to Burdett Smith 3 Oct 1888. In Smith, 1889

29. 'Tongue of silver, heart of gold'

1. FJ 15 Dec 1888
2. SMH 30 Oct 1888
3. SMH 1 Nov 1888
4. *Argus* 29 Oct 1888
5. FJ 3 Nov 1888
6. SMH 31 Oct 1888; FJ 3 Nov 1888
7. SMH 7 Nov 1888
8. SMH 11 Dec 1888
9. SMH 12 Dec 1888; Long nominated Wentworth, Bland, George Nichols, Cowper and Martin
10. SMH 18 Dec 1888; FJ 22 Dec 1888
11. FJ 10 Nov 1888 refers to articles in the *Times*, *Pall Mall Gazette* and *Standard*.
12. Inglis, p. 28
13. FJ 29 June 1889
14. FJ 10 Nov 1888
15. FJ 10 Sept 1892
16. FJ 10 Nov 1888
17. Donovan, p. 441
18. FJ 16 Feb 1889
19. Dalley to Lady Martin 15 Oct 1886, MLMSS 2425/5
20. Dalley to Mary Martin 29 Aug 1886, MLMSS 2425/6
21. H.F.M., p. 17
22. *Argus* 29 Oct 1888
23. FJ 10 Nov 1888
24. Myers, p. 1
25. 'Fifty years in the making of Australian history', 1892
26. SMH 3 Nov 1888
27. SMH 29 & 31 Oct 1888
28. FJ 17 Nov 1888
29. FJ 30 Aug 1890
30. FJ 30 July 1892
31. FJ 7 Sept 1895
32. FJ 25 May & 19 Sept 1896 & 2 Jan 1897
33. FJ 24 April 1897
34. FJ 12 Oct 1889, 11 Nov 1899 & 6 Jan & 31 March 1900

Bibliography

Archival collections

Catholic Archdiocesan Archives Sydney (Moran correspondence)
Mitchell Library (mainly J.R. Clarke, Kendall, Loftus, Manning, Martin, D. O'Connor, Parkes, Stephen and Towns collections)
National Library of Australia (Dalley to Erskine and to Loftus; Stenhouse correspondence microfilm)
State Records New South Wales (Special Bundle, The Soudan Contingent 1885)
University of Melbourne Archives (Archer correspondence)
University of Sydney Archives (Senate minutes, Alexander Oliver papers)

Newspapers

Argus, Melbourne
Australasian, Melbourne
Australian, Sydney
Bathurst Free Press
Brisbane Courier
Bulletin, Sydney
Chronicle, Sydney
Daily Telegraph, Sydney (*DT*)
Empire, Sydney
Evening News, Sydney (*EN*)
Freeman's Journal, Sydney (*FJ*)
Goulburn Herald
Southern Cross, Sydney
Sydney Mail (*SM*)
Sydney Morning Herald (*SMH*)
Sydney Punch
Sydney Times
Sunday Sun, Sydney
Wagga Wagga Express
Yass Courier

Articles

Bennett, J.M., 'Sir Julian Salomons – Fifth Chief Justice of New South Wales', *Journal of the Royal Australian Historical Society*, vol. 58, 1972, pp. 101–11
Bennett, J.M., 'Sir Frederick Darley – Sixth Chief Justice of New South Wales', *Journal of the Royal Australian Historical Society*, vol. 63, 1977, pp. 40–59
Bladen, F.M., 'Daniel Henry Deniehy', *Sydney Quarterly Magazine*, Jan. 1884, pp. 194–206
Blair, D., 'Daniel Henry Deniehy: a Recollection', *Centennial Magazine*, vol. 1, 1889
Blair, D., 'Henry Parkes in 1850', *Centennial Magazine*, vol. 1, 1889
Boldrewood, Rolf, 'The Birthday of the Sydney Grammar School', *Sydneian*, April 1898, pp. 5–6
Dalley, W.B., 'A Plea for Horace Walpole', *Sydney University Review*, no. 1, 1881, pp. 7–17
Dalley, W.B., 'Charles Lamb', *Sydney University Review*, no. 4, 1882, pp. 329–47
Dalley, W.B., 'Henry Kendall', *Sydney*

University Review, no. 4, 1882, pp. 430–33

Dalley, W.B., 'Pensées', *Centennial Magazine*, vol. 1, 1888

Deniehy, D.H., 'How I Became Attorney-General of New Barataria' (1859), in Martin, E.A., *Life and Speeches of Daniel Henry Deniehy*, McNeil and Coffee, Sydney, 1884

Donovan, J.T. (J.T.D.), 'William Bede Dalley: A Sketch', *Austral Light*, August 1897

Dowd, B.T., 'William Bede Dalley: Scholar, Orator, Patriot and Statesman', *Royal Australian Historical Society Journal and Proceedings*, vol. 31, 1945, pp. 201–48

Dowd, B.T., 'Daniel Henry Deniehy: Gifted Australian Orator, Scholar and Literary Critic', *Royal Australian Historical Society Journal and Proceedings*, vol. 33, 1947, pp. 57–95

Heney, T., 'William Bede Dalley', *Sydney Quarterly Magazine*, Dec. 1888, pp. 296–301

H.F.M., 'William Bede Dalley', *New Triad*, 1 June 1928, p. 17

Kirkpatrick, R., 'Survival and Persistence: A Case Study of Four Provincial Press Sites', *Australian Studies in Journalism*, vol. 5, 1996, pp. 158–88

McGuanne, J.P. (J.P.M.), 'Men of the Days Long Past: William Bede Dalley', *Austral-Briton*, 11 March 1916, pp. 10–12

McMinn, T., 'Conservatism in Decline: The Parker Ministry, 1856–1857', *Journal of the Royal Australian Historical Society*, vol. 64, 1978, pp. 182–91

Melleuish, G., 'Daniel Deniehy, Bede Dalley and the Ideal of the Natural Aristocrat in Colonial New South Wales', *Australian Journal of Politics and History*, vol. 33, 1987, pp. 45–57

Mooney, C., 'St Mary's Seminary 1838-1852: Educating the Sons of Respectable Catholic Families', *Australasian Catholic Record*, vol. 71, 1994, pp. 475–84

Mortensen, R.G., 'Slaving in Australian Courts: Blackbirding Cases, 1869–71', *Journal of South Pacific Law*, vol. 4, 2000, pp. 1–22

Myers, F., 'William Bede Dalley', *Lone Hand*, vol. 1, 1907, pp. 1–4

Nairn, B., 'The Governor, the Bushranger and the Premier', *Journal of the Royal Australian Historical Society*, vol. 86, 2002, pp. 114–33

Prendergast, A., 'The Benedictine Schools and Students of Colonial Sydney', *Journal of the Australian Catholic Historical Society*, vol. 21, 2000, pp. 67–79

Rutledge, M., 'Edward Butler and the Chief Justiceship, 1873', *Historical Studies*, vol. 13, 1968, pp. 207–22

Saunders, M., 'Parliament and the New South Wales Contingent to the Sudan in 1885: The Dissection of a Debate', *Journal of the Royal Australian Historical Society*, vol. 70, 1985, pp. 227–50

Saunders, M., 'Australia's First Peace Movement?', *Labour History*, vol. 49, 1985, pp. 38–50

Saunders, M., 'Peace Dissent in the Australian Colonies: 1788–1900', *Journal of the Royal Australian Historical Society*, vol. 74, 1988, pp. 179–99

Stephen, A.E., 'Numantia: A Place of Disillusioned Aspirations', *Royal Australian Historical Society Journal and Proceedings*, vol. 31, 1945, pp. 249–76

Wynne, R., 'Archdeacon John McEncroe (1795-1868)', *Australasian Catholic Record*, vol. 32, 1955, pp. 216–17

Books

Amos, K., *The Fenians in Australia 1865–1880*, University of New South Wales Press, Sydney, 1988

Australian Dictionary of Biography, Melbourne University Press, from 1966, and www.adb.online.anu.edu.au

Barker, T., *A History of Bathurst*, vol. 1, Crawford House Press, Bathurst, 1992

Barrett, M., *King of Galong Castle: The Story of Ned Ryan 1786–1871*, Canberra, 2000

Barton, G.B., *Literature in New South Wales*, Government Printer, Sydney, 1866

Barton, G.B., *The Poets and Prose Writers of New South Wales*, Gibbs, Shallard & Co, Sydney 1866

Bennett, J.M. (ed.), *A History of the New South Wales Bar*, Law Book Company, Sydney, 1969

Bennett, J.M., *Sir James Martin*, Federation Press, Sydney, 2005

Bertie, C.H., *The Story of Old George Street: A chapter in Old Sydney*, Tyrrell's, Sydney, 1920

Birch, A. & Macmillan, D.S., *The Sydney Scene 1788–1960*, Melbourne University Press, 1962

Blacket, W., *May It Please Your Honour*, Cornstalk, Sydney, 1927

Bolton, G., *Edmund Barton*, Allen & Unwin, Sydney, 2000

Campbell, T.W., *George Richard Dibbs: Politician, Premier, Patriot, Paradox*, Canberra 1999

Dalley, W.B., *Opinions of the Attorney General (the Honourable William Bede Dalley) from March 1875 to February 1877*, Government Printer, Sydney, 1877

Denison, Sir William, *Varieties of Vice-Regal Life*, Longmans, Green & Co, London, 1870

Farrell, J., *How He Died and Other Poems*, Angus & Robertson, Sydney, 1905

Fitzgerald, C.C.P., *Life of Vice-Admiral Sir George Tryon KCB*, William Blackwood, Edinburgh, 1898

Fogarty, R., *Catholic Education in Australia 1806–1950*, Melbourne University Press, 1959

Fowler, F., *Southern Lights and Shadows*, Sampson Low, London, 1859

Froude, J.A. *Oceana or England and Her Colonies*, Longmans, Green & Co., London, 1886

Garran, R.R., *Prosper the Commonwealth*, Angus & Robertson, Sydney, 1958

Grainger, E., *Martin of Martin Place*, Alpha Books, Sydney, 1970

Hirst, J.B., *The strange birth of colonial democracy: New South Wales*

1848–1884, Allen & Unwin, Sydney, 1988

Hogan, J.F., *The Irish in Australia*, Ward & Downey, London, 1887

Hyndman, H.M., *The Record of an Adventurous Life*, Macmillan, London, 1911

Inglis, K.S., *The Rehearsal: Australians at War in the Sudan 1885*, Rigby, Adelaide, 1985

Jordens, A-M., *The Stenhouse Circle – Literary Life in mid-Nineteenth Century Sydney*, Melbourne University Press, 1979

Lehane, R., *Forever Carnival: A Story of Priests, Professors and Politics in 19th Century Sydney*, Ginninderra Press, Canberra, 2004

Loveday, P. & Martin, A.W., *Parliament, Factions and Parties: The First Thirty Years of Responsible Government in New South Wales 1856–1889*, Melbourne University Press, 1966

Martin, A.W., *Henry Parkes: A Biography*, Melbourne University Press, 1980

Martin, A.W., *Letters from Menie: Sir Henry Parkes to his Daughter*, Melbourne University Press, 1983

Moran, P.F., *History of the Catholic Church in Australasia: From Authentic Sources*, Oceanic Publishing, Sydney, 189?

Molony, J.N., *An Architect of Freedom: John Hubert Plunkett in New South Wales 1832–1869*, ANU Press, Canberra, 1973

O'Farrell, P., *The Catholic Church and Community in Australia: A History*, Nelson, Melbourne 1977

O'Sullivan, J., *The Bloodiest Bushrangers*, New English Library, London, 1974

Palmer, G., *Kidnapping in the South Seas: Being a Narrative of a Three Months' Cruise of H.M. Ship Rosario*, Penguin Colonial Facsimiles, Melbourne, 1973

Parkes, H., *Fifty Years in the Making of Australian History*, Longmans, Green & Co., London, 1892

Pearl, C., *Brilliant Dan Deniehy*, Nelson, Melbourne, 1972

Piddington, A.B., *Worshipful Masters*, Angus & Robertson, Sydney, 1929

Polding, J.B. *The Letters of John Bede Polding OSB*, ed. M. Xavier Compton et al., Sisters of the Good Samaritan, Sydney, 1994–98

Polding, J.B., *Documents and Resource Material Relating to the Episcopacy of Archbishop John Bede Polding OSB*, ed. M. Xavier Compton et al., Sisters of the Good Samaritan, Sydney, 2001

Powell, A., *Patrician Democrat: The Political Life of Charles Cowper 1843–1870*, Melbourne University Press, 1977

Saunders, M., *Britain, the Australian Colonies, and the Sudan Campaign of 1884–85*, University of New England, Armidale, 1985

Sheldon, J.S., *The Big School Room at Sydney Grammar School*, Sydney Grammar School Press, 1997

Shine, T., *The Australian Portrait Gallery and Memoirs of Representative Colonial Men*, Southern Cross Publishing Co., Sydney, 1885

Stargardt, A.W., *Australia's Asian Policies: The History of a Debate*

1839–1972, Institute of Asian Affairs, Hamburg, 1977

Thompson, R.C., *Australian Imperialism in the Pacific: The Expansionist Era 1820–1920*, Melbourne University Press, 1980

Travers, R., *The Phantom Fenians of New South Wales*, Kangaroo Press, Sydney, 1986

Vamplew, W. (ed.), 'Australians: Historical Statistics', vol. 10 of *Australians: A Historical Library*, Fairfax, Syme & Weldon Associates, Sydney 1987

Walker, R. R., *The Newspaper Press in New South Wales, 1803–1920*, Sydney University Press, 1976

Walsh, G., *Daniel Deniehy: A Portrait with Background*, Department of History, University College, UNSW, Canberra 1988

Walsh, K.J., *Yesterday's Seminary: A History of St Patrick's Manly*, Allen & Unwin, Sydney, 1998

Woods, G.D., *A History of Criminal Law in New South Wales: The Colonial Period 1788–1900*, Federation Press, Sydney, 2002

Pamphlets

Buchanan, D., Political Portraits, Davies and Co., Sydney, 1863

Smith, R.B., The New South Wales Soudan Contingent: A Few Historical Notes, Government Printer, Sydney, 1889

Dalley, W.B., Speech Delivered at the Masonic Hall, May 20, 1872, Edward F. Flanagan, Sydney, 1872

Dalley, W.B., Speech Delivered in the Legislative Council on Certain Resolutions Submitted to that Chamber, Gibbs, Shallard & Co., Sydney, 1879

Dalley, W.B., Sydney Platforms & European Cabinets: An Address to the Catholics of New South Wales on the Education Question, F. Cunninghame and Co., Sydney, 1879

Parkes, H., The Case of the Prisoner Gardiner, George Robertson, Melbourne, 1876

Rosebery, A.P.P., Australian Speechlets 1883–1884, 1884

Other documents

Colonial Office records, Australian Joint Copying Project, CO 201

Muir, D.K., 'William Bede Dalley (1831–1888): A Further Perspective', typescript lodged at Mitchell and other research libraries

New South Wales Parliamentary Debates

Votes and Proceedings of the Legislative Assembly, NSW

'Report of Royal Commission into Certain Alleged Cases of Kidnapping of Natives of the Loyalty Islands', Government Printer, Sydney, 1869

Picture credits

p. 8 & spine Brendon Kelson

p. 19 Sadd, H.S. The Most Reverend John Bede Polding OSB. nla.pic-an9997459. National Library of Australia

p. 27 *Illustrated Sydney News*, November 1875, mfmNX 189. National Library of Australia

p. 34 *Sydney Mail*, 19 December 1874, mfmNX1. National Library of Australia

p. 47 Sadd, H.S. The Honourable Sir Alfred Stephen. nla.pic-an9847107. National Library of Australia

p. 55 Patrick Francis Cardinal Moran, *History of the Catholic Church in Australasia*, Sydney 189?. N282.94 MOR. National Library of Australia

p. 69 Government Printing Office collection, State Library of New South Wales

p. 90 *Illustrated Sydney News*, November 1874, mfmNX 189. National Library of Australia

p. 92 Lady Viola Tait collection. Portrait of Gustavus Vaughan Brooke. nla.pic-vn3600518. National Library of Australia

p. 102 Sadd, H.S. Revd. John Dunmore Lang, DD. nla.pic-an9650315. National Library of Australia

p. 112 *Town & Country Journal*, 1 March 1873, mfmNX 442. National Library of Australia

p. 125 *Sydney Punch*, 14 October 1865, NX 1325. National Library of Australia

p. 139 Sadd, H.S. H.R.H. Prince Alfred. nla.pic-an9281419. National Library of Australia

p. 139 *Illustrated Sydney News*, February 1868, mfmNX 189. National Library of Australia

p. 152 G.M. Mathews collection. Portrait of William Macleay. nla.pic-vn3793260. National Library of Australia

p. 169 Moore, May. Portrait of Henry Kendall. nla.pic-an3084988. National Library of Australia

p. 180 'A Romance of Dalley Mansion Estate', 1911, mcN 2225 JAFpHIST 1171. National Library of Australia

p. 189 Sadd, H.S. The Honorable Sir James Martin. nla.pic-an9721325. National Library of Australia

p. 196 *Illustrated Sydney News*, April 1875, mfmNX 189. National Library of Australia

p. 212 *Illustrated Sydney News*, January 1877, mfmNX 189. National Library of Australia

p. 228 Sadd, H.S. The Most Reverend Roger Bede Vaughan OSB. nla.pic-an9860722. National Library of Australia

p. 246 & back cover Archives collection, Manly Warringah &

Pittwater Historical Society. Acc. 422(36)

p. 261 Government Printing Office collection, State Library of New South Wales

p. 269 *Illustrated Sydney News*, January 1886, mfmNX 189. National Library of Australia

p. 275 *Illustrated Sydney News*, November 1883, mfmNX 189. National Library of Australia

p. 276 Portrait of Charles Badham. nla.pic-an22932041. National Library of Australia

p. 303 *Illustrated Sydney News*, August 1887, mfmNX 189. National Library of Australia

p. 305 *Illustrated Sydney News*, December 1884, mfmNX 189. National Library of Australia

p. 307 *Bulletin*, 6 December 1884, mfmNX 141. National Library of Australia

p. 310 *Illustrated Sydney News*, September 1879, mfmNX 189. National Library of Australia

p. 312 *Illustrated Sydney News*, March 1885, mfmNX 189. National Library of Australia

p. 317 Sketch by Monty Scott. Private collection

p. 324 *Illustrated Sydney News*, April 1885, mfmNX 189. National Library of Australia

p. 325 *Bulletin*, 7 March 1885, mfmNX 141. National Library of Australia

p. 332 *Bulletin*, 28 March 1885, mfmNX 141. National Library of Australia

p. 335 C.C.P. Fitzgerald, *Life of Vice-Admiral Sir George Tryon KCB*, William Blackwood, Edinburgh, 1898. 920 FIT, National Library of Australia

p. 343 *Illustrated Sydney News*, August 1885, mfmNX 189. National Library of Australia

p. 344 *Illustrated Sydney News*, August 1885, mfmNX 189. National Library of Australia

p. 348 *Illustrated Sydney News*, August 1885, mfmNX 189. National Library of Australia

p. 349 *Bulletin*, 8 August 1885, mfmNX 141. National Library of Australia

p. 350 *Illustrated Sydney News*, August 1885, mfmNX 189. National Library of Australia.

p. 361 John Oxley Library, State Library of Queensland. Image number 57131.

p. 363 His Excellency Lord Carrington. nla.pic-vn3665726. National Library of Australia.

p. 367 *Illustrated Sydney News*, August 1886, mfmNX 189. National Library of Australia.

p. 370 Ferguson collection. Portrait of Sir John Robertson, nla.pic-an23492568. National Library of Australia.

p. 376 Sadd, H.S. The Honorable Sir Frederick Darley. nla.pic-an9484579. National Library of Australia.

p. 376 Portrait of Sir Patrick Alfred Jennings. nla.pic-an24228786. National Library of Australia.

Index

A

Aaron, Dr Isaac 170, 188
Abbott, Joseph 316, 402
Ainger, Alfred 260
Albert, Prince 408
Alfred, Duke of Edinburgh 12, 139–141, 146, 149, 153
Allen, Caroline 144
Allen, (Sir) George Wigram 191, 219
Allen, William 52
Anderson, George 271
Antill, Major-General John 10
Archer, William 230, 231, 234, 235, 368
Archibald, J.F. 245
Arnold, Matthew 398
Arnold, William 142
Aspinall, Butler Cole 144
Auld, Very Rev. John 403

B

Badham, Professor Charles 10, 112, 142, 155, 172, 173, 179–181, 186, 187, 194, 203, 217–219, 229, 230, 247, 259, 262, 276, 283, 293, 307, 393
Bainbridge (née Dobbins), Catherine 14, 82, 141
Baker, Exekiel 255
Barker, Bishop Frederick 238
Barry, Bishop Alfred 324, 373, 378, 379, 403
Barton, George 111, 112
Barton, (Sir) Edmund 11, 259, 266, 283, 299, 300, 306, 307

Battye, Mrs 48
Bayley, Lyttleton Holyoake 68, 69, 71, 75, 77, 79, 80, 83
Beach, Bill 365, 377
Beaconsfield, Lord 245, 246, 251
Belmore, Governor Lord 138, 154, 174, 250
Bennett, J.M. 30
Bennett, Samuel 74, 103, 104, 105, 130
Berry, Alexander 71
Bertie, C.H. 17
Bertrand, Henry Louis 128
Besnard, Nicholas 164
Blacket, Wilfred 43
Black, John 78
Blair, David 22, 23, 121
Blake, Dr Isidore 148
Blake, Isidore 134, 136
Bland, Dr William 22, 74, 402
Bourke, Governor Sir Richard 13, 34, 55, 96, 408
Bourke, Richard jr 96
Bow, John 101, 193
Bowman, William 54, 55
Brassey, Lord Thomas 9, 388
Brennan, Patrick 127
Bright, John 216
Britten, Frank 101
Broadhurst, Edward 270
Brooke, Gustavus Vaughan 92, 93, 129
Broomfield, Frederick 381
Broughton, Bishop William 95
Brown, Stephen 209, 216
Brown, Thomas (Rolf Boldrewood) 18, 189

Browne, Thomas (journalist) 189
Brunel, Isambard Kingdom 86
Buchanan, David 129, 130, 133, 162, 166, 167, 185
Bulletin, The 12, 245, 308, 319, 348, 381
Burdekin, Marshall 126, 289
Burdekin, Mary Ann 20
Burdekin, Sydney 289
Burdekin, Thomas 20
Burke, Edmund 216, 262
Burke, James 116
Burke, Mickey 108
Burns, Robert 66
Burton, Sir William 89
Butler, Edward 11, 24, 29, 154, 160, 174, 177, 189, 195, 207, 231, 290
Butler, Professor Thomas 10
Butler, Thomas 113, 170, 174, 229, 254
Byrnes, Henry 48
Byrnes, William 31

C

Cameron, Angus 266
Campbell, Dr Allan 145
Campbell, John 31
Campbell, Robert 28, 29, 31, 51, 52, 533
Campbell, William 162
Cape, William T. 18, 19, 97, 171, 237
Carnarvon, Earl of 195, 199, 218
Carrington, Governor Lord Charles 357, 359, 362, 363, 368, 371, 374, 378, 380, 391, 401, 402, 404
Carrington, Lady 371, 378, 389
Carroll, John 136
Cassim, Mahomet 106
Charles, Captain 17
Charters, Daniel 101
Cheeke, Alfred 131, 136, 137, 144, 146, 179, 183, 198, 199, 202

Cheeke, George 179
Cheeke, Selina 179, 389
Chiniquy, Charles 221
Chisholm, Caroline 251
Clarke, Jacob 257, 260, 393
Clarke, John & Tom 133–137, 143, 188
Clipsham, Rev. Paul 324
Cobden, Richard 216
Cohen, Henry 351
Coleridge, Samuel Taylor 258
Collins, Michael 404
Columbus, Christopher 228
Combes, Edward 193, 195
Connell, Mick 137
Conroy, John 145
Cook, Captain James 165, 166, 408
Cooper, Sir Daniel 52
Cooper, Walter 170
Copeland, Henry 263, 264
Cordini, Joseph 295
Cowper, Charles jr 107
Cowper, (Sir) Charles 27–31, 35, 40, 43, 46, 47, 50, 51, 53–57, 59, 60, 62, 64, 68, 69, 71, 74–79, 84, 87, 88, 90, 92, 99, 105, 106, 112, 113, 116, 118, 124–126, 158, 162, 163, 165, 166, 168, 171, 177, 201, 289, 370, 383, 402
Cox, George 288, 299
Cubitt, Arthur 41
Cummins, Larry 209
Cuthbert, John 185

D

Daggett, John C. 156, 157, 158
Dalley, Catherine sr 15, 82, 141, 155
Dalley, Charles 182, 405, 407, 408
Dalley, Eleanor Jane (née Long) 179, 180, 181, 185, 241, 244, 245, 246, 372, 373
Dalley, Eleanor jr 181, 372

Dalley, Hannah 15
Dalley, James 15
Dalley, John Bede 182, 206, 293, 372, 377, 408
Dalley, John jr 15, 18, 19, 20
Dalley, John sr 13, 14, 17, 21, 31, 74, 82, 155, 173, 179
Dalley, Mary 180, 241, 405
Dalley, Richard 15, 82, 92, 97, 155, 173, 182
Dalley, William Bede
  acting premier 9, 300–400
  childhood 15–21
  election campaigns 28–39, 47, 51–53, 54–55, 74, 75, 78, 87, 88, 162–164, 177, 178, 190, 194, 195, 261, 263, 290, 355
  houses 12, 181, 182, 233, 246, 251, 257, 262, 320, 394
  illnesses 20, 42, 149, 151, 220, 239, 240, 261, 276, 288, 299, 304, 325, 342, 343, 352, 366, 369, 370, 372, 382, 389, 392, 398–400
  in court 10, 11, 28, 43, 44, 45, 47, 48, 58, 59, 62, 68, 72, 88, 100–105, 108–110, 116–118, 120, 127–137, 144, 145, 146, 148, 155, 157–159, 160, 168, 169, 171, 173, 183, 184, 186, 187, 188, 189, 197, 242, 255, 291, 302–304
  in government 12, 62–67, 68–69, 195–205, 206–210, 214, 222, 263–353
  in Legislative Assembly 12, 40–43, 45, 46, 49, 50, 51, 56, 57, 60–64, 65, 66, 67, 69–71, 77, 78, 79, 99, 106
  in Legislative Council 12, 89, 166–168, 171, 182, 184, 197, 202, 210, 212, 217, 220, 222–224, 226, 231, 236–240, 248–249, 267–270, 272–273, 281, 286–287, 288–301, 320, 329, 352–353, 357, 365, 369–370, 371, 383, 385, 387–388
  journalism & literature 44, 49, 93, 111–114, 118, 122, 124, 126, 127, 141, 142, 147, 150–154, 155, 159, 170, 172, 175, 176, 183, 185, 194, 199, 200, 211, 221, 227, 229, 230, 237, 243–247, 250, 251, 254, 258, 260, 262, 267, 270, 367, 371, 381, 398
  law reform 45, 49, 62, 207, 208, 223, 226, 264, 265, 266, 272, 275, 276–277, 281, 290, 378
  legal opinions 197, 198, 200, 209, 210, 266, 269, 270, 289, 306
  marriage & family 12, 82–84, 155, 173, 179–181, 182, 206, 241, 244, 245, 257, 260, 292, 371–372, 405
  monuments 9, 367, 402, 403, 407, 408
  NSW Centennial celebrations 387, 391–392
  on university Senate 186, 217, 218, 219
  public speaker 9–10, 25, 29–31, 33–34, 36, 37, 42, 46, 47, 51, 76, 84, 89, 94, 96, 107, 129, 132, 138, 142, 162, 165, 168, 171, 172, 173, 190, 217, 227, 232, 242, 244, 250, 252, 256, 257, 259, 260, 270, 275, 276, 279, 281, 283, 292, 293, 307, 308, 316, 322, 327, 328, 339, 341, 347–352, 354, 355, 369, 374, 375, 377, 381, 383–386, 389, 391, 392, 393, 394
  relations with Catholic Church 19,

46, 53, 55–58, 64–65, 70–71, 114, 119, 154, 161, 163, 167, 181, 203, 211, 228, 230, 234, 235, 255, 360, 361, 362
response to Russian threat 327, 335, 337, 338, 382
Sudan commitment 9, 312–317, 318–330, 341–345, 346–349, 365, 382, 385, 390, 400, 402
visits to England, Ireland and Europe 83, 85, 86, 90–95, 97, 98
views on
   Chinese 12, 49, 120, 225, 227, 248, 249, 265, 396, 397, 398
   constitution, representative government 29, 30–35, 42, 46, 53, 55, 61, 75, 77, 96, 165, 203, 209, 220–221, 223, 226, 239, 266, 272, 300, 355, 371, 388
   criminal law, sentencing 45, 102, 115, 135, 191, 192, 203, 208, 217, 225, 265, 291, 379
   divorce 57, 166, 185, 291, 293
   economic & financial issues 34, 71, 266, 281, 297, 306
   education 34–38, 46, 75, 78, 171, 203, 213, 234–237, 241
   Empire, foreign policy & defence 9, 60, 158, 165, 199, 213, 257, 268, 282, 284, 285, 286, 305, 310–312, 314, 322, 329, 334, 341, 347, 351, 365, 369, 385, 390
   federation 286
   flora & fauna 220, 239, 267, 272, 293, 341, 376
   honours & distinctions 251, 279, 336, 367
   land policy 33, 36, 50–51, 75, 88, 206, 214, 238, 261, 277, 297–300
   legal profession 43, 69, 76, 190, 199, 224, 231–232, 264, 267, 272, 293, 341, 364, 376
   liquor licensing 58, 268
   public health 353
   religious & national differences 12, 25, 49, 55, 114–115, 140, 141–149, 221–222, 233–238, 248–250, 256–257, 309, 316, 331, 341, 347, 361, 364, 383, 390–393
   role of politicians 66, 75, 85, 201, 205, 222, 223, 239, 263–264, 274, 276–280, 294, 302–303, 355–356
   role of the press 104, 114, 119, 189, 221, 257, 271, 279
   Sunday observance 288
   United States 268, 349, 368, 397
   water storage 296, 322, 343
Dalley, William Bede jr 181, 186, 377
Dalton, Rev. Joseph 293
Darley, Frederick 202, 267, 268, 271, 292, 329, 337, 375, 376, 377, 396, 401, 402, 404, 408
Darling, Governor Ralph 13
Darvall, John Bayley 47, 68, 103, 105, 117, 127
Davies, John 150
Davis, Bishop Charles 393
Dawson, John 54
Deniehy, Daniel Henry 10, 22–24, 29, 42, 50, 57, 62, 63, 65, 66, 68–71, 74, 76, 77, 79, 80, 83, 111, 120, 121, 186, 256, 270, 293, 370, 383, 399
Deniehy, Mary 270
Denison, Governor Sir William 26, 27, 30, 51, 89, 391
Derby, Lord Edward 285, 306, 310,

312, 315, 321, 327, 335–337, 340, 343, 352
Dibbs, John 242
Dibbs, Sir George 16, 242, 267, 276, 278, 281, 284, 306, 316, 343, 353–357, 381, 393, 402, 408
Dickens, Charles 113, 253
Dickinson, John 58
Dillon, John 236
Docker, Joseph 209
Donaldson, Stuart 27, 29, 30, 31, 61, 62
Donovan, J.T. 182
Dowling, James 148
Driver, Richard 78, 191
Duffy, Charles Gavan 24, 25, 26, 28, 84, 120
Duncan, William Augustine 151, 254, 255
Dunleavy, James 116
Dunn, John 116
Dunphy, Rev. 21
Dwyer. Rev. John 147

E

Eagar, Geoffrey 107, 141, 151, 163
Eason, George 164
Egan, Daniel 21
Empire 24, 32, 46, 74, 103–105, 152
Epaille, Right Rev. 21
Erskine, Commodore James 304, 305
Evening News 320
Express 253, 254

F

Fairfax, James 117, 118
Fairfax, John 32, 33, 35, 37, 38, 40, 117, 118, 271, 275
Farnell, James 216, 220, 222, 281, 297
Farrell, John 381
Faucett, Peter 60, 88, 129, 133, 145, 202, 215, 218, 272, 321

Fitzpatrick, Michael 206, 207, 216, 236, 253
Fitzpatrick, Thomas 194
Flood, Edward 265
Foley, Charles 100
Forbes, Archibald 257
Fordyce, Alexander 101, 193
Forrest, Very Rev. Dr John 221, 393
Forster, William 18, 42, 49, 62, 78, 87, 101, 105, 112, 161, 174, 177, 181, 192, 195, 200, 201, 213, 260, 383, 392
Fowler, Frank 52, 53
Francis, Saint 242
Freeman's Journal 55, 56, 58 113–115, 118, 125, 126, 127, 142, 170, 253, 254, 319
Fremantle, General Sir Arthur 365
Froude, James 318, 320, 363

G

Gardiner, Frank 17, 100, 101, 109, 110, 133, 191, 192, 193, 195, 218
Garran, Andrew 314, 371
Garrett, Thomas 197, 200, 206, 209, 214
George, Hugh 223
Gilbert, Johnny 116
Gillies, Duncan 366
Gipps, Governor Sir George 27, 95
Gladstone, William 216, 282, 313, 336
Gordon, Adam Lindsay 170
Gordon, General Charles 313, 314, 318, 321, 381
Gordon, Samuel 41
Graham, Major-General Sir Gerald 313, 315, 333, 407
Green, Richard 107
Gregory, Abbot 65, 70, 147, 154
Greig, Christina (née Dalley) 15, 82, 179, 182, 292, 405
Greig, William 82, 292

Grey, Sir George 346
Griffin, Gilderoy 366, 403
Griffin, James 136, 137
Griffin, Patrick & Michael 137
Griffith, Samuel 312, 340, 366
Griffiths, Archina 192
Gurney, Professor Theodore 218

H

Hall, Ben 100, 108, 116
Hampden, Governor Lord 9, 408
Hanson, William 74, 103, 104, 105, 130
Harding, Charles 323
Hare, Augustus 185
Hargrave, John 71, 118, 133, 136, 185, 188, 189, 199, 202, 215
Harpur, Charles 23
Harpur, Joseph 113, 170
Harte, Bret 381
Hartington, Lord 315, 337
Hart, James 65, 70
Hawkin, William 146
Haynes, John 245
Hay, (Sir) John 66, 218, 377, 401
Healy, Patrick 132
Henty, Thomas 14
Herald, Sydney Morning 32, 35, 43, 102, 104, 115, 271, 320
Heydon, Jabez King 70
Hezlett, William 212
Hicks, W.H. 169, 247
Hill, Richard 192
Hogarth, Miss 405
Holtermann, Bernhardt 278
Hosie, William 109, 110
Huenerbein, Charles 317, 323
Hume, Frederick 317
Hutchinson, Frank 181, 401
Hyndman, Henry Mayers 161

I

Inglis, K.S. 326
Innes, (Sir) George 207, 250, 271
Intercolonial Convention 1883 283–287, 309
Isaacs, Robert 101, 105, 109, 110, 112, 117, 118, 137, 144, 145

J

Jackson, 'Stonewall' 134
Jefferis, Rev. James 324
Jennings, (Sir) Patrick 229, 235, 307, 357, 365, 368, 375–378, 380, 403, 408
Jervois, (Sir) William 311
Joachim, William 197, 198
Johnson, Charles 148, 149
Jones, James 177

K

Keightley, Henry 108, 109
Kelly, Rev. William 401
Kendall, Charlotte 258, 259, 374
Kendall, Frederick 259
Kendall, Henry 23, 169, 170, 186, 188, 228, 243, 248, 258, 259, 262, 374, 375
Kennagh, Patrick 137
Kennedy, Rev. 245
Kimberley, Lord 158
Kinder, Henry 128
Knutsford, Lord 407
Krauss, Wilhelm 187
Krefft, Johann 198

L

Labouchere, Henry 27
Lackey, John 204
Lamb, Charles 260
Landor, Walter Savage 250, 274
Lang, Rev. Dr John Dunmore 61, 72, 76, 85, 89, 94, 99, 102, 103, 112,

114, 117, 118, 162, 163, 165, 185, 211, 221, 260, 402, 408
Lanigan, Bishop William 236
Lehane, Jeremiah 129
Leichhardt, Ludwig 20
Lewin, Ross 156
Lilley, Charles 173
Loftus, Governor Lord Augustus 270, 283, 302, 310, 312, 315, 321, 323, 326, 335, 336, 340, 343, 345, 352, 353, 357, 358, 368, 369, 393
Loftus, Lady 302
Longmuir, Captain James 187
Long, Isabella 179
Long, William 179, 206
Long, William jr 179, 378, 402, 404
Lorenzo the Magnificent 250
Lover, Samuel 93
Lucas, John 223
Lutwyche, Alfred 62, 68, 72

M

Macarthur, James 57
Macarthur, Sir William 218
Macaulay, Lord 216
Macintosh, John 83
Mackellar, Dr Charles 342, 344, 345, 352
Mackinlay, Denis 159, 160
Maclean, Harold 192
Macleay, William 99, 113, 147, 152, 177, 199, 218, 232, 239, 247, 270, 392
Macquarie, Governor Lachlan 371, 391
Mahdi, the 313, 315
Mahony, Rev. Francis Sylvester 253
Manning, Sir William 132, 158, 195, 198, 201, 217, 219
Manns, Henry 101, 102, 106
Martin, A.W. 153
Martin, Charlotte 373

Martin, Eleanor 241, 358
Martin, Emily 345
Martin, Lady Isabella 179, 241, 345, 358, 359, 372, 373, 382, 389, 399, 405
Martin, Mary 372, 405
Martin, (Sir) James 10, 18, 29, 30, 31, 32, 33, 40, 41, 43, 47, 48, 62, 64, 65, 66, 68, 71, 74, 75, 77, 79, 83, 84, 86, 88, 101, 102, 104, 105, 107, 109, 110, 112–114, 117–119, 124–126, 130, 133, 144, 151, 154, 162, 163, 168, 171, 174, 177, 179, 185, 187, 189, 199, 200, 202, 215, 217, 218, 229, 233, 241, 268, 271, 307, 312, 321, 327, 329, 336, 340, 341, 346, 358, 359, 369, 370, 372, 373–375, 383, 398
McCarthy, Rev. Tim 108
McElhone, John 262
McEncroe, Edward 127
McEncroe, Archdeacon John 50, 102, 127, 149
McGuanne, J.P. 17
McGuinn, Rev. Denis 116
McGuire, John 101
McIlwraith, Thomas 283
Melville, Ninian 243, 248
Melville, Robert 104
Middleton, John 109
Milford, Samuel 68, 101, 118
Moloney, Patrick 394
Montgomery, Walter 144
Moore, Charles 140
Moore, J. Sheridan 170
Moran, Cardinal Patrick 9, 293, 324, 358, 360, 361, 370, 373, 378, 379, 384, 385, 389, 394, 402, 403, 408
Morgan, George 187
Morris, Augustus 280
Morton, George Ross 112, 155
Mort, Thomas Sutcliffe 270, 408

Munday, William 145
Murphy, James 84
Murphy, Very Rev. Francis 19
Murray, Bishop James 401
Murray, Terence Aubrey 77
Myers, Frank 180, 379, 380, 406

N

Newcastle, Duke of 93
New Guinea 199, 283, 285, 305, 309, 310, 311, 312, 330
Newman, John Henry 217, 230, 233, 368, 398, 401
Newry, Lord 138
Norfolk, Duke of 231
Northbrook, Lord 312

O

Oakes, Francis 14, 31
O'Brien, Annie 182
O'Brien, Dr James 393
O'Connell, Daniel 21, 102
O'Connor, Daniel 294, 330, 365, 374, 399
O'Connor, William 100
O'Farrell, Henry 140, 142, 143, 144, 145, 146, 147, 150, 152, 176, 177
O'Haran, Rev. Dr Denis 378
Oliver, Alexander 16, 251, 258, 260, 340, 355, 368, 375, 398, 399, 402
Oliver, Celia 399
O'Mara, Thomas 392
O'Neill, Michael 164
O'Quinn, Bishop James 255
Osborne, John 332
O'Shanassy, Sir John 197
Osman Digna 313, 315, 333
O'Sullivan, Richard 127, 132, 142, 170
Owen, Robert 71, 185
Oxford, Edward 144
Oxley, John 41

P

Palmer, Captain George 157, 158
Palmerston, Lord 58, 103
Parker, Henry 27, 30, 31, 42, 46, 62, 68, 101
Parkes, Clarinda 93, 98
Parkes, Menie 92, 93
Parkes, Robert 98
Parkes, (Sir) Henry 12, 24, 29, 32, 33, 35, 42, 46, 47, 50, 51, 55, 57, 61, 67, 76, 77, 86, 88, 90, 91, 93–95, 97, 98, 99, 124, 126, 136, 138, 140, 141, 143, 145, 146, 148–154, 162, 163, 168, 171, 174, 176–178, 189, 191–193, 195, 199–201, 204, 207, 209, 210, 212–214, 216, 221, 222, 225, 226, 231, 234, 236, 237, 239, 240, 248, 255, 260, 261, 263, 266, 271, 286, 289, 290, 296, 300, 302–304, 310, 321, 322, 331–334, 337, 352, 354, 355, 357, 368, 370, 371, 378, 379, 381–383, 387, 388, 395, 396, 406
Paterson, John 164
Patteson, Bishop John 159, 185
Peel, Sir Robert 216
Peisley, John 109
Piddington, Albert Bathurst 120, 276
Piddington, William 32, 296, 357, 367
Pigott, William 203
Plunkett, John Hubert 35, 37, 40, 42, 55–57, 63, 67, 70, 71, 75–77, 88, 102, 112, 124, 126, 155, 383
Polding, Archbishop John Bede 18, 19, 21, 70, 119, 147, 154, 161, 163, 167, 211, 217, 219, 237, 252, 294, 390
Pope Leo XIII 230
Porter, Sir Joseph 295
Pritchard, William 156, 157

Q

Quinn, Bishop Matthew 173
Quong Tart 320

R

Ranken, George 257, 280, 331
Redman, William 54, 55
Reed, William B. 183
Reid, George 259, 289, 290
Renwick, Dr Arthur 217, 263
Reynolds, John 184
Richardson, Colonel (later Major-General) John 315, 327, 333, 337, 338, 345, 346, 354, 404
Riley, Alban 381
Roberts, Colonel Charles 315, 346, 354, 368
Roberts, George 58
Robertson, (Sir) John 12, 18, 43, 50, 55, 63, 76, 79, 86, 87, 89, 91, 92, 94, 99, 115, 120, 121, 151, 152, 154, 158, 161–163, 165, 168, 174, 177, 179, 185, 190, 194, 195, 197, 199–202, 204, 206, 209–213, 214, 216, 221–223, 227, 234, 235, 240, 255, 259–261, 263, 264, 277, 279, 297, 308, 327, 330, 331, 333, 337, 341, 346, 348, 357, 359, 365–370, 374, 384, 389, 392, 401–404, 408
Robinson, Governor Sir Hercules 179, 191–193, 195, 199, 209, 213, 218, 222, 337
Rolleston, Christopher 159
Rosebery, Lord Archibald 282, 314, 403, 407
Ross, Alexander & Charles 100
Ross, Dr Andrew 146
Ross, Robert Scott 75
Rowe, Richard 111
Russell, Henry 217
Russell, Lord 87
Ryan, John Nagle 316

S

Sala, George 328
Salomons, Julian 376
Samuel, Saul 161, 311, 315, 317–319, 333, 335, 337, 338
Sani, Tommaso 268
San Just, Don Eduardo 156
Scott, Annie 131
Scott, Bill 136
Scott, Dr John 104, 105
Scott, Sir Walter 172
Scott, Thomas 41
Scott, William Henry 131
Scratchley, Major-General Peter 311, 312
Service, James 283, 284, 305, 306, 346
Shaw, Alexander 160, 161
Sheahan, John Philip 129
Simpson, George 169, 401
Smith, Professor John 218, 225
Smith, Robert Burdett 400
Speer, William 163
Stacey, Henry 146
Stanley, Lord 63
Stenhouse, Nicol Drysdale 10, 22, 23, 52, 111, 121, 122, 129, 155, 169, 186, 247, 293
Stephen, Lady 233
Stephen, Sir Alfred 47, 49, 72, 100, 105, 108, 110, 128, 129, 132, 133, 135, 136, 157, 168, 189, 191, 192, 198, 199, 201, 203, 207, 208, 216, 229, 233, 240, 263, 264, 266, 268, 272, 290, 291, 296, 303, 312, 329, 337, 340, 372, 385, 388, 392, 397, 402
Stewart, Ellen 48
Stiff (old *Punch* man) 112
St Ignatius Loyola 228
Street, John 14
Strickland, Sir Edward 293, 313, 314, 329

Stuart, (Sir) Alexander 12, 16, 201, 203, 211, 216, 261, 262, 264, 266, 274–276, 278, 280, 283, 284, 289, 300, 302, 308, 323, 336, 340, 341, 343, 345, 346, 352–356, 358, 363, 367, 400, 402, 407
Sturge, Joseph 114
Suttor, Francis 289
Suttor, William 330
Swan, N. Walter 229
Swift, Jonathan 250, 290
Sydney Punch 9, 12, 111, 125, 126, 142, 151, 153, 155, 169, 170, 211, 247
Sydney Times 113, 183

T

Tait, John 364
Taylor, Adolphus George 265, 288, 289, 300, 306
Taylor, Sir Henry 120
Thackeray, William Makepeace 113, 183, 245, 253, 280
Therry, Rev. John 15, 21
Therry, Roger 44, 46, 48, 59, 68
Thomson, Sir Edward Deas 217, 232
Thornton, George 52, 59, 60, 357
Tooth, Robert 52
Towns, Robert 156, 158
Trollope, Anthony 113, 172, 183, 185, 199, 200
Trotter, Miss 389, 405
Tryon, Rear Admiral (Sir) George 312, 327, 335, 339, 346, 358, 365, 372, 378, 399, 407

U

Unwin, Frederick Wright 20

V

Vane, John 108, 110, 116
Vaughan, Archbishop Roger Bede 181, 217, 219, 228, 229, 233, 235, 237, 241, 244, 252, 253, 255, 324, 360
Verdon, Sir George 346
Victoria, Queen 138, 144, 256, 305, 319, 339, 363, 366, 383, 385, 408

W

Walker, David 350
Walpole, Horace 251
Walsh, Constable William 133, 135
Walsh, Kevin 360
Want, John Henry 187, 188, 303, 353
Wardell, William Wilkinson 119, 269, 388, 409
Watson, James 163, 164
Wearne, Joseph 163
Webb, Edmund 132
Webb, William 302, 304
Weekes, Elias 60
Wentworth, William Charles 22, 24, 31, 58, 74, 89, 186, 402
West, Rev. John 46, 56, 103, 118, 183, 223
White, James 9, 408
White, Thomas 224
Wilkes, Joseph 59
Williams, John 158
Wilshire, James 51, 52, 53
Wilton, Edward & Thomas 132
Windeyer, William Charles 11, 99, 103, 128, 163, 214, 272, 376, 378–380
Wise, Charley 48
Wise, Edward 48, 101, 103, 104, 109, 116, 118, 129
Wise, Frances 48
Wiseman, Cardinal 194
Wolseley, General Lord Garnet 313, 319, 339
Woods, Greg 145, 208
Woods, John 292

Woolley, Professor John 23, 111, 112, 129
Wright, Francis 343, 351, 353, 356

Y

Young, Governor Sir John 89, 102, 119, 371, 391

www.ingramcontent.com/pod-product-compliance
Lightning Source LLC
Chambersburg PA
CBHW071801080526
44589CB00012B/638